Reaching for the Moon

The Struggle for Integration in Prince Edward County and America

Reaching for the Moon

The Struggle for Integration in Prince Edward County and America

John J. Festa

Manakin Publishing LLC

Reaching for the Moon: The Struggle for Integration in Prince Edward County and America

Published in the United States by Manakin Publishing LLC.
This book is protected by the copyright laws of the United States of America. Any reproduction or unauthorized use of the material contained herein is prohibited without written permission of Manakin Publishing LLC. This is the galley manuscript (Galley Number VI, August 11, 2013).
When distributed a percent of the price from every copy sold will be donated to the Robert Russa Moton Museum. You are also encouraged to make a donation to the Robert Russa Moton Museum at 900 Griffin Boulevard, Farmville, VA 23901, phone number (434) 315-8775 (www.motonmuseum.org).

Acknowledgment and thanks are offered to John A. Stokes and his publisher for permission to reprint certain portions of his book *Students on Strike- Jim Crow, Civil Rights, Brown and Me*. Reprinted by arrangement with National Geographic Society from the book *Students on Strike- Jim Crow, Civil Rights, Brown and Me* by John A. Stokes, © copyright 1999 John A. Stokes.

Thanks to my friends at the Robert Russa Moton Museum for their permission to use information on their web site and from the book, *They Closed Their Schools: Prince Edward County, Virginia 1951-1964*, © Copyright 2008 Robert Russa Moton Museum, Farmville, Virginia.

Credit for the cover picture of the Virginia Civil Rights Memorial on Capital Square belongs to my friend Fred Landa. Fred's diligent pursuit resulted in getting just the perfect shot for this book.

The title *Reaching for the Moon* is a quote from Barbara Rose Johns describing how it felt to be sixteen year old, and a black female, in 1951, fighting to integrate her High School in Prince Edward County, Virginia.

> "It seemed like we were reaching for the Moon."
> —Barbara Rose Johns, 1951

ISBN: 9780615832128
Contact: manakinpublishing@gmail.com
August 11, 2013, All rights reserved.

To Mary, John, Joseph, Lydia, and Frank the foundation that provided me support, strength, and wisdom throughout my life.

ACKNOWLEDGMENTS

I received great support from the institutions and staff of the: Library of Virginia, Virginia Commonwealth University, Library of Congress, Robert Russa Moton Museum, and Virginia Historical Society.

The author acknowledges the approval from John A. Stokes and his publisher for permission to include certain portions of his book *Students on Strike- Jim Crow, Civil Rights, Brown and Me*. Reprinted by arrangement with National Geographic Society from, *Students on Strike- Jim Crow, Civil Rights, Brown and Me* by John A. Stokes, © Copyright 1999 John A. Stokes.

The Robert Russa Moton Museum for their help in researching and providing permission to use information on their website and from the book *They Closed Their Schools: Prince Edward County, Virginia 1951-1964*, © Copyright 2008 Robert Russa Moton Museum, Farmville, Virginia. The museum Director, Lacy Ward, was always available to answer questions and provide any help I requested.

I have had a number of friends who upon learning of my untamed idea to write my first book, did nothing to dissuade me and offered consistent and sturdy encouragement throughout this project. Thank you all: Beryl, Jackie & John, Linda, Liz, Maria & Dave, Mack, Michelle, and Vince.

One such friend, Fred Landa offered to provide the cover picture for this book. Fred provided me numerous shots to select from of the Virginia Civil Rights Memorial on Capital Square. Thank you Fred your talents are much appreciated.

Thank you to my talented editor, Nina Erb. In spite of being handicapped with me as both the author and her father she helped me make the words match my passion and guided me through my combat with the English written word. Long live the comma!

A final thank you to my wife Terry Festa who helped with some of the editing and, most importantly gave me the space and encouragement I needed to finish this eight year project.

I LYTP.

CONTENTS

CONTENTS *(continued)*

FORWARD

I vividly remember in 2004 reading an article in my hometown paper, the *Richmond Times-Dispatch*, that tangentially referred to something called massive resistance. The article associated this with schools being closed in a place called Prince Edward County. I might have been a recent arrival to the South from New England, but it still bothered me that I never heard about the student-led strike or the school closings. After some research found that Prince Edward County closed their public schools for five years rather than comply with court ordered desegregation. Not only was this a revelation to me, I found that a lot of my friends, relatives, and colleagues, both here in Virginia and up north in New England, had never heard the details of Prince Edward County's integration struggle. I was mystified that anyone would close their public schools—never mind for five years. My search for both the truth of what happened and the why, has led me to complete the book that you now hold in your hands.

This particular book project has become an educational journey that at times seemed to have no end. While I did my research to further my understanding and curiosity of race in America, I certainly had the problem of knowing when enough was enough. Deciding when to stop researching is an all too common story even among professional historical authors. I became hooked as I learned about the sacrifices of so many noble Virginians, both black and white, and the more I learned, the more questions I had and the more I felt compelled to understand the how and why of all of this. I also became more and more in awe of those courageous and patient—beyond patient—black Americans who never gave up on the American dream.

Early on in my journey, to my surprise and delight, I found on busy State Route 15 in Farmville, Virginia the Moton High School. While it was an empty shell in 2004 and looking somewhat cold and forlorn, it was still standing and strongly exhibited that sense of "place"— a feeling that something special had happened here.

Mostly local folks, including some of the 1951 student strikers, have preserved this "place" that represents a stepping stone in the American civil rights struggle as a National Historic Landmark, and they aspire for Moton to become a first class civil rights museum and learning center. The Robert Russa Moton Museum is committed to the preservation and positive interpretation of the history of civil rights in education, specifically as it relates to Prince Edward County and the role its citizens played in America's struggle to move from a segregated to an integrated society. I remain an enthusiastic supporter and volunteer of the Moton Museum and suggest you visit their website (www.motonmuseum.org) and the museum in person to learn more about this historic struggle. If you do visit, you will see a strong correlation between the six gallery exhibits at the museum and this book. Among the goals I established for this work was as a companion or supplement for visitors to the Moton by providing the background and details for what they would see and experience at the museum. I think this is especially important for youngsters so they understand that we all stand on the shoulders of giants—even if, as in this case, they were the slender shoulders of a usually shy and quiet sixteen-year-old girl.

So why write a book about this less-than-noble time in our American history that many wish to forget? Some wish to bury those painful memories surrounding the struggle to integrate America's schools in the 1950s and 1960s. And some have a hard time justifying in their own minds, never mind to the rest of us, why they were on the wrong side of the civil rights movement. I believe that today most Americans are just glad we made it through those dark days, and remain grateful to those inspiring Americans who had the tenacity to use peaceful protest and the courts in forcing us to live up to our ideals.

The short answer to the questions *why this book and why now*, is that I felt compelled to understand not only what happened in 1951, but why it happened and why it mattered. As this book neared completion, I attended a lecture at the University of Virginia Miller Center on Monday, January 18, 2011. The Pulitzer Prize winning writer Isabel Wilkerson was discussing her new book *The Warmth of Other Suns*. In response to my question about why she wrote her book, she indicated that she felt profoundly compelled to tell the story of those brave, black folk who left the Jim Crow South for points West and North, and in their own very personal way changed America for the better. Like her, I felt compelled to tell the story of the brave children who jumped into the unknown world of civil disobedience on April 23, 1951, to gain some measure of justice and a decent high school education.

I also saw from my reading and research that no book fully covered the entire 13-year struggle to integrate Prince Edward County public schools with the information I wanted to know. Certainly no book has chapters that directly correspond to the Moton gallery exhibits. Most of these pre 2010 books either focused on the strike or the legal case or only the briefest details regarding how these two historic events were related and played off each other. Also, with the passage of 50-plus years, some of the key participants have become talkative. For a long time no one on either side of this issue wanted to bring up all the hurt and embarrassment associated with closing the public schools for five long years. Today, new and exciting information has become available through individual interviews, numerous oral history projects, and also Barbara Rose Johns' *Diary* surfaced in 1999, nine years after she passed away.

I am indebted to the authors of these four seminal works, as they collectively build the foundation of the historical record of the 13-year struggle:

- Richard Kluger, *Simple Justice: The History of Brown v. Board of Education and Black America's Struggle for Equality,* Vintage Books, 2004.
- Bob Smith, *They Closed Their Schools: Prince Edward County, Virginia 1951 — 1964,* Robert Russa Moton Museum, 2008.
- John A. Stokes with Lois Wolf, Ph.D. *Students on Strike - Jim Crow, Civil Rights, Brown, and Me,* National Geographic, 2008.
- Neil Vincent Sullivan, *Bound For Freedom: An Educator's Adventures in Prince Edward County, Virginia,* Boston Little Brown, 1965.

My hope is that those historically minded individuals, who want a complete picture of the 13-year struggle, will find this book meets that need. Additionally, those students of *Brown v. Board* and the Prince Edward County integration struggle will find new and insightful information that was not available to the earlier authors. And finally, for those visitors who go through the Robert Russa Moton Museum six gallery's and decide they want to know more of the what and why that they experienced in the exhibits this is a convenient enabler to assist with learning more.

Now, a word about "the N word." In February 2011 a new edition of Mark Twain's classic novel *The Adventures of Huckleberry Finn* was issued. The editor has expunged all instances of the N word—which appears more than 200 times in the original text—and in its place he has added the term "slave." I have made no such error in sanitizing history. If you are offended by the word "negro" or "nigger" good, you should be. In nearly every case where I cite those words, it is used by the speaker as a derogatory, denigrating, and hurtful term. You will also notice that the word Negro is often not capitalized in some of the referenced quotes which is also a faithful translation and reflection of the times. After all, do you really need to capitalize a piece of property you buy and sell or a race you marginalize to the point of disenfranchisement? You may also see quotes where white men are referred to by Mr. and blacks are called by their last name or "a negro."

Feisty Barbara Rose Johns', who you will read a lot about here, was often angered when white customers and white salespeople assumed inappropriate and unwelcomed familiarity in addressing her mother by her first name instead of the customary greeting of Mrs. Johns (read as respect reserved only for whites). Of course, the white patrons who visited the Johns rural store demanded and received the very measure of respect they so carelessly denied their black neighbor.

I also draw your attention to my deliberate use of the full name, in many cases, of those heroes who put their all on the line for a better future. My purposeful attempt was to honor them and contradict the previous 350 years of editorial slight to them and their race.

———————

So difficult it is to show the various meanings and imperfections of words when we have nothing else but words to do it with.

—John Locke

Chapter One

STRIKE

That day, when the curtains opened it was my sister on stage rather than the principal. I was totally shocked. She walked up to the podium and she started to tell everyone about the fact that she wanted us to cooperate with her because the school was going out on a strike. I remember sitting in my seat and trying to go as low in the seat as I possibly could because I was so shocked and so upset. I actually was frightened because I knew that what she was doing was going to have severe consequences.

—Joan Johns Cobb, younger sister of Barbara Rose Johns

Time Line for Chapter One
Strike
(1951)

1892. Vernon Johns born (April 22, 1892–June 11, 1965). Johns was an American minister and civil rights leader who was active in the struggle for civil rights from the 1920s to his death in 1965. He is considered by many as the father of the American Civil Rights Movement, having laid the foundation on which Martin Luther King, Jr. and others would build. He was also Dr. King's predecessor as pastor at Dexter Avenue Baptist Church in Montgomery, Alabama. Johns' was born in Darlington Heights section of Prince Edward County, Virginia. As the uncle of Barbara Rose Johns he was influential in her life.

1939. Robert Russa Moton High School built and named after local born black leader Robert Russa Moton (August 26, 1867 – May 31, 1940). Moton was the President of Tuskègee Institute (1915 – 1935).

1949, October. Reverend Leslie Francis Griffin became pastor of the First Baptist Church in Farmville. The Reverend Griffin was one of the few leaders of the Prince Edward County struggle who stayed in the county and continued to fight for the entire 13 year struggle. He was a mentor to the student strikers, leader of the black community, president of the local NAACP, and the plaintiff in *Griffin v. County School Board of Prince Edward County* that finally brought an end to the five years of public school closing which forced the start of integrated schools in Prince Edward County.

1950, October. Barbara Rose Johns recruited John and Carrie Stokes, her first two and most important committee members, for the Robert Russa Moton Student Strike Committee. Both John and Carrie Stokes were influential seniors at Moton and key leaders during the student strike.

1951, April 23, Monday, 11 a.m. The Moton students go on strike for a new school. Barbara Rose Johns becomes their leader and spokesperson.

1951, May 7, Monday. Moton students end the strike and the entire student body returns to school.

1951, May 23. Attorney Spottswood Robinson files the students' lawsuit. The case was named *Davis v. County School Board of Prince Edward County.*

1951, June. Barbara Rose Johns leaves Prince Edward County. After finishing her junior year at Moton, Barbara is sent by her parents, fearing for her safety, to live with her uncle Vernon Johns in Montgomery, AL.

1951, July 3. School Board declines to renew Moton high School Principal Jones' contract.

Detailed Time Line for the Two Week Strike

1951   Moton Student Strike (April 23, 1951 – May 7, 1951).
- Monday, April 23, 11 a.m. The Moton students go on strike for a new school. Barbara Rose Johns becomes their leader and spokesperson.

- Tuesday, 24th. Students meet with superintendent of the school board which does nothing to settle the stalemate.

- Wednesday, 25th. First meeting with NAACP attorneys Hill and Robinson. They met with the students in the Rev. Griffin's church in downtown Farmville, Virginia.

- Thursday, 26th. Over 950 students and parents meet in Farmville, Virginia with Lester A. Banks, executive secretary of the Virginia Chapter of the NAACP and vote to continue the strike, and importantly, to now fight for integrated schools versus just a new segregated school.

- Friday, 27th . Strikers continued to meet with their lawyers, parents, and mentors. The first article about the strike appears in the *Farmville Herald.*

- Monday, 30th. M. Boyd Jones the Moton High School principal, sends a letter to the Moton parents urging them to send their students back to class.

- Tuesday, May 1st. Rev Griffin and John Lancaster (president of Moton PTA) send a counter-letter urging parents to stand with the students and not return them to school at this time.

- Wednesday, 2nd. The student strike committee received strong support and encouragement from their private meeting with John Lancaster the Moton PTA president.

- Thursday, 3rd. Over 1,000 Prince Edward County blacks meet at the First Baptist Church in Farmville, Virginia, with the student strike leaders and the NAACP attorneys to discuss and sign the petition of non segregation.

- Friday, 4th. *Farmville Herald* published a complete list of the names of parents who signed the petition of nonsegregation.

- Sunday, 6th. A ten-foot high cross is found burning in front of the Robert Russa Moton High School.

- Monday, 7th. Moton students end the strike and the entire student body returns to school.

Chapter One
STRIKE
(1951)

And then there were times—I just prayed—God please grant us a new school. Please let us have a warm place to stay where we won't have to keep our coats on all day to stay warm. God, please help us. We are your children, too.

—Barbara Rose Johns' *Diary*, found in 1999 by her daughter nine years after her death

On April 23, 1951, Farmville, Virginia became one of those places, like Bunker Hill or the Sea of Tranquility, that trumpet the greatness that is American courage and freedom. It was a partly sunny day with mild temperatures in the mid 60s. All in all a pretty unremarkable day, except that at 11 a.m. a group of courageous students were going to change America forever.

As the Robert Russa Moton High School auditorium's thick green stage curtains were drawn back, there stood Barbara Rose Johns at the speaker's podium. This bright, normally shy, 16-year-old, African American girl was on a mission to gain a decent school. She did not believe it was fair or right for her schoolmates to be forced to attend classes in deplorable conditions while white students had a modern school less than a mile away.

Barbara Rose Johns announced that this assembly was for students only, and the student leaders were going to take the Robert Russa Moton High School on strike. Their parents had been pleading for many years with the Prince Edward County School Board for a new high school, but to no avail. Now the students were going to take matters into their own hands by going on strike for a new school.

She asked the teachers to leave since this meeting was called by students for students. Her teachers glanced at each other to see if anyone knew what was going on and where Principal Boyd might be. Beyond the small group of 20 or so students comprising the student strike committee, no else knew what was happening, or what would happen next. Some of the teachers started toward the stage. A few of them got to the front of the auditorium and demanded Barbara and her student strike committee leave the stage and all students return to their classes immediately.

Barbara Rose Johns, this time in a louder voice, again asked the teachers to leave. This was not a good beginning; there was a lot of confusion in the school auditorium. The strike could have ended before it even began as students and teachers alike wanted to know what was going on. Barbara knew she needed to gain control of events. "Some teachers tried to rush onstage and seize Johns, so Johns took off her shoe and pounded it on the podium, 'I want you out of here,' she yelled." This time most of the teachers grudgingly complied and left the students to make history, although, none of them knew that at this moment.

While the students loved their teachers (a point that was carefully considered in the planning to call the strike), they were mindful that the teachers involvement in the strike could mean their jobs. The white school board might choose to retaliate against their school administrators and teachers, and there would be little anyone would be able to do about it in the 1951 segregated South.

You can also imagine that, as black teenagers in 1951, the students' fear of punishment by the school, their parents, and the county's white leaders was a very real concern. Every student in that auditorium had to wonder how much trouble they were now trying on and would one size fit all?

Nothing like this had ever happened before at the all black Robert Russa Moton High School. The students, teachers, and administrators were all black. It was not a usual occurrence for a white person to even set foot in the school. In fact, many whites later remarked that they had never taken notice of the poor conditions of the school even though they drove by it daily. It was just that a Negro school was not of much interest to those in the white community. Prince Edward County, Virginia had a completely segregated public school system that was mirrored throughout much of the South. A normally orderly school, Robert Russa Moton sat alongside busy State Route 15 on the southern edge of Farmville, in the rural community of Prince Edward County, about 60 miles south-west from state capital in Richmond. The students, teachers, and principal knew their roles and they all scrupulously followed the script; a script rooted in the Jim Crow laws and customs of the South.

Prince Edward County, the American South, and the rest of America were in for a shock because things were about to change.

What would possess a 16-year-old, black girl in southeast Virginia, the start of the northern most end of the South's so-called Black Belt, to stand up to her school, her teachers, and the powerful white community? One answer could be the scene that was in front of Barbara Rose Johns in that overflowing auditorium. The school was designed and built to house 180 students and yet it was overcrowded from the day it opened in 1939. In 1951, Robert Russa Moton had 450 students crammed into a school with only seven permanent classrooms.

More likely though, it was the "temporary" tar paper shacks now being used for classrooms that had the students freezing all winter long and using umbrellas inside when it rained. Or maybe it was the fact that for some classes there were no text books, and when there were, they would often be worn out hand-me-downs from the white school up the street. Adding further insult to injury, were the derogatory racial slurs a few of the white students penned in those books—knowing that the Moton students would be receiving them next.

In any event, it was clear she was angry. Despite her teachers' exhortations to get down from the stage, and their wonder of how she dare call an unauthorized assembly and what was the meaning of all this; she started to speak—she spoke the truth that every student at Moton knew.

As she built a case for action, she reminded her classmates of the deplorable conditions they were forced to endure at Robert Russa Moton. The auditorium had no permanent seating, worn floors, and even the curtain she just passed through was worn and needed replacement. As many, as four classes were held daily in the auditorium. For many the most embarrassing indignity was being forced to hold classes in a broken-down old school bus in the school parking lot. The students were, at times, forced to share ripped or incomplete text books, too often not having enough for everyone in the class. She recalled the broken desks they used and, in some cases, there simply were not enough desks for the entire class. Supplies were meager, with hardly enough of the most basic supplies like pencils and paper.

She reminded her peers about the three tar paper shacks that the students were forced to use as classrooms. While the main school was outdated and overcrowded from the day it opened in 1939 with only seven classrooms and an auditorium, conditions had reached the point that the white school board attempted some measure of diminution by constructing temporary classrooms in 1948. Each of the tar papered buildings housed two classrooms, meaning more than half the classrooms at the Moton were in those drafty, leaky, cold buildings, or in the makeshift auditorium, or the refuge of last resort a school bus in the parking lot. When visitors would drive by the school on busy State Route 15, they would sometimes stop and ask the students what those chicken coops were doing next to the school? This became a constant source of embarrassment for the students, administrators, teachers, and parents alike. And as if the black community needed a reminder, the tar paper shacks became a constant token of their second-class citizenship in segregated Prince Edward County.

Particularly galling was the white high school just up the street, Farmville High School, which seemed like paradise compared to their raggedy old Moton. Farmville High School was a sound building large enough to comfortably house their students, with central heating in the winter, new desks for every student, and adequate supplies and text books. Barbara Rose Johns got to see these inequities firsthand about a year before the strike when she and another Moton student were asked to help retrieve a few boxes of old textbooks that were no longer wanted at the white school. Barbara was in awe of the facilities that included a garden, gymnasium, and cafeteria.

Years later, Barbara Rose Johns spoke about that day in the auditorium: "It was time that Negroes were treated equally with whites, time that they had a decent school, time for the students themselves to do something about it. There wasn't any fear. I just thought—this is your moment. Seize it!"

—————— PLANNING THE STRIKE ——————

The forward to this book describes the Moton Museum and the six galleries that tell the story of the Prince Edward integration experience. In Gallery I a visitor to the museum will step back into 1951, taking a seat in the school's auditorium that has been restored to the look of that fateful day in April 23, 1951. You will see a video showing 16-year-old Barbara Rose Johns, rallying her peers with a persuasive argument to join her and walk out in protest of "inferior educational facilities."

By all accounts, it was Barbara Rose Johns who came up with the idea of the strike. She had read about how some white students at a school up north had used a strike to get better dining room facilities. Since it worked for them, she was determined to make it work for Prince Edward County. As an African American, 16-year-old junior at the Robert Russa Moton High School, Barbara knew she would need help if she was to execute an effective strike and gain facilities equal to the white schools. She referred to the enormity of the difficulties in achieving her goal of a decent school as, "if we were reaching for the Moon."

As she tried to come up with a plan that could lead to a better or new school, she decided to consult with a few select students. In October 1950, she approached John and Carrie Stokes, well-respected seniors at the high school, to be the first to join her strike planning committee. It is believed that one of the reasons she approached them was that their parents were well respected in the community by both blacks and whites alike, and she was aware that they had both traveled outside of the South. Their experiences, like hers, would expose the myth that all blacks were tolerating the inadequate conditions Prince Edward County black students had to endure. John A. Stokes recalls Barbara speaking to him early on about a strike.

So we knew that we had a problem, so when Barbara came to us, Barbara Johns approached my twin sister and I, first she approached me, and Barbara was a very unusual person, she was very, very, very—very quiet, but highly intelligent, and when she approached me, I had heard this before about striking, about boycott and things like that, so it was nothing new, but she was so persistent, so around October I said, look, we'll look into it.

The students knew from the onset that secrecy was necessary if they were to have a chance of success. They had to keep it a secret so their parents wouldn't stop them. They also needed to keep their teachers out of the strike because they knew that the white school board would likely fire them if they were involved. The students were taught under unfair and difficult conditions by an all-black staff that was both dedicated and talented. They demanded high standards from their students and pushed them to excel. The students respected and loved their teachers.

John A. Stokes, Vice President of his Senior Class, remembers others talking about taking action to put pressure on the school board but ignored them because he didn't think their plans were well thought out. However, he not only trusted Barbara but believed that she could make it work. "But Barbara Johns was different. There was something very special and genuine about her that is really hard to put into words. There was something unique about her demeanor that commanded my respect. It made me not only trust her, but also have faith in her ability to take us to this promised land—a new school building. She was a very quiet person and very much a lady."

While Barbara Rose Johns was indeed a lady, she was also a bulldog when she got an idea in her head. For those she targeted to join her special strike planning committee, she was persistent and usually succeeded in convincing them to join. Barbara's mother related, "her daughter had a temper and she was sort of stubborn, and anything she believed in she was determined to continue to believe in and if you wanted to change her mind you had to give a lot of reasons."

Barbara very carefully went about selecting individuals for her committee because it would not have been successful if the individuals were not well respected, capable, and trustworthy. She also wanted to get a representative from each of the different areas of the county as well as from the different school classes. She eventually recruited 20 student leaders to join her on her strike planning committee.

As John A. Stokes recalls, the need to build a solid student coalition was paramount: "So the coalition group that started it moved forward and got other students. We had gotten other students to work with us, you see, and we selected those students very carefully, because we did not wish any of the students to be Uncle Toms and things like that."

An accurate list of exactly who was on the Robert Russa Moton High School strike committee remains difficult to validate due to the lack of official records and the uncertainty of memories impacted by the passage of 60 years. Most of the strikers seem to recall about 20 students involved in the planning. Nearly 60 years later on March 24, 2011 an article in the *Farmville Herald* identified the 20 individuals that were the planers and leaders of the student strike.

> *On Tuesday, The Herald asked John A. Stokes, a key member of the student strike planning committee and author of the National Geographic-published Students On Strike: Jim Crow, Civil Rights, Brown and Me, to share the names of those involved, so that credit might be publicly given as the 60th anniversary approaches.*
>
> *"This is the group that started the situation. Remember, it started with only a few of us...We picked others to join us as we moved forward," Stokes told The Herald in an email with the two lists.*
>
> *The original Strike Committee of Robert Russa Moton High School was, according to Stokes: Carrie Stokes, John Watson, Hodges Brown, Catherine Coles, Barbara Johns, Irene Taylor, John Stokes, Carl Allen, Louise*

Reed, Donald Coles, Willie Walker, Joseph Jones, Loreda Branch, Thelma Allen (Hampden Sydney), Melvin Watkins, John Monroe, Claude Cobbs, Meattear West, Agnes Woodson and Floyd Bland.

"This is the original group that did the initial groundwork for the strike on 23 April 1951," Stokes said in the email.

Barbara Rose Johns started holding meetings on the cinderblock bleachers at the school's athletic field, or in one of the tar paper shack classrooms, or in private homes; anywhere that would allow the students to keep their secret until the time was right for a strike. At the very first meeting, John A. Stokes recalls, "I'll never forget her words. She said, 'I'll die for the cause.'" He knew she was right, and also knew he could not live with himself if he did not support her plan. Then and there they started planning the strike. "We knew it was not going to be easy, but we believed we could pull it off."

Since the plan needed to be secret, they started calling it the "Manhattan Project." This allowed them to discuss it without using the word strike which would have alerted the adults. As the sister of Barbara Rose Johns, Joan Johns Cobb, recalled: "My sister was sort of an introvert and she stayed to herself a lot. She was very studious, always reading books and going to the woods to, I guess, meditate. She never told me anything. And afterwards, I questioned her and asked her why she didn't mention it. She said it was because she couldn't afford to tell anyone because it may have gotten out and it had to be a secret."

Miss Inez Davenport, the Moton music teacher, was someone who Barbara Rose Johns could confide in. When discussing the conditions of the school, Miss Davenport said to her, "Why don't you do something about it?" With that statement, Barbara said she, "decided to think about that." She didn't forget that statement, "for it stuck with me for several days and out of it was conceived the idea of the strike."

While the students at the time, and later as adults, always maintained they conceived and planned the strike without any teacher or parental knowledge, there is now evidence, surfacing 54 years after the fact, that there was at least some adult input.

At least one adult was aware the students were planning some form of protest. On February 11, 2005, the *Richmond Times-Dispatch* published an article in which Mrs. Inez Davenport Jones, age 51 at the time of the interview, discussed her role in the 1951strike. At the time of the strike Miss Inez Davenport was single, but engaged to Principal Jones. She was the Moton music teacher and, importantly, a mentor to Barbara Rose Johns. At a 1999 Moton reunion, Mrs. Jones revealed publicly, for the first time, that she was aware of the strike before it occurred and offered Barbara some advice on how to deal with the parents and Principal Jones. "Inez Jones said she recalled hearing students venting their frustrations and working out a plan. She said she told Johns not to let the students inform their parents of the plan and to trick her husband, the principal, into leaving the building. Jones said it was several days into the strike before she told her husband of her involvement."

There is other evidence that points to meetings between the students and Reverend L. Francis Griffin days before the strike. Bob Smith interviewed the Reverend on July 5, 1961 about his meeting with the students as they finalized their plans. "They wanted to ask me one question, just one question," Griffin recalled. The students wanted advice on whether to tell their parents they were planning a strike. Up to this point the entire effort was to be a secret until the strike was called making it harder for the adults, white or black, to stop the protest. This question surfaced because one of the strike committee members was against striking without informing their parents first.

...Mr. Griffin, who was summoned to the school and found the student leaders behind locked doors: .... There was one boy who dissented, he went against the idea. All he said was that they should get the consent of their

*parents, and the others disagreed. They wanted me to
advise them on this, and I advised them to take a vote
among themselves. They did and all but this one boy
voted against telling their parents first.*

Then there was the fact that the students had made the protest
signs at the school ahead of time and stored them at the school as
well. It seems plausible that as small as Moton was, those
placards would have been discovered. One can envision a
particular music teacher, for instance, looking the other way as
art supplies were used to make the signs.

One wonders just how much help the students were given.
Rosa Parks had her protest well planned with flyers printed and
attorneys all lined up ahead of being arrested. Given the tenor of
the early 1950s and faced with the formidable task of taking
down the Jim Crow establishment in the South, strategic thinking
and tactical preparation was just plain smart.

And finally, months after the strike when Barbara returned
with her Uncle Vernon to Montgomery, Alabama, to escape
possible violence and retaliation in Prince Edward County, she
was shortly joined by another exile from Virginia. Soon after
being fired from his principal position due to the strike, Boyd
Jones moved in the summer of 1951 to Montgomery, as well, to
pursue his doctorate at Alabama State College. He also promptly
joined Mr. Johns' church. I will leave it to the reader to connect
the dots even if they are circumstantial dots.

––––––––––

The students had used the six months since Barbara Rose Johns
first approached John A. Stokes to good use by monitoring the
School board's discussions regarding a new school and
meticulously preparing for a strike if that became necessary. On
Sunday, April 22, 1951, a critical meeting of the committee
members of the "Manhattan Project," so named because of the
need for secrecy, was hosted by John A. Stokes at his family's
farm about three miles south of Farmville. While the majority
was in favor of going forward with a strike the next day, some

were concerned that they could be imprisoned. With a little help from John's older brother Leslie, they quickly realized that 450 students would completely overwhelm the small Farmville jail. As part of the meeting, they reviewed their individual roles, ensuring everyone was ready. They even checked if the weather would support their planned march from the Robert Russa Moton School to the offices of the Board of Education in downtown Farmville. The weather was going to be fine with partly sunny skies and temperatures in the mid 60s.

John A. Stokes discusses the students planning and research in preparing for the strike, in an oral history he gave to the Virginia Civil Rights Movement Video Initiative on March 21, 2010. He also contrasts the value of Negro schools with white schools. As you will read the students used these facts to their advantage when meeting with the school board following the walk out.

So to go back in what you asked me, we knew that in order to do something, it was just so hopeless, in order to do something we had to develop a plan, and the plan was to get the students out of the school, protest, because we knew it wasn't going to last over five or seven days. We knew that the board of supervisors, board of education, Mr. McIlwaine would say, look, we'll put a new building up, and we knew that was going to be it, but it didn't happen that way. They rebelled against us, and they called us a few names that I can't put on tape and became very, very upset with us because of the fact that they felt that we were doing something wrong, and they failed to realize that we knew that the 14 or 15 schools in the county, the property was only worth around $330,000. You know, they didn't think that we as young kids would know all this. And that we knew that the properties that their buildings were on were worth $1,200,000. That's a difference in around $870 some thousand dollars, so this was not equality. This was not equality at all.

So, and see, I think they played us real cheap because of the fact that they did not think that we had the abilities to do what we did. So once we walked out and some students did come back, of course, and—but we had planned it, we had planned it very well, when those students hit the grounds we would have cars and take them on home. And it happened for about three days. And after then they did not come back to school on the buses anymore.

──────── **THE PLAN WORKS** ────────

The students had a narrow window of opportunity on the day of the strike. Their plan relied upon effective delegation, subterfuge, and split accuracy timing for a strike to take hold and achieve their goals before they could be shut down by the adults. They had correctly anticipated that their teachers and administrators would attempt to step in before they were able to march and picket.

Task one that Monday, April 23, 1951, was to get Principal M. Boyd Jones to leave the high school. They could only expect him to be out of the building for a few hours, but that would be enough if they stayed on schedule. A number of students were assigned to plant themselves at specific locations in Farmville to make calls into the school office pretending to be adults notifying the principal that some of his students were creating problems downtown. Remember, this is 1951 in Farmville, Virginia; Negroes did not create problems in town or anywhere else for that matter, or at least not for very long. Shortly before 11 a.m., Principal Jones received a call from a muffle-voiced individual with information that two of his students were at the Greyhound bus terminal causing a ruckus. As was expected, he got in his car and headed to that location. As soon as he was seen leaving the building, Barbara Rose Johns had four students distribute to each classroom notes that she had prepared alerting teachers to a special emergency meeting in the auditorium at 11 a.m. An interesting coincidence exploited by Barbara, was to use the initial "J" from her last name to mimic the "J" used by Principal

Jones at the bottom of his notes. The teachers didn't necessarily assume anything was wrong because it was not abnormal for the principal to call an emergency meeting even for issues like littering on the schoolyard or other infractions of school policy; Principal Jones was known as a stickler for following the rules.

——— SARDINES IN A CAN ———

We now return to the scene at the opening chapter of this book with the student body and 25 teachers crammed into the Moton auditorium for an "official assembly," and a few key members of the strike committee sitting on stage behind the drawn curtains.

The auditorium was the largest space in the school. During normal school hours, the students were forced to use it as an assembly area with folding metal chairs since there was no permanent seating, and at other times the auditorium became a classroom with as many as four different classes running simultaneously. It also served as their gymnasium and lunch room. The layout of Moton had the auditorium central to the permanent classrooms with a small library and the principal's office at one end, and at the other end, an elevated stage that stood at a height of 32 inches with four sets of stairs at each corner of the stage. One would need to pass through that open area to get to the other parts of the school, thereby creating a disturbance to classes being held there. It measured 35 feet by 14 feet- 6 inches or 507.5 square feet. If you consider there were close to 400 students at the assembly that day, this divides out to about 1.26 square feet per person. John A. Stokes was not exaggerating when he said, "we were packed in that room like sardines in a can."

Amid the chaos, Barbara Rose Johns was aided by John A. Stokes, who stood up and helped get his fellow students to quiet down. Then together they said the Lord's Prayer and sang a song.

While most of the teachers left voluntarily as Barbara and her strike committee had hoped, she did need to repeatedly ask a few teachers to leave before all but one complied. The one male teacher who refused to leave had to be ushered out of the auditorium by a few of the beefier members of the Robert Russa

Moton football team. He was sequestered in one of the classrooms behind a closed door with guards standing by to make certain he would stay put until the meeting was over.

It is important to point out that in no way were the students striking against their teachers, but against poor school conditions. They respected and loved their Moton teachers and went out of their way to have them absent from the meeting so they would hopefully be spared from losing their jobs or other disciplinary action by the white school board.

This belief illustrates the naivety of the strikers. The Prince Edward County School Board was almost certainly going to hold Principal Jones responsible for what occurred in his school, and just as certainly would use him as a scapegoat to ward off criticism from the Board of Supervisors and white citizens. Jones was already labeled a troublemaker by the School Board for his repeated requests for supplies and a new school. Maybe it was a good thing that the students did not understand this most likely of outcomes or they may never have struck a blow for freedom that day.

Barbara's sister Joan Johns Cobb describes how she experienced the strike first hand in an oral history she gave to the Congress on Racial Equality in 1991.

That day, when the curtains opened it was my sister on stage rather than the principal. I was totally shocked. She walked up to the podium and she started to tell everyone about the fact that she wanted us to cooperate with her because the school was going out on a strike. I remember sitting in my seat and trying to go as low in the seat as I possibly could because I was so shocked and so upset. I actually was frightened because I knew that what she was doing was going to have severe consequences. I didn't know what they were going to be but I knew there were going to be some. She stood up there and addressed the school. She seemed to have everyone's attention.... At one point, she took off her shoe and she banged on the podium and said that we were going to go out on strike and would everyone please cooperate and "don't be afraid, just follow us out." So we did. The entire student body followed her out.

We walked out to the school grounds and awaited further instructions. Then later we were just loaded on the buses and went home, as usual. But I do remember being shocked and frightened ... not knowing what was going to happen next. Because I knew that you did not do anything in the community to upset the white establishment. And I knew something very bad was going to happen as a result of it.... It was April 23, 1951.

——— BARBARA JOHNS SPEAKS ———

Barbara Rose Johns was the first speaker to address the students. She stood behind the podium and started out by reminding the students just how poor their school conditions were, especially when compared to the much better facilities for the white students in town. She told them that things would never change unless they, the students, joined together and insisted on a new school. At that moment she was not talking about an integrated school, but improving the conditions at her segregated black school. Integration would come later, but not very much later.

As an adult Barbara Rose Johns wrote about her recollection of standing on the stage and what she said to the students.

I do not remember exactly what I said that day, but I do know that I related with heated emphasis the facts they knew to be the truth—such as the leaking roofs, having to keep our coats on all day in winter for warmth. Having to have the gymnasium classes in the auditorium, inadequate lunchroom facilities and food, etc. My sister says that I reminded her of a politician standing on a platform denouncing the sins of his opponent and promoting his own ideas with such intensity that you automatically believed and followed instructions. I don't know about this—but I do know we mapped out for those

students...our wish that they would not accept the
conditions of our school and they would do
something about it.

John A. Stokes spoke about how the auditorium was warm
and stuffy with students standing in the wings of the auditorium
and "soon everyone was at a fever pitch." What struck him as
they were chanting another cheer was that every single student
was singing and hollering, even the ones who were usually quiet,
or doubting, or unlikely to join something as provocative as a
strike. He remembers thinking, "that we're on a roll" now and
"no one was seated" as the students loudly sang out, "two bits—
four bits—six bits—a dollar—all for the strike stand up and
holler."

During one of the cheers, John recalls suddenly seeing his
mother at the entrance door taking in the whole scene. He also
remembers seeing other parents starting to enter the auditorium.
Apparently, as the strike was just getting started, one of the
female students had run up Route 15 towards downtown
Farmville screaming that there was a riot at the high school and
that the entire student body was having an angry meeting in the
auditorium. To set the record straight, there never was a riot and
the strike committee kept everything peaceful and orderly.

In Stokes' memoir, he recollects being stopped cold when his
mother suddenly appeared at the back of the auditorium.

There stood Ms. Alice Marie Spraggs Stokes, my mama,
with her girlfriend Mrs. Daisy Anderson. I froze.
However in the world did she find out about what was
going on? Who told her? Was she going to make us call
the whole thing off? Most of the students knew her. So
did most of the people in the community—the teachers,
preachers, merchants, and others. They all respected her.
She appeared calm and composed, but I could see that
she was evaluating the entire situation. She took it all in.
Blocking out the noise and excitement engulfing her, she
looked directly at me. Recovered from my frozen state, I

gathered myself, went down the stage steps and
approached her.
"Mama," I said.
She looked me dead in the eyes and asked, Son are you all
all right?"
"Yes, Mama," I answered.
She repeated, "No, I mean are you all all right?"
Again I answered, "Yes, Mama."
She turned and very calmly said, "OK, Daisy, let's go!"
She and her friend turned and walked out. WOW! What
a relief. ...

After Mama, left the room I knew all systems were go.
I knew that I would have Daddys support, too. If Mama
had said to me, "Boy, you are calling this thing off," I
would not be writing this book today. I would've said to
the students, "Ladies and gentlemen, head back to your
classes. The strike is off."

This is another instance where the strike could have been stopped in its tracks. Stokes' dramatically reminds us that in 1951, Negro teenagers did not disobey adults. It was also true that while some parents were not in favor of pursuing the student strike, most backed it even if it was with "lots of reservations and some fear." A few of the parents had been trying for years to get the school board to provide a new school for the black students, but they were given the runaround time after time. The parents, once they learned of the planned strike, could have put a halt to it any time they chose. However, Mrs. Stokes left her son to his business and the other parents present did the same.

This opportunity to support or end the strike is further evidence of the courage demonstrated not just by the students, but by their parents. The parents knew far better than the students the reprisals that were likely to follow from the white power structure in terms of being harassed, fired, or prevented from getting loans to run their farms, or possibly worse. The parents had a lot at stake and took a giant leap of faith in allowing the strike to continue. Of course they all wanted the same thing, a decent school for their children. You only had to look to the tar paper shacks on the school's front yard to understand their dissatisfaction.

JONES RETURNS

When Principal Jones finally got back to the school, he found the students inside the auditorium and pleaded with them to stop the strike and return to class. He told them this was not the way to get a new school. Barbara asked him, a number of times, to go back to his office, and eventually he did. From interviews Mr. Jones gave years later, it seems clear that the Moton Principal was in deep sympathy with the students and was doing his best to walk a narrow line between his support for the students and a new school, and his obligation to the school board.

Soon the students marched outside the building carrying picket signs that they had made ahead of time. The student-made signs spoke to the urgent need for a new school and the elimination of the embarrassing tar paper shacks. The student carried signs proclaiming:

WE WANT A NEW SCHOOL OR NONE AT ALL

DOWN WITH TAR PAPER SHACKS

WE WANT A NEW SCHOOL

WE ARE TIRED OF TAR PAPER SHACKS—WE WANT A NEW SCHOOL

The students originally considered picketing until the school board set a start date for the construction of the much-needed new school. However, the picketing didn't last long. An edict from the superintendent's office asserted that if the students did not return to class, they were to get off school property or face arrest for trespassing. There was no returning to class so the students began making their way home in the usual manner to face some very interesting conversations around the dinner table that night.

As the day's strike wore down, the student strike committee had a chance to meet with the principal and restate their position that they would not return to class until they were promised a new school. They were dismayed to hear that Mr. McIlwaine, the superintendant of schools, refused to meet with them. And, as an indication of just how separated the races were in Prince Edward County, not a single white person was reported to have stepped on the school grounds or entered Moton the day of the strike to see what was going on: not the superintendant, not a single school board member, not the police, nor anyone from the county or city government. It seems they just did not take the students or the strike very seriously, and seeing to the needs of some Negro children was apparently not a priority.

The students did, however, have an opportunity to meet with Mr. John Lancaster, the president of their school PTA. He, along with his committee, had been leading the charge to get a new school for the colored students, but was repeatedly turned down by the school board. He became a mentor; a source of strength and supporter for the students.

The students also met that day with another person who was to become instrumental not only throughout the strike, but through the whole 13-year odyssey that Prince Edward County had just unknowingly embarked upon. The Reverend L. Francis Griffin, the pastor of the first Baptist Church in Farmville, gave the students his complete support. He offered his church as a meeting place and, as the president of the local chapter of the NAACP (National Association for the Advancement of Colored People), was the first to come up with the idea of contacting the lawyers in the NAACP's Richmond office for legal help.

——— NAACP ———

Following their meeting with reverend Griffin Carrie, Stokes and Barbara Rose Johns called the Richmond NAACP office that day only to find the lawyers either out dealing with other cases or busy in conference. Undeterred, they called back again later that afternoon and spoke to attorney Oliver W. Hill Sr. It seems as though Barbara Rose Johns was not very good at taking no for an answer. Oliver W. Hill Sr. recollects his first encounter with the passionate Johns.

On the afternoon of the first day of the strike, Barbara Johns called our office at about 5:00 p.m. At the time of the call, Spot, Martin and I were working on a motion for further judicial relief in the Corbin v. Pulaski. We were planning to go to Christiansburg, Virginia that week in preparation for our hearing in the case. The plaintiff in that case, Mathama, Corbin, was the son of a dentist and had to ride approximately 60 miles daily to a consolidated schools serving all of the Negro students for a number of communities including the counties of Pulaski and Montgomery and the town of Radford.

Regarding the Prince Edward situation, Barbara Johns told us that they were on strike; however, I stated they didn't need to continue to strike because they had made their point. I said to her besides, "We've already filed a suit in Clarendon County, South Carolina challenging the constitutionality of separate schools there." I added that one case was enough to establish the legal principle. For these reasons I urged her to lead the students back to school. Having appeared before the school authorities in Prince Edward County on a number of occasions during the 10 year period before the initiation of the Prince Edwards suit, I was familiar with the deplorable school system about which they were complaining.

Nevertheless, Barbara Johns pleaded their case so strongly, and I did not feel comfortable terminating our discussion on the telephone, that I said, "All right. We're coming through Farmville Wednesday morning. We will leave Richmond a little earlier and we will stop by and talk to you." She said, "All right." She told me that they would be at Reverend Griffin's church. Reverend Griffin was an outstanding leader in the turbulent years leading *to, during and after the closure of the Prince Edward County Public Schools. In the <u>Davis</u> case, Griffin participated as an activist, and assumed a similar role in a suit involving his own children.*

That afternoon, they followed up their call with a letter to the NAACP attorneys explaining their particular situation and the remedies they were seeking. Carrie Stokes and Barbara Rose Johns drafted the letter telling the attorneys about the strike and asking them to come to Farmville on Wednesday, April 25, 1951. They even offered to help with a place to stay if they needed to stay overnight, since in the 1951 Jim Crow South, there were no hotels for black people in Prince Edward County. After the letter was typed by Carrie Stokes, another member of the strike committee delivered it directly to the post office. It was hand delivered to the post office in part to get it to Richmond as soon as possible and partly out of concern with the letter being intercepted.

——— THE KEY MEETINGS ———

Herein lies the tragedy of the age: not that men are poor,—all men know something of poverty; not that men are wicked,—who is good? Not that men are ignorant,— what is Truth? Nay, but that men know so little of men.

—W. E. B. Du Bois, *The Souls of Black Folk*, 1903

Tuesday, April 24th brought day two of the strike which promised to be another busy day for the student leaders. Once again, the students detailed planning was paying off.

The strike committee maintained a checkpoint just outside the high school grounds. The purpose was to intercept any students who had not heard about the strike and were intending to attend class that day. The committee recognized that if even one student showed up for school, the strike could be in jeopardy and ultimately fail. They had addressed this contingency by pre-staging automobiles that were loaned to them by local black businessmen to take the few students who arrived at the school back home.

On day two of the strike, eight students arrived at the school; all had been absent the day before so had not heard of the strike and had no idea what was going on. It was Carrie Stokes and Catherine Coles who explained the situation, being careful to make clear why they had to go home. Stokes reports that not one of them gave the strikers any trouble and simply got in the cars and allowed the students to drive them home.

While students today have cell phones, in 1951, in rural Prince Edward County and especially for the black population in that area, many did not even have phones in their homes. So for those students out of school on Monday, there was no easy way of contacting them. One might ask why they hadn't learned about it from TV or possibly the radio. It would have been impossible for them to hear about it because there was absolutely no news coverage concerning the strike until several days later. So the student strike committee had correctly anticipated that some of their peers would unwittingly show up for class, and they had prepared a ready response.

Later that afternoon, 19 members of the student strike committee were able to meet with the superintendent of Prince Edward County Schools, Mr. McIlwaine. The Robert Russa Moton High School Student Strike Committee Members who met with School Superintendent T. J. McIlwaine on April 24, 1951 were, according to Stokes: Agnes Woodson, John Monroe, Barbara Johns, Carrie Stokes, Irene Taylor, John Stokes, Joseph Jones (Bo), Louise Reed, Hodges Brown, Willie Walker, Thelma Allen (from Hampden Sydney), Edwilda Allen, John Watson, Floyd Bland, Loreda Branch, Donald Coles, Catherine Coles, Matteauer West, and Claude Cobbs.

John A. Stokes recalls the superintendent chose not to meet with the students in his office, but in one of the symbols of county power, the county court room. He also chose to sit in the judge's raised chair while motioning the students to sit below him, an obvious attempt to intimidate them. The students were neither intimidated nor unprepared and got right to their point.

When would the date be established for construction of a new high school for blacks in Prince Edward County?

Superintendent McIlwaine explained that any decision about a new school was up to the school board. There were some funds put away for the new school, but they only amounted to one-third of the school's actual cost. He also reminded the students that the amount of taxes black people paid was only 10 percent of the taxes collected in Prince Edward County, and said that the strike was making things worse since it was costing the county school system $100 for every day the students stayed out of school. He insisted that the tar paper shacks were only temporary, and that representatives from the board upon visiting the Robert Russa Moton School had found it in good and adequate condition. All creditability was lost with the students as he went on to say that every piece of furniture in their high school was just as nice as any other school in Prince Edward County and their agricultural building was the most up to date in the county. The students knew he was wrong and believed that he had never stepped foot in the Robert Russa Moton High School.

The students had done their homework and were ready with their counter arguments. They addressed the obvious inequality in tar paper shacks for blacks versus a completely outfitted brick school for whites. While the black and white student populations were about even in Prince Edward County, the property value of the white schools was estimated to be around $1.2 million while the Negro schools were valued at $327,000. Then there was what the county chose to spend per pupil; spending $817 on each white student compared with only $194 for each black student.

As the meeting ended Mr. McIlwaine said, "he was a Christian and that he would pray for the school system." He was emphatic that the students could not demand the board give them a new school and offered the students his advice to, "take things as they come instead of by force" since force in Prince Edward County would inevitably lead to a "hatred among the people." The students were not satisfied in the least with the meeting or any of Mr. McIlwaine's answers. It was clear to them that he intended to continue to stall for the foreseeable future. The foreseeable future to the students looked like more of the same and they were the ones who were suffering today in those tar paper shacks.

———————

After their frustrating encounter with the superintendant, the students were contacted by the Rev. L. Francis Griffin with some encouraging news. The NAACP attorneys—Oliver Hill and Spottswood Robinson—had a conversation with Griffin earlier that day and indicated they were impressed with the children's case, as outlined in their letter. In fact, they said, the next day (Wednesday, April 25) they were heading to a meeting in Blacksburg some 163 miles from Richmond, and would be willing to make a detour to meet with the strikers in Farmville.

As they drove from Richmond to Farmville for their meeting with the students, Hill recalled listening on the radio to the news reports about the student strike in Farmville. He recalls that he and the other NAACP attorneys were fully prepared to strongly counsel the students to return to class immediately. Hill was no stranger to the conditions in Prince Edward County and had been to Farmville to investigate the school conditions numerous times over the last ten years. He said that he knew the Robert Russa Moton students, "were up against a most deplorable situation." A major reason Hill would council for a return to school, was that in all his previous trips to Prince Edward County, he found the Negro community was predominated by the "old guard" who were not willing to rock the boat. In a 1961 interview, Hill offered his candid assessment that, "in very few of the counties would you find people you would regard as militant. Most of them were long-suffering, just wanted to get some relief....It was when the younger group came along that all this changed." While it is easy to see how Barbara Rose Johns and John A. Stokes fit into this younger group of new militants, the Reverend L. Francis Griffin equally represented this new vanguard of activist. Griffin was still early into his ministry and one of those new activists who had begun to make their presence known and, importantly, willing to rock the boat. Griffin is also the one individual who stood by the strikers, the *Brown v. Board* plaintiffs, and the children displaced from five years of no public school and he supported the community through the turbulent return to public education in 1964. The Reverend L. Francis Griffin was there, at great personal cost, throughout the entire 13-year ordeal.

Another issue weighing on the minds of the NAACP attorneys was the recent decision, made by the national organization of the NAACP, to use their scarce resources only to fight segregation versus just asking for equal facilities. While Hill was very skeptical that the Negroes in Prince Edward County were willing to take on this fight, he was more concerned that the students had picked the wrong fight because the NAACP had just recently made the turn to an all-out assault on segregation. He was about to learn that Barbara Rose Johns and her strike committee were very willing to not just demand equal facilities, but also willing to attack at the heart of Jim Crow—the segregated public schools.

——— OLIVER W. HILL, SR. ———

Here are the transcripts from an interview with Oliver W. Hill, Sr. conducted on November 13, 2002 as part of the Virginia Civil Rights Movement Video Initiative. Hill makes the point that until the NAACP broke the back of separate but equal, none of the protests of the 50s and 60s would have had the impact they did. As long as the South could hide behind "separate but equal," via the egregious 1896 Supreme Court decision in *Plessy versus Ferguson*, all other efforts would be frustrated and of limited effect. That is why the strike and the resulting Supreme Court case of *Davis v. Prince Edward County* were so important. Hill and the NAACP were betting it all in 1951 that they could defeat 55 years of legal precedent that had forced blacks to accept second-class citizenship. Hill spoke about the Prince Edward County case in an oral interview he provided in 2002.

INTERVIEWER: Well, with that in mind tell me about the Prince Edward County School Case.

HILL: All right, well, the Prince Edward County School case in 1939, a brand new school was opened down in Prince Edward, it was over crowded the day it opened, to show you how much planning they did, and starting in early 40s I went down there several times, before I went in the Army, trying to get the school board to do something about the situation.

Their remedy was to put up cardboard shacks and run stove pipes from one to another, and then down into big oil bed—drums to heat the schools, so that meant those kids would have to leave the main building in bad and inclement weather, and go from one school to the other building to another, or in—if the weather was real bad, slick out, or snow, or mud, and they kept promising to do something about it.

They always got rid of me. Of course, I used to appear before a lot of boards of supervisors for Negroes because when Negroes appeared, they asked them, what do you want, John, or Jim? And they would try to tell them, and they would cut them off, tell them they was going into executive session.

Well, at least when I appeared, they at least sat and listened to me, and then   do—whenever they want to do, any time we talk, finish talking, then they always go into executive session so we couldn't hear the discussion.

But anyway, that was—that situation continued. I went into the Army, and came out. Well, in the mean time, we filed suits in several places. And one of the suits we filed was against a group in Pulaski County, [inaudible] a dentist. We filed—because he was about 60 or 70 miles from the school over in Christiansburg. It was a consolidated school. They took care of kids in the City of Radford, Pulaski and Montgomery County and somewhere else and all. I have forgotten now. And they hadn't done anything about it. So we were planning a motion for further relief, and one Monday afternoon, the telephone rang and a young lady name Barbara Johns, her uncle was one of—the famous fiery Baptist preacher named Vernon Johns. Vernon Johns was a firebrand, and he was the one who had been down in Montgomery County for the previous five years before Martin Luther King came there. He was all fired up. He was a firebrand if there ever was one, but he was very eccentric.

But anyway, Barbara Johns called, and I answered the phone and asked if we would finish up—in my book there's a picture of us sitting at a table—and asked what we were doing on the afternoon. They called Martin, Spot and I. But I happened to be nearest to the telephone, so I picked up—answered the telephone, she was telling me, she told me how they had gone out on strike, and the reason and everything that was going on, very orderly, and she wanted us to represent her.

I said, you don't need no representation. I said, we have already filed suit in Prince Edward—I mean in Darlington County, South Carolina, challenging segregated schools, and we don't need but one suit to prove a point, so what you ought to do, you all are seniors, you go on back to class, you made your point and go on back to school the next day.

Well, she pleaded so hard that I asked her, well, I'll tell you what, we'll be going up to Christiansburg on Wednesday morning, this is Monday evening, on Wednesday morning, and we'll leave earlier and stop by Reverend [inaudible] church. You'll be there in the Sunday school room, and we'll talk with you, talk it over there.

And that's what we did. On our way up there, we still intended to tell the kids to go on back to school, but we got there, they had such high morale, and so well organized, and could state their case so nicely, we didn't have the heart to turn them down. So we told them if they were no longer filing suit on the theory of separate but equal, but if their parents would back them in a suit challenging constitutionality of the segregation laws per se, we'll take the case. And that we would be going up to Christiansburg and we'd be coming back through there Thursday night. This was early Wednesday morning, and we would be coming back through there Thursday night, and have the parents there and we will go over it then.

But the point I wanted to make is I think—I don't think I made it up to this time, although I've done a lot of talking, is that we refused—when I say "we" I'm talking Negroes, refused to recognize the fact that until we got Plessy versus Ferguson overruled, declared to be unconstitutional, we wouldn't have gotten to first base with anything else.

But my point, let me go back and make this point, as I say, until, as long as segregation was constitutional, we wouldn't have gotten to first base with the sit-ins, and the marches and all that stuff. You had to break that law and make it possible for us, at least on paper, to be first-class citizens.

——— NAACP ATTORNEYS ———

The meeting location was set for the First Baptist Church at 100 South Main Street in downtown Farmville where Griffin was pastor. That Wednesday, April 25th, the students and a small group of parents and supporters assembled. The lawyers from Richmond chose to meet privately with the 19 student strike committee members. In part, the lawyers wanted to hear from their potential clients directly, and to also test their resolve and courage. The lawyers explained that while their cause was "just," the NAACP was no longer interested in fighting for separate but equal schools.

The NAACP had correctly determined that to sustain a quality education for all America's children, separate but equal needed to be eliminated in favor of fully integrated schools. The fight now was for a fully integrated school system. So if the students were to get help from the NAACP, they would have to change their objective to go after the larger prize of a fully integrated Prince Edward County school system. The students gained the lawyers' support that the strike should continue until the NAACP could consider their request, and for their part the students needed to consider the NAACP's policy on only fighting for integration. Oliver Hill recalls, "we found them [the Robert Russa Moton students] so well organized that we didn't have the heart to break their spirit."

In a 2003, as part of the Virginia Civil Rights Movement Video Initiative, John A. Stokes describes to the interviewer (Ronald Carrington) the first meeting on Wednesday, April 25, 1951 with the NAACP attorneys, and to his later embarrassment, Stokes' misinterpretation of Spottswood Robinson's race.

INTERVIEWER: Let's get back to that meeting. Did that meeting with Oliver Hill, the first meeting with Oliver Hill and the students, did that, what they were doing in terms of asking you guys those hard questions, did that dissuade you or how did it impact on the strike you all were doing?

STOKES: When Mr. Oliver Hill and those came to us and following that particular meeting, it really cemented us more firmly in our belief that we were right, they told us before they left, they said, you are right, you are right, but we have never seen a bunch of students with so much guts to try something like that, and that's why we asked you all these questions. They told us the reason. And you know, because of their rationale we trusted them. We knew we could trust them. We knew we could lean on them.

And of course the Reverend Griffin by being a mentor that he was, you know, sort of took us under his wing like a chicken does, you know, just like a hen does, you know, and to protect us, he guided us in the direction to move from that point. He said you can always use this facility whenever you wish to have any meeting you want to have.

INTERVIEWER: Tell me about the meeting with the attorneys from the NAACP.

STOKES: Yeah. Spottswood Robinson, Dr. Henderson. Mr. Tucker could have been there. I don't remember that other person. I remember Mr. Henderson very, very well, but he was a cool cat, you know, he was real calm. Spottswood Robinson, boy, he walked the dogs on us that night. He was something, you know. In fact, amazingly enough, I said something that I got very ashamed of in later years, Spottswood Robinson was so hard on us telling us, you know, you know what you are doing, and that's what he started with. Then he said some of the students sometimes, you know, do things and then they regret it and things of that nature.

So then near the end of his conversation I raised my hand, I said, sir. He said, yes. I said, you know, I can understand why you are having a problem with us. He said, why is that? I said, because you are white. And he never corrected me. He was such a man. He never corrected me. Reverend Griffin called me to the side, he said, young Stokes, let me tell you one thing. There are such people as light-complected Negroes, you know. The word was Negroes then, not black, you know. And I felt like I wanted to go through the floor, you know, here I am the President of New Farmers of America, you know, and I here I misinterpreted who the man was, and because I permitted my emotion, I realized then I permitted my emotion to get in the way of my thinking pattern. And we went on from there.

And they told us, they said, we are going to come back through Farmville, we are going to Pulaski, Virginia, and when we come back if you are not—if you have decided not to go back to school we'll take your case, and they kept their promise. And that was the most amazing thing, they actually kept their promise and listened to what we had to say.

The student strike committee was now in a quandary. Should they change course and move towards the larger prize of integration or simply stay the course hoping for a better, but still segregated school? The one thing they knew for sure was that none of them wanted to go back to school as things now stood. They now knew they were in for a fight and the powers to be were simply not going to cave after a three-day strike. They also were committed, if needed, to go it alone without the NAACP's help. It's worth pointing out just how embarrassing it was for them to go to a school that had tar paper shack classrooms. These awful tar paper shacks by now had become a rallying cry—like Bunker Hill, or the Alamo, or Pearl Harbor in their day—that motivated the students to fight on. The students knew that others had better and were fed up with being second class citizens. They were determined that something was going to change.

——— PTA MEETING ———

As the students were thinking about what to do next, they received news that more help was on the way from the NAACP. Mr. Lester A. Banks, Executive Secretary of the Virginia Chapter of the NAACP, was willing to come to Farmville and speak to the students and their parents. Reverend L. Francis Griffin helped to arrange his visit and participation at a Robert Russa Moton High School PTA meeting on the evening of Thursday, April 26, 1951.

Over 950 students and parents turned out to hear the NAACP leader speak. They opened the session by singing a hymn, "Nearer, My God to Thee." The Reverend Griffin offered a prayer and spoke of the need for cooperation among the community members, encouraging the parents to stand by their children and their demands. Next to speak was Barbara Rose Johns as the selected spokesperson for the student strikers. She gave an impassioned speech where she recalled the lack of decent facilities and resources, and the miserable conditions of the tar paper shack classrooms. She discussed their recent meeting with the Superintendent of Prince Edward County Schools and the strikers' opinion that the superintendent was only interested in creating more delays. She went on to say that the students were prepared to move beyond just requesting a new school. They were now willing to fight for an integrated Prince Edward school system. "She ended by pleading with the parents to back the students in their stand against the white power structure."

For the first time, Barbara Rose Johns was publicly announcing that the student strike committee had decided that, with the NAACP's help, they would now be fighting for nothing less than a fully integrated school. The students were keenly aware that any delay could weaken their position and the possibility of continued help from the NAACP. John Stokes recalls the debate and how close the vote within the committee was on whether to fight for integration or just insist on a new school.

We knew that before Mr. Banks spoke at the school, we had to decide what we're going to do. We were afraid of non-segregation, not just because how the white power structure would retaliate but because we knew integration would dismantle our education system. We were very proud of our teachers. They were the ones who taught us how to be leaders. They were our motivators and role models. We knew we would lose them and these benefits when we were no longer separate schools for blacks and whites. When the strike committee finally voted, non-segregation won by only one vote! That's how close it was. That's how close we came to not making history. Once the decision was made, we were all united behind it.

Mr. Banks then took the podium. He started out by sharing that since its founding 42 years ago, the NAACP had been working to prepare the Negro, "for the progress and leadership, which are due us." He went on to say, "we as Negroes should not be satisfied with what we have been given. We are Americans and should enjoy all the rights, privileges, and amenities as anyone else."

But Mr. Banks was just warming up, as he continued, "there is no such thing as separate but equal. If it is separate and equal today, it will be unequal tomorrow. Equality is a little deeper than that." He pointed out that should the black community of Prince Edward County choose to back down on the issue of segregated schools, they could possibly hinder the civil rights struggle for years to come.

Now the parents had their turn to speak. Some voiced their very real concern that some of the Prince Edward County whites would see fit to take retribution on the parents' ability to earn a living, obtain a loan, or purchase daily necessities in the local stores. There was some concern that if the strike continued, it would encourage Klan violence. One of the parents discussed his feelings that the students should have informed their parents before they actually went on strike. Mr. Banks responded by saying, "you are saying that your child, or your children, or these children should have informed you. But the reason they did not inform you was because if they had informed you, we wouldn't be here today. There never would have been a strike." By the end of the meeting, the majority of parents voted by a show of hands to support the student strike and stepped up to the idea of demanding an integrated education system in Prince Edward County.

Over the next few days, the student strike committee was once again busy, meeting with their lawyers, their mentors, parents, and other leaders in the black community. The NAACP lawyers were drafting up a petition for nonsegregation that would outline the essential merits of their lawsuit against Prince Edward County. It was decided that there would be a meeting the following week at the First Baptist Church, on Thursday, May 3, 1951, to formally present and sign the petition. This document was the first step in petitioning the courts for integrated schools.

Student strikers knew this meeting would be the critical test, because there was a huge difference between voting in a closed meeting by a simple show of hands versus actually signing your name to a legal document.

A fact of life in 1951 was that America was a land where being black and standing up for your rights carried risks. John A. Stokes offered his perspective that, "living in the Jim Crow South was always scary for blacks," but even more so when you decided to challenge the very core of segregation and white power.

—— A DECISION POINT ——

Some men see things as they are and say Why?
I dream things that never were and say Why not?

—Robert F. Kennedy

While the student strike committee was busy getting ready for the May 3rd meeting where the nonsegregation petition would be presented and signed, Principal M. Boyd Jones, under orders and pressure from the school board, sent a letter to all of the school's parents saying that the superintendent had authorized him to request all students to return to school. If they failed to do so, there would be, "grave consequences which must be suffered by those who persist in violating the compulsory attendance laws," and the students and their parents would, "be subject to punishment upon the recommendation of the division superintendent." The letter was signed by Mr. Jones and all the teachers at the school. This was the school board's way of not only trying to end the strike, but sidestepping any blame for themselves by holding Mr. Jones solely responsible for the student strike.

The strikers received immediate help from Reverend L. Francis Griffin and Mr. John Lancaster who provided their own letter to the parents. It identified their personal support for the strike and the fight for integrated schools, and implored the parents to ignore Mr. Jones' letter and keep their children home. The strikers hand delivered copies of the letter to every Negro family in Prince Edward County. The parents followed their advice and kept their children at home. Obviously, the school board had no idea just how committed the students and parents were, but they were about to find out.

In preparation for the May 3rd meeting, the student strike committee had a private meeting with John Lancaster, the Robert Russa Moton PTA president, and the students felt his words were both an encouragement and inspiration.

> *We have been trying to get the people in charge of the school system to treat us in a fair and respectful manner ever since my own Daddy was the president of our PTA. These people have not been fair to us, and they have never respected us; they have lied to us; they have actually cheated us; they have robbed us of our educational rights. Boys and girls, you have done a wonderful job. You've done a brave thing. We are not going to let you down. We are very proud of you, and we're going to support you. There is a saying by us farmers you cannot scald the hogs until the water is right. Y'all have the water just right, so let us go forth and scald the hogs. Let us stand together and fight for our rights. You children are our future. You children are good for us. Keep on keeping on.*

Meanwhile, the local Farmville press was starting to wake up to the strike and, in particular, was getting more and more interested in the local student leaders. On April 27th , the first article about the strike appeared on the front page of the *Farmville Herald*. The headline read "**Robert Russa Moton students claims unjustified board feels now**." The article restated the school board's position that they were working on providing the new school for the Negroes, the tar paper shacks were just temporary, and the students had no grounds for a strike.

The student strikers were now being repeatedly pressed by *Farmville Herald* reporters to be granted access to their private meetings. In one instance the reporters just showed up where the students were meeting and when they were denied entry, the next article in the *Farmville Herald* appearing on May 1st expressed shock and dismay that a group of Negro teenagers had the nerve to shut the paper's white reporters out of their meeting. A *Herald* report posed these rhetorical questions: "I asked the question where do they learn their manners?" and, "What were they trying to hide?" The article did have an impact in stirring up the angry feelings of the white community. The student strikers were even called communists and un-American by some white adults.

Meanwhile, some of the white students from Farmville High School signaled their willingness to join the strike, but their parents wouldn't allow it. Based on comments made to the strikers and their parents, a few members of the Prince Edward County's white community supported the strike and a few more supported a new school for the Negroes. However, the majority were clearly in favor of retaining a segregated school system.

——— MAY 3, 1951 ———

Reverend Griffin sent out the notice for the Thursday, May 3, 1951, meeting indicating the purpose was to discuss and sign the petition of nonsegregation. It was scheduled to start at 8 p.m. and would be held at his church, the First Baptist Church located in downtown Farmville. In the notice, he told the black community, "REMEMBER. The eyes of the world are on us. The intelligent support we give our cause will serve as a stimulant for the cause of free people everywhere." His message to the parents was straight to the point, "there will be no excuses. Every man must stand for his children this one night. Just stand!"

While the meeting was not announced publicly, beyond the black community, there was enough concern for public safety by town law enforcement officials that checkpoints leading in and out of Farmville were manned by state police. The strikers knew that there were plenty of white spies reporting on their activities. They were also aware that a small group of Negroes who didn't approve of what the students were doing were also reporting back to white officials.

The student strike committee had arranged to meet with their lawyers and Reverend Griffin prior to the main meeting. As they arrived, they could barely get through the crowd to squeeze through the church basement door to attend the pre-meeting.

It was determined at that time, who would have a speaking role and who would sit in the pulpit at the front of the church with the lawyers and other leaders of the community.

The First Baptist Church was one of the largest churches within 60 miles of Farmville and could seat 500 people, but with many more standing in the aisles, that night the church was packed. The *Afro-American* reported that the meeting was attended by close to 1,000 folks. The student strikers had done their job in getting the word out for this important meeting.

The Reverend Griffin opened the meeting with a prayer. Next to speak were the lawyers Robinson and Hill who outlined the NAACP's new approach in attacking segregated schools. Then Barbara Rose Johns, representing the strike committee, spoke about the deplorable conditions of the current Robert Russa Moton High School, the right of the students to a decent education, and their commitment for an integrated school system. The formal presentations were concluded with a question and answer period. This is where the sparks flew.

During this session, the former Moton principal, Mr. J. B. Pervall, spoke. He criticized the strike and the strike leaders, and then went on to criticize the attorneys accusing them of coming into our "quiet pastoral community" and "disturbing the peace." Mr. Pervall was a well known supporter of the go slow approach and the status quo. John A. Stokes considered him, "a stooge of and an ally of Superintendent McIlwaine."

The head of the Virginia NAACP, Mr. Lester Banks, chose an indirect method to answer Mr. Pervall's comments. He reminded the crowd that they were there to reaffirm their commitment for a non-segregated school, which was the only sustaining way to ensure their children would receive a decent education; an education that they deserved and was now being denied them.

What happened next represents one of those moments when someone stands up, stands tall, and seizes the moment to make history. The Richmond *Afro-American*, provided coverage of the meeting and wrote, "Barbara Rose Johns reminded the audience of the tar paper shacks and challenged Pervall with unmistakable metaphors of white oppression and black accommodation to it." "Don't let Mr. Charlie, Mr. Tommy, or Mr. Pervall stop you from backing us." she retorted back to the audience.

A more impassioned account comes from John A. Stokes who recalls this pivotal moment in the meeting. Mr. Lancaster returned to his seat after addressing the audience following the comments from Mr. Pervall, and then Barbara Rose Johns gave her reply.

> *As he headed back to his seat, Barbara Johns popped up as though shot out of a cannon. I've never seen her move so fast. She really lit into the stooge. She told the crowd to ignore him. She did two things that young people back then didn't dare do to adults. She raised her voice, and she called him an Uncle Tom,—a traitor to his people. She crushed him with her words. When she finished, the former principal just turned and walked to the back of the room. I can still hear the thunderous ovation Barbara received when she finished her comments. I do believe that at that very moment her impromptu speech elevated her to another level in the eyes of our people. She was no longer just a 16-year-old student. She became a Superstar, an instant heroine. Her comments spoke volumes and profoundly reflected the feelings and frustrations of our community. Flash bulbs lit the room, and her picture was splashed on the front page of newspapers all over the state.*

The last person to speak was the pastor of the church they were meeting in, the Rev. Griffin. He began, "Mr. Pervall has a right to speak...," and continued, "Anybody who would not back these children after they stepped out on a limb—is not a man. Anybody who won't fight against racial prejudice—is not a man. And to those of you who are here to take the news back to Mr. Charlie, take it—only carry the tale straight."

The *Afro-American* reported that at the end of the meeting, 1,000 persons lifted their voices as inspirational tones filled the church with the words of "America the Beautiful." Coincidentally, a May thunderstorm was just getting started. There was a blast of thunder and a spark of lightning outside, but that was no match for the thunderstorm that had started inside the church. This storm of "segregation or not" would engulf Prince Edward County for the next 13 years.

———

When the students collected the petitions that had been circulating throughout the evening, they counted nearly 200 signatures, although only one was needed to file the lawsuit. The NAACP lawyers indicated that the students could return to school on Monday morning May 7, 1951, because for now, their work was done. Some of the students had tears in their eyes as they thanked their parents for their courage and support because they knew just how much was being risked. Yet, their parents believed in them and their cause. John A. Stokes correctly called it, "an amazing act of bravery during such a dangerous era. Those who signed knew they were risking life and limb."

If the strike had been halted, there would have been no Prince Edward County participation in the *Brown v. Board of Education* Supreme Court filing. It is fair to say, based on the NAACP strategic vision to strike down segregated schools, that *Brown v. Board* would have happened with or without Prince Edward County, but in any case, the Moton students picked this battle, not the NAACP. It is also fair to say, it took a lot of courage from the parents when it came time to sign their names to a petition to sue the white school board in 1951. The parents' signing the petition of nonsegregation was the first step in petitioning the courts for integrated schools.

Fifty-one years later on November 13, 2002, in an interview by the Virginia Civil Rights Movement Video Initiative, Oliver W. Hill, Sr., recalls the May 3rd meeting. Please note that as with many of these oral history used in *Reaching for the Moon* the speaker is recalling events from 50 or 60 years ago and as in the case of Hill, he was 95 years of age when he provided this oral history.

We came back Thursday night, the parents was there with the kids, and the parents—a hundred to one—100 percent agreed to back the children. Somebody though raised the question, said, well, this is a county affair, maybe we ought to bring it before the whole county. That's what we wanted to do, so we agreed. And this was Thursday, so we agreed to hold a meeting the following—not the next day, Friday, but a week from the following day, Friday, and we got there that Friday evening Spot and I, they had the meeting—of course they had it in the church, in the sanctuary, you know, and the place was full, standing room only. And the News Leader had a reporter down there.

And they argued about it, and it was 90 to one—I mean 90 percent of the people wanted to pursue the case, so we agreed to it. But one of the principal employer was—a man was principal of the school over in Cumberland County, but he lived in Greensville County, and—I mean lived—not in Prince Edward County. And we could understand his problem. He was trying to protect his job. So that was it.

Now, as a consequence of the strike by the pupils—as a consequence, they fired the principal of the high school, [inaudible] and they fired the county—what was known as the county agent, agricultural agent, man named—I think his name was Lancaster, because they figured they were active NAACP people. They figured—they really had put the kids up to it, but the main proponent of the strike and carrying out and getting the principal out of the school on the date was Barbara Johns. That one mistake we made in filing the suit, we named the plaintiffs alphabetically, but we should have—it should have been Barbara Johns

*versus Prince Edward County instead of Davis versus
Prince Edward County.*

The happenings of this night would send an important message to
the powers that be; the Prince Edward County black community
was unwilling to continue with disadvantaged facilities for their
children. Also noteworthy was the fact that the meeting was
allowed to proceed without any harassment from any official or
unofficial white organizations or groups. The town fathers were
wary enough of the gathering though, that as previously
mentioned, the State Police were ordered to set up check points at
the major roads leading into town; and a military contingent from
nearby Camp Pickett was mobilized, in case things got out of
hand. Fortunately, lack of violence was to become a hallmark of
the entire struggle in Prince Edward County—unless you count
denying a child an education for five years as a violent act.

Following the meeting, Prince Edward County remained
uncannily calm with blacks and whites continuing to cordially
greet each other on the streets in downtown Farmville, but of
course the school case would never have been discussed. This
was the other hallmark of Prince Edward County and in general
the Jim Crow South; blacks and whites did not really know each
other and rarely exchanged more than a few pleasantries. If they
had talked, they would have found that they shared a belief in the
American dream for their children albeit one segregated and the
other integrated and still they both wanted what was best for their
children. This would be the central question Prince Edward
County, half black and half white, would struggle with for the
next 13 years.

——— CONSEQUENCES ———

In the days following the meeting, some of the parents were
approached by influential whites and pressed to remove their
names from the petition. The local paper made it easy to target
the petitioners' since every parent who signed the petition of

integration was listed in alphabetical order in *The Farmville Herald*. Very few of the parents, chose to backpedal and they remained steadfast in their commitment for better schools. Attorney Spottswood Robinson however, wasted no time—only a month had passed from the start of the strike—when he filed the lawsuit in the Virginia court system on May 23, 1951 (*Davis vs. PEC*).

During this turbulent time, while there were no reports of violence, there was always the fear among blacks that acts of violence or other retributions might take place. Many of the students described this time as a feeling of "holding ones breath and walking on egg shells." In fact, three days after the petition for nonsegregation was signed, a cross was found burning at the Robert Russa Moton schoolyard. John A. Stokes discusses how he was informed about the cross, its implications for the Prince Edward County blacks, and how the white community, police, and press discounted the cross burning.

Just three days after the petition was signed, our fears came to a head. On Sunday morning, May 6, my Aunt Mary called to tell me that a cross was burning in the Robert Russa Moton schoolyard. I heard about the Ku Klux Klan burning crosses across the Jim Crow South as a tactic to scare blacks, but I had never actually seen one. The cross on our school campus stood more than 10 feet high and was 7 feet across. It was made of green wood, so it did not burn well, but the kerosene-soaked rags that had been used to set the fire were still hanging from the cross. The colored community wanted the F.B.I. to investigate, but the local police dismissed the cross burning as just a prank. No one even remotely associated with law enforcement ever pursued the incident.

A photograph showing Thelma Allen, Admore Joyner, Ronnie Matthews, and me standing in front of the charred symbol of hate is published in the Richmond Afro-American newspaper on May 8, 1951. It was the only photograph of the incident ever published. Since white newspapers never covered the story, few if any whites heard about it. But I saw that symbol of hatred with my own eyes. It was very frightening experience. Living in the Jim Crow South was always scary for blacks, but tensions were running especially high in the aftermath of the strike and the petition signing. News of the cross burning spread like wildfire the entire black community went into "cover me" mode. This meant that we protect ourselves and our loved ones from the threat of violence by arming ourselves. Because of the terror we felt, we kept loaded guns in our homes at all times. It even reached a point where there was no shotgun shells left to buy in the surrounding area.

We were ready to fight because we did not want a lynching or anything like that to take place. We had seen evidence of foul play in our community before, but no one had ever been killed or shot. We wanted to keep it that way. Colored boys who had moved up north to work sent word that they were on standby to come to Prince Edward County in case there was a conflict or confrontation between the coloreds and the whites. They were ready to leave their jobs and come down and fight besides their relatives if necessary. That's how serious the situation was during the time following the strike....

We don't know why no physical action was taken against blacks in the county during this stressful time, but I have always thanked God we were spared.

Stokes recalls that after he and a few other Moton students saw the remnants of the burned cross, they decided they needed to talk to the one person who had been their leader from day one. They wanted Barbara Rose Johns to help them make sense of this hateful symbol. They drove out to Barbara's home "to talk with the person they had relied upon so heavily." Because "Barbara was calm and suggested that teenagers had been responsible," she helped keep her peers from overacting and making things worse.

The week the students returned to class, the editors of the *The Farmville Herald* voiced their displeasure with the petition and any Negro who signed the document. The paper, along with many of the county's white residents, seemed genuinely puzzled that the Negroes were unhappy with conditions in the county. The *Herald* reaffirmed its belief that the majority of the Negroes of Prince Edward did not want, "nonsegregation." The villain in the *Herald*'s view was now, "a vocal minority, craftily led, and agitated by outside influences."

Following the return of the students to their classes, Mr. Jones, the Robert Russa Moton principal, was closely questioned by the school board about his role in the strike and eventually fired. On July 3, 1951, the Prince Edward County School Board made the announcement that Mr. Jones' contract would not be renewed. They went to great pains to say that he was not fired, but that his contract was simply not renewed. The Moton students and parents collected hundreds of names on a petition urging the retention of Mr. Jones as principal, but the school board would not reinstate him. Clearly he was blamed for the strike and the current predicament. The school board seemed oblivious to the fact that the conditions they allowed to fester created this strife within the county.

In this same timeframe, John Lancaster, the high school's PTA president, was fired from his job as the county agent for the black farmers of Prince Edward County. He was accused by his supervisors in Blacksburg of being too friendly with Reverend L. Francis Griffin and spending time with Griffin on the student strike when he should have been doing his agent job. They also accused him of holding a party at his house for NAACP lawyers. For his part, Lancaster vigorously denied he was working for social change on state time.

Reverend Griffin was starting to feel the pressure too, from some of the more timid members of his church. They did not like him rocking the boat and some were afraid of additional retributions. In fairness, some blacks were flat out against integration or any association with whites and preferred segregated schools.

While some of the retribution took the form of petty threats or verbal abuse, other forms were more threatening. Some of the county's black farmers discovered that their crops were no longer worth anything because they could not sell them in Farmville. Some of the farmers were no longer able to get credit from the banks to plant a new crop or replace needed equipment. For folks who were living on the edge of poverty and barely making ends meet, this had the effect of threatening not just of their livelihood, but their farms, their homes and their very survival.

Edwilda Allen was the 13-year-old that Barbara Rose Johns had recruited for the strike committee. She recalls how elated her mother, Vera Allen, was when she found out about the strike. "They were all excited, smiling, like they'd [the students] done something big." While her "daddy" was self employed her "momma" worked for the county school system as an elementary teacher. "I kind of knew somebody was in trouble," Edwilda said. "My father was self-employed, so they couldn't do anything to him, but my mother worked for the county. They did not renew her contract that fall and revoked her Virginia teaching license. All through my teen-age years, she worked in North Carolina."

Barbara Rose Johns' time in Prince Edward County was coming to an end. She was starting to receive disturbing threats and a cross was burned in front of her house too. Taylor Branch writing about Barbara's departure from Prince Edward County in his civil rights book, *Parting the Waters*, said, "The idea that non-adults of any race might play a leading role in political events had simply failed to register on anyone—except perhaps the Klansmen who burned a cross in the Johns' yard one night, and even then people thought their target might not have been Barbara but her notorious firebrand uncle."

With the close of the school year and rumors of threats continuing against her, Barbara's parents decided she should leave Prince Edward County and live with her uncle Vernon Johns in Montgomery, Alabama. Barbara would finish out her remaining year of high school in Montgomery. Of course she was forced to leave her family, friends, and strike co-conspirators behind. Leaving her home must have been difficult for the sixteen-year-old and doubly difficult for her fellow strikers that had so heavily leaned on this quiet leader.

Vernon Johns learned of the strike and the suit by letter because the Johns' household in Farmville had no telephone service. Vernon Johns returned to Farmville in the spring of 1951 at the urgings of his brother, Barbara's father. He listened to his brothers' concern regarding the cross burnings, and potential for harm to his daughter.

The following is taken directly from Taylor Branch's *Parting the Waters*. He interviewed Barbara Rose Johns in December 1983 and provides one of the few direct insights into her personal feelings regarding the strike and how she chose to handle her exile from Prince Edward County. These few paragraphs are about all we have that provide insight into Barbara's years of stoic silence following those fateful few weeks in 1951.

There was a tense scene in the kitchen when Vernon Johns arrived from Montgomery. His brother Robert, a farmer 20 years younger than he, who had always been meeker and more practical, made no secret of his fear. Nor did his wife. Both of them were consumed with worry over the safety of their head strong daughter—now banished to her room during the summit conference—and with all the violence and risk, they did not welcome the fact that uncle Vernon was so plainly "tickled" by the trouble in his native county. They asked him to take Barbara home with him to Montgomery until tempers calmed. Vernon agreed, and Robert begged him to be careful on the long trip. He had always believed that his older brother was a terrible driver, especially when he was quoting all that poetry.

Barbara Johns changed from student leader to student exile the very next morning, as her parents piled her into uncle Vernon's green Buick with some cheese and milk and a very large watermelon, but without a word of explanation. It embarrassed her that her legendary uncle

*stopped on the side of the road to eat the watermelon, like
the stereo typical Negro, and her resentment grew as he
failed to say anything or ask a single question about her
astonishing achievement. She speculated furiously about
his silence. Perhaps he exhorted Negroes to stand up for
themselves but really wanted to take all the risk himself.
Perhaps he wanted to protect her as a family member, or
as a young girl—though either would violate her image of
him. She listened to the poetry and wondered whether she
could ever comprehend what a person of such age and
presence was really like. Finally, she decided that the
most likely explanation for his silence was that he was
proud of her but simply refuse to complement her, as he
refuse to complement people all his life, for fear of
implying that he expected less. This theory caused her
pride to overtake her resentment, and she resolved never
to mention her feats in Farmville to anyone in
Montgomery.*

With Barbara exiled to Montgomery, the Johns family would
before long, have to face the tragic loss of their home under
mysterious circumstances. Barbara's sister Joan Johns Cobb
relates how the family found out that their house in the
Darlington Heights section of the county had burned to the
ground and the ensuing disruption to their lives.

*One weekend [in 1954] we traveled to Washington D.C.
to visit one of my relatives, my aunt. And when we came
back—actually before we got home—my uncle called up
my aunt's house to tell us that our house was burning.
And when we got back, we saw our house in flames—in
ashes really. And to this day, we don't know what
happened to our house.... I remember we had to live with
my grandmother...during my senior year in high school....
Then in 1955 we moved to Washington, D.C. ...*

The strike had come off, the suit was filed, and now the consequences had begun to be felt by Jones, Lancaster, Griffin, 13-year-old Edwilda Allen and her family, Barbara Rose Johns and her family, and a score of other Prince Edward County blacks. Because this was to be a protracted battle, there would be more consequences in store for both the white and black communities. In fact, the Prince Edward County case was to become the longest running civil rights legal case the Supreme Court has ever administered. Barbara and her peers' initial request for a decent school was to launch Prince Edward County, Virginia, and the nation into a 13-year odyssey that, at times, seemed completely out of control, destined to never be resolved, and a fight were many would feel there was no winner.

Chapter Two

A CHILD SHALL LEAD THEM

The wolf shall dwell with the lamb,
and the leopard shall lie down with the kid,
and the calf and the lion and the fatling together,
and a little child shall lead them.
The sucking child shall play over the hole of the asp,
and the weaned child shall put a hand on the adder's den.
They shall not hurt or destroy in all my holy mountain:
for the earth shall be full of the knowledge of the Lord
as the waters cover the sea.

—Isa. 11:6

Time Line for Chapter Two
A Child Shall Lead Them
(1935–1991)

1935. Barbara Rose Johns was born in New York City. At eight she moved to Prince Edward County, her family's ancestral home. In 1951 as a sixteen-year-old, African American, junior at the overcrowded Moton High School she conceived, planned, and led a student strike for a new school and then abruptly changed her course to fight for an integrated school. After being sent away for her safety that spring, she went on to graduate from college, marry, and raise five children in Philadelphia. Her efforts culminated with the Supreme Court striking down "separate but equal" in the 1954 landmark *Brown v. Board of Education* case. In 2008, she was recognized for her part in the civil rights struggle with a life-size bronze that is part of the Civil Rights Memorial on Capital Square in Richmond. A portrait of Barbara Rose Johns, commissioned by the Moton Museum in 2010, was prominently displayed in the Virginia Capitol rotunda. She died in 1991 and is buried at Triumph Baptist Church in the Darlington Heights section of Prince Edward County.

1955, March 2. Fifteen-year-old Claudette Coleman was arrested for refusing to give up her seat on a Montgomery, Alabama bus.

1955, December 1. A forty-two-year-old Rosa Parks was arrested and thrown in jail because she too refused to give up her seat on a Montgomery, Alabama bus for a white person.

1957, September 24. The Little Rock Nine, including fifteen-year-old Elizabeth Eckford and fourteen-year-old Carlotta Walls Lanier, had to daily walk through the gauntlet of an angry white mob as part of their struggle to integrate Little Rock Central High School in Arkansas.

1960, November14. As one of the youngest children to ever take on segregation, six-year-old Ruby Bridges Hall faced angry mobs in her effort to integrate William Frantz Elementary School in New Orleans. Ruby was famously captured by Norman Rockwell in his painting, *The Problem We All Live With.*

1963, May. The Children's Crusade was the name bestowed upon a civil rights march by hundreds of school students in Birmingham, Alabama. Initiated and organized by Rev. James Bevel, the purpose of the march was to walk downtown to talk to the mayor about segregation in their city and attempt to effect some change. Many children left their schools in order to be arrested, set free, and then to get arrested again the next day.

A CHILD SHALL LEAD THEM
(1935–1991)

It was time that Negroes were treated equally with whites, time that they had a decent school, time for the students themselves to do something about it.
We wanted so much and had so little.....We had talents and abilities here that weren't really being realized, and I thought that was a tragic shame, and that's basically what motivated me to want to see some change take place here....There wasn't any fear... I just decided, 'This is your moment. Seize it.'

—Barbara Rose Johns

April 23, 1951 was a day for miracles. What else would you call a sixteen-year-old, African American, youngster leading a protest of 450 black students in racially divided Virginia? Why weren't the student strike leaders thrown in jail? Clearly the powers to be just did not take the students very seriously. If blacks as a group were marginalized in 1951, what status was assigned to a group of black teenagers? That left sixteen-year-old Barbara Rose Johns, as a black and a female, at about the bottom of the of the power base in south-central Virginia.

This was all before Rosa, before Martin, before Little Rock, and before the bridge outside Selma. Barbara Rose Johns started a firestorm that morning; a storm that would burn down the walls of segregation across America. Barbara Rose Johns did not argue the legal case at the Supreme Court or march on that cursed bridge outside Selma or join the march on Washington, but before all that in April of 1951, she summoned the courage to make her stand and simply say this is not right, this cannot continue, and I will not take it anymore. As one of the five cases ultimately bundled under *Brown v. Board,* the Prince Edward

County case that Barbara helped start was the only one initiated by students.

Many historians believe the April 23, 1951 Robert Russa Moton student-led strike was the start of the protesting and activist phases of the modern civil rights movement. Certainly the strike was one of the few, if not the only, child-led protests that occurred without adult approval. Because they were groundbreakers, this just makes them all the more courageous. If Thurgood Marshall was called Mr. Civil Rights, Rosa Parks was the Mother of the civil rights movement, Dorothy Height its Godmother, and Rev. Marin Luther King its Father, then Barbra Rose Johns seems to have a legitimate claim to the title "The Daughter of the Civil Rights Movement."

——— EARLY LIFE ———

Barbara Rose Johns was born in New York City in 1935. Her parents had hoped that they would find greater opportunities in New York City than their home in rural Southside, Virginia. The family certainly had deep roots in Prince Edward County. Barbara's grandparents and parents were all born there. Her father owned the land he farmed in the Darlington Heights section of Prince Edward County. And most significantly her uncle the Rev. Vernon Johns, was born there, started preaching there, farmed there, and owned a small rural store there that Barbara and her family managed. While Barbara remained adamant that her Uncle was never consulted about the strike. She nonetheless looked up to him and his activism had a profound impact on her thinking and values.

When Barbara was 14 months old, the family moved back to Prince Edward County from New York. Then in 1942 they headed to Washington, D.C., where her mother was able to find work with the government and her father entered the Army. In 1943 at the age of 8, Barbara and her siblings moved back to the county to live with her grandparents. She wrote in her *Diary* that, "My days at my grandmother's house were fun filled and chore filled." She remembers creeping out of bed late at night to listen at the door to the adults talking about "slaves and slave stories." While none of them had been a slave, they still held close the stories that were passed down from generation to generation. Upon moving back to Prince Edward County, Barbara was enrolled in the Mary E. Branch Elementary School in Farmville, where she remained through the eighth grade. She then started at the Robert Russa Moton High School in 1948 and quickly became involved in clubs and the student council.

Author, Bob Smith talks about Barbara Rose Johns' early work experience at the family store as she was growing up in Prince Edward County. The narrative demonstrates how even as a 12-year-old she was an independent, intelligent, young black woman who had developed an expectation early on that she would demand fair treatment from both blacks and whites. In this regard, her mother felt this defiant attitude was a reflection of her Uncle Vernon Johns.

> *When Barbara was 12 and 13 she worked in the store, waiting on customers, when school was out. Of the job, she recalls, "I used to feel proud that I was able to give this service rather than go to them for service.... My father was on good terms with all the white around.... They would come, some of them, and sit around and play cards... Well they were all poor dirt farmers, you know, and it didn't matter much to them... One white farmers wife used to come over and talk and sit. I remember she had a daughter and I used to think she was such a beautiful girl. She went to Farmville and got a job in the five and 10 and I came in one day and she just turned away.... All the times we had talked and just this little thing turned her head...."*

Barbara Rose Johns was not in awe of whites. She had read the classics, she had a keen mind, she was a student leader at Moton, and she had traveled. She also witnessed her outspoken uncle take on whites nearly every day, and usually get away with it. While Barbara often argued with her uncle Vernon, she told Bob Smith, "My uncle was always outspoken and I used to admire the way he didn't care who you were if he thought that something was right. It used to be an admirable thing to me the way he would handle white men who would have an argument with him." Barbara's mother related that, "her daughter had a temper and she was sort of stubborn, and anything she believed in she was determined to continue to believe in and if you wanted to change her mind you had to give a lot of reasons.... She was very outspoken, a little like her uncle Vernon in that respect."

Nonetheless, Barbara could still be hurt by the pettiness of those whites stuck in the strait jacket of their carefully manufactured Jim Crow world. In a February 12, 1961, letter to author, Bob Smith, she discusses an experience she had as a teenager with a clerk at the five and ten store in downtown Farmville.

> *I remember as a youngster getting a special surge of pride out of discovering that the superior white man wasn't too superior after all. This came from visiting the Roses and Newberry's five- and 10-cent stores in Farmville and finding out that the sales girls couldn't count worth a darn. Example: I remember getting several (say five) 10-cent items and one 19-cent item. Instead of figuring 69 cents right off the bat, she got pencil and pad and wrote a list of five 10- and one 19-items and then added up to be 79 cents. I asked her to recheck and she came up with 59 cents. Instead of taking advantage of her ignorance I got a greater kick from taking each item and counting them correctly out for her and seeing her face turned crimson red and muttering 'Oh, yes, that's right.'*

─────── **SERENE FIRE** ───────

Because Barbara traveled, she was able to see for herself that some blacks in both the North and the South had much better schools than segregated Prince Edward County provided for their

Negroes. She became less and less tolerant of the attitude adopted by many blacks in the county that "this is just how it is." She also, along with her classmates, felt deeply embarrassed by the tar paper shacks on the lawn surrounding the school. Barbara Rose Johns characterized these temporary classrooms as, "depressing, demeaning places." She felt their mere presence demeaned her school, her race, and most of all her own sense of self worth. You can read the hurt and anger in her *Diary* when she discusses these makeshift facilities, shabby equipment, and the lack of science laboratories, and a gymnasium. Starting with her enrollment as a freshman at Moton in 1948, Barbara felt as if her life had changed. She not only became increasingly involved in activities at Moton, but her dissatisfaction with Prince Edward County and their attempt at providing "separate but equal schools" grew and grew.

Barbara Rose Johns had an interesting personality; a mix of an intelligent dreamer, hard working tactician, and a strongly willful yet often introverted personality. Because of her shyness she seemed in many ways the most unlikely person to lead the Moton school strike. Sixty years later, the Reverend Samuel Williams Jr. said he needed only two words to describe Barbara, "Serene, Fire." So in the end she turned out to be the perfect leader to step forward at that moment in 1951 to lead the student protest—*a child will lead them.* You can sense her passion as she talks about her dreams for a new school in her unfinished Diary.

But I spent many days in my favorite hangout in the woods on my favorite stump contemplating it all. I sat by the creek while Sadie Red [the family farm horse] *drank and I thought about it. My imagination would run rampant—and I would dream that some mighty man of great wealth through God and his kind generosity built us new school building or that our parents got together and surprised us with this grand new building and we had a big celebration—and I even imagined that a great storm came through and blew down the main building and splattered the shacks to splinters—and out of this*

*wreckage rose this magnificent building and all the
students were joyous and even the teachers cried.*
Note: the author added "[the family farm horse]" for
clarity.

As discussed above, Barbara was somewhat naive, believing
that once the white community became aware of the deplorable
conditions at Moton, they would rush in to either fix their school
or build them a new one. Nonetheless, while allowing herself
many moments of fantasizing about a new school, she also had a
practical side that knew it would take action to turn that new
school into reality. Taking action would require extraordinary
leadership and project management skills that not many sixteen-
year-olds possessed. Perhaps it was a result of the adult
responsibilities she assumed in the Johns' household. Barbara
was tasked with raising her three younger brothers and younger
sister because her mother was in D. C. working during the week.
Her daddy was busy either farming or minding the store they ran
in rural Darlington Heights. By the time Barbara Rose Johns was
16, she was used to being in charge of a household, working in
the family store, helping in the fields, and being responsible for
her siblings. You can gauge for yourself just how much
responsibility this 16-year-old undertook on a daily basis from
her own recounting of her teen years.

*Around September to May—we went to school daily. I
arose early in the morning to fix breakfast and lunch for
my sister and brothers, and to see that they were properly
dressed for school. My mother had returned to her job in
Washington to help supplement the income produced by
the farm whose primary paying crop was tobacco.....*

*I was "mother" to my siblings and therefore arrived
home each day from school—not with frivolous
considerations of what I wanted to do—but already I had
begun formulating in my mind as I rode the bus home
which foods I would prepare for supper that evening.*

I had a great deal of responsibility thrust upon my shoulders both outside in the fields and inside the house. In addition, when I needed extra money for another pair of shoes, or club money, etc, I went to what was referred to as the "billet woods" where we would cut down a load of timber, take it down and get paid.

——— STARTING HIGH SCHOOL ———

Barbara Rose Johns' life seemed to take on many more dimensions with her enrollment as a freshman in Moton. "Her classmates remember her during her freshman and sophomore years as a quiet girl, intelligent, and active in school affairs. Barbara joined the drama guild, the new homemakers of America, the high school chorus, and she was elected to the student council. She traveled a good deal as a result of her involvement with these groups. She began to think that the Moton High School was a blight on the county, on all Negroes in the county, and on her." Even in the South there were pockets of improving conditions. Barbara had a chance to visit black high schools in Newport News, Lawrenceville, and King George; all newer modern brick buildings with central heating and much advanced over the facilities afforded to blacks in Prince Edward County.

In her book *The Warmth of Other Suns,* Isabel Wilkerson details how from 1900 to 1970 six million southern born African Americans voted with their feet by heading north and west in rejection of the oppressive Jim Crow South. And once settled, they shared stories with the folks back home of a better life in general and better school facilities for their children in particular. Barbara and her peers at the Moton, all knew someone who had escaped the oppressive segregation in the South for better conditions beyond the borders of the Jim Crow states. The fact that there was a better life over the border fired their own dissatisfaction with the white supremacy they faced daily, and one can draw parallels to the 18th century slaves dreaming of their freedom lying just across the border in the free States.

The genesis of Barbara Rose Johns' dissatisfaction with conditions at her school can be traced to her exposure to school systems outside of Prince Edward County, where blacks had real science labs, shops stocked with power tools, a gymnasium, central heating, and hot food in a sit-down cafeteria. Why not in Prince Edward County too, was her question?

And then there was the all-white Farmville High School which she could look at from a distance, but would not be welcomed to enter. She also heard from the boys in her class who worked around Farmville High School and spoke admiringly of the excellent equipment in the shops. In many ways, she glamorized what the whites had because, except for one quick trip, she could not enter the white school, but only look through the windows. The students continued to discuss all of these things at lunch but no one ever did anything to improve their situation. Barbara did have a favorite teacher that she felt she could talk to and confide in, Ms. Davenport.

Barbara went to Ms. Davenport: I told her how sick and tired I was of the inadequate buildings and facilities and how I wish to hell (I know I wasn't this profane speaking to her but that's how I felt) something could be done about it. After hearing me out she asked simply, "Why don't you do something about it?" I recall smiling at her dropping the subject, and going about my other activities but I didn't forget that statement, for it stuck with me for several days and out of it was conceived the idea of the strike.

——— MONUMENTIS EVENTS CAN TURN ——— ON SMALL MATTERS

Another inequity that the black students at Moton had to endure, was riding in dilapidated hand-me-down buses that had been abandoned by the white school system. These buses had no working heat and would often break down. After months of contemplation about the conditions at Moton, it was a school bus that unexpectedly provoked Barbara into action. She describes a busy morning in the fall of 1950 in her *Diary*.

One morning—I was so busy rushing my brothers and sister down the hill to school, that I forgot my own lunch and had to rush back up the hill to retrieve it. In the meantime, the bus arrived, picked them up and left me standing there by the roadside waiting to thumb a ride with whoever came by.

About an hour later, I was still waiting, when the "white school bus" drives by—half empty—on its way to Farmville High School. It would have to pass by my school to get to that school and I couldn't ride with them.

Right then and there, I decided indeed something had to be done about this inequality—but I still didn't know what. All day my mind and thoughts were whirling and as I lay in my bed that night—I prayed for help—that night whether in a dream or whether I was awake, but I felt I was awake, a plan began to formulate in my mind. A plan I felt was divinely inspired because I hadn't been able to think of anything until then. That plan was to assemble together the student council members whom I considered the "Crème de la Crème" of the school council. They were smart and thinkers. I knew them and trusted them and I was a part of them. From this we would formulate plans to go on a strike. We would make signs and I would give a speech stating our dissatisfaction and we would march out the school and people would hear us and see us and understand our difficulty and would sympathize with our plight and would grant us our new school building and our teachers would be proud and the students would learn more, and it would be grand— and we would all live happily ever after. Fully confident that all of this would transpire, I arose early the next morning, rushed to get everyone out, could hardly wait to get to school to call this meeting.

The very next day at school she gathered a few close confidants together, including John and Carrie Stokes, and started to plan for the strike. Then in April 1951, she launched her strike for a decent school. By late spring, with her parents fearing for her safety, she was sent out of the county to live with her uncle Vernon Johns in Montgomery, Alabama and complete her senior year of high school. Barbara would never again live in Prince Edward County. She lived out the rest of her life in relative peace. Attending Spelman College in Atlanta, Georgia for two years before deciding to marry, she did continue on at Spelman and graduated in 1956. She and her husband, Reverend William Powell, raised five children—four girls and one boy. Her commitment to education moved her to become a librarian, a profession she continued on with until her death in 1991. At age 56 she passed away in Philadelphia. Fittingly, she returned to Prince Edward County to be buried at Triumph Baptist Church in Darlington Heights, on the very same road where that half-filled white school bus went roaring past her in 1950.

——— A HERO IS DISCOVERED ———

As a measure of the respect and admiration Barbara Rose Johns has gained in the last decade, Virginia's Governor Robert McDonnell, in his January 18, 2010 inaugural address, chose to use Barbara's own words to demonstrate their shared commitment to education. One can only think this notoriety would have brought a wry smile to the shy, but determined woman who never went looking for fame. In talking about a shared value for education with Barbara Rose Johns, the Governor said: "It was in seizing the opportunity of equality and education that a courageous 16-year-old girl named Barbara Johns, memorialized behind this majestic Capitol at the Virginia Civil Rights Memorial, stood up and walked out of Robert Russa Moton High School in Farmville 59 years ago this spring."

Later in his address, the Governor went on to remark on her courage, "Barbara Johns was willing to risk everything for the simple opportunity of a good education. Surely, 60 years later, we can work together to provide that opportunity to all Virginia children."

Recognition by the Governor and others is fitting, but is it even possible for us today to truly understand how impossible it all must have seemed in 1951? Those of us who did not experience these tumultuous times firsthand cannot truly appreciate the hurt and fear these 13 years wrought on all sides. Of course, 13 years seems small when compared against the 250 years of slavery and 80 years of Jim Crow segregation. One of the manifestations of this hurt was a code of silence many of the participants on both sides of the issue observed for decades following the strike and especially the protracted school closing. Because of this code of silence and Barbara Rose Johns' own reluctance to talk, she has only recently been "discovered" by historians, educators, and journalists.

Writing in 1988, Taylor Branch conjectured that because Barbara Rose Johns was a teenager, she got little fame in the 1950s for her achievement and was all-but-forgotten in the 1980s. Taylor Branch put the Barbara Rose Johns role in perspective in his Pulitzer-winning *Parting the Waters: America in the King Years 1954-63*. "The case remained muffled in white consciousness, and the schoolchild origins of the lawsuit were lost as well on nearly all Negroes outside Prince Edward County. The idea that non-adults of any race might play a leading role in political events had simply failed to register on anyone—except perhaps the Klansmen who burned a cross in the Johns' yard one night, and even then people thought their target might not have been Barbara but her notorious firebrand uncle."

Barbara's sister Joan recalls that, "following the strike not too many people asked her any questions about what happened during that time. Barbara was not the type of person to talk much about what happened. She only talked if you asked her questions about it. Other than that, she didn't have much to say about what happened. After she settled down and raised a family, I don't think she was active at all that I recall."

Taylor Branch goes on to make the point that, had the student strike begun 10 or 15 years later, say in 1961, "Barbara Johns would have become something of a phenomenon in the public media." From interviews with Barbara, Branch reports that during her exile in Montgomery, she and her uncle Vernon followed reports of the landmark Brown case, but never in their wildest dreams did they believe that the authorities in Farmville would close the entire public school system for five years rather than face integration. "Long before it was over, Barbara Johns would begin carrying a permanent sense of guilt for stirring up the trouble on principle but then leaving others to bear the consequences of the movement. She thought it was a fault she shared with her uncle."

During an interview, aired on April 21, 2011, by the Virginia PBS show *Virginia Currents,* Joy Cabarrus, then an adult, discusses her remembrances as a 12 years old of the strike meeting in the Moton auditorium. She also remembers how Barbara carried guilt into her adult hood for those of the lost generation. The show was timed to coincide with the opening of Gallery number I at the Moton Museum and to recognize the 60th anniversary of the strike. Cabarrus described the burden Barbara Rose Johns carried to her grave, "She died feeling guilty that she was the cause of the children not getting their education for those four years. She felt guilty."

———— CHILDREN AND CIVIL RIGHTS ————

If a child washes his hands he can eat with kings.

—Chinua Achebe. *Things Fall Apart: A Novel*

A part of our history that is often overlooked or downplayed is the pivotal role children played in the making of America. Consider the Virginia Colony in 1607 and the key role 12-year-old Pocahontas played as the liaison between John Smith and her father the Chief of the Powhatans, and later with her marriage to John Rolfe and their trip to England to meet the Queen.

Would Lewis and Clark have made it to the Pacific without Sacagawea, a 15-year-old Shoshone with child, while acting as interpreter, cook, and guide in 1804?

Children were also instrumental in the civil rights struggle. We can place at the top of the list our own Barbara Rose Johns who led the Moton protest in 1951. She was the first and only child to lead a protest in the modern civil rights era. This book in general and this chapter in particular, appropriately devote much attention on Barbara Rose Johns, but there are other notable heroes of the civil rights movement.

On March 2, 1955, 15-year-old Claudette Colvin from Montgomery, Alabama was arrested for refusing to give up her bus seat for a white man. She was tired that day, and loaded down with school books, and had had enough of Montgomery's segregated bus laws that relegated blacks to a second-class-citizenship. Nine months later Rosa Parks, at the age of 42, followed her by also refusing to give up her seat and was arrested because she refused to comply with those same segregated bus laws in Montgomery. While Claudette never received the fame of the adult Rosa Parks, the 15-year-old was there first. She was also a complete surprise to the local NAACP who was unprepared and somewhat unwilling to support a child activist at that time. This story is well documented in a compelling book about Claudette by Phillip Hoose, *Claudette Colvin: Twice Toward Justice.* The students in Prince Edward County, likewise, appeared suddenly and unexpectedly to the Virginia NAACP. Fortunately for the Moton students, they received the full support of their local and state NAACP offices.

Blacks protesting their treatment on public transportation go back to before the Civil War. The first African American to protest discrimination on public transportation was 24-year-old Elizabeth Jennings Graham (1830–1901) who was arrested in 1854 in New York City for refusing to get off a public streetcar when directed by the white conductor. She sued the Third Avenue Railroad Company and won, thereby requiring the company to order all its cars desegregated.

Then there was the courageous 15-year-old Elizabeth Eckford, one of the Little Rock Nine. The photo of her walking through a gauntlet of angry white citizens in her effort to attend

Little Rock Central High School in September 24, 1957 remains an iconic image of the civil rights movement. Her classmate Carlotta Walls Lanier, the youngest of the Little Rock Nine, wrote a book about her experiences. As 14-year-old Carlotta walked up the stairs of Little Rock Central High School, she only wanted to make it to class without being torn limb from limb by the white mob confronting them.

One of the youngest children to take on segregation has to be 6-year-old Ruby Bridges Hall. In 1960, she shouldered the hopes of an entire race as she walked with her head held high through her own gauntlet of angry whites that were intent on preventing her attendance at the William Frantz Elementary School in New Orleans. She and her parents responded to a call from the NAACP and volunteered to participate in the first attempt to integrate the New Orleans School system. She was to attend William Frantz Elementary School as a first grader, and after the usual delays and legal wrangling, the first day of the court ordered integration was set for November 14, 1960. It was necessary for a squad of U.S. Marshals to escort Ruby through a frantic mob of whites blocking the front of the school. This day was famously captured by Norman Rockwell in his painting, *The Problem We All Live With*. Ruby said later, that she survived her daily walk into the school by praying for those who were screaming hate at her. Markedly it was left to a 6-year-old to show the adults how to be grown up and compassionate.

As an adult, Bridges described the scene on that first day of school. "Driving up I could see the crowd, but living in New Orleans, I actually thought it was Mardi Gras. There was a large crowd of people outside of the school. They were throwing things and shouting, and that sort of goes on in New Orleans at Mardi Gras." Former U.S. Marshal Charles Burks recalled his impressions of little Ruby. "She showed a lot of courage. She never cried. She didn't whimper. She just marched along like a little soldier, and we're all very proud of her."

As soon as Ruby entered the school, all the white parents went in and brought their own children out. All but one of the white teachers refused to teach if a black child was enrolled. Only Barbara Henry, a new teacher from Boston, Massachusetts, willingly agreed to teach Bridges. For over, a year Ms. Henry taught her alone, "as if she were teaching a whole class." The Bridges family suffered for their decision to send Ruby to William Frantz Elementary; her father lost his job, and her grandparents, who were sharecroppers in Mississippi, were turned off their land once their white overlords found out they were connected to "that" Ruby Bridges. She is now celebrated as the first African American child to attend an all-white elementary school in the South.

Reflecting on the pivotal role and inspiration young people provided to the early Civil Rights struggle, Reverend Martin L. King put it well, "The blanket of fear was lifted by Negro youth." This was never truer than in the first week of May 1963. The Children's Crusade was the name bestowed upon a civil rights march by hundreds of school children in Birmingham, Alabama. Initiated and organized by Rev. James Bevel, the purpose of the march was to walk downtown to talk to the mayor about segregation in their city and attempt to effect some change. Many children left their schools in order to be arrested, set free, and then to get arrested again the next day. Not all the movement leaders where in favor of using children in this way on the "front lines." Malcolm X was opposed to the event because he thought it might expose the children to violence. He said, "Real men don't put their children on the firing line."

On May 2, 1963, over a thousand African American children marched in the Children's Crusade singing, "We Shall Overcome." The children were sprayed with water from high-power hoses that could blast off clothing. They were also attacked by vicious German shepherds and, by the end of the day, police had arrested 959 boys and girls. These May protests by children were to become one of the pivotal moments in the civil rights campaign. While Birmingham police chief Eugene "Bull" Connor ordered fire hoses and dogs used on the children, the students remained nonviolent. This was one of the events that helped achieve the 1964 Civil Rights Act. These images of the attacks were shown on national and international television news shows and the front pages of leading newspapers. These pictures conveyed powerful messages, and many Americans became disgusted by what they saw. The police had not protected the protesters, but had helped to attack them instead. Those in power from Alabama like Governor George Wallace and police chief Eugene "Bull" Connor, made for an ugly juxtaposition to innocent, courageous, and nonviolent children.

With Barbara Rose Johns' leading the way, other child activists made real progress in the fight for civil rights. It seems odd to say or even write the phrase "child activist" as if the two words do not naturally fit in the same thought. Perhaps using children in this way seems contrary to our sensibilities because we all feel the need to protect our children, not place them in jeopardy. This is not meant to criticize those leaders in the NAACP who chose this path, but to recognize the bravery and sacrifice of those children activists. This small summary of vital roles played by children in the civil rights campaign is meant to recognize the important yet largely unheralded role children played to bring America a measure of equality.

All of this brings us back to Barbara Rose Johns who asked no adult for permission to begin her fight. She and her student committee picked the place and time for their protest. Barbara's fight is significant because what she started went all the way to the Supreme Court, and once "separate but equal" was struck down for the schools, all the rest of the segregated laws and customs became untenable and were ultimately overturned. While the massive protests, freedom rides, lunch counter sit-ins, and marches of the 60s were vital to the success of the civil rights movement, without *Brown v. Board* changing the legal basis for discrimination, it remains doubtful that the rest would have been successful. U.S. Rep. John Lewis, at a ceremony commemorating the 48th anniversary of *Brown v. Board of Education* at Topeka's First United Methodist Church, spoke to the importance of *Brown*. "Had there been no May 17, 1954, I'm not sure there would have been a Little Rock. I'm not sure there would have been a Martin Luther King Jr., or Rosa Parks, had it not been for May 17, 1954. It created an environment for us to push, for us to pull."

Barbara Rose Johns represents the first of a long line of child heroines who chose to fight inequality and injustice in the post-

World War II era. While most were black, and a surprising number of these child leaders were female, there are also instances of white children marching with their black sisters and brothers.

Barbara won the initial rounds of the Prince Edward County fight. Within six months of the strike, the county purchased the land and started the process in earnest to build the black students a new, modern high school. In 1954, the Supreme Court voted unanimously that "separate but equal" was unconstitutional and children like Barbara Rose Johns had indeed been put at a disadvantage with segregated schools.

You may be wondering, if Barbara helped win one of the biggest prizes in the civil rights fight, why she is not more widely known? She was, and remains, an iconic figure in Prince Edward County, but even 60 miles away at the capital city of Richmond, she was little known for most of the last 30 years. Barbara Rose Johns has begun to gain some measure of the honor she deserves with the establishment of the Robert Russa Moton Museum in 1999, the dedication of the Civil Rights Memorial on Capital Square in 2008—which features a life size bronze of Barbara Rose Johns leading the student strike—and the unveiling of her portrait in 2012 by the Governor of Virginia. Her portrait hung in that states Capitol rotunda until the Moton Museum completed Galley I. The very Capital that was built with slave labor, housed the Congress of the Confederacy, and passed the anti-integration massive resistance laws of the 1950s.

Chapter Three

TAR PAPER SHACKS

More than sixty years ago he said in prophetic warning: "This nation cannot endure half slave and half free: it will become all one thing or all the other." With equal truth, it can be said today: no more can the nation endure half privileged and half repressed; half educated and half uneducated; half protected and half unprotected; half prosperous and half in poverty; half in health and half in sickness; half content and half in discontent; yes, half free and half yet in bondage.

My fellow citizens, in the great name which we honor here today, I say unto you that this memorial which we erect in token of our veneration is but a hollow mockery, a symbol of hypocrisy, unless we together can make real in our national life, in every state and in every section, the things for which he died.

Twelve million black men and women in this country are proud of their American citizenship, but they are determined that it shall mean for them no less than any other group, the largest enjoyment of opportunity and the fullest blessings of freedom. We ask no special privileges; we claim no superior title; but we do expect in loyal cooperation with all true lovers of our common country to do our full share in lifting our country above reproach and saving her flag from stain or humiliation. Let us, therefore, with malice toward none, with charity for all, with firmness in the right as God gives us right let us strive on to finish the work which he so nobly began, to make America the symbol for equal justice and equal opportunity for all.

—Robert Russa Moton, *Draft of the Lincoln Memorial Dedication Keynote Speech.* This is a portion of the original draft of Moton's speech. The speech was intended for the May 30, 1922 dedication of the Lincoln Memorial. This version of the speech was never given because white censors objected to Moton holding the country to task for failing the black man following reconstruction. See Appendix I for the entire speech text of this more radical version and also Appendix II for the toned down version that Moton ultimately provided at the dedication.

Time Line for Chapter Three
Tar Paper Shacks
(1619–1951)

1619. Dutch traders bring the first Africans from Angola, Africa to Jamestown and exchange them for goods.

1852. Uncle Tom's Cabin published by Harriet Beecher Stowe.

1857. Supreme Court in *Dred Scott v. Sandford* ruled that any person descended from Africans, whether slave or free, is not a citizen of the United States, according to the Constitution. *Dred Scott v. Sandford*, 60 *U.S. 393 (1857)*.

1860. Abraham Lincoln gave his Right Makes Might speech at Cooper Union, New York, New York.

1862. Lincoln issues the preliminary Emancipation Proclamation.

August 26, 1867. Robert Russa Moton was born (August 26, 1867 – May 31, 1940). He was an African American educator and author. He served as an administrator at Hampton Institute and was named principal of Tuskegee Institute in 1915 after the death of Dr. Booker T. Washington, a position he held for 20 years until retirement in 1935. The Robert Russa Moton High School was named after him.

1868. The 14th amendment, providing equal rights to blacks is passed.

1869 to 1877. During much of the Reconstruction era, the federal government assumed political control of the former states of the Confederacy.

1870. The 15th amendment, giving black male citizens the right to vote is passed.

1892. Vernon Johns (April 22, 1892—June 11, 1965) was born. He was an American minister and civil rights leader and Uncle to Barbara Rose Johns.

1896. Supreme Court in *Plessy v. Ferguson* ruled that segregation in America was constitutional. This one ruling doomed the black man and the South to seventy-five years of segregation by providing the legal underpinnings of the South's Jim Crow laws.

1948. Prince Edward County adds three "temporary" wooden buildings, covered with tar paper around the central Robert Russa Moton High School brick building to address unbearable overcrowding.

1949, October. Rev. Leslie Francis Griffin's father passes away and he becomes the pastor of the First Baptist Church in Farmville, Virginia following in his father's footsteps.

1951. James J. Kilpatrick named editor of the *Richmond News Leader.*

Chapter Three
TAR PAPER SHACKS
(1619–1951)

Dare we dream of a golden day when the bestial War shall rule no more.
But instead—the gentle Prince in the Hall of Brotherly Love in the City of Peace.

—D. W. Griffith, *The Birth of a Nation*, 1950

If you visit the Robert Russa Moton Museum you will find in Gallery II, *The Tar Paper Shacks*, the background and context for the events that led up to the student strike in1951. The gallery paints a vivid picture of what life was like in the segregated South and why the Moton students were motivated to strike for a decent school. For those of you who did not live through these times, this chapter was constructed to provide you an overview of the first 399 years of race relations in America, Virginia, and Prince Edward County. No small task in a single chapter, and well beyond the scope of Moton's Gallery II. Nonetheless, the reader should be prepared to see an America profoundly different than what exists today. This overview paints a picture of a country steeped in racism and segregation. You are encouraged to not just look at the hate, but see that even in the darkest moments, somehow, this group of Americans singled out for unconscionable aggression still found the courage, wisdom, and hope to keep moving forward toward a better future.

We start our review with the arrival of the first slaves from Angola at Jamestown in 1619, then describe the 250 years of slavery both in the North and South, address the Civil War and Emancipation, move on to Reconstruction, which all too quickly transitioned to 100 years of Jim Crow segregation, discover the great black migration, introduce Robert Russa Moton and his instrumental involvement in World War I to promote the fair treatment of the black soldier, the new world order following World War II, and finally the specific Prince Edward County conditions that led to the 1951 strike.

If you were born after 1980 you might assume that America was always as it is today. To my young readers, read on, and you can begin to understand and appreciate the sacrifice and courage our civil rights leaders invested to free all of us, first, from a slave nation, and then from a hundred years of corrupt segregation. To those unfamiliar, beyond a few sound bites, with our country's first 399 years of race relations, this overview will provide a summary of the unbiased truth of America's transition from a slavery state with a constitution built to codify blacks into perpetual servitude, to the run-up to the modern civil rights movement. The intended purpose is to allow you to appreciate our Moton heroes and heroines all the more. In many ways they led the way for the final push of the modern civil rights advancements we enjoy today. While much of this 399 years of history is just plain ugly and shameful, you will note a persistent theme that blacks, no matter how disenfranchised, never gave up on themselves or their vision for their rightful opportunity to earn a piece of the American dream.

This 399 year journey in America starts with violence. Blacks, for the most part—certainly this is true from 1619 to 1807—did not ask to come to America. As slaves they were prevented from leaving and as emancipated men they were encouraged by whites—Lincoln and others—to migrate back to Africa. Blacks refused to leave because America was now their home and, more important, they had caught on to the dream of being an American. They fully expected that Jefferson's promise that "all men are created equal" would include them.

──────── **WHY SUCH A FUSS** ────────

Why was segregation so bitterly disputed in Prince Edward County with neither side willing to give an inch? Education is vitally important in its own right, and then mix in the need to do what is best for your children, and we can start to understand why a line was drawn in the sand by both parties. That is not to say that this fight was just about education and the young. Maybe more important, this was a fight for a culture and way of life. For many whites, sending their children to school with blacks was a giant step toward their ultimate fear—miscegenation; the mixing of the races and intermarriage. This was viewed by many whites as the ultimate abomination and became the rallying cry for those opposed to an integrated society. The proof of this is that it took until 1967 for the courts to strike down the Virginia law prohibiting mixed marriages, and decades more for even a modicum of acceptance of mixed race couples in the Old Dominion. Perhaps Robert Russa Moton best captured the emotions of race relations in the early and mid 20th century when he wrote in his autobiography, *Finding a Way Out,* about the "negro problem," or perhaps he should have called it the "white problem." "For a great many years I entertained the idea that while the Southern man thought logically and clearly on economic, political, religious, and other questions affecting the welfare and progress of the country, here was one question upon which he did not *think* at all, but rather *felt*– that on this matter he had definite, fixed opinions about which argument was unnecessary and upon which nothing further could be said." While Moton made his observation in 1920, he rather pointedly captured the tenor that continued to polarize the South and Prince Edward County during the 1950s and 1960s.

One of the vital roles America public schools assumed is preparing our most precious possessions, our children, to not just learn and prepare for a productive life, but become schooled in the responsibilities of good citizenship.

> *Of all the instruments for the maintenance of a government, the public school is recognized as the most powerful. The strength of America has been in the transformation of people from other parts of the world into American citizens loyal to a new country and to a new way of life full of opportunities for the common man. The building of this citizenship has been the duty primarily of the American public school system. It is the backbone of our democracy.*

—Patrice Preston-Grimes, assistant professor in the Department of Curriculum, Instruction, and Special Education of the Curry School of Education at the University of Virginia, Charlottesville, Virginia, 2010

Herein lies the heart of the problem that was facing both sides of the Prince Edward struggle; they each saw a radically different America. One side wanted the full rights and responsibilities of American citizenship and the other wanted to maintain blacks in the role of a second-class citizen and keep them subservient and dependent upon whites.

———— A COLD NORTH WIND ————

Even though the start of slavery in the American colonies can be traced to a Dutch ship arriving at Jamestown in 1619 with 20 slaves, or possibly they were indentured servants, it is worth noting that, "the African presence in the New World was more than a hundred years old by the time these twenty Angolan slaves found themselves in Jamestown... ." Black men were part of the Spanish conquest of the Americas as slaves, free men, and even conquistadors.

Let us start our look at slavery in one of the greatest slave ports in all the New World. For most of the early 1700s, New York City was the port were most slaves entered what was to become the American Colonies. One reason to start in the North is to reinforce the point that slavery and racism were not just a Southern disability, but in all too many meaningful ways the entire country was complicit and vested in its maintenance.

Slavery had a long demise. Indeed, slavery's long history in New York indicates the importance of black labor to the region between 1626 and 1827. "As in the South, black slave labor was central to the day-to-day survival in the economic life of Europeans in the colonial North, and no part of the colonial North relied more heavily on slavery than Manhattan." Slave labor supported the survival of the first European settlers in Dutch-governed New Amsterdam in the 16th century. "By the first decade of the 1700s, forty percent of New York's households contained at least one enslaved African; the largest proportion of any of the northern settlements." In the 18th century, the British sought to heighten white New Yorkers' reliance on slave labor and the slave trade in order to make Manhattan the chief North American slave port and thereby an economic center. As British New York became known as a hub of slave labor, few European laborers, free or indentured, chose to emigrate there. Under both the Dutch and the British, slaves performed vital agricultural tasks in the rural areas surrounding New York City. By the end of the 16th century, New York City had a larger black population than any other North American city. "The ratio of slaves to whites in the total population was comparable to that in Maryland and Virginia. In the 18th century, only Charleston and New Orleans exceeded New York City in number of slaves."

Connecticut stood out amongst all of New England as the only colony where blacks were legally disenfranchised from their forced arrival in 1660 until reconstruction. The first blacks came to Connecticut soon after the first settlements were founded near Hartford and along the coast. Colonial records note black servants as early as 1660, and there is evidence that at least a few blacks lived in Connecticut as early as 1640. Slavery was also not an exclusively racial institution; it applied to Indians and whites as well. Habitual white criminals were periodically sold into servitude in the West Indies. As the black population increased, Connecticut's lawmakers enacted more and more laws to control their slave population. The so-called Black Code was a series of laws passed between 1690 and 1730 that described the rights and responsibilities of slave and master.

By 1690 the Black Code had formalized slavery in Connecticut. Black servants were required to carry passes outside their hometowns or be treated as runaways. Blacks were not allowed to sell items without proof of ownership or written permission from the owner. Blacks were liable to whippings for offenses like disturbing the peace or "offering to strike a white person." Blacks found outside after 9 p.m. without a pass could be whipped.

Connecticut did emancipate their slaves in 1848, but they were only a little better off free than they had been as slaves.

They could testify in court and own property, but their place was still at the bottom of society. They could not vote; nor were they welcome as social equals in the educational and social institutions of the state. Almost simultaneous with the movement toward suffrage was the disfranchisement of Connecticut's blacks. Theoretically, free blacks who amassed enough land could have voted, but in 1818 a state law specifically denied blacks the vote. By 1847, Connecticut was the only New England state to disfranchise blacks. Blacks were voting regularly in Massachusetts before the Civil War. In 1847 and 1865 the Connecticut General Assembly convincingly voted down black suffrage. Only with the passage of the Fifteenth Amendment in 1869 could blacks vote in Connecticut.

Before leaving the early colonial era, a word about Phillis Wheatley. Historian Gary Nash wrote that, during her time she was to become "the most famous African women in America…" In 1761, she was only seven years old when the slave ship *Phillis* came to Boston to sell its human cargo. A prospering tailor John Wheatley purchased her and named her for the ship that brought her from Africa. Phillis Wheatley was writing and being published in an era where women of any color were not supposed to write for public consumption. Phillis not only wrote pamphlets in support of the revolution, she became famous for her poetry and anti-slavery positions. Even though she was enslaved, she became the first woman in North America to publish anything for public purchase. Her book of poetry published in 1773, *Poems on Various Subjects, Religious and Moral*, was widely read in America and England.

Twas mercy brought me from my Pagan land,
Taught my benighted soul to understand
That there's a God, that there's a Saviour too:
Once I redemption neither sought nor knew.
Some view our sable race with scornful eye,
"Their colour is a diabolic dye."
Remember, Christians, Negroes, black as Cain,
May be refin'd, and join th' angelic train.'

—Phillis Wheatley, *Poems on Various Subjects, Religious and Moral*, first published in 1773

Singularly, because she was a black, Phillis Wheatley had to endure an inquisition from 18 learned Bostonians to substantiate that she indeed was the author of her poems. Many refused to believe a black was capable of writing such sophisticated poems, nevermind one who was also a women and still only a teenager, at 17. She indeed was the author and when she turned 19 she sailed to England to promote her book and assist the burgeoning abolitionist movement in that country. Upon her return to Boston she was freed by her owners and continued to write and be published until her death at the young age of 30. Wheatley is just one of thousands of blacks who in spite of slavery, Jim Crow laws, and segregation rose above circumstance to attain great accomplishments. Of course, each time the white man had to act surprised all over again.

Sometimes we can learn about ourselves best from the view of an outsider. In his book *North of Slavery*, Leon F. Litwack discusses French nobleman Alexis de Tocqueville's American tour and his impressions and views of race relations in the Northern parts of the United States in 1831.

Most Northerners, to the extent that they thought about it at all, rebelled at the idea of racial amalgamation or integration. Instead, they favored voluntary colonization, forced expulsion, or legal and social proscription. The young and perceptive French nobleman Alexis de Tocqueville, after an extensive tour of the United States in 1831, concluded that Negroes and Whites form separate communities, that they could never live in the same country on an equal footing, and that the oppressed race—the Negro—consequently faced ultimate extinction or expulsion. Having associated the plight of American Negroes with the institution of slavery, Tocqueville expressed his astonishment at conditions in the North. "The prejudice of race," he wrote, "appears to be stronger in the states that have abolished slavery then in those where it still exist; and nowhere is it so intolerant as in those states where servitude has never been known."

Where statutes made no racial distinctions, Tocqueville found that customs and popular prejudice exerted a decisive influence. While some white schools admitted Negroes, especially before 1820, most northern states either excluded them altogether or established separate schools for them. Of course, in the South education for blacks was legally prohibited and for most slave holders a dangerous idea as well. In spite of the odds against them, a few blacks did learn to read and write; it was always under a cover of secrecy lest they be punished.

Although Negroes and whites could legally intermarry in most northern states, public opinion would not permit it. Where Negroes possessed the right to vote, they often faced vigorous resistance at the polls. They might seek redress in the courts, but only whites served as judges, and although they were legally entitled to sit on juries, the public would again not allow it. Segregation was omnipresent in the North and blacks found discrimination confronting them in public places, including churches, transportation, and cemeteries. "Thus the Negro is free," Tocqueville concluded, "but he can share neither the rights, nor the pleasures, nor the labor, nor the afflictions, nor the tomb of him whose equal he has been declared to be; and he cannot meet him upon fair terms in life or in death."

On the eve of the Civil War a Scottish poet, journalist, and songwriter, Charles Mackay, who was making a similar tour of the United States, wrote of his impressions of the North and attitudes toward the black man. Mackay summarized what he had seen and heard during his multicity tour of the North.

We shall not make a black man a slave; we shall not buy him or sell him; but we shall not associate with him. He shall be free to live, and to thrive, if he can, and to pay taxes and perform duty; but he shall not be free to dine and drink at our board — to share with us the

deliberations of the jury box — to sit upon the seat of judgment, however capable he may be — to plead to our courts — to represent us in the legislature — to attend us at the bed of sickness and pain — to mingle with us in the concert-room, the lecture-room, the theater, or the church, or to marry with our daughters.
We are of another race, and he is inferior. Let him know his place — and keep it.

—Charles Mackay, Life and Liberty in America: or, Sketches of a Tour in the United States and Canada in 1857—1858

Negroes in the North understood from the beginning that education was the key to not only their individual success, but one way as a race they could gain some measure of respect from the white community with the hope that this would lead to full equality. Of course the rules varied from state to state. In New England, the local school committees often assigned Negro children to separate institutions, and in Ohio and Pennsylvania they allowed Negroes to go to school with whites unless 20 or more could be accommodated in separate facilities.

"By 1860, some small and scattered communities established integrated education, but the large cities, including New York, Philadelphia, Cincinnati, and Providence became a haven, by correcting existing abuses and making the Negro schools equal to those of the whites." Leon F. Litwack documented in his *North of Slavery: The Negro in the Free States, 1790–1860* the experiences of Fredrick Douglass' with his own daughter. When Frederick Douglass' daughter entered Seward Seminary in Rochester, school authorities assigned her to a room separate from the whites and appointed a teacher to instruct her. "Douglass protested the school's action and withdrew his daughter. The principal told him that perhaps prejudice would subside after a few terms and she could then be accorded equal privileges."

——— THE SOUTH ———

Moving along to the South, we can turn to one who is noted for his blunt assessments, General U. S. Grant, who wrote in his iconic memoir a pointed perspective of the South's views on slavery and their constitutional rights to enslave the Negro. "The South claimed the sovereignty of states, a claim the right to go years into confederations such states as they wanted, that is, all the states that where slavery existed. They did not seem to think this course inconsistent. The fact is, the Southern slave-owners believed that, in some way, the ownership of slaves conferred a sort of patent of nobility — a right to govern independent of the interest or wishes of those who did not hold such property. They convinced themselves, first, of the divine origin of the institution and, next, that that particular institution was not safe in the hands of any body of legislators but themselves."

In February 1861, only a few weeks after Louisiana seceded from the Union, Randall Lee Gibson enlisted as a private in a state army regiment. The son of a wealthy, sugar planter and valedictorian of Yale's class of 1853, Gibson was a longtime supporter of secession. Conflict was ultimately inevitable, he believed, not because of states' rights or the propriety or necessity of slavery. Rather, a war would be fought over the inexorable gulf between whites and blacks, or what he called, "the most enlightened race and the most degraded of all the races of men." In large measure, because Northern abolitionists were forcing the South to recognize "the political, civil, and social equality of all the races of men," Gibson wrote, "the South was compelled to enjoy independence out of the Union."

The notion that the American Civil War turned on the question of black and white was hardly an intuitive position for Gibson or for the South. Although Southern society was wholly dependent on slavery, the line between black and white had always been permeable. Since the 17th century, people descended from African slaves had been assimilating into white communities—albeit at a trickle. It was an inalterable migration, which was covered up even as it was happening, its reach extending into the most unlikely corners of the South. While

Randall Gibson was committed to a hard-line ideology of racial distinction, there was a secret narrative of his family's story that lay buried with his ancestors. For, you see, Randall Gibson was a descendant of a black man.

Gibson's siblings proudly traced their ancestry to a prosperous farmer in the South Carolina backcountry named Gideon Gibson. "What they didn't know was that when he first arrived in the colony in the 1730s, he was a free man of color. At the time the legislature thought he had come there to plot a slave revolt." The governor interrogated him and learned that he was a skilled tradesman, had a white wife and had owned land and slaves in Virginia and North Carolina. He declared the Gibsons to be "not Negroes nor Slaves but Free people." Then the governor granted them hundreds of acres of land. The Gibsons soon intermarried with their Welsh and Scot-Irish neighbors along the frontier separating South Carolina's coastal plantations from Indian country. "It did not matter if the Gibsons were black or white—they were planters." Once again, the Gibson story proves that there is no separate black history, but blacks like everyone else are inseparably intertwined within one mosaic that is the United States. However, unlike most Americans today blacks were here from almost the beginning; and they had from the beginning a singularly profound impact on America.

──────── **CIVIL WAR ENDS** ────────

Returning to Grant, as his time as the commanding general of the army was coming to and end, the last act of his role in the civil war played out in and around Prince Edward County. While pursuing Lee on his retreat from Petersburg on the night of April 7, 1865 he was able to bring that terrible war to its end on the door step of Prince Edward County. Grant describes how it was in Farmville that he came upon the idea to reach out to Lee to start negotiations for his surrender. It seems rather poignant that both the Civil War and segregation all surrendered within a few miles of Farmville. Of course there was almost a hundred year gap between these two monumentis events. Grant's recollections of the night of April 7, 1865 as told in his memoirs:

I rode in to Farmville on the seventh, arriving there early in the day. Sheridan and Ward were pushing through, away to the south. Mead was back towards the High Bridge, and Humphreys confronting Lee as before stated. After having gone into bivouac at Prince Edwards Courthouse [Farmville, Virginia], Sheridan learned that seven trains of provisions and forage were at Appomattox, and determined to start at once and capture them; and a forced march was necessary in order to get there before Lee's armies could secure them.... This fact, together with the incident related the night before by Dr. Smith, gave me the idea of opening correspondence with Gen. Lee on the subject of surrender of his army I therefore wrote him on the following day.

Grant continues, in describing his accommodations while he stayed in Farmville, "I know that I occupied a hotel almost destitute of furniture at Farmville, which had probably been used as a Confederate hospital. The next morning when I came out I found a Confederate colonel there, who reported to me and said that he was the proprietor of that house, and that he was a colonel of the regiment that have been raised in that neighborhood. He said that when he came along past home, he found that he was the only man of the regiment remaining with Lee's army, so he just dropped out, and now wanted to surrender himself. I told him to stay there and he would not be molested. That was one regiment which had been eliminated from Lee's force by this crumbling process."

History buffs know well that Lee stayed in that very hotel the night before Grant. Some say the great generals stayed in the very same room and bed within hours of each other. What really matters is that within a few days on April 9, 1865, only a few miles across the Prince Edward County line in neighboring Appomattox, Lee surrendered the Army of Northern Virginia to Grant. The surrender essentially ended America's most deadly war. Immediately following the war the South entered into a period called Reconstruction. Unfortunately, after less than 10 years of reconstruction, blacks in the South would see their dreams for emancipation turn into a 100-year nightmare called Jim Crow. The next section investigates this missed opportunity.

———— RUN UP TO RECONSTRUCTION ————

To understand reconstruction, it is useful to investigate the years leading up to the Civil War and, importantly, the tenor of white and black relations. Prior to and during the Civil War, blacks had to struggle with a divisive American psyche that permeated the thinking of many, if not most Americans in both the North and South, who did not believe blacks were American citizens. While many believed slavery was wrong, few of them were willing to go the next step and allow free association between blacks and whites. In his first Inaugural Address on the East Portico of the Capitol on March 4, 1861, Lincoln got right to the point in his usual profound manner, when he captured both the tenor of the times, and the essence of the strife at hand.

"One section of our country believes slavery is right and out to be extended," he tartly summarized, "while the other believes it is wrong, and ought not to be extended. That is the only substantial dispute."

While the expediency to end a long, costly war drove Lincoln to eventually emancipate the slaves, his preferred solution to the "Negro Problem" was to ship them all back to Africa. After all, in 1857 the United States Supreme Court in *Dred Scott v. Sandford* ruled that any person descended from Africans, whether slave or free, is not a citizen of the United States, according to the laws and Constitution of the United States. *Dred Scott v. Sandford*, 60 *U.S. 393 (1857)*, was a ruling by the U.S. Supreme Court that people of African descent imported into the United States and held as slaves or their descendants, whether or not they were themselves slaves, were not protected by the Constitution and could never be U.S. citizens. The court also held that the U.S. Congress had no authority to prohibit slavery in federal territories and that, because slaves were not citizens, they could not sue in court. Furthermore, the Court ruled that slaves, as chattel or private property, could not be taken away from their owners without due process. The Supreme Court's decision was written by Chief Justice Roger B. Taney. The effects of this decision were far reaching and consequential:

- Enabling the rise of the Republican Party over the Whig Party;
- Forming the core of the argument for the Lincoln–Douglas debates; and
- Directly leading to the election of President Abraham Lincoln and ultimately the American Civil War.

In some ways this manifesto for a slave state was so over the top that even armed conflict would become tenable rather than admit the Declaration of Independence was so hollow. This ruling and the vehemence of the southern defense helped the North, finally, to understand just how deep and strong was the attachment of the South to slavery.

An interesting side note to this period is the story of one strong-willed woman who went from Slavery to the White House. Elizabeth Keckley (1818-1907) was a slave in Prince Edward County, living on the campus of the then struggling Hampton-Sydney College. Her master Colonel Armistead Burwell, was the college Steward. After a life of slavery, (being sold, hired out and moved all over the country) she ultimately purchased her freedom in St. Louis and moved to Washington D.C. She opened a dress shop and was a manntuamaker for the Washington elite. In short order she went from creating fashionable dresses for the wives of Southerners like Mrs. Jeff Davis to having the run of the White House and the confidence of Mary Todd Lincoln. Of course nearly all the Southerners were soon to decamp from D. C. and the Federal government with the election of Abraham Lincoln.

Recall that following the election of Abraham Lincoln in 1860, South Carolina adopted an ordinance of secession on December 20, 1860, and Mississippi did so on January 9, 1861. Davis had expected this but waited until he received official notification; then on January 21, the day Davis called "the saddest day of my life", he delivered a farewell address to the United States Senate, resigned and returned to Mississippi and soon after was elected to the Presidency of the Confederate States.

Arriving in Washington, D.C. by the spring of 1860 she used her perseverance and considerable dress making skills to ingratiate her with those of influence; she was able to distinguish herself among the notable women of society in the nation's capitol who sought out her dressmaking skills. Among her clients were Varnia Davis, wife of Jefferson Davis, and Mary Anne Randolph Custis Lee, wife of Robert E. Lee. She was an eyewitness to much of the history surrounding the demise of slavery. In a strange coincidence her master in St Louis, 1840 until 1854, was Hugh A. Garland the noted attorney who successful argued the *Dred Scott* case that most historians believe directly precipitated the Civil War. Immediately following Lincoln's assassination, the only person Mary Todd Lincoln asked to be sent to the White House to console her was Elizabeth Keckley.

Years later her tell-all book about her time in the White House was written to defend Mrs. Lincoln and gain sympathy for her former patron, but much to her dismay only became more fodder for May Todd Lincoln's detractors. More information on her fascinating life can be found in books referenced under Bibliography items number172 and number173.

The marginalization of blacks did not stop with emancipation, or the end of the Civil War, or the Fourteenth Amendment. Lincoln's vision for the future, like most of his countrymen, did not include an America where a black could enjoy the full fruits of citizenry, even if his forced labors had helped make the America that whites then enjoyed. In this Lincoln was in step with most of the country during this period. Paradoxically the two great emancipators of the civil war, Lincoln and Grant, left a lasting legacy for decades of continued and significant injury to blacks through their appointments to the Supreme Court. Both Presidents appointed only men who reflected the countries racist sentiments; to the ruin of the black man and America for the next century.

─────── **RECONSTRUCTION** ───────

Following the end of the Civil War, the country went through a period called Reconstruction. The main aim for the Union was to unify the country, bring the South back into the Union, and transition the slaves into a productive labor force. While some Republicans wanted the black man to be the equal of whites, most of America was not willing to go anywhere near that far.

Following the assassination of Lincoln the South was surprised and encouraged by President Johnson's stated intention, to return the South to the management of their own affairs. Between September and December of 1865, every Southern state enacted their own version of what came to be called Black Codes. Their very evident purpose was to reduce free blacks to a new kind of legal servitude distinguished by all the disadvantages of chattel slavery and none of its advantages. The small town of Opelousas, Louisiana wasted no time in getting their new "Negro Problem" under control. In an ordinance passed immediately after the war, the town made a law that declared, "no negro or freedmen shall be allowed to come within the limits of the town of Opelousas without special permission from his employers. …Whoever shall violate this provision shall suffer imprisonment and two days work on the public streets, or pay a fine of five dollars. …Any negro found on the streets of the town after ten o'clock in the evening had to work for five days on the public streets or pay a $5 fine." The ordinance further provided:

> *No negro or freedman shall be permitted to rent or keep a house within the limits of the town under any circumstances. . . . No negro or freedman shall reside within the limits of the town . . . who is not in the regular service of some white person or former owner. . . . No public meetings or congregations of negroes or freedmen shall be allowed within the limits of the town. . . . No negro or freedman shall be permitted to preach, exhort, or otherwise declaim to congregations of colored people without a special permission from the mayor or president of the board of police.. .. No freedman ... shall be allowed*

to carry firearms, or any kind of weapons.... No freedman
shall sell, barter, or exchange any article of merchandise
within the limits of Opelousas without permission in
writing from his employer In the parish of St. Landry it
was required that every negro [is] to be in the service of
some white person, or former owner. ...

What precipitated this punitive action against blacks?
Southern plantation owners fearing that they would lose their
land was part of the issue. More to the point, having convinced
themselves that slavery was justified, planters feared African
Americans wouldn't work without coercion. The Black Codes
were an attempt to control them and to ensure they did not claim
social equality. The Black Codes granted African Americans
certain rights, such as legalized marriage, ownership of property,
and limited access to the courts. But the Black Codes denied
them the rights to testify against whites, to serve on juries or in
state militias, or to vote, or to express legal concerns publicly. In
addition, poll taxes were imposed in every Southern state,
ranging in amounts from Georgia's $1 per head on every man
between the ages of 21 and 60, to $2 in Alabama on every person
between the ages of 18 and 50, and to $3 in Florida. A black man
could not buy or rent land except in a city. South Carolina
required that a black man pay an exorbitant fee to engage in trade
or open a store. Nor, in that state, could he serve on juries.
Unemployment was treated as a crime, and the unemployed could
be sentenced to a work prison.

In response to planter's demands that they not lose control of
their black labor pool, the Black Codes declared that those who
failed to sign yearly labor contracts could be arrested and hired
out to white landowners. Some states limited the occupations
open to African Americans and barred them from acquiring land,
and others provided that judges could assign black children to
work for their former owners without the consent of their parents.
When Negroes could not pay the fines and costs after legal
proceedings, they were to be hired at public auction by the sheriff
to the highest bidder. In South Carolina persons of color
contracting for service were to be known as "servants," and those

with whom they contracted, as "masters." You can forgive Southern blacks if all this sounded slightly familiar.

One unexpected response the Black Codes elicited was to outrage Northern public opinion, because it seemed the South was creating a form of quasi-slavery to negate the results of the war. After winning large majorities in the 1866 elections, the Republican's responded by placing the South under military rule. They held new elections in which the Freedmen could vote. Suffrage was also expanded to poor whites. In 1866 these new governments repealed all the Black Codes. On April 9, Congress overrode President Andrew Johnson's veto thereby enacting the Civil Rights Act of 1866. The act confers citizenship upon black Americans and guarantees equal rights with whites. Thus begins the era of Reconstruction that forced, for a time, so many changes to life in the South.

The Civil Rights Act of 1866 and the Fourteenth Amendment were milestones in the fight to give former slaves equal rights. The Civil Rights Act was groundbreaking because it was the first piece of congressional legislation to override state laws and protect civil liberties. More important, it reversed the 1857 *Dred Scott v. Sanford* ruling by the U.S. Supreme Court, which stated that blacks were not citizens, which had effectively reinforced slavery. In giving former slaves citizenship, the Civil Rights Act also gave them—at least in theory—equal protection under the law.

The ratification of the Fourteenth Amendment guaranteed that from that point onward, no one in the United States—even a Supreme Court justice or president—could deny a black person citizenship rights on the basis of racial inequality. Constitutional law would now forever stand in the way. Of course, true equality did not just spring forward and the next remaining steps would not be taken for another hundred years. But the Fourteenth Amendment was a necessary step.

––––––––––

While the Civil Rights Bill of 1866 was groundbreaking there was more to do, much more, to ensure the equal treatment of blacks. Unfortunately, little would be accomplished as the country back slide into the Jim Crow era. The changing tenor of the country, away from Reconstruction, can be portrayed by the saga of the Civil Rights Act of 1875. This federal law was proposed by none other than Senator Charles Sumner and Representative Benjamin F. Butler (both Republicans) in 1870. The act was passed five years later by Congress in February, 1875 and signed by President Grant on March 1, 1875.

The act's purpose was to guarantee that everyone, regardless of race, color, or previous condition of servitude, was entitled to the same treatment in "public accommodations" (i.e., inns, public conveyances on land or water, theaters, and other places of public amusement). If found guilty, the lawbreaker could face a penalty anywhere from $500 to $1,000 and/or 30 days to one year in prison. However, the law was rarely enforced, especially after the 1876 presidential election and withdrawal of federal troops from the South.

Almost from the beginning, while clearly needed, the passage of the act was no sure thing and required enormous concessions that would contribute to holding the black man back for almost a hundred years. In an effort to gain support for the passage of the 1875 Civil Rights Bill, three-term Representative Stephen Kellogg of Connecticut stripped the bill of all references to education. Black members vigorously defended the education clause, preferring almost unanimously the Senate version of the bill. John Lynch contended that increased federal funding for education was the most harmless provision of the bill. "All share its benefits alike," he said. Richard Cain sharply admonished his southern colleagues: "Examine the laws of the South, and you will find that it was a penal offense for anyone to educate the colored people there.... You robbed us for two hundred years. During all that time we toiled for you. We have raised your cotton, your rice, and your corn.... And yet you upbraid us for being ignorant—call us a horde of barbarians!" In a harbinger of fights to come it was education that was the final sticking point to passing the bill. The bill called for federal funding and oversight of public education across America, and especially the South, and in particular called for the education of the Negro. Traditionally, states and local municipalities controlled public schools. It would be sarcasm to simply say that throughout the South, local prejudice led to uneven educational opportunities.

By the time the Civil Rights Bill came to a vote, the measure had been gravely wounded. As the 1875 Civil Rights Bill was coming to closure there were desperate pleas from its supporters. "Spare us our liberties; give us peace; give us a chance to live; …place no obstruction in our way; give us an equal chance," Richard Cain pleaded. "We ask no more of the American people." James Rapier despaired, "I have no compromise to offer on this subject…. After all, this question resolves itself into this: either I am a man or I am not a man." Minutes before the final measure came to a vote in the House, Members passed Kellogg's amendment eliminating all references to public education, 128 to 48. A motion replacing the House version with the Senate bill failed soon afterward, 148 to 114. The battered Civil Rights Bill finally passed 162 to 99. The measure provided no mechanism to regulate public schools, but stipulated equal use of public transportation and accommodations regardless of race. It also prohibited the exclusion of African Americans from jury service. The legislation passed the Senate on February 27. On March 1, President Ulysses S. Grant signed it into law. Many were thankful that Republicans, who were within days of being relegated to a minority status within the government, managed to steer such a bill through the chamber at the conclusion of a lame duck session. While the bill represented a considerable legislative victory, in their desperation to pass the measure, Republicans had left the Civil Rights Act of 1875 in such a weakened state that it did little to impede the oncoming creation of a system of segregation in the South. Moreover, the limited protection it did afford would soon be stripped by the courts.

And, in 1883, in a decisive step toward Jim Crow, that is exactly what the highest court in the land did. The *Civil Rights Cases*, 109 U.S. 3 (1883), were a group of five similar cases consolidated into one issue for the United States Supreme Court to review. The decision itself involved five consolidated cases coming from different lower courts in which African Americans had sued theaters, hotels, and transit companies that had refused them admittance or excluded them from "white only" facilities. The Supreme Court declared the Civil Rights Act of 1875 unconstitutional on the basis that although the Fourteenth Amendment prohibits discrimination by the state, it does not give the state the power to prohibit discrimination by private individuals.

Many of the 1875 Act's provisions were later more strongly enacted in the Civil Rights Act of 1964 and still later the Fair Housing Act, this time using the federal power to regulate interstate commerce. You can mark down 1875 as the point in history were Congress and the America people made their last gasp on Reconstruction and began to turn away from the Negro. It would be almost another 90 years before a civil rights bill would again be passed by Congress. In reflecting on the disillusionment that all to quickly followed Emancipation, with the dawn of the Black Codes and Jim Crow, W. E. B. DuBois summed up the state of the black man in one sentence: "The slave went free; stood a brief moment in the sun; then moved back again toward slavery."

––––––––––

For much of the Reconstruction era, from 1869 to 1877, the federal government assumed political control of the former states of the Confederacy. Voters in the South elected more than 600 African American state legislators and 16 members of Congress. Black and white citizens established several progressive state governments that attempted to extend educational opportunities and civil and political rights to everyone.

As federal troops either withdrew or consolidated in a limited number of Southern cities, the white planter class again regained the upper hand. The 1873 Depression further distracted Northern voters and they became decreasingly interested in Southern Reconstruction. With unemployment high throughout the mid-1870s, and hard currency scarce, Northerners were more concerned with their own financial well-being than in securing rights for freedmen, punishing the Ku Klux Klan, or re-admitting secessionist states. Reconstruction efforts stalled when Democrats capitalized on these depression conditions and took control of the House of Representatives in 1874.

Then they were almost entirely erased after the compromise that elected Republican, Rutherford B. Hayes president in 1877. An informal deal was struck to resolve the disputed election that came to be called the *Compromise of 1877*. In return for the Democrats' acquiescence in Hayes's election, the Republicans agreed to withdraw federal troops from the South—essentially ending Reconstruction. The *Compromise* effectively ceded power in the Southern states to the Democratic Redeemers.

This is what led to denying black men the right to vote through legal maneuvering and violence as a first step in taking away their civil rights. Beginning in the 1890s, Southern states enacted literacy tests, poll taxes, elaborate registration systems, and eventually whites-only Democratic Party primaries to exclude black voters. The laws proved very effective. In Mississippi, fewer than 9,000 of the 147,000 voting-age African Americans were registered after 1890. In Louisiana, where more than 130,000 black voters had been registered in 1896, the number had plummeted to 1,342 by 1904.

Pulitzer Prize winner and noted Jeffersonian scholar Annette Gordon-Reid spoke at the Philadelphia Free Library on February 8, 2011, about her new book on Andrew Johnson. She talked about how much easier it was for her to forgive or understand the behavior of slaveholders in the 1700s and early 1800s than those individuals who let the "opportunity of reconstruction" following the Civil War slip through their fingers. The immediate aftermath of the Civil War found the South ready to take just about any remedy the North was obliged to dish out. Unfortunately with Andrew Johnson's help they were allowed to kill reconstitution and resume their legacy of a white supremacist state. Annette Gordon-Reid talked about, "being angry that blacks had to endure" another hundred years of discrimination and segregation, "when reconstruction could have made such a difference in lifting up a black man and in promoting racial healing." And, hence, we move on to investigate the Jim Crow era next.

———— **CREATING JIM CROW** ————

As much good as the 1954 *Brown v. Board* did to free the black man from Jim Crow a corollary of harm can be attributed to the *Plessy v. Ferguson* decision. This one act played into the hands of segregationist and did as much or more harm than any other measure by providing the necessary legal underpinnings to support almost a hundred years of the American apartheid we call Jim Crow. In 1890 a new Louisiana law required railroads to provide, "equal but separate accommodations for the white, and colored, races." Outraged, the black community in New Orleans decided to test the rule.

On June 7, 1892, Homer Plessy agreed to be arrested for refusing to move from a seat reserved for whites. Judge John H. Ferguson upheld the law, and the case of *Plessy v. Ferguson* slowly moved up to the Supreme Court. On May 18, 1896, the U.S. Supreme Court, with only one dissenting vote, ruled that segregation in America was constitutional.

———————

The shift of political power in the South was supported by a series of sweeping Supreme Court rulings. The 1883, *Civil Rights Cases*, declared the Civil Rights Act of 1875 unconstitutional. There was more harm to come from the court of last resort. All throughout the 1870s and 1880s, the court continued to weaken the gains made during Reconstruction. The first of these were the 1873 Slaughterhouse Cases, so named because they involved a suit against a New Orleans slaughterhouse. In these cases, the conservative Supreme Court ruled that the Fourteenth Amendment protected U.S. citizens from rights infringements only on a federal level, not on a state level. In 1876, the Supreme Court ruled in *United States v. Cruikshank* that only states, not the federal government, could prosecute individuals under the Ku Klux Klan Act of 1871. As a result, countless Klan crimes went unpunished by Southern state governments, who tacitly condoned the violence.

The post-Civil War Supreme Court made up of Lincoln and Grant appointees had repeatedly struck down radical Republican legislation and issued rulings that were devastating to black civil liberties. The court reflected that in the 1870s most Americans were clearly against slavery, but not in favor of an integrated society. As it turned out, blacks would not regain the support of the federal government until the civil rights movement of the 1960s.

Yet, some in that era saw that, despite the disastrous decisions of the Supreme Court, the court was still fungible. Robert Russa Moton wrote in his 1929 book *What The Negro Thinks*, "Except for a few state legislators, the Supreme Court of the United States is still all that stands in a legal way between the Negro and civil and political extinction." He went on to write:

> *Public sentiment still effectively eliminates the Negro from equitable consideration of all those matters of common welfare for which government exists. Where Negroes are found in largest numbers the declaration of leaders on public matters are generally understood to have no reference to black men. To talk about the rights of citizenship does not mean the Negro—that was settled by disenfranchisement. Good citizenship applies to white people; a black man is encouraged to be a good Negro. Government of the people, for the people, and by the people does not as yet include black people. Education for all children does not mean for black children! So in all public matters it is accepted that the Negro is concerned and included only incidentally...in an equal and un-grudging share in the opportunity and privileges of American life.*

To gauge just how omnipresent Jim Crow was, we can look to Claudette Colvin, the forgotten bus heroine from Montgomery, Alabama, discussed in Chapter Two. She learned early in life, at four years old, what happened when even an innocent action could suddenly be deemed an insult by whites in the Jim Crow South. In 1943, Claudette was standing in line at a general store in her hometown of Montgomery when a little white boy cut in front of her. For some reason the little white boy was intrigued with her hands being white on the inside and kept asking to see them, and seemed to think it all very funny. She held up her hands palms out and let the little white boy touched his hands to hers. Claudette's mom came running didn't say a thing and hauled off and gave her a strong backhand slap across the face. She said, "don't you know you're not supposed to touch them?" The white boy's mother nodded and said, "that's right." Claudette's lesson at four years old was to never touch another white person again.

Claudette grew up in central Alabama during the '40s and '50s where the Jim Crow laws were firmly controlling every aspect of black and white life. Blacks were born in separate hospitals, buried in separate cemeteries, and worshiped in separate churches. The Jim Crow laws were in place to accomplish three main objectives:

    (1) keep the races separated,
    (2) keep blacks as second-class citizens and subservient,
    (3) and keep blacks poor, thus ensuring the availability of
    an economically disadvantaged labor force.

Claudette also learned that respect was a one-way street. While she always had to use Mr. or Miss. or Mrs. when addressing a white person they would likely never return the favor to a black adult; often calling them by their first name or a derogatory term like Boulet or girl. "I knew plenty of white people, and they knew me. You had to be very careful around them. They never called the adults Mr. or Miss. or Mrs.: they use their first names instead." This idea of always looking over your shoulder and never knowing when an innocent remark or action would provoke the wrath of a white is a theme one reads consistently that kept blacks uneasy when whites were near.

I have always been made sad when I have heard members
of any race claiming rights and privileges, or certain

badges of distinction, on the ground simply that they were members of this or that race, regardless of their own individual worth or attainments. I have been made to feel sad for such persons because I am conscious of the fact that mere connection with what is known as a superior race will not permanently carry an individual forward unless he has individual worth, and mere connection with what is regarded as an inferior race will not finally hold an individual back if he possesses intrinsic, individual merit.

—Booker T. Washington in his autobiography *Up From Slavery*

——— MONTGOMERY ———

As time marched on, it seemed like segregation was always the way of the South. After all, multiple generation had grown up in this system and for most whites it was expected to continue into the foreseeable future. One place, Montgomery, Alabama, became tantamount with the image, deliberately cultivated to keep blacks in their place, of a two-fisted version of segregation. One result of this segregation was limiting the job categories open to blacks. By 1950, nearly three in five black women in Montgomery were working as maids for white families, and almost three quarters of the employed black males mowed lawns and did other kinds of unskilled labor. "The average black worker made about half as much money as the average white. The only professional jobs open to blacks were… pastoring a black church and school teaching, which was open because of segregated schools."

For many who lived through the 1960s civil rights movement, Montgomery is synonymous with the bus strike. Since blacks were not allowed to live in white neighborhoods they needed to travel across town to their jobs as yard boys and maids. This is why the buses were so necessary to blacks in Montgomery. Taking the bus was a daily insult. A black rider had to sit in the segregated section at the back of the bus, and if the bus was full, would have to give up his or her seat to a white person. Even entering the bus was humiliating for black passengers; a black rider would enter through the front door like the white passengers and drop their dimes in the fare box near the driver. If even one white person was in the white section the blacks were required to get back off the bus and reenter through the rear door.

Sometimes whether through meanness or neglect, the driver, who was always white, would leave the black passenger standing on the curb as they closed the doors and pulled away. Blacks learned to detest the number 10 in Montgomery. Each bus had 36 seats. The first four rows of seats would hold 10 passengers and were reserved for white passengers only. Imagine standing in the black section of the bus when there were perfectly good seats empty, but they happened to be in the front which was reserved for whites only. Blacks also knew that the bus drivers were extremely conscientious and sometimes very aggressive in enforcing the rules on their buses.

Having to stand up at the end of a long day within plain sight of empty seats was a constant reminder that you are a second-class citizen. The 10 empty seats became an obsession to weary workers, wrote Jo Ann Robinson, an English professor at Alabama State College at the time. "The number ten became a damnable number... Nobody wanted that number on anything that belonged to him. And being packed together inside a small tube magnified the rudeness of segregation." There were no Negro drivers, recalled Martin Luther King, Jr., of the Montgomery buses. "It was not uncommon to hear [drivers] referring to Negro passengers as... black cows and black apes." Reminds one of the insult the tar paper shacks became for the blacks of Prince Edward County.

Unfortunately this wasn't just about insults, since blacks were routinely beaten, or, in severe cases, killed in incidents associated with enforcement of the rules for properly riding the buses in Montgomery. In 1952, a man named Brooks boarded a bus, dropped a dime in the fare box, walked down the aisle toward the back. The driver shouted at him to come back and get off and re-board through the rear door like blacks were supposed to do. Well Brooks said he rather walk and he asked for his dime back. An argument ensued and it soon became overheated and the police were called. The police felt it necessary to shoot Brooks who later died of his injuries. The officer claimed Brooks resisted arrest and the coroner ruled the death a justifiable homicide.

——— JUMP JIM CROW ———

So where did the name Jim Crow come from? In the late 18th century minstrel shows featured white performers who smeared burnt cork on their faces and made fun of African Americans. A popular song by Thomas "Daddy" Rice is credited with popularizing minstrel shows with the song "Jump Jim Crow" which he said he learned from a black singer. Eventually, the moniker of Jim Crow represented the whole system of laws and customs that segregated black and white Americans in the South. Some of the Jim Crow rules were intended to keep the races separated, and some were just plain silly. Claudette Colvin talked about how going downtown in Montgomery to shop would make her angry. "We could shop in white stores- they take our money all right- but they wouldn't let us try anything on. I never went into a fitting room like white people did. The sales lady would measure me and then go get a dress or the blouse and bring it out. She hold it up and tell me it was a perfect fit and expect my mom to buy it. When we needed new shoes, my mom would trace the shape of our feet on a brown paper bag and we carry the outline to the store because we were not allowed to try shoes on."

Of course there were the odd oasis of kindness and humanity even in Claudette's Montgomery. St. Jude Hospital was one such place where blacks were treated with kindness. St. Jude opened in 1951 as one of the first racially integrated hospitals in that part of the South. The hospital would provide an entire range of services to blacks or whites including health social, services and education. Father Harold was the founder and manager of St. Jude's. He was noted for his refusal to put up the iniquitous white and colored signs found everywhere else in the South.

—— **SLAVERY REDUX** ——

A book by Douglas A. Blackmon, *Slavery by Another Name*, is a revealing treaty of the little-understood re-enslavement of blacks in the early 20th century. Blackmon chronicles how prisoners were sold as forced laborers to coal mines, lumber camps, quarries, and farm plantations. Thousands of other African Americans were simply seized by Southern landowners and compelled into years of involuntary servitude. Companies like U.S. Steel, looking for cheap and abundant labor, took advantage of armies of free black men laboring without compensation. Black labor was forced through beatings and physical torture to do the bidding of white masters for decades after the official abolition of American slavery. This neo-slavery exploited legal loopholes and leveraged federal policies that discouraged prosecution of whites for continuing to hold black workers against their will.

In the summer of 1906, W. E. B. DuBois and a team of more than a dozen researchers chose Lowndes County, Alabama as the location for the first large-scale study and documentation of the current conditions of blacks. DuBois later called the project his "best sociological work." DuBois documented that for many black sharecroppers they lived or died on the whim of their white overseers who they still called master. Their broken down log cabins, meager food, and ragged clothing were little enough but, it could all be taken away from them if they didn't toe the line. The report was destroyed by the federal government because of the political firestorm it was expected to create. Not one to ever be intimidated, three years later, DuBois turned to fiction to get his message published. He wrote a novel based on what he found in Lowndes County, *The Quest for Silver Fleece*, which portrayed the African American struggle in the early 1900s. One of the books main characters was Colonel Cresswell who lived in a sprawling mansion far from town, surrounded by endless broken down cabins inhabited by his terrified black tenants. Colonel Cresswell and other whites bought and sold sharecroppers at will, substituting the sale of their alleged debts for rent in supplies as a proxy for the sale of the humans themselves. Black men and their families were routinely sold for $250 in Lowndes County. Black families who resisted their sale to other whites were subject to brutal violence and the confiscation or burning of their meager homes and few possessions. Once under a labor contract to a white man, blacks knew they would almost certainly never be free of it. Creswell summed up his business philosophy when he professed, "cheap cotton depends on cheap niggers." In the DuBois novel maturing black girls complied with the sexual advances of Col. Cresswell's son for the simple reason that, "he was our master."

It was W. E. B. Dubois who created the construct he called the "double consciousness." This was one of the key insights from his study of 20th century African American life. In his classic work, *The Souls of Black Folk* (1903), Dubois captured the essence of living in a racially divided society as: "this sense of always looking at one's self through the eyes of others... of measuring one's soul by the tape of a world that looks on in an amused contempt and pity. One ever feels his two-ness as an American, a Negro; two souls, two thoughts, two unreconciled strivings; two warring ideals in one dark body, whose dogged strength alone keeps it from being torn asunder [emphasis added]."

Ironically, the contradiction of being forced to live by one set of rules, and yet often acting inconsistently with those rules, is not unique to African Americans. White Americans also experienced a similar "two-ness" of sorts during colonial times. The Founding Fathers, for example, crafted democratic ideals and citizenship practices that they were willing to fight for; yet they excluded women and enslaved Africans from receiving those same rights and privileges. As slaveholders themselves, George Mason, Thomas Jefferson, George Washington, and James Madison "lived lives cushioned by slavery." In Roger W. Wilkins, *Jefferson's Pillow: The Founding Fathers and the Dilemma of Black Patriotism* he devotes much of his book to documenting and explaining this duality as practiced by the Founding Fathers. "They created a nation conceived in liberty and dedicated to the proposition that whites should be supreme. They celebrated freedom while stealing the substance of life from the people they owned." The complexities and duality of their thinking and consequences of their acts remain with us today, with both the descendants of the former enslaved and their masters struggling to make meaning of their interwoven roles and relationships in American history and our national culture.

——— POVERTY ———

In his book about Franklin Roosevelt, Jean Edward Smith strikingly describes the rural poverty facing both whites and blacks in the South. This anesthetizing poverty was one of the drivers in creating the Tennessee Valley Authority to help develop the great potential of the nation's great river basin and one of the most poverty-stricken regions of the country. Smith describes the region as beyond poor. "The Tennessee River and its tributaries, spilling into seven Southern states, drained an area of 64,000 square miles. Flood it might be more precise. But once fertile bottomland was sadly depleted; the forests were cut over; the thin soil of the uplands was eroded, crisscrossed with gullies, and unable to contain the annual runoff from devastating spring rains. Income in the region was less than half the national average. Only two out of every hundred farms had electricity. Infant mortality was four times greater than elsewhere, pellagra and tuberculosis were epidemic, medical care was sparse, and cementation was primitive. There was no industry to speak of, little commercial life, and few prospects other than further descent into squalor."

Smith points out that the Rural Electrification Administration (REA), that FDR created as part of the new deal in 1935, was critical to the survival of the region. Nothing has done more to eliminate rural poverty than bringing electricity to the countryside. In 1935 only 11% of American farms had electricity; in Mississippi, less than 1%. This numbing poverty affected both white and black residents of the South. At least in this one measure they were equal.

——— NAACP FIGHTS LYNCHINGS.———

In an effort to control the back population, whites used the hangman's noose as a symbol of terror. Even today, this symbol of intimation and hate creates an almost guttural reaction from those old enough either have lived through these times or been schooled by their family in the fear and meaning of this hate symbol. The lynching era encompassed roughly the five decades between the end of Reconstruction and the beginning of the Great Depression. African Americans were tortured and killed for a wide variety of alleged crimes, without even the slightest opportunity for any legal due process. Some blacks did fight back; in spite of laws to prevent their ownership of firearms, many blacks stood guard of their homes with shotguns during troubled times. During the tense days during and following the Moton 1951 strike, John Stokes father guarded their rural home with a loaded shotgun. There are, "2,805 [documented] victims of lynch mobs killed between 1882 and 1930 in ten southern states. Although mobs murdered almost 300 white men and women, the vast majority almost 2,500 of lynch victims were African American. Of these black victims, 94 percent died in the hands of white lynch mobs. The scale of this carnage means that, on the average, a black man, woman, or child was murdered nearly once a week, every week, between 1882 and 1930 by a hate-driven white mob."

In many ways the Old Dominion was a safer place for blacks than the deep South. Again, the premise of degrees fueled the circumstances a black would have to reconcile in attempting to deal with these situations. The range of circumstances could cover: everything from some loose talk by whites, pointed verbal harassment, specific acts of intimation to keep you in line, or a hanging. Most of the time, blacks couldn't tell whether the Klan was just sending them a message or they were in imminent danger. A review of the reported lynchings between 1882 and 1968 shows that Virginia lynched 83 blacks while Mississippi and Georgia lynched 539 and 492 respectively. Of the 13 Confederate states Virginia ranked last in per capita lynchings of blacks during this period. Considering total population, Virginia lynched 11 per one million people, compared to Mississippi, the most deadly state, with 184 lynchings per one million people. A panelist at a civil rights conference in Richmond discussing this period said, perhaps Virginia missed a golden marketing opportunity, "Visit Virginia- Fewest Lynchings in the South."

Nonetheless, Virginia blacks knew the meaning of finding a hangman noose on their door. Even John Stokes talks about this real concern, growing up in relatively docile Prince Edward County.

In an effort to draw attention to this travesty, Tuskegee Institute kept the most reliable statistics on lynchings throughout the United States. While even one person lynched by a mob is one too many, the relevance to our story is that during the entire 13-year struggle for desegregation in Prince Edward County, no one reported being physically attacked. The South and especially segregation was never a monolith. There were always state and then local differences to contend with. Something that would be permitted in a large city would not be tolerated in the rural Black Belt. For blacks, racism could go in a blink from insulting to physical harm or death. One was never sure what that sneer might mean and the unpredictability of racist behavior provided a deterrent to retaliation by unbalancing their confidence and reinforcing that duality W. E. B. Dubois wrote about. "In addition to the punishment of specific criminal offenders, lynching in the American South had three entwined functions: *first,* to maintain social order over the black population through terrorism; *second,* to suppress or eliminate black competitors for economic, political, or social rewards; *third,* to stabilize the white class structure and preserve the privileged status of the white aristocracy." Tolnay and Beck authors of *A Festival of Violence: An Analysis of Southern Lynchings, 1882-1930* make the disturbing point, "Lethal mob violence for seemingly minor infractions of the caste codes of behavior was more fundamental for maintaining terroristic social control than punishment for what would seem to be more serious violations of the criminal codes."

Further, it was no accident that in Virginia they not only lynched less than the rest of the South but, overall had a reputation as maintaining a less violent approach to blacks. In terms of the segregation fight in the 1950s and 1960s Virginians believed in the rule of law and importantly felt that any violence would hurt the white cause in the courts and with U. S. public opinion. The white powers, at both the state and the county levels, made it frequently clear to their own hotheads that violence would not be tolerated and would be viewed as counterproductive to their segregation agenda. That is not to say that preventing a child from attending public school until she is 11 is not in itself a form of violence. However, both sides did work at largely keeping violence out of the equation and, despite many fears and mostly rumors; no one was ever physically harmed in Prince Edward County during the 13 year struggle.

Racism and lynching were certainly not the exclusive purview of the American South, nor reserved exclusively for African Americans. While the Northern states did significantly less lynching, they were complicit in a host of profound ways; whether by benign neglect, housing discrimination, job discrimination, or even limited school segregation. The North seemed to lean toward riots as their weapon of terror. Witness the New York City Draft riots in 1863 where blacks were murdered in the streets. The Chicago Race Riot of July 27, 1919 became one of the worst racial conflicts in a summer that featured widespread racial unrest across America. During the riot, dozens died and hundreds were injured. That period was named the "Red Summer of 1919" because over 25 race riots swept a bloody path across many Northern cities. With the Great Migration of African Americans to the industrial cities of the North and post-World War I tensions, frictions between the races boiled over. Overcrowding and increased African American militancy by returning WWI veterans all vying with whites in a competitive labor and housing markets contributed to this visible racial schism.

Other ethnic groups were also singled out for special treatment. On March 14, 1891, eleven Italian immigrants were broken out of jail, beaten, shot with hundreds of rounds, and hanged in New Orleans. Of course, these Italians, mostly from Sicily and Southern Italy, possessed swarthy complexions and were viewed with suspicion and contempt by the white Protestant elite ruling New Orleans. Akin to Negroes, Italians were "not quite white" and subject to a racial prejudice only slightly subtler than that reserved for the black man. The riot took place on a bright sunny morning. By ten o'clock, a crowd of thousands was gathered by the Parish Jail, with many of them shouting, "Yes, yes, hang the dagoes!" This event was one of the largest multiple lynchings in American history and was an attempt to ensure Italians remained in their place at the bottom of the hierarchy. Well almost the bottom.

——— THE HUMAN COST OF SEGREGATION ———

The reasons behind the creation, development and refinement of Jim Crow in the South went well beyond simple racism. In his 1955 book called *The Strange Career of Jim Crow,* C. Vann Woodward takes the opportunity to refute many of the myths surrounding Jim Crow. On the one hand, he demonstrates at great length that segregation was not a mere expression of racism but, in fact, a complex and corrupt outworking of many political and economic interests in the impoverished, post-Reconstruction South. He also shows conclusively that segregation took time to develop. It was not, as its supporters claimed, the way things had always been, or even the way things had come to be immediately following the Civil War, but had actually arisen 30 and even 40 years later, starting with the removal of Northern troops. This, along with the disintegration of Republican influence, increasing economic distress, and a national distaste for "taking up the black man's burden" by whites allowed successive Populists and Democrats to consolidate power. The fact that these actions had the direct result of limiting white exposure to the threat of competing with blacks was not lost on both sides. These effects were also combined with a series of Supreme Court rulings adding a legal sanctioning to segregation that became the final ingredient to the production of a wicked stew which tried to beat the black man down for almost a hundred years.

Woodward has a unique ability to understand this peculiar time in our history and he provides a detailed analysis of racial attitudes following the Civil War. He demonstrates that slavery had required the proximity and interaction of blacks and whites, which could not be reversed overnight; that Northern Republicans, Southern Conservatives, and Southern Radicals all had reasons to court black citizens; and reminds us that with the

North virtually running the South for a period of years, segregation would not have been allowed immediately after the war.

He then makes a compelling case that, "….the true rise of Jim Crow came about, in the 1890's, due to a confluence of factors: 1) Northern withdrawal from Southern affairs; 2) the changes in Northern attitudes towards colored people's as America became an Imperialist power; 3) the crushing depression of the 80's, which added fuel to racial animus; 4) the concurrent rise of the Populists who were more than willing to play the race card; and 5) the series of Supreme Court rulings which sanctioned separation."

After chronicling the rise of Jim Crow Woodward provides his insight into its demise, which was going on even as he wrote the several editions of his book. He identifies a number of factors, besides the Civil Rights movement, which contributed to Jim Crow's fall: Northern migration, improving attitudes towards colored peoples, the reversal of course by the Supreme Court, and the improved economic condition of the nation generally. In chronicling this rise and fall of Jim Crow, he demonstrated that segregation was a gradual rather than an immediate and natural response to the end of slavery and showed that many factors besides race led to the adoption of segregation policies.

We can do no better than the learned sociologist W. E. B. Du Bois to contribute to our understanding of race relations in the South in 1903. In her introduction to the 2003 edition of W. E. B. Du Bois *The Souls Of Black Folk*, (originally published in 1903) Farah Jasmine Griffin provides a graphic picture of the Jim Crow South and what cost blacks were made to pay.

> *The Souls Of Black Folk introduced a unique and singularly eloquent voice to contemporary discourse on race in the United States. It appeared at a time when "separate but equal" had been ruled to be the law of the land in the infamous Plessy v. Ferguson decision of 1896.*

Black Southerners had been successfully disenfranchised and were suppressed economically, socially, and politically through Jim Crow segregation, sharecropping, tenant farming, debt-peonage, and the rise of the chain gang. If this were not enough, they were systematically terrorized by white supremacist organizations such as the Ku Klux Klan. Thousands of blacks were lynched between 1880 and 1920. In the midst of all of this, their supposed racial inferiority was taken for granted in popular culture and academic discourse. Thomas Dixon's white supremacist play The Leopard's Spots appeared on Broadway to large audiences in 1903, and in 1905 Dixon published the best-selling The Klansman, the basis for D. W. Griffin's film The Birth of a Nation and a praise song to the Ku Klux Klan. This is the context that gave birth to Souls.

JIM CROW LAWS

Today it seems such a difficult exercise in trying to muster the words that can do justice to the spirit of the period. It is especially important that young people have an understanding of how omnipresent and destructive were the laws and customs of the Jim Crow South. When speaking to young people all of this just does not seem relevant to their world and experiences. Every high school student should read Richard Kluger, who wrote the definitive treaty on *Brown v. Board*, entitled *Simple Justice,* for a creditable citation of the black experience in the 1951 Jim Crow South. If they are not disturbed by the stupidity of it all, perhaps the sheer volume and scope may give them some pause to reflect on the enormity of the challenge facing the nation at that time. In any event, here is a partial list of some of the Jim Crow rules and laws:

- *Florida did not permit white and black students to use the same editions of some textbooks.*
- *In Arkansas, white and black voters could not enter a polling place in the company of one another.*

- *In Alabama, a white woman was forbidden to nurse a black man in the hospital.*
- *North Carolina required racially separate washrooms in its factories. South Carolina required them in their cotton mills. Four states require them in their mines.*
- *In six states, white and black prisoners could not be chained together.*
- *In seven states, tuberculosis patients were separated by race.*
- *In eight states, parks, playgrounds, bathing, and fishing, and boating facilities, amusement parks, racetracks, pools, circuses, theaters, and public walls were all segregated.*
- *Ten states required separate waiting rooms for bus and train travelers.*
- *Eleven states required Negro passengers to ride in the back of buses and streetcars.*
- *Eleven states operated separate schools for the blind.*
- *Fourteen states segregated rail passengers on trips within their borders.*
- *Fourteen states segregated mental patients.*
- *Seventeen states require the segregation of public schools, four other states permitted the practice if local communities wished it, and in the District of Columbia the custom had prevailed for nearly ninety years.*
- *In Birmingham, Alabama, 1930, it shall be unlawful for a negro and white person to play together or in company with each other in any game of cards or dice, dominoes or checkers.*
- *In Nebraska, 1911, marriages are void when one party is a white person and the other is possessed of one-eighth or more Negro, Japanese, or Chinese blood.*
- *In Maryland, 1924, any white woman who shall suffer or permit herself to be got with child by a negro or mulatto...shall be sentenced to the penitentiary for not less than eighteen months.*

- *In Oklahoma, 1915, the Corporate Commission is hereby vested with power to require telephone companies in the State of Oklahoma to maintain separate booths for white and colored patrons when there is a demand for such separate booths.*
- *Restricted real-estate covenants were prevalent in both the North and South. In communities across the country, property owners signed agreements called restrictive covenants. These contracts barred African Americans and sometimes other groups-including Jews, Asians, and Latinos-from many neighborhoods. In this covenant from Arlington County, Virginia, in the 1940s, the purchasers agreed never to sell their house to "persons of any race other than the white Caucasian Race."*

——— VOTING WITH YOUR FEET ———

It took a World War One (1914- 1918) to slow the flow of European immigrants into the United States. In an effort to prevent mass migration from a war torn Europe, starting in 1915 emigration to the United States was drastically reduced. While at the same time the call for industrial workers in the Northeast and Midwest was rising to meet war production needs. To help fill the void, previously segregated factories began hiring African Americans from the rural South. Over the course of the war and the next several decades, large numbers of African Americans moved from the former slave-holding South to the industrial Midwest and Northeast. So many African Americans made the journey north that the entire period is known as the Great Migration. During the war, more than 1 million blacks left the poor, rural South for better jobs in the North, radically altering the racial balance of the United States. Before 1910, the black population of Chicago was 2 percent; by 1970 the figure was 33 percent, and much of that change happened during the years immediately following the war. One of the great lasting legacies of World War I was its influence on the racial makeup across the United States.

Between 1915 and 1970, more than 6 million African Americans moved out of the South to cities across the Northeast, Midwest, and West. This relocation resulted in massive demographic shifts across the United States. Between 1910 and 1930, cities such as New York, Chicago, Detroit, and Cleveland saw their African American populations grow by about 40 percent, and the number of African Americans employed in industrial jobs nearly doubled.

Looking over the broader sweep of history Ira Berlin describes four distinct migrations that Africans and then African Americans undertook in his book, *The Making of African America- The Four Great Migrations:*

1. The first migration was the forced deportation of Africans to North America during the seventeenth and eighteenth centuries. Over 400,000 Africans landed in mainland North America, mostly along the Atlantic coast, during this period.

2. A larger migration occurred from the Atlantic seaboard to the southern interior during the first half of the nineteenth century. This second migration was even larger than the first as nearly one million men and women were moved by their slave owners into the Deep South to cultivate new lands with cotton, tobacco and rice.

3. The period of the middle decades of the twentieth century saw six million blacks flee the Jim Crow South to Northern and Western cities. This migration, sometimes referred to as the Great Migration, helped transform America as we now know it and was largely driven, like most immigration to the United States, as a step toward a better life.

4. Finally, at the end of the twentieth and the beginning of the twenty-first centuries, people of African descent entered the United States from all over the world— Africa, the greater Caribbean, South America, and Europe—again changing the composition, character, and cultures of the black population of the United States.

In an NPR interview, Isabel Wilkerson said, "The Great Migration had such an effect on almost every aspect of our lives—from the music that we listen to the politics of our country to the ways the cities even look and feel, even today." In fact this Great Migration had a profound impact on Barbara Rose Johns and John S. Stokes in allowing them to visit Northern cities where they were able to see for themselves that all blacks were not taught in tar paper shacks without adequate text books and forced to endure extreme overcrowding.

——— DR. MOTON'S LEGACY ———

As it turns out, World War I was the high point in the influence of Dr. Robert (Major) Russa Moton, for whom the Prince Edward County High School for blacks was named. Dr. Moton repeatedly pushed for a role for black troops that went beyond the stevedore and mess cook role to which they had routinely been relegated. Because of his influence with President Woodrow Wilson, black soldiers were allowed to fight in battle, and many units made significant contributions, impressing their French officers with their bravery and coolness under fire. Why French officers? Seems the U.S. Army officers were largely unwilling to have blacks fight in or next to their units so most black fighting units were assigned to the French sectors and reported directly to French officers. Moton was also able to see for himself the conditions of the black soldiers in France because President Wilson sent Moton to France to inspect black troops and report back to him.

When Robert Russa Moton entered the world, the South was still clinging to the vestiges of slavery. Born only two years after the Civil War ended, he was raised by parents who had been slaves most of their lives. He grew up on the sprawling Vaughan plantation in Prince Edward County, Virginia. He was born just east of Prince Edward County in neighboring Amelia County, yet spent most of his childhood living in and going to school in Prince Edward County. J. Samuel Williams Jr., one of the original Moton strikers and long time civil rights activist, noted in his recent book concerning Moton's home in Prince Edward, "His place of abode still stands stately in the 'Rice' hamlet of the county." His mother, Emily, was in charge of the big house and his father, Booker, was made foreman or "head man" of the field hands. The Moton's understood that their son, while blessed by emancipation, would be handicapped if he did not receive a good education. Education had always been dear to his mother Emily, so much so that she risked her life by secretly learning to read while a slave. But even in freedom, she concealed her rudimentary reading ability from the plantation master and misses, lest they take offense or outright prohibit her book work. Each night, under the fear of discovery, she shared her limited knowledge with her son.

During one of their late night lessons, they were discovered by the mistress of Vaughan plantation. To their surprise and delight the masters of the plantation did not reproach them. In fact, the master allowed his youngest daughter to teach both mother and son. Moton's early experience of learning how to read impressed upon him the great value of education and stirred in him a thirst for new ideas, greater knowledge, and a deeper understanding of the world around him.

When the time came for Robert Moton to go to college, his poverty did not discourage him. He worked in a lumber yard and eventually saved enough to attend Hampton Institute. After graduating from Hampton, Moton began working for the school as Commandant overseeing the discipline of young men. At Hampton, Moton became exposed to the influential black thinkers of the day. Booker T. Washington became not only a mentor, but a dear and trusted friend. Together Moton and Washington traveled throughout the South and the North, talking to black groups in the South about racial progress and Northerners about the necessary funds for their respective schools.

In 1905, Moton married Elizabeth Hunt Harris, who died the following year. In 1908, he met and married Jennie Dee Booth, a home economics instructor at Hampton. Together they raised five children. Jennie worked alongside Moton and equally matched his commitment to improving the lives of African Americans.

Over the next decade, Robert Russa Moton became one of the most recognized names, not only in the black community, but in

America. At the death of his friend and mentor, Booker T. Washington, Moton left Hampton and became the second president of Tuskegee Normal School. Under Moton's leadership, the Tuskegee endowment grew from $2.2 million to $7.7 million. With such an endowment Moton transformed Tuskegee into one of the premier institutes dedicated to training and educating African Americans. During the 1925–1926 academic year, Tuskegee announced its first college-level courses. Soon after, the institute offered its first B.S. degrees in Education and Agriculture.

Moton's influence on African American society in the '20s, '30s and '40s is unparalleled. In 1922, when speakers were being considered to deliver the keynote address for the upcoming dedication ceremony of the Lincoln Memorial, Moton was the obvious choice for whites and blacks alike. President Harding delivered remarks, as did Robert Lincoln, the memorialized President's son. But the primary task fell to Moton, who had by now grown accustomed to addressing men and women of political importance. This address, however, was different. With one speech, he had the power to reach tens of thousands with a message of racial unity and progress. The Harding administration had seen fit to censure Dr. Moton's speech in deference to the Southerners in the audience. As noted by Lincoln scholar Harold Holzer, the dedication ceremony in 1922, hosted by President Warren G. Harding, represented efforts for "sectional, not racial reconciliation."

When it came time to deliver his altered speech Moton stood with his trademark dignity and grace and looked out over the crowd numbering well over fifty thousand. His words were to the point and got to the heart of racial circumstances in the 1920s: "In the name of Lincoln, twelve million black Americans pledge to the nation their continued loyalty and their unreserved cooperation in every effort to realize in deeds, the lofty principles established by his martyrdom." wrote the son of former slaves. Kay Coles James, President and Founder of *The Gloucester Institute* said, "You can't overstate the importance of place and the significance that can have on the message," continuing on she points out that, "Before Obama stood on the steps of the Lincoln Memorial, before Martin Luther King gave his powerful speech, he [Moton] stood on those steps. He stood there and challenged a nation."

Forty years before the Rev. Martin Luther King Jr. climbed the steps of the Lincoln Memorial to share his dream for racial equality with the world, Robert Russa Moton did the same. He praised Lincoln for being willing to make a stand and unravel the thread of inequality that had been woven into the fabric of our nation. On behalf of the "Negro" people of the nation, Moton pledged, "With malice toward none, with charity for all, we dedicate ourselves and our posterity, with you and yours, to finish the work which he began, to make America an example for all the world of equal justice, equal opportunity for all." After delivering these final words full of hope for unity and equality, Moton looked to the blacks and whites in the audience to gauge the measure of his remarks. He had to search for the black faces because they were only allowed to sit in the extreme back of the crowd in a special roped off section—"for colored only." Moton did not allow such ironies in his life to deter him from his mission of racial progress.

Moton is not often remembered today, or if remembered, he is usually not given the credit he deserves. While some cast him as a black apologist along with his lifelong mentor Booker T. Washington, others understand the significant role he played in educating Southern blacks and his continual push for equal rights. His relationship with Julius Rosenwald, the Chairman of the Board for Sears and Roebuck, led to hundreds of Rosenwald Schools being built throughout the South to educate black students. He was instrumental in gaining increased responsibilities for black soldiers in World War I; and was largely responsible for the construction of a veteran's hospital in Alabama for black soldiers returning from that war. Despite protest from the white community and threats by the Ku Klux Klan, Moton saw to it that black administrators and doctors governed the facility. While W. E. B. DuBois praised Moton's fight to have the hospital staffed by black medical professionals, he was often critical of Moton's lack of militancy. Although DuBois had a less harsh opinion of Moton than his predecessor, Washington, it was only slightly so. In 1917 he informed the Commission on Inter-racial Co-operation that, "Major Moton is a fine fellow, but weak in the presence of white folks." DuBois was not only reacting to the generic appeasement approach favored by Washington and Moton, but specifically he was attacking their industrial education model. By the early 1900s, this model was being debated vigorously by those who favored only training blacks for teaching and industrial occupations, versus those who demanded the same academic curriculum as in white universities. Wealthy white philanthropists from the North, like Rockefeller, Rosenwald, and Carnegie, sided with Moton in part because this served their own financial interests for a ready pool of inexpensive farm and factory labor. However, they failed to convince many students, parents, or intellectuals that blacks should settle for only a lower-level university education. Author James D. Anderson summed up the situation facing black educators and students alike: "The basic philosophy underlying the Hampton-Tuskegee program for the training of black leaders remained unchanged. It was still a program of interracial harmony predicated on a social foundation of political disfranchisement, civil inequality, racial segregation, and the training of black youth for certain racially prescribed economic positions." By 1925, Fisk University was leading the charge to a more rigorous academic program for blacks. Other black colleges and universities slowly followed suit. Washington and Moton both had strong roots at the Hampton Institute, in Virginia, yet, in 1927 the students there went on strike for improved standard of instruction and more qualified instructors. Robert Coles, one of the leaders of the student revolt, said, Hampton's new students possessed "a DuBois ambition" that would not mix with "a Booker Washington education." Moton would eventually change his position and lead Tuskegee in offering academically challenging bachelor degrees.

Moton served as an advisor to presidents: Wilson, Harding, Coolidge, Hoover, and Franklin D. Roosevelt. Countless universities and organizations honored Moton, including the National Negro Business League, which elected him president; a role that he served in for more than 20 years. Dr. Moton was not afraid to cast racism in the ugly, hurtful light it deserved. Rather than cast him as an apologist, it may be fairer to say he was careful to pick his battles. In his 1929 book, *What The Negro*

Thinks, he talks about the experience of a black man buying a train ticket in just about any southern city.

> *With some such experience wrinkling in his bosom the traveler approaches the ticket window. If, to avoid the rush that develops as train time approaches, he decides to purchase his ticket early, he is really not surprised if the agent tells him it is too soon to buy a ticket. He retires to his seat in some discomfiture, to return when the train is called, and he observes the agent selling tickets to white patrons. He takes his stand at the window for Negroes, and there he waits and waits and waits until every white passenger is sold a ticket and then impatiently asked, "Where are you going?" with barely time enough to get his luggage aboard the train. Sometimes there is not time enough left to purchase the ticket, and the hapless passenger is rebuked by the gate man for not having a ticket; a porter at the train growls his reproaches, and the conductor voices his contempt for the stupidity that boards a train without a ticket.*

Moton intended his book as a bridge for education of whites about the hidden world of black life in the 1920s. Moton took the measure of racially divided America and how the Negro reacts to segregation in his 1929 book, *What The Negro Thinks*.

> *In the midst of all this the Negro thrives. Segregation, disenfranchisement, prejudice, injustice, lawlessness—in spite of them all he prospers. Above it all his voice rises singing; and the notes of his joy has become the symbol of our modern America. Whatever he hides in his heart, whatever he may think in the back of his head, he turns to the world a smiling face, and in spite of itself, the world, when it stops to look, is captivated by that smile; when it stops to listen, it is thrilled by that song. And all the while he presses steadily onward, resolved to let nothing hold*

him down, to let nothing crush his spirit, to let nothing to feed his steadfast purpose of establishing his claim of equal right to life, liberty, and the pursuit of happiness and demonstrating even the most skeptical that essentially all men are created equal, determined to let no man, no movement drag him down so low as to make him hate his fellow man.

How much notice of Moton's worthy life did the 1951 student strikers use as their inspiration? Did they take notice of their school's namesake? The records of the time are silent regarding Moton the man. Nonetheless, like him, they were a hundred percent committed to education and using every legal method at their disposal to change unequal to equal; thereby improving the lot of the black man and indeed all men. In this they were united.

———— SUNDOWN TOWNS ————

Charles Wiley recalled that, "My grandmother used to tell us all about the old homestead that was up in Forsyth County, which was strange to us, because we always heard that there's no black people in Forsyth County. That's what we were always told. There used to be a saying that we even as young kids heard, 'Don't let the sun go down on you in Forsyth County.'" Charles Wiley describes this example of the phenomena now know as a "Sundown Town," from the 2007 documentary film *Banished*. While the demographic remnants of these Whites Only towns still linger today it was just another strategy employed by white supremacists to restrict and segregate blacks. In the early 1900s, there were more than 1,000 African Americans in Forsyth County, Georgia, comprising 10 percent of the population. But in 1912, whites violently expelled all the black residents from the county. Even today, as part of the burgeoning metropolitan Atlanta region, Forsyth County is home to slightly more than 175,000 people, and blacks are only 2.6 percent of that population.

Starting in 1864 and continuing for the next six decades, whites in town governments across the US violently purged black residents from their communities. Occurring across much of the U.S., with significant activity along the Mason-Dixon line, even today—as with Forsyth County—blacks are notably absent from these counties and a significant black population is often a few miles away in an adjoining county. This occurred in places like Washington County, Indiana; Comanche County, Texas; Polk County, Tennessee; Lawrence County, Missouri; Harrison County, Arkansas; and Marshall County, Kentucky. This listing is only the tip of the iceberg, as there were thousands of these special towns across America.

During the 2007 Sundance Film Festival the documentary film *Banished* was screened to a nearly universal pronouncement of, "I had no idea that went on in America!" Not a surprising insight based on the scrawny effort we make in teaching history to our high school and university students. After spending most of his life as a sociologist, historian, teacher, and researcher James W. Loewen advocates that most of the history books we hand out to our high school students today are "an embarrassing blend of bland optimism, blind nationalism, and plain misinformation." All the more reason to value any insight this documentary can offer us. The film is about four U.S. cities that represent many communities that violently forced African American families to flee in post-Reconstruction America. The film defines a sundown town as, a town that does not allow a certain race or group, most notably African Americans, in after sundown, resulting in the complete exclusion of this group from the town. Black people found in a town after dark were often brutally beaten or imprisoned. However, African Americans were allowed in during the day because they provided a number of services for white families, including housecleaning, landscaping, and cooking.

These towns cultivated a reputation for extreme racism with legal and illegal means of enforcement to ensure the whiteness of their town. The enforcement tactics employed by the residents and the law officials in sundown towns were meant to directly contribute to a town's reputation. James W. Loewen summarizes this culture of fear in his book *Sundown Towns: A Hidden Dimension of American Racism*, "The best way to stay all-white, many communities concluded, was to behave with such outrageous hostility to African Americans who happened by or tried to move in that a reputation for vicious white supremacy circulated among African Americans for many miles around." Surprising to many is that "the overwhelming majority of sundown towns were in the North" or the border states. This is because the South had such a high percentage of blacks and black servants that eradicating all African Americans from a community would completely destroy the social structure and economy of the town. However, northern whites could more easily eradicate blacks from their communities without much difficulty or backlash. Loewen wrote in 2005, "something significant has been left out of the broad history of race in America as it is usually taught," namely the establishment between 1890 and 1968 of thousands of "sundown towns" that systematically excluded African Americans from living within their borders. "Located mostly outside the traditional South, these towns employed legal formalities, race riots, policemen, bricks, fires, the hangman's noose, and guns to ensure a homogeneously Caucasian community—and some of them continue such unsavory practices to this day."

Loewen's eye-opening history traces the sundown town's development and delineates the extent to which state governments and the federal government, "openly favor[ed] white supremacy" from the 1930s through the 1960s and "helped to create and maintain all-white communities" through their lending and insuring policies. "While African Americans never lost the right to vote in the North... they did lose the right to live in town after town, county after county." This forced expulsion drove African Americans into urban ghettoes and this legacy continues today to have ramifications for the lives of whites, blacks, and the social system at large.

——— BIRMINGHAM ———
THE NEGRO PROBLEM

Throughout the late 1950s and the early 1960s, challenges to the system of racial laws and customs were too often met with violence. The singer Nat King Cole was attacked during his performance at Birmingham's municipal auditorium in 1956.

Jefferson County, Alabama, is significant because of its size—
over a thousand square miles—and its position completely
surrounding the city of Birmingham. In 1958 the Ku Klux Klan
lit 18 crosses throughout Jefferson County and, over the course of
the year, paraded through black neighborhoods. The clan burned
11 schools a year after that. For many, Birmingham was often
cited as the most racist city in America; and for others it was a
good example of how to handle "the Negro problem." During the
early 1960s when others Southerners were beginning to see that
change was inevitable the good folks of Birmingham, especially
their elected and appointed authorities, remained steadfast in their
insistence on segregation. The iconic Eugene "Bull" Connor, the
Commissioner of Public Safety, became famously known as the
"fist of Jim Crow."

During the 50s and 60s Condoleezza Rice grew up in
segregated Birmingham under the rule of Bull Connor. She
discusses the struggle her parents were faced with to provide her
a safe, nurturing, and stimulating environment. "In some ways
the task was hard and complex, yet straightforward at the same
time. The hard part was obvious: Birmingham was the most
segregated big city in America, and daily life was full of
demanding reminders of the second class citizenship accorded to
blacks. Whites and blacks lived in parallel worlds, their paths
crossing uneasily and only in a few public places." In her book
released in 2010 Condoleezza Rice talks about how her parents
loved each other and unconditionally loved her and together they
"wove the fibers of our life—faith, family, community, and
education—into a seamless tapestry of high expectations and
unconditional love.... Somehow they raise their little girl in Jim
Crow Birmingham, Alabama, to believe that even if she couldn't
have a hamburger at the Woolworth's lunch counter, she could be
president of the United States."

She went on to say, "So how can I say that there was a
straightforward way for black parents to nurture their children?
Well, ironically, because Birmingham was so segregated, black
parents were able, in large part, to control the environment in
which they raised their children. They rigorously regulated the
messages that we received and shielded us by imposing high
expectations and a determined insistence on excellence. It took a

lot of energy for her parents to channel us in the right direction, but we became neither dispirited nor bitter." Regarding the schools, "The City put fewer resources into the black schools, so they were substandard in an already poor state system. But the teachers were dedicated, and they produced remarkable results. In these circumstances, teachers could demand the best of their students without any racial overtones. Teachers had high expectations and were pretty tough on low performers. 'To succeed,' they routinely reminded us, 'you will have to be twice as good.' This was declared as a matter of fact not a point for debate." In his memoirs, Moton strike leader John A. Stokes has similar things to say about his upbringing in Prince Edward County. In large measure this confidence instilled by his parents and teachers was possibly the one indispensible ingredient that supported his bold move as one of the strike leaders in 1951.

Rice traced her attitude and drive to succeed to her parents. "All of these elements—extended family, community, school, and churches—conspired together to convince me and my peers that racism was 'their' problem, not ours. Whatever feelings of insecurity or inadequacy black adults felt in the appalling and depressing circumstances of Jim Crow Birmingham, they did not transfer it to us. For the children of our little enclave, Titusville, the message was crystal clear: we love you and we will give you everything we can to help you succeed. But there are no excuses and there is no place for victims."

In many ways Condoleezza Rice paints a vivid picture of how many of the Moton strikers were brought up with a similar belief; that they were just as good as anyone else and much was expected of them. They became the first black generation that felt racism was not their problem and they felt it was their obligation to work hard and take on the system when improvements were appropriate. All of this ties back to our Prince Edward County student strikers in general and Barbara Rose Johns' in particular who by sixteen-years-old was already responsible for a household, and raising her brothers and sisters, and like Rice did not lack confidence or conviction.

─── **TO WAR** ───

After the years of abuse heaped upon the black man, as chronicled in this chapter alone, it seems amazing that when the call went out for volunteers to serve in World War I, blacks joined in record numbers. When the United States declared war against Germany in April of 1917, War Department planners quickly realized that the standing Army of 126,000 men would not be enough to ensure victory overseas. The standard volunteer system proved to be inadequate in raising an army, so on May 18, 1917, Congress passed the Selective Service Act requiring all male citizens between the ages of 21 and 31 to register for the draft. Even before the act was passed, African American males from all over the country eagerly joined the war effort. They viewed the conflict as an opportunity to prove their loyalty, patriotism, and worthiness for equal treatment in the United States.

When it came to the draft, however, there was a reversal in usual discriminatory policy. Draft boards were comprised entirely of white men. Although there were no specific segregation provisions outlined in the draft legislation, blacks were told to tear off one corner of their registration cards so they could easily be identified and inducted separately. Now instead of turning blacks away, the draft boards were doing all they could to bring them into service, southern draft boards in particular. One Georgia county exemption board discharged 44 percent of white registrants on physical grounds and exempted only 3 percent of black registrants based on the same requirements. As a cruel joke, it was not uncommon for southern postal workers to deliberately withhold the registration cards of eligible black men and have them arrested for being draft dodgers. Although comprising just 10 percent of the entire United States population, blacks supplied 13 percent of inductees.

How is it that the black man remained consistently loyal to the United States? Even though blacks endured 250 years of slavery—followed by a promising yet devastatingly short and incomplete reconstruction period, which then heralded in the apartheid era that lasted until 1965—they were always able to see the promise that was America and had hope, maybe this time, they would gain their slice of the American dream. They saw the promise in the Declaration of Independence, if not in the authors' deeds, and they wanted America to meet its promise of freedom for all. In World War I most white officers were conflicted as to whether blacks should carry guns and help with the fighting. All of these questions "whether a black man can fight," were a replay from the American Revolution and the Civil War. General Washington did not want blacks in his continental Army because he questioned their fighting skills and saw the future conflict about slaves demanding their freedom after the war. A near desperate Lincoln, in the second half of that struggle, finally allowed blacks to enlist. So again in 1917, white officers refused to lead or even fight alongside black troops, promoting the myth that the black man could not fight, or were not smart enough to grasp the intricacies of modern warfare and tactics, and could not be trusted. So, once again, the American black males had to prove themselves, again, as capable and able fighters; as if all the other blood they shed for America never happened.

While still discriminatory, the Army was far more progressive in race relations than the other branches of the military. Blacks could not serve in the Marines, and could only serve limited and menial positions in the Navy and the Coast Guard. By the end of World War I, African Americans served in cavalry, infantry, signal, medical, engineer, and artillery units, as well as serving as chaplains, surveyors, truck drivers, chemists, and intelligence officers. Although technically eligible for many positions in the Army, very few blacks got the opportunity to serve in combat units. Most were limited to labor battalions. The combat elements of the U.S. Army were kept completely segregated. The four established all-black Regular Army regiments were not used in overseas combat roles but instead were diffused throughout American held territory. There was such a backlash from the African American community, however, that the War Department finally created the 92nd and 93rd Divisions, both primarily black combat units, in 1917. As discussed previously, using his considerable influence, Dr Robert Moton led the cry calling for blacks to have equal treatment by the Army. Because of his influence with President Woodrow

Wilson, blacks were eventually allowed to fight and many units made significant contributions, impressing their French officers with their bravery and coolness under fire. As previously discussed, most blacks that saw combat; saw it under French officers because white U.S. Army officers were unwilling to have blacks fight in or next to their all white units. Black fighting units were assigned to the French sectors and reported directly to French officers. Additionally, Moton was able to see the conditions of the black solder in France first hand because Wilson sent him to France as his representative to inspect black troops and report back to him.

While in France, the humiliation of the Negro continued. Military staff officers seemed to go out of their way to prejudice the minds of the French people against the Negroes in order that they might be held down to the same status they had in the, United States. General Ervin, who succeeded General Ballou in the command of the 92nd Division—complying with the wishes of his staff—issued among other regulations, Order No. 40—a proclamation that Negroes should not speak with or to French women. Carrying out this order, the Military Police overseas, undertook to arrest Negroes found talking to French women while the white privates and officers were not under any similar restrictions. This led to a serious misunderstanding between the French and the Americans and to a number of brawls in which the white and black soldiers entangled themselves. In addition to orders issued with a design to prevent Negro soldiers overseas from coming into social contact with French civilians, French officers were also advised not to present any semblance of mixing socially with Negro officers, especially not to eat with them, and also not to praise the Negro in the presence of white Americans for any military action in which he participated.

In order to ensure the segregation in America came across the Atlantic, the American officers who were of a racist bent succeeded in having issued, on August 7, 1918, from General Pershing's headquarters, guidance to French officers on the proper interactions between blacks and whites.

This document began with the observation that "it is important for French officers in command of black American troops to have an idea as to the position occupied by the race in the United States." The Negroes were referred to as a "menace of degeneracy which had to be prevented by the gulf established between the two races," and especially so "because of the fact that they were given to the loathsome vice of criminally assaulting women, as evidenced by the record," they said, "they had already made in France." The French were, therefore, called upon, "Not to treat the Negroes with familiarity and indulgence which are matters of grievous concern to Americans and an affront to their national policy." The Americans, it continued, "are afraid that the blacks might thereby be inspired with undesirable aspirations." It was carefully explained that although the black man as a citizen of the United States is regarded by the whites as inferior, with whom relations of business and service only are possible, that the black is noted for his want of intelligence, lack of discretion, and lack of civic and professional conscience. The French army then was advised "to prevent the rise of any pronounced degree of intimacy between French officers and black officers, not to eat with them, not to shake hands or seek to talk or meet with them outside of the requirements of military service." They were asked also "not to commend too highly the black American troops in the presence of white Americans."

French officers and French civilians, as a rule, could not understand why the black soldiers should not be treated identically as white American soldiers; when French officers were alone with Negro officers, the latter were treated with the utmost friendliness and consideration, and it was only when in the presence of American officers that they reluctantly observed the official order, inspired by race prejudice, which positively forbade them from fraternizing with Negro soldiers and officers.

Thus it was that race prejudice in the Army was carried overseas to plague the black man fighting for his country.

───── **THE SOUTH: 1920 TO 1945** ─────

Three key occurrences converged in the Southern states between the Great Depression and the end of World War II to mark the region as bedrock of racial, political, and social turmoil. These events were: (1) the organized calls to end to public violence against African Americans, (2) discriminatory treatment of African American veterans and newly registered voters, and (3) increased demands from African Americans to improve public schooling conditions and opportunities. A brief description of these events provides us additional insight into the tensions and contradictions that teachers and students at Moton High School would face daily in their efforts to gain a fair education in a segregated society.

In 1939, the NAACP's goals for equal rights were clear: mob violence and lynching must stop, and equal treatment for all in the courts and schools must begin. This position was fueled by a long history of documented brutality. Between 1900 and 1946, for example, of the 1,973 people in the U.S. who were killed by lynching, 1,771 were African Americans. African American press accounts of the upsurge of mob violence caused concern within NAACP leadership, especially when reports surfaced on the mistreatment of African American veterans in the South and on alleged police brutality against those who defied local segregation laws. The NAACP position was clear: violence against all people had to be addressed because "as long as the terror of lynching mob [hung] over anyone in America, there [was] no possibility of the enjoyment of full civil rights by either Negroes or underprivileged Whites."

Secondly, a backlash against African American advancement after World War II showed a temporary, yet significant, gain in voter registration numbers in one Southern state. A rise in discriminatory voter registration laws, threats of "economic reprisals," random acts of violence, and the lack of united African American leadership in the state's rural areas were key problems. Tensions surfaced in many Southern communities when African

Americans could not vote in key primaries, or general elections, or were directed to pay poll taxes to register to vote, or had to pass literacy tests to cast their ballots. This was disappointing to many African Americans, who believed that they would finally gain equal rights because they had proven their loyalty to the United States, again, during the recently finished war. Although African American labor leader A. Philip Randolph was one of a vocal few who questioned whether African Americans should be loyal and expect to fully participate in a system that upheld Jim Crow laws, others maintained a heightened sense of racial and political consciousness and demonstrated that their basic American loyalty remain[ed] unquestioned.

Third, efforts to improve African Americans' educational access gained momentum in the postwar era. NAACP efforts to crack the higher education admissions ceiling persisted, resulting in a series of court decisions that paved the way for African Americans to attend public colleges and universities. The successful outcome of those decisions laid a foundation for the U.S. Supreme Court's hearing of the *Brown v. Board of Education* case in 1954. Clearly, racial discrimination extended to K-12 schools, as evidenced by unequal salaries, poor facilities, and unfair educational policies that kept African Americans in segregated public school environments.

Teaching self-respect and decision-making on a more social level, the teachers reported elementary and high school activities that stressed an orderly environment and respect for the rights of self and others. They set clear codes of conduct for students' behavior and enforced classroom rules throughout the school year. The purposes were not merely punitive, but designed to instill self-discipline and to reinforce thoughts and actions that contributed to wise decision-making.

Given the racially oppressive climate and the social systems that supported it, African American students in the segregated South had to learn how to adjust their social behavior when outside of the confines of their classroom and school. These measures were essential to their safety, and in some cases, to their survival. Although the outsider's (white) interpretation may describe this behavior as passive or non-confrontational, internalizing and not acting on aggression might have kept many students from physical harm. In the teachers' minds, they were saving their children from, rather than sacrificing them to, the whims of potential verbal insult, mob violence, and white brutality. For example, when students traveled together away from school, they could be physically or emotionally harmed if they violated social rules of segregation, especially in public spaces (e.g., do not use public restrooms or water fountains marked "White only"). However, the teachers also used the trips to provide a "window to the world" to give students a truer sense of what life could be outside of the relative safety of their local community. Given that the physical separation of the races was instituted and enforced by prevailing local laws, many African American teachers described the need to filter out negative stereotypes and images from the younger children, especially in public places. This is yet another example of the duality W. E. B. DuBois wrote about. Teaching students how to develop and maintain a state of double-consciousness without succumbing to its negative effect was considered a skill as necessary as reading and writing.

Unlike school desegregation movements of the modern civil rights era that featured K-12 students on the front lines, some teachers of the pre-*Brown* period chose not to put their children at the forefront of the struggle, but shielded them physically and psychologically from a racially tense environment. Their empowering responses to the double-consciousness dilemma, studied by DuBois, conveyed courageous role models that transcended the established patterns of the times. They believed that until a civic community truly reflected the common good for all, their students must understand the two-ness of their lives and become prepared to navigate its complexities outside of the safety of their segregated school settings. With the support of local African American communities, the teachers modeled democratic principles that none could exercise, but all hoped to realize fully in the coming decades. In a sense, their teaching was walking a line between not letting go of that Jeffersonian promise of citizenship yet, equipping their students with necessary survival skills in an era rife with political inequities and social contradictions.

—— **THE VIRGINIA WAY** ——

The Virginia General Assembly is the oldest legislature in the Americas. While credited with many progressive ideas, like the statutes for religious freedom, they spent nearly 350 years making laws to control and demean their black residents of Virginia. It is true that in Virginia there were less hangings and violence directed to blacks than in the states of the deep South. That should not imply that those who controlled Virginia in the mid 1900s—in particular the Byrd political machine and the powerful Richmond newspapers—were not just as ardent segregationist as those in the more violent deep South.

Ed Peeples, noted civil rights advocate created a magazine in the early '60s (called the *Ghost*) expressly for the purpose of calling out the Virginia white power structure on their less-than-equal policies and practices. The "Virginia Way" was a phrase developed by the pro-segregation editor of the *Richmond News Leader,* Douglas S. Freeman and extolled in editorials by the *News Leader's,* James J. Kilpatrick to describe the strenuous, legal-based opposition to integration, though always within the confines of Virginia's gentlemanly code. In the *Ghost* Peeples sarcastically poked fun at the "Virginia Way" by noting in his magazine that in Virginia "we are able to segregate like gentleman," not like those "rubes in Alabama who give segregation a bad name."

Of course the segregationist approach in Virginia, as well as the rest of the South, started as part of the post-Reconstruction agenda to address their labor issues—read this as their black problem—that was sweeping the South. On February 16, 1901, the General Assembly passed an act calling for the election of delegates to serve in Virginia's fifth constitutional convention. On June 12, 1901, one hundred delegates (88 Democrats and 12 Republicans) assembled in the old hall of the House of Delegates at the Capitol in Richmond. The Democrats had successfully pushed through a referendum for a new constitution by campaigning for electoral reform and better state government. The Virginia Democratic Party's real agenda was one that mirrored public sentiment throughout the South by favoring disfranchisement of blacks, whose support of the Republican Party made it a powerful political factor. Eliminating the black vote became the real work of the Convention of 1901-1902.

The main question for the delegates was how to eliminate the black vote without violating the Fifteenth Amendment to the U.S. Constitution. Eventually they proposed that under Virginia's new constitution, a man would be eligible to vote if he could satisfy one of the following three requirements: he could read or understand the state constitution; he had paid taxes on property worth at least $333; or he was either a U.S. or Confederate veteran or the son of a veteran. All three conditions were loopholes designed to protect white voters. Further narrowing the pool of possible voters, minimum requirements were set for age, residency, and literacy, and a poll tax requirement was also instituted.

The Constitution of 1902 also provided for the revision of the county court system, the creation of the State Corporation Commission, and the direct election of certain officials. It also codified the practice of the day, for the first time, that "white and colored children" must be educated in separate schools.

Before the convention met, the General Assembly had passed an act requiring that the proposed constitution be ratified by the voters of Virginia. They became unsure of how the new constitution might fare with voters, especially those who were about to be disfranchised, the Convention instead took the unusual step of proclaiming it the law of the commonwealth. The new constitution became law on July 10, 1902. The old poll books were purged, and the Virginia electorate was cut in half. Both the poll tax and the literacy requirements remained in effect in Virginia until they were overturned by the federal courts and Congress in the 1960s.

On March 20, 1924, the Virginia General Assembly passed two laws that had arisen out of contemporary concerns about eugenics and race: SB 219, entitled "The Racial Integrity Act" and SB 281, "An ACT to provide for the sexual sterilization of inmates of State institutions in certain cases", henceforth referred to as "The Sterilization Act."

The Racial Integrity Act required that a racial description of every person be recorded at birth and divided society into only two classifications: white and everyone else, who were lumped under the heading defined as colored (including American Indians). It defined race by the "one-drop rule," defining as colored persons with any African or Indian ancestry. It also expanded the scope of Virginia's ban on interracial marriage (anti-miscegenation law) by criminalizing all marriages between white persons and non-white persons. In 1967 these laws were overturned by the United States Supreme Court in its ruling on *Loving v. Virginia*. From 1969 to 1971, state legislators under Governor Mills Godwin rewrote the state constitution; finally removing the last vestiges of the Jim Crow laws. In 1989 a groundbreaking event occurred in Virginia. Douglas Wilder, a former Virginia State Senator, became the first African American elected as governor in the United States.

———— IRENE MORGAN ————

In 1944 electing a black Governor would have seemed incredulous. The Virginia legislature was worried about winning the war in Europe and Pacific. There was another war of sorts that erupted on the roads of the Virginia. On July 14, 1944, Irene Morgan boarded a bus to take her from Gloucester, Virginia, to Baltimore. As she was passing through Richmond she was informed by the bus driver that she was defying Virginia's 1930 law segregating seating by rows. In one of those spontaneous decisions that can change history, she refused to move. The bus driver stopped in Middlesex County, Virginia, and summoned the sheriff, who tried to arrest Morgan. She tore up the arrest warrant, kicked the sheriff in the groin and fought with the deputy who tried to drag her off the bus. "If something happens to you which is wrong, the best thing to do is have it corrected in the best way you can," said Morgan. "The best thing for me to do was to go to the Supreme Court." A state court rejected her argument, but in 1946 assisted by lawyer Thurgood Marshall, the U.S. Supreme Court ruled 7–1 that Virginia had no right to impose segregation beyond its borders. If it seems Mr. Marshall was everywhere at once, it is because he was; at least in those places where he could make a difference for the cause. Segregation on interstate bus travel was coming to an end. It took Rosa Park's similar refusal in Birmingham, Alabama, in 1955 to extend the same principle to bus travel within a state. Then, in 1960, through *Boynton v. Virginia*, the Supreme Court extended the *Irene Morgan v. Commonwealth of Virginia* ruling to bus terminals used in interstate bus service. Nonetheless, even after the law was successfully challenged many African Americans were ejected or arrested when they tried to integrate such facilities. In 1961, hundreds of volunteers from across the country traveled to the South to test compliance with the *Boynton* decision by riding from Washington, D.C., to New Orleans. Known collectively as the Freedom Riders, they encountered little opposition beyond derogatory remarks as they traveled through Virginia. Violent resistance, however, was encountered from South Carolina to Alabama, where at one point buses were set on fire.

Morgan's arrest in 1944 and subsequent court ruling inspired the 1947 Journey of Reconciliation, during which 16 activists from the Chicago-based Congress of Racial Equality rode on interstate buses through the Upper South to test the enforcement of the Supreme Court's ruling. The activists divided themselves between Greyhound and Trailways bus lines and usually rode with an interracial pair in the white-area of the bus, with the other activists disguised as disinterested observers in the racial sections that applied to them. The group traveled uneventfully through Virginia, but once they reached North Carolina they encountered violence and arrest. By the end of the Journey, the protesters had conducted over 24 "tests" and endured 12 arrests and repeated mob violence. A remarkable exchange occurred between the judge and the defendants when a North Carolina court sentenced noted civil rights activist Bayard Rustin and others, in a flagrant violation of the Irene Morgan decision, to 22 days on a chain gang for their participation in the Journey. Judge Henry Whitfield expressed his distaste for the entire episode, and in particular with the white men involved. Igal Roodenko (February 8, 1917–April 28, 1991) was a white, Jewish U.S. civil rights activist, and pacifist who rode the bus with black activist Bayard Rustin. In April of 1947 they were both arrested in North Carolina for deliberately violating a North Carolina law requiring segregated seating on public transportation. At their trial, Rustin and Roodenko were both convicted. Rustin was sentenced to 30 days on a North Carolina chain gang. The judge then turned to Roodenko and said, "Now, Mr. Roodenko (sic), I presume you're Jewish." "Yes, I am," Roodenko replied.

"Well, it's about time you Jews from New York learned that you can't come down bringing your nigras with you to upset the customs of the South." Just to "teach [him] a lesson," the judge sentenced him to 90 days on a chain gang – three times the length of Rustin's sentence.

The 1947 Journey of Reconciliation, far ahead of its time in its use of tactics of nonviolent direct action, inspired the highly publicized Freedom Rides of 1961, also organized by CORE, that had a significant impact on the Kennedy administration initiating the civil rights legislation that was passed in 1964. A more immediate benefit from these 1947 civil rights actions came by way of helping to lay the ground work for translating bus seating inequality to the inequality of segregated schools, thereby paving the way for the 1954 Supreme Court *Brown v. Board* decision.

——— BLACK EDUCATION ———

All of the first 350 years of the black experience in America was always about degrees of control by whites. While slavery was hardly monolithic there were some hard truths. Often, the field hands were unmercifully whipped while the house slaves were given considerable freedom. On some plantations, all the slaves were treated well; just short of making them free. When Thomas Jefferson returned from France in 1789, his slaves ran down the mountain to greet him, unhitched the team of horses that were pulling his carriage and proceeded to bodily haul him and his carriage up the mountain as a sign of their affection and joy upon the master's return. Slavery was different from plantation to plantation and especially state to state. And so it was with the educational experiences of whites and blacks across America. In some places, a very few, some blacks were getting an adequate education. In some states they had integrated schools, mostly in the North, with some having segregated facilities that were almost equal to white facilities. While there were some variations on the theme, for the South in general it was overwhelmingly about inadequate facilities.

To meet the enormous desire for education among African Americans following emancipation, northern charities helped black communities start thousands of new schools in the South. One of the largest programs was the Julius Rosenwald Fund, established in 1914 by a Sears Roebuck and Company executive. The fund required matching contributions from local communities. We have already discussed Dr. Robert Russa Moton's involvement and assistance to the Rosenwald schools. Even in the poorest rural areas, black men and women, held fundraisers, donated land, and built schools with their own hands. In fact, throughout the period between emancipation and the May 1954 *Brown v. Board* decision, blacks contributed many more private dollars per capita than whites to support education in America. This was despite already paying taxes for supposedly equal facilities. Americans have long believed that a healthy democracy depends in part on free public education. The nation's founders stressed that an educated citizenry would better understand their rights and help build a prosperous nation.

In a 1984 address to students and teachers, President Ronald Regan quoted Thomas Jefferson to make the point that education and democracy are codependent.

> *Thomas Jefferson noted... "If you expect the people to be ignorant and free, you expect what never was and never will be." The ongoing experiment called democracy, the longest continuing experiment in human history, cannot exist without an informed citizenry, and cannot exist, therefore, without you.*

Certainly no one understood this better than the former slaves living under the rule of Jim Crow. They had seen firsthand what ignorance yielded for them and their descendents, and were willing to make any sacrifice for their children to be educated, with the hope that this would lead to attaining their rightful piece of the American dream. Beginning in the early 1800s, the federal government and the states encouraged a public school system, albeit largely under local control. For millions of children, the American public school movement opened new opportunities. But millions of others were excluded because of their race or ethnicity. From the onset a segregated education was designed to confine these children to a subservient role in society and second-class citizenship.

Before the 1860s most of the South had only a rudimentary public school system for whites only. After the Civil War, Southern states ultimately created a dual educational system based on race. These separate schools were anything but equal. Yet, the commitment of African American teachers and parents to education never faltered. They established a tradition of educational self-help and were among the first Southerners to campaign for universal public education. They welcomed the support of the Freedmen's Bureau, white charities, and missionary societies. While black communities, many desperately poor, dug deep into their own resources to build and maintain schools that would meet their children's needs and reflected their values, they were keenly aware of the inequities forced upon them and never stopped pushing the white school boards for their fair share. Nonetheless, by the height of the Jim Crow era the gap for blacks in public school funding was increasing at a meteoric rate. In 1900, the disparity in the per capita expenditures upon the two racial groups was "60 percent in favor of the whites, but in 1930 this disparity has increased to 253 per cent."

——— CARRY ME BACK TO OLD VIRGINIA ———

In Virginia, the first general state school law was passed in 1796. It was unfunded and a non-compulsory law. The idea that a Virginian would tax himself to educate the poor or would assume responsibility for the education of someone else's children was not part of the thinking of that time. The general education law of 1796 was dependent upon the willingness of any county to accept the responsibility for free education, so progress under this act was almost nil. The first steps toward the beginning of modern education came with the establishment of a statewide liberty fund in 1810. The state put money aside for the education of the poor and eventually for the University of Virginia and Virginia Military Institute. Of course educating blacks, who were under bondage, was never part of the plan. Nonetheless, even for whites Virginia made little progress in broadly applying public education until Reconstruction following the end of the Civil War.

During Reconstruction, while Virginia was still under federal oversight, legislation was put in place for educating both races. The state constitution was changed in 1870, called the Underwood Constitution of 1867, to ensure education of both races. However, in practice this had the effect of universally stopping any broad move to have public education in both the elementary and secondary schools. Once federal oversight of the South ended in 1876, whites created sufficient laws to put in place the two society system we have come to call Jim Crow. By 1902, Virginia held a state convention to bring about the necessary corrections, as viewed at that time by the whites, to the Underwood Constitution of 1867.

The main problem to address was what to do about educating black children and ensuring that the races did not mix. In reality, this meant how little can we spend on the black schools and not force a return of the federal government oversight. The South, in general, learned that they could basically get away with completely disfranchising their black population and enforcing a form of caste system that guaranteed white supremacy. While not exactly the system of slavery that some longed to return to, the Jim Crow system ensured a steady supply of black house maids and field hands. Blacks were demoted to a second-class citizenship as enforced by state law.

In the early 20th century, education for blacks was not simply a concern about raising taxes. Whites in the South and North generally were opposed to Negro education because of deep racial prejudice first and, secondly, economic considerations. The following quotes from Virginia educators and local newspapers of the day portray just how ardent the "keep them ignorant and on the farm" sentiments were. In the early 20th century the debate was not whether to have black high schools, but whether blacks should be educated at all.

The Richmond Times-Dispatch editorialized that black education was "a needless expense that made hotbeds of arrogance and aggression out of black schools" and pointed out that "many families distinctly prefer nurses and cooks who cannot read and write."

Paul Barringer, the chairman of the faculty at the University of Virginia, argued in 1900, "whites should cease to support free school for the blacks" because they tended "to make some negroes idle and vicious" and "others able to compete with whites."

The Farmville Herald was blunter in identifying the problem of educating blacks: "When they learn to spell dog and cat they throw away the hoe."

Given this attitude, it should be no surprise that black schools by design were chronically shortchanged throughout the period leading up to the 1954 *Brown v. Board* decision. In many ways, as unfair as the conditions were at the Robert Russa Moton High School, they were far better than the conditions that existed for many blacks in the deeper South. In the early 1950s, there were still plenty of counties that had no high school for their black students.

Nonetheless, for the Moton strike leaders, their vision was firmly fixed with an all-consuming gaze on the white Farmville High School. They wanted the same facilities or the opportunity to attend Farmville High, and, in large measure, they had become emboldened because they were the first generation to be brainwashed by their parents and teachers into believing they could accomplish anything they set their mind to. Even in the Jim Crow South, hope of a decent education began to take root.

———— PRINCE EDWARD '40S AND '50S ————

Life for blacks in Prince Edward County was, in many ways, the same as for their peers throughout the South. If you followed the rules and obeyed the social customs you stood a good chance of not being jailed, or beaten, or killed. The NAACP saw that the freedom fight could best be fought by educating their children and that meant pushing for equal and eventually integrated schools. While integrating the nation's schools was the first priority of the civil rights movement in the '40s and '50s, the denial of equal access to public accommodations affecting all blacks was a secondary goal. Blacks could not use restaurants, bathrooms, water fountains, public parks, beaches, or swimming pools used by whites. They had to use separate entrances to doctor's offices and sit in separate waiting rooms. They could only sit in the balcony or in other designated areas of theaters. They had to ride at the back of streetcars and buses.

The public face of segregation in Farmville was omnipresent. Negroes could walk down the street and enter a restaurant, but they could only have the food as takeout; there were no seats for them. If they went into the drugstore they dare not sit at the counter—that was just was not done. And blacks were not able to enter the town's only moving picture show.

Farmville had an interesting mix of unwritten restrictions that were overlaid with a veneer of cordial, gentlemanly conduct— The Virginia Way. A respected black man walking in the downtown section would find that both blacks and whites would greet him cordially. However the conversations between the adults of different races were limited to pleasantries or business. Black and white adults did not socialize, period. As John A. Stokes found out, black and white children were allowed to play with each other, but once the white children became teenagers they were instructed by their parents to not hang around with any Negroes.

Blacks always had to have certain wariness when around white folks. Vincent West, an African American Richmond native, who grew up in the Jackson Ward neighborhood during the '50s, helped explain this: "Your parents taught you to maintain vigilance around white people, lest some simple perceived slight or violation of a well understood social code, could turn into a tongue lashing or worse." Mr. West called this mindset an "eternal wariness." Contributing to this was the fact that, even growing up in urban Richmond, Mr. West recalled that, "it was a rare to see a white person in my neighborhood because segregation was that pervasive. The only white visitors to the neighborhood were for business purposes. The most frequent were the men that sold life insurance policies with five and ten cent a week premiums, the area or corner grocers, the police, and our family doctor."

In his memoirs, John A. Stokes recalls an incident when he was 12 years old of having to hide among the bushes and brambles alongside Route 15 just outside Farmville. He emerged from the roadside bushes bleeding and his clothes were ripped because in his rush to get off the road he landed in a thorn bush. No he did nothing wrong and he wasn't fleeing from home but, simply practicing the survival skill his parents taught him. "Whenever and wherever colored children are walking after dark, we are taught to take cover in ditches and gullies, behind bushes and trees, and culverts, or in any safe hiding place as soon as we hear or see a car approaching us from the front or rear." As a 12 year old in 1943 Stokes daily existence was dictated by decades-long practices and laws supporting Jim Crow. During this time in the South, it was not unusual for colored boys and girls to be taunted, hurt, and even killed, especially if they are caught alone at night. Stokes went on to say, "The white authorities blame us. They ask, just why are you all out at this time of night anyhow?"

——— PRINCE EDWARD COUNTY SCHOOLS ———

By 1951, in Prince Edward County there were 15 Negro schools for an estimated Negro student population of 2,000. The total value of these properties was around $329,000 because all but two of the schools were of wood construction, with no toilet facilities or indoor plumbing, and only used either wood or coal or kerosene stoves for heat. If you see the pictures of these facilities the word that comes to mind is "shacks." For the white population, there were seven schools for an estimated 1,400 students with a total property value of $1,200,000 with each of their seven schools constructed of sound brick design, with indoor plumbing, indoor flush toilets and modern central hot water heating. That is a 73 percent difference to the disadvantage of the black students. In 1951, the school per capita property value for white students was $817, while for each Negro student it was $194. Remember, the law of the land was separate, but equal.

When John Stokes and his twin sister Carrie started elementary school their first problem was just getting there. At that time the only public school buses in Prince Edward County were the ones that took white kids to the white only schools. The twins had to walk miles along the gravel shoulders of US Route 15 to get to a school in Farmville. Imagine those cold winter days trudging along and then the white school bus passes you by, yet those buses are off limits to you. And sometimes the white students would taunt them and spit upon them. The Stokes twins were lucky because after a few months a colored company started running a school bus that they could pay a dollar a month to ride on. Yes their parents were already paying taxes for supposedly equal facilities, but…. They also attended the only elementary school for blacks in all of Prince Edward County that was a brick building. The dozen or so other elementary schools scattered throughout the county were mostly one or two room school houses with a coal stove for heat, and no indoor water or toilets. Stokes talks about his friend Jack Jeffers, a white friend, who had a hard time understanding why the two boys had to go to different schools and why Jack's school was so much better than John's. The two boys played together since their homes were not far apart as long as they didn't do it in public. Jack would often ask, "why don't they want you to learn?" Stokes early on figured out the answer to Jack's question. "But eventually I came to realize that by denying us transportation to school and schools that were grossly unequal to the ones white children attended, the white power structure was programming us to fail. This realization would play a pivotal role in the events that would unfold my senior year at Robert Russa Moton High School."

——— MOTON ———
IT WAS MUCH MORE THAN JUST A SCHOOL

The Robert Russa Moton High School was built in 1939 by Prince Edward County for Negro children in the colonial-revival style common to many school buildings of that era. It replaced several smaller one-room wooden schools scattered around the county. It had six classrooms and an office arranged around a central auditorium. It had no cafeteria or restrooms for teachers. Built originally to serve 180 students it was hopelessly overcrowded almost the day it opened and by the 1950s with 450 students it had, at its best, become a daily source of irritation for teachers and students alike. At its worst, it was an inadequate facility that was holding the students back both academically and athletically. In 1948/1949 the County built long temporary buildings to house the overflow. The outsides were covered with a felt-like black material commonly referred to as roofing paper, the structures were quickly labeled "tar paper shacks." They were as ugly as they were uncomfortable. These tar paper shacks became a rallying cry during the two week strike, in 1951, and for the subsequent law suit's.

In 1953, following the strike and the filing of the student's suit, Prince Edward County made an effort to undermine the student's pending law suit by fast tracking the building a new high school for Negroes. The original R. R. Moton building had many uses over its life: starting out as a high school, then a grammar school when all the county public schools were closed in 1959 the building housed one of the elementary schools as part of the Free School, once public school resumed in 1964 the building was a grammar school, and finally today houses the Robert Russa Moton Museum.

The building was closed in 1993 after 56 years of service. At that time the Martha E. Forrester Council of Women launched a movement to preserve it as a memorial to the struggle for civil rights in education. While some in the county would have been happier to see the old school torn down, as if erasing the shame of the 13-year segregation struggle, the historic building was saved. In 1998, Robert Russa Moton School was declared a

National Historic Landmark. Moton Museum was established in 2000 and an energetic Museum Director, Mr. Lacy Ward was hired to guide the building's transformation from an abandoned school to a world-class civil rights museum. The old high school is now a museum dedicated to preserving the historic structure and allowing future generations to learn about the strike and the efforts to integrate education in the County, Virginia, and America. You can read more about the Museum and plan a visit from their web site: www.motonmuseum.org. If you go, stand on the stage where Barbara Rose Johns and John A. Stokes addressed their fellow students and close your eyes for a moment; you might just be inspired to right some wrong, or at the least write a book.

The Robert Russa Moton High School was named after Robert Russa Moton who was born in an adjoining county and grew up in Prince Edward County. Dr. Moton is best known as the successor to Booker T. Washington, president of Tuskegee Institute. Earlier in this Chapter we covered Dr Moton and his contributions to education in 20th century America.

The Robert Russa Moton main building was a sturdy structure and in better shape than many of the schools throughout the South and certainly better than those schools in the outlying rural areas of Prince Edward County. Of course this reference is to the actual brick structure not the tar paper shacks. In many locales throughout Virginia and the South, blacks went to schools with grades one through twelve all in the same building. Many of these buildings were really nothing more than shacks. These one-room schoolhouses may sound quaint, but imagine trying to get a modern, quality education in that substandard environment. In some cases, principals were forced to conduct fundraising to have enough money just to buy desks, books, and basic school supplies like pencils and paper.

As discussed previously in this chapter, the legal underpinning of this two-color system was the infamous 1896 *Plessy v. Ferguson* Supreme Court ruling that made "separate but equal" the rule of the nation. This ruling supported segregation and was based on the fallacious premise that as long as facilities were equal, separate was acceptable to the law of the land. As John Stokes and his family well knew, what passed as equal was interpreted solely by the whites in power and rarely if ever approached truly equal.

The statistics tell the story and provide stark evidence of the sham that separate but equal was in Prince Edward County. Prior to 1923, the highest level of education a black student could reach in Prince Edward County was the sixth grade. With continual pressure by the parents of black students, the county added a seventh grade. It's also interesting to note that in the 30 years since the passing of the 1896 *Plessy v. Ferguson* ruling the county constructed one and only one high school for blacks, in 1927. In fact, it was the first brick school for blacks in the county. Meantime, during this same period six high schools for whites were built. So where did the Prince Edward County blacks attend high school prior to 1927? The reality was that most of them never went beyond the sixth grade. A few attended high school in adjoining counties or left the area entirely in order to continue their educations.

John A. Stokes talks about the overcrowding in his memoir, how black students were so hungry for learning that they quickly filled the building and how one person commented on the number of students in the school by saying, "they are coming out of the windows!" By the time John and his sister Carrie were attending Robert Russa Moton High School, the school designed for 180 was packed with more than 450 students. Throughout this period, the parents of the Moton students continued to press their case with the school board for some relief from the overcrowding. The school board's remedy was to build six tar paper shack classrooms on the lawn of the school. This is how the tar paper shacks came about.

By 1951, those tar paper shacks held about half the classes at Moton, so most students had at least one class a day, or more, in the tar paper shack classrooms. Of course, the really unlucky students might find themselves being taught in a broken-down bus behind the school. The students were injured by more than physical discomfort, they were often embarrassed by these eyesores, especially when folks who were traveling to Florida and other places would come by; they would ask the students "Where are the cows?" because, you know, they looked like barns or chicken coops. "They leaked when it rained," said John A. Stokes in an interview at his home in Lanham, Maryland. "Each shack had a potbelly stove that roasted students near it while leaving those in the back chilled. There was no plumbing, no running water. Students had to use secondhand books, they had no science labs or cafeteria, and their school buses broke down constantly."

In some ways being more worldly made the situation worse for some of the students. They had traveled in and outside Virginia and had seen much better black school. Barbara Rose Johns and John Stokes were two of the strike leaders that had seen for themselves these better facilities and wondered why they should settle for second-class status. "Barbara knew what other schools had. She had seen schools with cafeterias and science labs," Edwilda Issac said. "In the tar paper shacks, coals would pop out of the holes in the stoves. Everything was leaking. In our biology classes, we had one frog. The teacher was the only one with a microscope. Every single book we ever had was a discarded book from Farmville High School. When you find out there is something better than what you have, it gives you extra courage." At the time of the strike Edwilda Issac was a 13-year-old student at Moton and a friend of Barbara Rose Johns' sister Joan.

Joan Johns Cobb was a first-year student at Moton when the strike occurred. She shares her remembrances of life at Moton in an oral history she gave to the Congress on Racial Equality in 1991.

The school we went to was overcrowded. Consequently, the county decided to build three tarpaper shacks for us to hold classes in. A tarpaper shack looks like a dilapidated black building, which is similar to a chicken coop on a farm. It's very unsightly. In winter the school was very cold. And a lot of times we had to put on our jackets. Now, the students that sat closest to the wood stove were very warm and the ones who sat farthest away were very cold. And I remember being cold a lot of times and sitting in the classroom with my jacket on. When it rained, we would get water through the ceiling. So there were lots of pails sitting around the classroom. And sometimes we had to raise our umbrellas to keep the water off our heads. It was a very difficult setting for trying to learn.

John Stokes shared, in an oral history he gave to the Virginia Civil Rights Movement Video Initiative in March 2003, describing how he felt about the education that was afforded to him in Prince Edward County. Stokes said, "...when you speak of the educational environment in Prince Edward County, Farmville, Virginia, even now it sort of brings tears to my eyes because of the fact that I knew it was deplorable, but as I grew older I realized how devastating it really was for us without us even realizing it. In the first place, my twin sister and I could not start in school until we were eight years old because there was no bus for black children. There were two buses for whites only that passed by our house every morning and picked up Jack Jeffreys, Bill Schueler, these were the white boys that I played with, these were the kids that's I played with, and yet my twin sister and I could not ride those buses."

———— EFFORTS FOR A NEW HIGH SCHOOL ————

The post-World War II 1940s saw a tremendous increase in Negro high school enrollments. Prince Edward County saw a 118 percent increase from 1940 to 1950. This is why the Robert Russa Moton was hopelessly overcrowded well before the 1951 strike. The situation at Moton is also a testament to how highly education was valued in the black community. "By 1947 some 377 students were stuffed into a school originally designed to handle a maximum of 180." And still, Principal M. Boyd Jones, who arrived at Robert Russa Moton that year, told of going out and beating the bushes for even more students. This was a testament to his and the black communities devotion to the education of their children. "Yet with each new student the crowding problem touched a fresh dynamic peak. John Stokes recalls, "Sure we were crowded. You know the auditorium? Well, we held two or three classes in the auditorium most of the time, one on the stage and two in the back. We even held some classes in a bus."

A Parent-Teachers Association was formed by the Robert Russa Moton parents in an attempt to gain some relief from the overcrowding. They made numerous appeals to the Board of Education which up to 1951 had only accomplished the building of three tar paper shacks on the lawn surrounding the Robert Russa Moton School. In fact, the school board was making some real progress, but this was never clearly communicated to the parent's or students. In a very real way these visible reminders of inequality made things even worse for the very blacks they were meant to appease. After the strike it is telling and sad how many whites commented that they never saw the tar paper shacks on the Moton lawn even thought they passed the school many times a day. The black condition was that invisible to them.

While the school board made a lot of false moves initially; by October 1947 a survey of both the white and black schools in the county showed a considerable amount of money was needed to bring them all up to par. By this time Maurice Large, who was the young head of his own construction firm, had taken over as chairman of the school board. "Large felt the need for new facilities for the Negro high school students, but he believed that only a carefully modulated political campaign in the county could bring approval of a local bond issue. He was not aware of the need for haste." He supported studying the problem by having a survey done in the county's schools by a committee of the State Board of Education. This would highlight the problem, he thought, and give the school board some ammunition for its bond campaign. The survey was undertaken and completed in October 1947. It called for a considerable expenditure to bring both the white and Negro facilities up to par. "It found Robert Russa Moton 'inadequate' and recommended that it be converted into an elementary school and that Mary E. Branch elementary school nearby be converted into a high school with full facilities for 600 pupils."

The school board developed economic tables in an effort to show that Prince Edward County could afford to improve their school. The tables demonstrated that the county ranked 33rd among 100 counties in income per school child and 44th in taxable wealth. This placed Prince Edward above the medium for both these measures and in the top one third of the state in income per school child.

Recall that the Moton students of the post-WWII era were the first generation that parents and teachers had convinced that they were just as good as anyone else and they could accomplish anything they set their mind to. Author Bob Smith, who wrote his book on the Moton strike in 1965, does a terrific job of capturing the history and, more importantly, the feelings surrounding the tar paper shacks. Smith reports that, "the shacks were deeply resented across the whole spectrum of Negro society."

In March 1948, the Prince Edward County school Board met with the state Board of Education to discuss the county's infrastructure needs. It was agreed by both the state and county officials that permanent adequate schools were necessary to deal with the overcrowding at the Robert Russa Moton school. In spite of this in June 1948 Large and McIlwaine presented a plan for temporary structures to relieve congestion at the Robert Russa Moton to the Board of Supervisors. The Board of Supervisors agreed to fund temporary structures not to exceed $25,000. It should be noted that the stopgap measures were being employed elsewhere in Virginia. While it is debatable if the county was serious about building permanent structures in 1948, it's clear that the powers to be felt it was necessary to sell the county on these large expenditures.

The obstacles that the school board saw before it in June, 1948, were formidable, then. It had to sell a big bond issue for public schools to people traditionally lukewarm to the idea of public education. It had to sell a big bond issue primarily for a Negro public school to people whose history had not conditioned them to regard Negro education as necessary or desirable.

So, while the board worked to wind up its political support, the Negro high school students would have temporary buildings. The structures had a five-year statutory limit upon their use, but many of them built in the 1930s and early 1940s had outlived their legal limit. Across the state to demand for literacy funds loans exceeded the funds ability to pay. That Prince Edward school board got permission to build three of the tarpaper buildings in 1948 – 1949 and soon afterward appointed a three-man committee to find a site for a new Robert Russa Moton high school.

This is how the tarpaper shacks came to be built. Their meaning was imprisoned in this history. It has something to do with the South's ancestral dissatisfaction for mass education, the scars left by the Civil War, the real poverty, the Penny Wise tightfistedness of the Byrd administration, and the unexpected demand of the Negro of the 1940s for high school education. All of these in one manner or another were villains of the piece.

Yet the chief villain is no less difficult to see for all of the help it had. The white high school that was built in the same period as Robert Russa Moton embodied the hope rather than just the well-founded expectation of increasing enrollment. Robert Russa Moton was built without the expectation, but, more importantly, without the hope. The bond issue that the school board handled so gingerly would've been troublesome enough if it had to do only with the improvements to a white schools. The fact that it dealt primarily with Negro school improvements made it a matter for profound contemplation all around. The real villain of the piece was segregation – or, rather, the cumulative set of attitudes of white toward Negro that make up segregation's cause and effect.

Years later someone close to the situation in the county for many years observed that there would have been no trouble if the shacks have been put up on the grounds of the white school for use by the white students. This may be true. But of course they would not have meant the same thing at all. They might have looked the same. They might have inspired the same complaints. They would not have stood as fresh evidence of an inferiority that a white man's history strained to impose on the Negro.

The shacks at Robert Russa Moton did not cure the overcrowding problem, although they helped. They did raise new and ugly questions that the county eventually would have to answer in pain. They stood as symbols – with a new and potent meaning that the law soon would invoke – of the failure of "separate" to be "equal" in the schools of the South.

The actuality that, in 1947, the school board was considering a Negro high school for 600 pupils' points to some level of awareness by the white school board that Moton was terribly overcrowded. Additionally, they had started to understand that the expected enrollment of Negro high school students would likely increase in the future. Today it seems a matter of course that we should all have a high school education. But in America and in the rural South in particular, that idea was just starting to gain traction and in this case the black community was way ahead of their white counterparts.

During this time a profound leadership shift was occurring within the local black community. Reverend L. Francis Griffin assumed the chair of the PTA committee that was pleading and pushing the school board for a new school. This is the same Revered Griffin, who, long before the NAACP announced its policy that segregation was unacceptable and that they would use the courts to bring about its demise had both preached and openly discussed the need for integration to truly move Negro civil rights to an equal footing.

While having Griffin lead the school committee was a big change in and of itself, another was the resignation of Willie Reed, a well-to-do local Negro contractor who had grown up and prospered under the system of segregation and was willing to work within this system. Reed's resignation from the PTA committee and Griffin's elevation to the chairmanship symbolized a change within the community that was equally significant and tragic, a change that the white community was completely oblivious to. Old habits die hard. Editor Barrye Wall of the *Farmville Herald* would continue to consult with Reed, believing he continued to represent the dominant opinion in the Negro community. He only learned later that this became less and less true after 1949. Thus, communication, or rather a communication failure, is also to blame for the initiation of the strike and the subsequent lawsuit and school closing.

In the spring of 1950, the all-black Robert Russa Moton PTA committee offered their assistance to the county school board in securing a site for the new school. It appears that white landowners were reluctant to have 600 Negroes residing in their midst. Around August 1950 the committee did indeed find some suitable land and an owner willing to sell. While all of this was going on in the summer of 1950, Superintendent Large chose to wait until November to get in touch with the land owner. By June of 1950, the school board felt things were moving along. They had an architectural sketch of the new proposed school, were in negotiations for the land and had a scheme to get the money. However, little of this was communicated to the black community, and the growing gulf in frustration was made worse because nothing was ever printed in the *Farmville Herald* or any of the other state papers about how far things had proceeded. In fact, in February 1951 Large had received approval for the purchase of the land from the Board of Supervisors and was in the final process to negotiate a deal. Of course, all of this became moot as the Robert Russa Moton students took matters into their own hands in April 1951. They had waited long enough; they were going to strike.

So, with plans for the new school almost set, why did Barbara Rose Johns and John A. Stokes lead the student strike? Was it as simple as a lack of communication between them and the white school board? The board was very reluctant to discuss publicly any plans for a Negro school in an effort to tiptoe around white sensibilities. Then there was the tradition that the white man did not go to the black man, but the black man came to the white with hat in hand, referential in demeanor and politely requested to speak. No one on the school board even considered it necessary or appropriate to address the black community and provide them an update on the new school plans. Unhelpfully, the local paper (*Herald*) never had one story about the new school. The *Farmville Herald* did not cover the school boards meetings. Editor Wall latter said, "I had very little knowledge of what was going on in the school board meetings." He went on to say, "I didn't know they [Moton PTA] were showing up there every month…I feel now that not reporting the school board meetings was a sin of omission. I wasn't aware or didn't recognize what was happing. Nobody else in the community was either…."

Within an environment of such poor communications, black parents and students became more and more frustrated and convinced, with no evidence to the contrary, that if something was to be done it was for them to take the initiative. After all, the shacks had by now become a sick joke, yet no one was laughing. You could make an argument that the strike was a result of a communication breakdown but, you would be missing the real root cause—segregation.

As the final trigger leading up to the strike, a tragic event struck Prince Edward County. On March 13, 1951, on an unusually foggy and rainy afternoon in Elam, Virginia, a school bus had not quite cleared the tracks, when a train blasted it in two, ripping off the back end of the bus, and taking with it the lives of five young people.

The five killed were Naomi Hendricks, 18, and her brother Dodson, 15; Christine Hendricks, 18, first cousin of the other Hendrick teenagers; Hettie Dungee, 17; and Winfield Page, 14. All five killed were Robert Russa Moton High School students returning home to the Prospect section of Prince Edward. This tragic accident occurred approximately one month before the student's walkout at Moton. Barbara Rose Johns lost her best friend in this event and many of the Moton strikers attribute this tragedy as the final straw that drove students and parents alike to support a strike. Many in the black community blamed the accident on the dilapidated condition of the bus. The failure of the bus's engine may or may not have been the cause, but, what is certain are the heightened emotions that resulted. The impact of the bus accident to the Prince Edward County black community was profound. There was anger that a hand-me-down bus caused the loss of five student's lives and hospitalized 10 other student's.

Just how impactful the legacy of this tragedy is to the community can still be seen, 58 years later, when on Saturday, May 30, 2009, the Martha E. Forrester Council of Women held a program of remembrance, "Gone But Not Forgotten," at the Robert Russa Moton Museum in honor of the five young Prince Edward students who lost their lives in the 1951 bus accident. During the program, the Virginia Department of Conservation and Recreation dedicated a plaque to be placed near the spot of the accident in honor of the five young lives lost.

———————

We can end this review that spanned 399 years of the Negroes' experience in the land of the free by sharing what Dr. Moton had to say in 1929. While the last 60 years have seen tremendous improvement, on balance, and yet for most of these 399 years, the Negro in America has been ill treated and maybe the most egregious sin made invisible. Therefore, it seems only fitting to give Dr. Moton the last word in this chapter covering Negro suffrage under Jim Crow, since he lived through some of the worst of it, yet always remained hopeful of a brighter future. His words are a sobering reminder of the pain endured on the black body and mind.

Any Negro, every Negro burns with indignation when he pays full first-class fare for a railroad ticket and then has to ride in a crowded, odorous, flimsy, dirty second- class coach. There is no word to describe the complex of his emotions when a Pullman ticket agent tells him he has no space, and then, going around the corner and calling the agent over the phone is told that there is plenty of space.

—Dr. Robert Russa Moton, author of *What The Negro Thinks,* 1929

Chapter Four

DAVIS V. PRINCE EDWARD

Had there been no May 17, 1954, I'm not sure there would have been a Little Rock. I'm not sure there would have been a Martin Luther King Jr., or Rosa Parks, had it not been for May 17, 1954. It created an environment for us to push, for us to pull.

We live in a different country, a better country, because of what happened here in 1954. And we must never forget it. We must tell the story again, over and over and over.

—U.S. Rep. John Lewis remarks at a 2002 ceremony commemorating the 48th anniversary of Brown v. Board of Education at Topeka's First United Methodist Church

Time Line for Chapter Four
Davis v. Prince Edward
(1951–1954)

1951, May 24. Kenneth Clark, a psychology professor at City College of New York came to Summerton, South Carolina, to interview the children and conduct a test using dolls of different colors.

1951, May 28. Thurgood Marshall, Robert Carter, and Spottswood Robinson brought the Carolina *Briggs v. Elliott* case before a three-judge panel at the federal courthouse in Charleston, South Carolina.

1951, June 25-26. The U.S. District Court for the District of Kansas heard *Brown v. Board of Education of Topeka*. At the trial, the NAACP argued that segregated schools sent the message to black children that they were inferior to whites; therefore, the schools were inherently unequal.

1952, October. The bundling of the *Brown v. Board* cases days before arguments were to be heard in *Briggs*, resulted in the Supreme Court announced a postponement. Three weeks later, the Court announced that it would also hear the Delaware cases, as well as *Davis v. Prince Edward County* and the District of Columbia case, *Bolling et al. v. Sharpe et al.*

Significance: The Supreme Court agreed to hear all five of the school desegregation cases collectively. This grouping was significant because it showed school segregation as a national issue, not just a southern one. As a strictly constitutional matter the U. S. Supreme Court eventually rendered a separate opinion on *Bolling v. Sharpe* because the 14th Amendment to the U. S. Constitution was not applicable in the District of Columbia.

1953, June. The Supreme Court ordered that a second round of arguments in *Brown v. Board* be heard in October.

1953, September 8. Supreme Court Chief Justice Fred M. Vinson unexpectedly dies before his court can rule on the *Brown v. Board* case.

1953, October 5. Chief Justice Earl Warren is sworn in and assumes his seat on the Supreme Court. He was selected by President Eisenhower to replace Vinson.

1953, December 7–9. Second round of arguments in *Brown v. Board of Education*.

1954, March 1. Chief Justice Earl Warren is confirmed by the Senate for the position of Supreme Court Chief Justice.

1954, May 17. Supreme Court issues a decree on the *Brown V. Board* case thus striking down 100 years of segregation.

Chapter Four
DAVIS V. PRINCE EDWARD
(1951–1954)

The arc of the moral universe is long but it bends toward justice.

—Dr. Martin Luther King

The Robert Russa Moton Museum, Gallery III covers the Prince Edward County court case that made up Virginia's contribution to the amalgamated law suit we know as *Brown v. Board of Education*. The Moton student strike case had made it all the way to the Supreme Court under the case name of *Davis v. School Board of Prince Edward County*. Gallery III covers this four-year period of legal wrangling.

———— MOTON STUDENTS FILE SUIT ————

The Moton students' suit, *Davis v. School Board of Prince Edward County,* was filed on May 23, 1951. While the suit was filed exactly one month after the student strike, it took three years to wind its way through the Virginia courts and Virginia appeal courts before the Supreme Court agreed to hear the case. It was always the NAACP's intention that these cases be heard in the highest court in the land. There are two reasons for this. The most important was only the Supreme Court could overrule itself. Recall that *Plessy v. Ferguson*, 163 U.S. 537 (1896), was the landmark United States Supreme Court decision that legalized the doctrine of "separate but equal." Secondly, a victory at this level could be applied nationwide, saving valuable NAACP resources. On May 17, 1954, the Supreme Court issued a ruling striking down separate but equal. However, this ruling was too long in coming for the original Moton strikers. By the time the ruling was issued many of the original strikers had moved on to college, jobs, or married life. Many left the county and never returned to live in Prince Edward County.

Moving swiftly, it took the NAACP attorneys Robinson and Hill only 30 days to file the lawsuit against Prince Edward County School District demanding the County integrate its schools. The case was called *Davis v. County School Board of Prince Edward County* and was filed on May 23, 1951, in the United States District Court for the Eastern District of Virginia, and Richmond division, under the civil action number 1333. You can see a mature, 1957, version of the order in Appendix III. The case listed 117 Robert Russa Moton High School students and 67 parents as the plaintiffs. If you read the complaint you will be struck by all the students listed as "infants" this was because they were underage and legally not considered adults. Of course throughout the two-week strike and the run-up to filing their suit these "infants" had surely acquitted themselves as very adult-like.

As expected, the county won the first round. The three-judge panel of the US District Court in Richmond unanimously rejected the students' request for non-segregated schools. The court based their decision on their assessment that the current school system had been of no harm to either race. Based on this development NAACP lawyers decided to combine the *Davis V. county school Board of Prince Edward County* case with three similar suits that had been filed across the United States, all with the same aim of striking down segregated education in America. This is how the famous *Brown v. Board of Education* class-action suit came to be. Lawsuits from Delaware, South Carolina, and Kansas were all combined into a single overwhelming indictment against the *Plessy v. Ferguson* separate but equal doctrine. While the court agreed to hear the D.C. case in conjunction with the *Brown* cases it was always treated separately from a legal perspective.

——— LEGACY ———
OF SEGREGATED EDUCATION

In the 1840s, Benjamin Roberts of Boston began a legal campaign to enroll his five-year-old-daughter, Sarah, in a nearby school for whites. The Massachusetts Supreme Court ultimately ruled that local elected officials had the authority to control local schools and that separate schools did not violate black students rights. The decision was cited over and over again in later cases to justify segregation. Black parents in Boston, however, refused to accept defeat. They organized a school boycott and statewide protests. In 1855, the Massachusetts legislature passed the country's first law prohibiting school segregation.

Segregation was a long-standing American tradition that was codified by law and enforced scrupulously by local boards of education that were reflecting their white constituents' desire for separation of the races. In 1884, Joseph and Mary Tape attempted to enroll their daughter Mamie at Spring Valley School in San Francisco. Principal Jennie Hurley cited school board policy against admitting Chinese children, and the Tapes took the case to court. On March 3, 1885, the California State Supreme Court said that state law required public education to be open to all children and ruled in favor of the Tapes. After the decision, the state legislature quickly passed a law allowing schools to establish separate facilities for "Mongolians." Other Asian parents continued the fight for integrated schools until their eventual victory in 1947.

By law, school districts in California segregated American Indian and Asian children. They also commonly placed Latino and African American students together in programs separate from whites. In the early 1940s, Felícitas and Gonzalo Méndez tried to enroll their three children in the local all-white Westminster Elementary School. When school officials refused, the Méndeze's joined other families and filed suit. On March 2, 1945, a group of parents, with the support of the League of United Latin American Citizens, filed a class action suit in federal court against segregated schools in Orange County (*Méndez v. Westminster*). They argued that separate schools violated the Fourteenth Amendment. Judge Paul J. McCormick ruled in favor of the parents, and appellate courts upheld his decision. In 1947, California Governor Earl Warren pushed through legislation ending school segregation for American Indian and Asian children. Remember that name; Warren will have more to say on this subject.

The American legal system is based on the principle of *stare decisis*—legal precedent establishes the law. The strategy of civil rights lawyers was to get the Supreme Court to make a series of judgments in support of racial integration. These judgments would establish legal precedents and the foundation for dismantling segregation in public schools. Some of the significant legal precedents they used to buttress their arguments in *Brown* were hard-fought legal victories going back decades:

- *Missouri ex. rel. Gaines v. Canada* **(1938)**
  In the 1930s, no state-funded law schools in Missouri admitted African American students. With guidance from NAACP lawyers, Lloyd Gaines, applied to the University of Missouri law school. Denied admission, Gaines was offered a scholarship to an out-of-state school. Gaines then sued the law school. When the case reached the Supreme Court, Charles Houston persuaded the justices that offering Gaines an out-of-state scholarship was no substitute for admission. The court ruled that the state either had to establish an equal facility or admit him.

- *Sipuel v. Oklahoma State Regents* **(1948)**
  Ada Sipuel was denied admission to the University of Oklahoma Law School in 1946. With the help of the NAACP she sued the school. Thurgood Marshall argued that separating black students, no matter what the conditions, denied them access to opportunities provided to others. The law school admitted Sipuel rather than continue the dispute. She went on to become one of the first African American women to sit on the board of regents of Oklahoma State University.

- *Sweatt v. Painter* **(1950) and** *McLaurin v. Oklahoma State Regents* **(1950)**
  Rather than admit Heman Sweatt to its law school, the state of Texas offered to create a separate program for African Americans. The University of Oklahoma accepted George McLaurin to its graduate program in education, but separated him from other students. Both students sued, and the U.S. Supreme Court ultimately ruled that dividing students by race in graduate programs

fell short of the legal standard of separate but equal. Interaction among students, the court said, was an integral part of the educational experience.

—— NAACP LEGAL STRATEGY ——

The principal black civil rights organization in the first half of the twentieth century was the National Association for the Advancement of Colored People, which sought the desegregation of public education from its inception. The NAACP's legal team in the 1930s began to challenge these inequalities in education. One early victory occurred in Norfolk, Virginia, in 1940, when the courts agreed that the city had to pay black and white teachers equitably. NAACP lawyers in Virginia continued to employ this strategy of challenging inequalities in numerous other school districts, and the pace of litigation accelerated after the close of World War II (1939–1945).

Virginia's public schools had been segregated racially since their forming in 1870. So, too, were the state's public colleges and universities. During and immediately following Reconstruction, black Virginians were able to pressure state and local authorities to provide support for their schools. They used the power of local organizations and the ballot. Following the disfranchisement of black voters by the 1902 Virginia Constitution, funding for black schools began to fall far short of what white schools received, and the discrepancies in salaries for teachers and administrators became stark.

The segregation of public schools went beyond issues of African Americans and whites. Members of Virginia's Indian tribes were also largely excluded from public education. While many tribes established mission schools early in the twentieth century, these schools often only went up to the seventh grade. Meanwhile, many Indian children, whose help was needed at home or in the fields, never made it past elementary school. Public high school was available only to American Indians who were willing to attend black-only schools, and most refused. Virginia's indigenous natives were sensitized to maintaining their cultural identity in the face of the Racial Integrity Act of 1924, which had deemed almost all Indians, for legal purposes, to be black. A number of the Powhatan tribes sent their children to the Bacone School in Oklahoma and to other such facilities, where they could complete high school and go on to earn the equivalent of a community college degree. Public schools were not opened to Virginia Indians until 1963.

To many African Americans, the success of the NAACP's cases against graduate and professional schools seemed to be a turning point. Thurgood Marshall and other NAACP leaders received hundreds of congratulatory letters and telegrams for their tremendous legal accomplishments in the 1940s and early 1950s. Marshall declared that total elimination of school segregation was the NAACP's next goal. The association's lawyers, he said, were now ready to attack the principle of segregation head-on. In 1950 Marshall was often quoted about the next steps, he said:

> *The complete destruction of all enforced segregation is now in sight. We are going to insist on non-segregation in American public education from top to bottom—from law school to kindergarten.*
>
> — Thurgood Marshall, 1950

In a harbinger of things to come, the Supreme Court issued a ruling in June, 1950, deciding the case of Heman Sweatt, a Negro applicant for law school at the University of Texas. Texas intended to seat Mr. Sweatt in his own law school as the sole student rather than allow him entry into the all-white classroom. Chief Justice Frederick M. Vinson wrote:

> *In terms of the number of the faculty, variety of course and opportunity for specialization, size of the student body, scope of the library, availability of law review, and similar activities, the University of Texas Law school is superior. What is more important, the University of Texas Law school possesses a far greater degree those*

qualities which are incapable of object measurement by which make for greatness in a law school. Such qualities, to name a few, include reputation of the faculty, experience of the administration, position and influence of the alumni, standing in the community, tradition, and prestige.

This ruling had a profound effect on the course of events within the NAACP. This one victory revised the strategy of demanding equal facilities in favor of fully integrated facilities. In September 3, 1950, the *New York Times* observed that, "by the Supreme Court's yardstick there is not a single state owned Negro school in the South that can measure up to similar white schools." With all this in mind, the NAACP quickly moved forward with their newfound strategy of attacking the heart of the problem—segregation. At a conference of NAACP attorneys in New York on September 1950, a resolution was drafted calling for a shift of emphasis. Henceforth there would be suits for desegregation in education rather than equalization. The presidents of the NAACP state conferences approve the measure at their annual convention in Boston later that September and further endorsed by the national Board of Directors in October. Aggressive NAACP leaders from Virginia wanted to send a public school desegregation case up to the Supreme Court from their state. In April 1951, it seemed to them that a case in Pulaski County, originally assumed for equalization, would fit the bill nicely. However as the attorneys became fully engaged with the Pulaski case it began to unravel with the untimely death of the plaintiff. W. Lester Banks, executive secretary of the state NAACP chapter, called the emergence of the Prince Edward case, an "act of providence."

———— BROWN V. BOARD OF EDUCATION ————

The next few sections review the four cases that made up *Brown* and the conjoined but separate D.C. case. At 32 years of age Mr. Oliver Brown, of Topeka, Kansas, was rebuffed in his attempt to enroll his 8-year-old daughter, Linda, at Sumner Elementary, a white school close to his home. She was required to go to an all-black school five miles away. This is how Mr. Brown lent his name to this most famous of civil rights cases. Additionally, the high court decided to simultaneously address a similar suit by the parents from the District of Columbia. The district of Colombia case has been a source of confusion to students of civil rights because, while technically not one of the *Brown* cases, the rulings were universally applied. Any of the Moton strikers would be quick to point out that only the Prince Edward case was student initiated and student led. Remember, the Prince Edward case was the surprise litigation pushed into the NAACP's lap by Barbara Rose Johns and her fellow strikers. Regardless of how the case came to the NAACP, to their credit, they vigorously prosecuted the suit to its ultimate successful conclusion.

The Supreme Court of the United States decided to address the segregation issue in one fell swoop by using the five cases to reexamine the "separate but equal" construct. The *Brown* decision would mark the end of the "separate but equal" precedent set nearly 60 years earlier in *Plessy* v. *Ferguson.* The court stated that "separate educational facilities are inherently unequal," and that school segregation violated the Fourteenth Amendment.

This decision was vindication for the students and parents of Prince Edward County especially considering their momentous decision to fight for the larger prize of integrated schools. Soon after the suit was filed, the second-guessing began and only became more pronounced as the legal case dragged on. Some might call the students naive because many thought they would see a resolution in a year or less. After all the justice of their case was plain for all to see; or at least that is how they saw it. Of course, the lawyers knew how risky bucking a hundred years of legal precedent and 300 years of racial divide would be. All of this contributed to making this victory sweet for the plaintiffs and for all who believed in equality.

The Supreme Court agreed to hear *Brown v. Board of Education* in June 1952. Deciding the case was difficult from the start. Differing social philosophies and temperaments divided the nine justices. Chief Justice Fred Vinson and several others doubted the constitutional authority of the Court to end school segregation. And all the justices worried that a decision to integrate schools might be unenforceable.

Kluger summed up what was at stake when he wrote that, "the Supreme Court had finally stopped stalling and agreed to be convened to hear arguments on whether the white people of the United States might continue to treat the black people as their subjects."

In 1952 the Supreme Court decided to hear school desegregation cases from across the country. When the trial began, everyone in the courtroom knew that the future of race relations in America hung in the balance. The attorneys for both sides believed that law and morality supported their arguments. A victory by the plaintiffs would mean that the highest court in the land officially endorsed the ideal of equal opportunity, regardless of race. Defeat would mean that the Supreme Court continued sanctioning a system of legal segregation based on the notion of racial inferiority and white supremacy. The case for the defenders of segregation rested on four arguments:

1. The Constitution did not require white and African American children to attend the same schools.
2. Social separation of blacks and whites was a regional custom; the states should be left free to regulate their own social affairs.
3. Segregation was not harmful to black people.
4. Whites were making a good-faith effort to equalize the two educational systems. But because black children were still living with the effects of slavery, it would take some time before they were able to compete with white children in the same classroom.

On the opposing side the civil rights lawyers of the NAACP Legal Defense Fund were much younger than their adversaries and had far fewer resources to prepare and bolster their cases. Much of their work was done at the law schools of Howard and Columbia universities. One of their biggest hurdles was overcoming the ruling law of the land. The *Plessy v. Ferguson* decision, they argued, had misinterpreted the equal protection clause of the Fourteenth Amendment—the authors of this amendment had not intended to allow segregated schools. Nor did existing law consider the harmful social and psychological effects of segregation. Integrated schools, they asserted, were a fundamental right for all Americans.

Lawyers for the plaintiffs relied on legal arguments, historical evidence, and psychological studies:

- In *Plessy v. Ferguson,* the Supreme Court had misinterpreted the equal protection clause of the Fourteenth Amendment. Equal protection under the laws did not allow for racial segregation.
- The Fourteenth Amendment allowed the government to prohibit any discriminatory state action based on race, including segregation in public schools.
- The Fourteenth Amendment did not specify whether the states would be allowed to establish segregated education.
- Psychological testing demonstrated the harmful effects of segregation on the minds and expectations of African American children.

Even before the Supreme Court issued their *Brown v. Board of Education* ruling in 1954, economic and political factors were already weakening segregation's hold on the Negro. Black migration to the northern cities began early in the century and had gathered pace through World War I, the Great Depression, and World War II. Segregation in factories and in the armed services gradually broke down as the Roosevelt and Truman administrations responded to legal and political pressure from blacks. In the next few sections we will look in some detail at each of the five cases the Supreme Court settled with the *Brown* decision.

——— VIRGINIA CASE ———

Moton High School is only a few miles away from the now tranquil farm land were the last battles of the Civil War played out. Nearly 86 years later, in 1951, African American students from Moton initiated a battle for access to equal education. Led by Barbara Rose Johns, a determined eleventh-grader, a group of students organized a strike for a better school. The students rallied not only their fellow classmates, an entire community, and an initially skeptical NAACP to their cause. Their courage and tenacity brought their demand for justice before the nation.

You may be wondering why they case started with the name "Davis?" Dorothy Davis was a ninth grader at the school and her name was selected at random to be first. You can read the case in Appendix III. As related previously the students are all noted as "infants" because from a legal sense they were under the age of consent.

In an oral interview many decades following the strike John A. Stokes answered the question; who is Dorothy Davis? And, why is the suit named for this 14-year old, Moton ninth-grader?

> *Dorothy Davis, Dorothy Davis' name became quite prominent in our lawsuit. Mr. Hill will support me on this. What happened is the fact that of the 117 names, and 69 parental – 117 student names and 69 parental names, they had to select a name, and it just so happened that they selected Dorothy Davis' name. It was at random more than anything else. He did not select the name of any of the students who were members of the caucus group, the nucleus of the group, he just selected a name, and that's the reason it went forward under Davis versus – initially, Davis versus Prince Edward County, that's how it went out initially. Dorothy Davis was a student whose name is listed as one of the plaintiffs in the case. Dorothy Davis is, you know, from Prince Edward County.*

Throughout the 13-year struggle, the state of Virginia reaffirmed its commitment to segregation and strenuously challenged the NAACP's arguments about the harmful effects of segregated education. According to the state's expert witnesses, blacks were intellectually inferior to whites; it was in everyone's best interest to separate the races. The federal district court upheld segregation in Prince Edward County, and the NAACP lawyers immediately appealed the decision to the U.S. Supreme Court.

In a move that proved to be futile, the county attempted to bolster their case in court by quickly building a new all-black high school. Soon after the students filed their suit, the county government leaders began working with renewed vigor, in an effort to show "equal" facilities and completed the new Robert Russa Moton High School in time for the start of the 1953 school year. The new school had room for 600 students.

The principal attorneys handling the students' case were Spottswood Robinson and Oliver Hill both from Richmond, and Robert Carter from the NAACP's New York office. The NAACP lawyers appealed the decision to the U.S. Supreme Court in time for the 1952 October term.

———— BROWN= 4+1 ————

With the certainty of hindsight it is inescapable that in this fight few brave souls changed a nation. When Thurgood Marshall launched the full-scale attack on segregation, the United States was very different from today. For some white Americans, changes in attitudes about race followed dramatic events in American society—the Depression, World War II, the integration of major league baseball by Jackie Robinson in 1947, and the desegregation of the armed forces in 1948. But deeply rooted feelings of white superiority continued to guide daily life in America and the South in particular. In five different communities across America, African Americans from various walks of life and generations bravely turned to the courts to demand better educational opportunities for blacks. Together with the NAACP these communities attempted nothing less than the destruction of segregation in the United States and the transformation of American society. Having just reviewed the *Davis* case from Prince Edward County, next we will review the other three *Brown* cases and the separate but conjoined District of Colombia case.

———— SOUTH CAROLINA CASE ————

In the heart of the cotton belt, where white landowners and business leaders had ruled Clarendon County, South Carolina, for generations, poor rural African Americans made a stand. They asked for a school bus for their children, and the county denied their request. Risking retaliation, they raised the stakes and demanded that their children have the right to attend the white schools.

Thurgood Marshall committed the resources of the NAACP's Legal Defense Fund to help this courageous community make a direct assault on legalized public school segregation. *Briggs v. Elliott* was filed in the United States District Court, Charleston Division on December 22, 1950. In no place in America was there a more just grievance against the starkly unequal, segregated schools than in Clarendon County. In the 1950s, Clarendon County, South Carolina, was the Deep South. Jim Crow laws and customs separated blacks and whites. Challenging this order, African Americans knew, could bring swift and severe consequences. The County had about 32,000 people and more than 70 percent were African Americans. Outside the towns of Summerton and Manning, the county was mostly rural and poor. Whites owned nearly 85 percent of the land, much of it leased to black tenant farmers. Two-thirds of the county's black households earned less than $1,000 a year, mostly growing cotton.

Because the school board refused to fund buses for black students, the county's 61 "colored" schools were scattered throughout the region. Most, like Liberty Hill Colored School, were small wooden structures that accommodated one or two classrooms. In the 1949-50 school year, for every dollar spent on a white child, only 24 cents was allotted for a black student. Not surprisingly, black adults in the county averaged just over four years of education. The white school in Summerton stood in stark contrast to the little more than shacks that blacks were schooled in. The county provided 30 buses to bring white children to a larger and better-equipped facility. White children from the Summerton area attended a red brick building with a separate lunchroom and science laboratories. Most rural black schools had neither electricity nor running water.

In the 1950s, things were changing in Clarendon County. A new generation of African Americans, many of whom had fought in World War II, saw a world of greater possibilities. The community's initial demand was small—a bus for children who had to walk up to nine miles to school. But the indifference of white officials stiffened the parents' resolve to seek more. At a meeting in the Liberty Hill African Methodist Episcopal Church in 1950, parents signed a petition demanding integrated schools. The omnipresent Thurgood Marshall filed the document with the United States District Court on December 22, 1950. Plaintiff Harold Briggs and 19 other parents in the county courageously signed the petition. Just as in Virginia, the federal district court ruled against the plaintiffs. And, likewise, their expected appeal reached the U.S. Supreme Court.

Harry Briggs's name appeared first on the complaint. A Navy veteran, he worked as an automobile mechanic. His wife, Eliza, was a maid in a nearby motel. Like many who signed the petition, they were fired from their jobs for their temerity to challenge white rule and eventually were compelled to leave Summerton to find work. To pursue the complaint the parents turned to Harold Boulware, the leading NAACP attorney in South Carolina to work on their behalf. Boulware knew that the national office of the NAACP was looking for school cases to challenge segregation, and he invited Thurgood Marshall to South Carolina. Boulware, also a graduate of the Howard University School of Law, was the first African American to pass the bar in South Carolina since Reconstruction.

On May 28, 1951, Thurgood Marshall, Robert Carter, and Spottswood Robinson brought the case before a three-judge panel at the federal courthouse in Charleston, South Carolina. The defendant was Roderick W. Elliott, a local sawmill owner and the school board chairman. The lawyers argued that segregated schools harmed black children psychologically and violated the Fourteenth Amendment's guarantee of equal protection under the law. Two of the three judges, citing the *Plessy v. Ferguson* decision of 1896, held that separate-but-equal facilities were constitutional and ruled against the parents.

J. Waties Waring, a member of the three-judge panel, wrote the dissenting opinion. He was one of the white southerners who stood up for justice at a time when many of his neighbors refused to see that change was upon them. As a supporter of equal rights, he endured both psychological and physical intimidation and eventually was forced to move from Charleston to New York City. For the parents and children of Clarendon County there only refuge now lay with the Supreme Court. The NAACP lawyers appealed the decision to the U.S. Supreme Court for the October 1952 term.

I am of the opinion that all of the legal guideposts, expert testimony, common sense and reason point unerringly to the conclusion that the system of segregation in education adopted and practiced in the state of South Carolina must go and go now. Segregation is per se inequality.

—Judge J. Waties Waring, in dissent, Briggs v. Elliott

———— THE TOPEKA, KANSAS CASE ————

Slavery was never legally established in Kansas, and racial separation there was less rigid than in the Deep South. School segregation was permitted by local option, but only in elementary schools. In 1950 the state capital, Topeka, operated four elementary schools for black children. African American parents and local activists from the NAACP challenged Topeka's policy of segregated schooling. They filed their case in U.S. District Court in 1951. Plaintiffs Oliver Brown and 13 other parents from Topeka had a three-judge federal court rule against them. The plaintiffs' appeal reached the U.S. Supreme Court.

In the early 1950s Topeka had a population of about 80,000. The city was an economic center for the surrounding farmlands. Hospitals and clinics were the largest employers, with the Atchison, Topeka, and Santa Fe Railroad headquarters located there. Many African American families had migrated to the city after the Civil War in search of land and opportunity outside the South. Just eight percent of the city's residents were black. Buses and railroads were integrated, but most restaurants, hotels, and other public places were usually segregated; by practice, if not by law.

Oliver Brown's name appears as the title for the most famous desegregation case in the nation's history, *Brown v. Board of Education*. He was a welder for the Santa Fe Railroad and a part-time assistant pastor at St. John African Methodist Episcopal Church. Attorney's John Scott and Charles Bledsoe of Topeka, joined by Robert Carter and Jack Greenberg of the NAACP's national office, presented the case to a panel of three federal judges. The NAACP attorneys again argued that segregated schools violated the Fourteenth Amendment and harmed black students. The judges conceded the damage caused by segregated education. Nevertheless, the Court ruled that white and black schools in Topeka were comparable and that segregation was consistent with the laws of Kansas and the Supreme Court's ruling in *Plessy v. Ferguson*. Federal district court judges Arthur J. Mellott, Delmas C. Hill, and Walter A. Huxman handed down their decision on the Brown case in June 1951. The NAACP attorneys appealed to the U.S. Supreme Court for the October 1952 term. Judge Huxman reinforced the reality that until the Supreme Court corrected a historic wrong there was no lower court in the land that could overrule *Plessy v. Fergusson*.

> *We weren't in sympathy with the decision we rendered. If it weren't for Plessy v. Ferguson, we surely would have found the law unconstitutional. But there was no way around it—the Supreme Court would have to overrule itself.*

— Judge Walter A. Huxman, reflecting on the decision in *Brown v. Board of Education*, 1970s

——— DELAWARE CASE ———

When the Civil War began, Delaware and other border states permitted slavery but refused to join the Confederacy. Issues of race in Delaware reflected this mixed heritage with both white and black people having misgivings about school desegregation.

Nonetheless, laws on segregation followed the state's Southern traditions. A small group of African American parents, upset when their children had to go past closer white schools to reach black ones, sought to challenge state-enforced segregation. Two cases from Delaware ultimately reached the U.S. Supreme Court as part of *Brown v. Board of Education*: *Bulah v. Gebhart* and *Belton v. Gebhart* were brought by two mothers of children in the Wilmington County schools, Sarah Bulah and Ethel Belton, who were joined by seven other parents from the community. Their primary grievance was that segregated schools far from their homes and neighborhoods created an undue burden on them and their children. A state court ruled in favor of the plaintiffs. An appeal to the state supreme court and the U.S. Supreme Court followed.

The city of Wilmington had a black population of about 17,000 out of 110,000 in 1950. Racial prejudice there was less conspicuous than in the rural counties and yet most public facilities were not segregated. Nonetheless, discrimination confined most African Americans to service and labor jobs. In the fall of 1950, members of the Wilmington branch of the NAACP coordinated an effort of black parents to register their children in white schools in Wilmington and surrounding communities. All were refused. African American attorney Louis Redding, working with the NAACP activists and parents, selected the cases that seemed likeliest to win. According to one NAACP member, Redding accepted no payment for his services. He directed the chapters instead to raise money for court costs.

Shirley Bulah endured a long daily walk to the Hockessin Colored Elementary School. Her mother, Sarah, asked the school board if her daughter could share a bus with white children or have a separate bus. When her requests were refused, she went to see attorney Louis Redding. All of this seemed silly to Mrs. Bulah since a perfectly good bus with enough space for her daughter, serving the nearby whites-only school, passed by her house every day. Mrs. Bulah had attempted to obtain transportation for Shirley on that bus, but she was told they would never transport an African American student.

Fearful of change, the pastor of the local African Methodist Episcopal Church opposed Sarah Bulah's lawsuit, and many black people stopped speaking to her. But her push for school integration had the firm support of the Wilmington branch of the NAACP. This was not unusual, for a black civil rights pioneer to not only have to take on the white power structure, but also endure the wrath from at least some of their own race. There was some of this also in Prince Edward County and contributed to the long silence by Barbara Rose Johns. One direct result of the lawsuit initiated by Sarah Bulah was to limit her popularity with the black folks in her town. It's interesting to note not a single one of her black neighbors joined her in the suit. Her minister, Rev. Martin Luther Kilson of the Chippey African Union Methodist Church, said:

> *I was for segregation. These folks around here would rather have a colored teacher. They didn't want to be mixed up with no white folks. All we wanted was a bus for the colored. Redding and some members of the NAACP encouched this issue of segregation. I hated to see them tamper with that little colored school next to our church. It was so handy.*

The other Delaware case involved Ethel Louise Belton, who was forced to travel two hours every day to Howard High School in Wilmington from her community of Claymont. The local white high school offered courses and extracurricular activities unavailable at Howard. Ethel's mother said, "We are all Americans, and when the state sets up separate schools for certain people of a separate color, then I and others are made to feel ashamed and embarrassed." Nine other black plaintiffs from Claymont felt the same way and joined her in a lawsuit.

In these two Delaware cases, the NAACP attorneys presented the same arguments the NAACP used in the other integration cases. Segregated schools harmed black children and violated the Fourteenth Amendment's guarantee of equal protection of the laws. Chancellor Collins Seitz ruled that African American pupils were receiving an inferior education and must be admitted to white schools. But he declined to strike down the principle of separate but equal. That responsibility, he said, belonged to the U.S. Supreme Court. The Delaware Supreme Court upheld his decision. Both sides were dissatisfied with the state court's decision and appealed the case. In December 1952, the Supreme Court agreed to hear the case and combined it with the three others discussed previously.

———— WASHINGTON D.C. CASE ————

Segregation in Washington, D.C., was a glaring example of the contradictions in American society. In the 1950s the city's government, including schools, was under the control of Congress. Its members proudly portrayed the city as the capital of the free world, where democracy and personal freedoms were defended against the threat of communist totalitarianism. Yet, most of the city's public facilities, schools, and housing were segregated by law or practice. Sparked by the protests of a local barber, a grassroots organization formed to expose this hypocrisy and demand equal treatment for all children.

Well-paid federal jobs drew thousands of African Americans to Washington and helped support a large community of well-educated professional and skilled workers. The reader may recall that Barbara Rose Johns' mother worked in D.C. during the week and only came home to Prince Edward County on the weekends. Between 1930 and 1950 the black population doubled to some 280,000, about 35 percent of the total population. Yet, along with a prosperous black community, Washington also had some of the nation's worst living conditions. The new migration strained limited city services, schools, and housing and this was nowhere more true that the segregated African American neighborhoods.

From the Civil War on, Washington had a segregated school system. As the population grew in black neighborhoods, the gap between white and black schools widened and overcrowding became a serious problem. Many African American schools went to multiple shifts, eroding the quality of education, while some neighboring white schools remained half empty.

Gardner L. Bishop was the father of a student at Browne Junior High School. In 1947 school authorities responded to crowded conditions at Browne by selecting two run-down former white primary schools for satellite classes. The school's PTA objected and demanded that white schools be opened for all students. Distrustful of the PTA's leadership, Bishop called on parents to boycott the school. With others, he formed the Consolidated Parent Group to present their grievances to the school board.

Howard University law professors James Nabrit and George E. C. Hayes were the attorneys in the lawsuit against segregated schools in Washington, D.C. Charles Houston had, before his death in April 1950, urged Bishop and the Consolidated Parents Group to seek out Nabrit to take over the legal fight. The first name on the lawsuit was Spottswood Bolling, Jr., a 12-year-old student. His mother, Sara, worked as a bookbinder in the General Services Administration. On September 11, 1950, Gardner Bishop escorted Bolling and 10 other African American students to Sousa Junior High. School, the school officials refused to admit the black students. On behalf of Spottswood Bolling and other students, James Nabrit filed suit against the president of the Board of Education, C. Melvin Sharpe. Nabrit argued directly that segregated schools were unconstitutional. The case was argued on December 10–11, 1952, before Judge Walter Bastian of the U.S. District Court. He dismissed *Bolling v. Sharpe* on the basis that separate but equal remained the law of the land. Nabrit and other lawyers were preparing to appeal the case when the Supreme Court asked to hear *Bolling v. Sharpe* as part of their *Brown* review.

——— THE DOLL TEST ———

One of the controversial and effective strategies developed by the NAACP to fight the segregation cases in court was the use of the doll test. On May 24, 1951, Kenneth Clark, a psychology professor at City College of New York, came to Clarendon County, South Carolina where the *Briggs v.* Elliott case originated from. Using dolls of different colors, he tested the Negro children of Scott's Branch school to measure how they felt about themselves. He asked the children to show him the "nice" doll, the "bad" doll, and the doll that "looks like you." Ten of the

16 children said the brown doll looked bad. Harry S. Ashmore in his book *Civil Rights and Wrongs: A memoir of race and politics 1944–1994* said of the doll test:

> *The NAACP launched a study of community attitudes under the direction of brilliant black psychologist Kenneth Clarke, whose findings on the effects of racial discrimination and children receive judicial notice in Brown I. Clark's team of social scientists filled an entire issue of the Journal of Social Issues, a publication of the American Psychological Association, and concluded that there was very little affirmative support for desegregation among white patrons of the affected schools.*

The results of these tests strongly suggested that forced segregation damaged the self-image of African American children. While this sociological study did not sway a South Carolina court, it became important when the case moved to the Supreme Court. The doll experiment was cited in the ruling and was often criticized by those opposing integration as poor case law and irrelevant to any legally interpretation of the Constitution. In fact, the Warren court would come to regret its inclusion in the brief because it was so often cited as a flaw in the decision.

> *The Negro child is made to go to an inferior school; he is branded in his own mind as inferior...You can teach such a child the Constitution, anthropology and citizenship, but he knows it isn't true.*

—Thurgood Marshall, concluding remarks, Briggs v. Elliott.

——— GROUNDWORK ———

The preceding section discussed each of the five cases that had a bearing on the *Brown* decision. Central to each case was the hard fact that the law of the land, as established by the Supreme Court in 1896 with *Plessy v, Ferguson,* was solidly segregationist. The NAACP invested wisely in the preparatory steps to achieving their *Brown* victory. This bold stroke by the Warren court was the result of over 30 years of hard, thoughtful work by NAACP activists, attorneys and plaintiffs.

Founded in 1909, the NAACP is the nation's oldest civil rights organization. Throughout the 1920s and 1930s, the association led the black civil rights struggle in fighting injustices, such as the denial of voting rights, racial violence, discrimination in employment, and segregated public facilities. Dedicated to the goal of an integrated society, the national leadership has always been interracial, although the membership has remained predominantly African American. The NAACP focused on five major areas from 1920 to 1950:

- anti-lynching legislation;
- voter participation;
- employment;
- due process under the law; and
- education.

At yearly conventions in different cities around the country, it drew attention to regional needs and interests and encouraged nationwide participation.

During the '30s and '40s, the NAACP chipped away at Jim Crow, specifically the fallacious premise of separate but equal. They forced the establishment of a separate graduate program for African Americans and the admission of blacks to the general university population when possible. Then they tackled inequality in pay, forcing the Southern states in particular to spend millions of dollars to provide the same pay for all teachers regardless of race and worked to raise the quality of black facilities.

In October 1938, attorney Thurgood Marshall filed a petition, on behalf of Norfolk, Virginia, teacher Aline Black, seeking salary equalization. Subsequently to the suit the school board fired her. Although the Virginia Teachers Association—a black teachers organization—agreed to pay her salary for a year while the case was taken to court, she moved to New York and the suit was filed instead on behalf of Melvin Alston, president of the Norfolk Teachers Association. In *Alston v. School Board of the City of Norfolk*, the Court of Appeals found that the salary inequality was based on race and violated the "equal protection" clause of the Fourteenth Amendment. The U.S. Supreme Court denied the school board's appeal, a decision that had national implications.

"WE WANT OUR TEACHERS EQUALLY PREPARED AND EQUALLY PAID" reads one of the signs at this June 25, 1939, parade in Norfolk protesting inequality between black and white schools. Overall, in 1937–38, the average salary of African American teachers was $526, slightly more than half the $1,019 average of white teachers. Teachers were prominent role models and highly visible members of black communities, which supported their battles for equal pay. Like many such events, this Sunday afternoon protest began at a black church although it was organized by the NAACP.

—Courtesy Library of Congress

Even though the NAACP was wining some victories, they recognized suing each county and city in the South and elsewhere would be costly and time consuming. By 1950 the NAACP was ready to move on and concluded that henceforth they would only take cases that challenged segregation directly. Towards the end of June 1950, the NAACP held a conference with 43 lawyers and 14 branch and state conference presidents to reassess the separate but equal approach and explore next steps. It was during this conference that it was determined all future education cases would, "be aimed at obtaining education on a non-segregated basis and that no relief other than that will be acceptable. Further, that all lawyers operating under such rule will urge their client(s) and branches of the association involved to insist on this final relief." Marshall understood that in order for this new strategy of attacking segregation directly to be successful, the entire NAACP community would need to be united. He sought and obtained a confirming resolution from the Board of Directors and the organization adopted it as their official policy. "The goal now, he declared, was to break up segregation, and nothing less would do." The board approved Marshall's stand. It was in many regards the most militant position the NAACP had ever taken in its 42 year history. This change in goals and strategy was a bit of a revelation to the Moton strikers. They were united around equal facilities, but it was anything but unanimous to switch their demands toward an integrated Prince Edward County.

When folks today think about the *Brown* case, this author included, they understand at its heart was the unfairness of forcing young black students into second-class schools. Yet what is sometimes lost are the black adults and children who were willing to sacrifice their comfort, safety and economic wellbeing to right this wrong. Clearly both students and parents demonstrated colossal courage and faith in sticking their necks out to be among the guinea pigs that the NAACP required in order to move their cases forward. As we have seen in this chapter, these civil rights pioneers were not always, at the time, thanked by the entire black community. Another aspect of the movement that is not usually discussed is how blacks used their brains to craft a strategy to defeat segregation and Jim Crow abuses. Even more important, these founders of the civil rights movement were willing to do the hard work over decades and exhibited enormous patience and foresight. When the NAACP decided that a legal strategy was essential to achieving any measure of equality, they found few competent black attorneys able to represent them. In response, Sam Houston was recruited to start a school of law at Howard University. Howard produced many of the attorneys who would go on to challenge segregation and directly argue the *Brown* case. Men such as Marshall,

Robinson, and Hill were all products of the Howard law school. The reality facing these civil rights pioneers is that it took all they had, including: sacrifice, courage, risking young children, parents who had to constantly worry about the safety of their children, and possible retribution from the white community. Further, an incredible amount of hard work by the legal teams was necessary, often using vastly inferior resources to outsmart some of the legends of the legal profession who chose to defend segregation.

Of course, as with any important cause, leaders were needed. Not just the ones like Martin Luther King but the leaders who were willing to stand on the front lines challenging Jim Crow and the status quo in the backwaters of America where there were no cameras and therefore danger was even more of a possibility. One of the concerns the NAACP and its lawyers had was the sustenance that even a single loss in court would provide to the segregationists.

———— THE LEGAL TEAMS ————

With the *Brown* v. Supreme Court trail, Marshall and his team had their work cut out for them because leading the opposition, charged with defending segregation, was perhaps the best Supreme Court attorney in America. The aristocratic John W. Davis, approaching 80 at the time of the *Brown* case, confidently told the court that the historical record showed Congress never intended to end school segregation when it passed the Fourteenth Amendment in 1868. The proof, he said, was that the Congress never acted to end segregated schools even after it passed the law. In fact, Congress had created a segregated public school system in the capital, Washington, D.C., in 1871, three years after the Fourteenth was passed. That led Davis to pose a question for the nine white men on the Supreme Court. Speaking with patronizing concern for black children, Davis asked, "Why should black children be taken from all-black schools where they were happy and inspired, and forced to attend integrated schools where they would be ridiculed and hated?" Davis contended that segregated schools were equal in the sense that they offered an appropriate education for blacks. Integrated schools, he predicted, meant the destruction of the existing nurturing, sanctuary that whites had created for the descendants of uneducated slaves. Davis used one of Aesop's fables to make his point, "The dog with a fine piece of meat in his mouth crossed a bridge and saw the reflection of the meat in the stream and plunged for it and lost both shadow and substance."

Opposing Davis was Thurgood Marshall. He was the undisputed field boss of the dozens of lawyers the NAACP had assembled to try the *Brown* case before the highest court in the land. Thurgood Marshall was leaving nothing to chance. He arrived in Washington 10 days before the *Brown* arguments were to start. Marshall was well suited both by his intellect and temperament to lead his team in their attempt to gain long overdue justice. Marshal had been involved in 15 previous Supreme Court cases, either as chief counsel making the oral argument or with a decisive voice in fashioning the brief. He was successful 13 times in arguing before the court. In some of Marshall's appearances before the court, he could be captivating and; in others he tended to be a bit on the dull side. As oral arguments started December 9, 1952, Richard Kluger writes, "On this day, he was at his best. He took the offensive from the start and he held it throughout the argument." Marshall not only had a thorough understanding of the law, but he had the right temperament to strike the balance between being confident and effective without appearing arrogant. He had a way, at just the right moment, of introducing an argument in some folksy down-home way that they made his point in a humble but profound manner. Oral arguments in this monumental case consumed the entire three days from Tuesday, December 9 to Thursday, December 11, 1952.

At 6 feet 3 inches, Marshall was a big, chain-smoking man who smiled throughout his presentation of the case before the Court. Speaking with the slight southern drawl of a Baltimore native, Marshall told the court that when Congress approved the Fourteenth Amendment to the Constitution—guaranteeing all citizens equal rights—it outlawed segregation. That meant, he argued, that Congress opened the doors to the nation's public schools for America's children, black and white.

Marshall's simple argument brought a simple rebuttal from the lawyer on the other side. He was a man with a childhood full of segregationist memories from his South Carolina birthplace. John W. Davis was the dean of American lawyers in the middle of the twentieth century. At the time, he had argued more cases before the Supreme Court than any other living lawyer. Davis had been solicitor general, the federal government's top lawyer before the high court, and for a time had reigned as president of the American Bar Association. Davis had also been the Democrats' presidential candidate in 1924. His stature and friendship with many of the justices on the high court is what prompted James Byrnes, the segregationist governor of South Carolina and former U.S. Supreme Court Justice, to ask Davis personally to argue the case before the high court.

The arguments in *Brown* took place in two stages. The first set of arguments was made in December 1952; a second round took place before the court in December 1953. More significant was that the presentation in '52 was given to the Vinson court and with his passing in September 1953, Warren assumed the Chief's chair and presided over the December 1953 arguments. During the 1953 presentation an interesting juxtaposition occurred as Marshall's wife sat next to Davis's daughter.

Paul Wilson, the assistant attorney general of Kansas who represented his state at the Supreme Court, said later that despite the many lawyers in the court, all eyes and ears turned to two men, Davis and Marshall. "The personalities of each seemed peculiarly appropriate to the cause that he represented...a duel between the champion of aristocracy and rationalism on the one hand and populism and humanitarianism on the other." The conflicting views that Marshall and Davis presented in *Brown* about American history, law, and race relations opened the door to arguments over affirmative action, busing, redistricting, and social justice that are still on the nation's agenda nearly 60 years later. The contrast between Marshall and Davis went beyond the colors of their skin. Marshall, then in his mid-40s, was accustomed to speaking to segregationist juries as well as openly bigoted judges. There was nothing coy about Davis's views on race. He had written that there were "anatomical differences" and "differences in intellectual processes, in tastes and aptitudes." Davis's suggestion to the Supreme Court that black people were better off in their own schools was an endorsement of the 1896

Supreme Court ruling in *Plessy v. Ferguson*, which declared the legality of separate but equal facilities for blacks and whites. The *Plessy* decision has always been a thin veil for racism. Separate schools never were equal, and the black school was always inferior due to lack of funding and most injurious to black youth the second class connotation that was the structural construct of segregation. But in Davis's segregationist mind there was virtue in separation, namely the opportunity for special attention to be given to the needs of black children. Blatant disparities in school funding, school facilities, and the quality of education did not seem to trouble him.

Marshall did not scream racism in response to Davis's argument. He did not want to risk angering the all-white justices. Arguing before a court produced by segregationist politics, Marshall decided the best strategy was to guard his tongue. Instead, he spoke about the well-being of black students. He said segregated schools in addition to being inferior facilities, acted to destroy the self-respect of black children and devastate their emotional well-being. Building on the argument, Marshall said segregation undermined the self-confidence of black children and their standing as equal citizens of the republic. Segregated schools were the basis for "humiliation" for Americans with black skin, the NAACP lawyer said, and it was not a matter of "theoretical injury" but "actual injury." Later, he came close to the edge of anger when he said anyone defending separate schools was showing, "an inherent determination that the people who were formerly in slavery... shall be kept as near that stage as possible... this court should make it clear that this is not what our Constitution stands for." This was the heart of the argument in *Brown*. And the Supreme Court, under Chief Justice Earl Warren, ruled 9-0 in favor of Marshall's argument.

On May 17, 1954, the court ruled that, "to separate black children from others of similar age and qualifications solely because of their race generates a feeling of inferiority as to their status in the community that may affect their hearts and minds in a way unlikely ever to be undone." Chief Justice Earl Warren, who read the decision from the bench, concluded with those monumentis words, "in the field of public education the doctrine of 'separate but equal,' has no place."

——— OLIVER WHITE HILL, SR. ———
(May 1, 1907–August 5, 2007)

Oliver Hill devoted his entire professional career to fighting for civil rights. He became the Moton students' champion and helped convince the NAACP to take the case. It then only seems fitting to spend some time looking at the man and his accomplishments.

Hill was all in favor of going after segregation directly. Before the NAACP changed tactics, Hill talks about his growing disillusionment with the equalization suits that the NAACP was introducing in the late '40s and '50s. The Virginia NAACP had successfully prosecuted four equalization suits between 1947 and 1950. Hill remembers that:

> *A lot of us didn't know much in the beginning. In the early days I felt that as soon as we got equal buildings we would be all right. But about that time (1948) a survey was made by a prominent group in Washington, D.C., where they actually had two school systems and where if there could be equality with segregation it would show up. The survey showed that inequalities were gross.... Later we tried a number of equalization suits around different places. It was quite obvious that we were going around in circles and not accomplishing anything.... We were learning that we might get a new building but we still ended up with inferior facilities.*

A prime example of the inequality Hill was citing could be seen in the new Robert Russa Moton High School—that was hastily built just for the county's black students—it was lacking adequate text books, had no science labs or gym equipment. The biology class was forced to function with only one microscope.

By May, 1950, the NAACP was aggressively pursuing the concept of equality. During this period Hill's partner, Spotswood Robinson shook up the school board of Cumberland County,

Virginia, which is next door to Prince Edward County, with proposals that seemed to cross the line into segregation. "In a stormy meeting in the Cumberland County schoolhouse, an irate board member threatened to 'shoot the first' Negro child who tried to enroll in a white school."

Hill was the most active NAACP attorney in Virginia and as the lead for the Prince Edward County case he is featured on the Civil Rights Memorial on Capital Square in Richmond with his equally courageous partner Spotswood Robison. In 2002, as part of the Virginia Civil Rights Movement Video Initiative, Oliver W. Hill Sr. describes his involvement in fighting massive resistance and provides insight for us today into the tenor of the times. He also discusses studying law with Thurgood Marshall. Note Hill was 95 when he gave this interview and his recall of events 70 years latter is remarkable if slightly disconnected.

INTERVIEWER: Whenever you are ready, go ahead and start.

HILL: I would like to start this program with a discussion of the significance of the movement that started in 1930. What had happened was—Dr. Mordecai Johnson, President of Howard University, had looked into the situation and found that sometimes cases went up to the Supreme Court that did not have a sufficient record for the court to act on properly, so he determined to make Howard University Law School, which from its inception in early—in the mid 19th Century, essentially, up to that time had been an evening school, he intended to make it a first-class law school, and he engaged the services of one of the most brilliant legal scholars and fine gentleman as you could locate, Charles Hamilton Houston.

Charlie was a son of a lawyer, and he was present in Washington. He was also one of the adjunct professors. Charlie decided what ought to be done is to have a full-time day school, cut out the adjuncts. Of course, that created a quite stir around Washington because most of

*the adjuncts and the other teachers, too, were either
lawyers or people working in—judges and things working
in the government service.*

*It also happened at that time a young man named—
Charles Garland's father died, left him with a large
estate. He was one of these bright young men, said, oh,
hell, I didn't earn it, I'm going to give it to the NAACP to
fight segregation. And he turned the money over to the
NAACP—he directed that money be turned over—that the
estate be directed to—funds of the estate be directed to
the NAACP.*

*And the determination was made, and at Charlie's
suggestion as to how the funds are to be best used, and it
was determined that the best use of it would be to fight
segregation. The suggestion was made that we file suits
all over the south and simultaneously challenge
segregation per se.*

*Charlie said, no, it would look like a stunt, and
furthermore, we didn't have the manpower, and
secondly—I mean thirdly, we'd be banging our heads up
against a stone wall in the early thirties to try to
challenge segregation head-on, and the results,
subsequent results proved him to be dead right.*

*All right. Charlie developed a very fine young faculty,
including his cousin, William Hastie, who later became
the first federal—Negro federal circuit court judge, one of
the first—one of the early federal judges, district court
judges. And he also had doctor—well, at that time he
wasn't a doctor—man named Andy Ranson, he graduated
Ohio State Law School. Hastie and Charlie had both
finished Harvard Law School. Andy Ranson had finished
as a member of the Order of Court, that's like Phi Beta
Kappa. Later, he became—got his doctorate in juris
prudence at Harvard.*

And I don't have anything to refresh my memory right now, and I can't [inaudible] a Jewish lawyer name Cohen. Then there was a very fine old gentlemen from out, one of them far west, like Iowa or Minnesota somewhere, they made the bulk of the—the backbone of the new faculty. But they also had, of course— including—they had a man named George—E. C. Hayes, was one of the best trial lawyers in the City of Washington, and Charlie's father was not quite the caliber of the others, but he was a fine man, constituted part of the faculty.

All right. Now, we started out, the first class had Thurgood Marshal. I went to law school to challenge segregation. I didn't know all this was happening. I mean, I had to learn that when I first became conscious of it, of course I knew it all the time, but became conscious of the fact that Congress back in the days—Civil War days had given Negroes all the Civil Rights of any white person, and it was the United States Supreme Court in the case known as Plessy v. Ferguson that had taken all those rights away from us and put us in a class, sometimes second, third and even as low as fourth class citizens, because any white person that got off the other side and came across the street had a legal status in the United States, he didn't have to have a penny in his pocket, but he had the status superior to that than the richest Negro in town.

All right. One of the first things Charlie instructed us on was that we was going to make the law school or—there was another young man—he wasn't a young man, he was a little older than the rest us of named Sweat. His brother had been—was a doctor in Detroit, and he had moved into what was known as a changing neighborhood, and white folks gave him seven days to get out, or else they were going to put him out, and so it was on the Friday that they said they were going to put him out the mob appeared, but he had gotten some of his friends to stay in the house with him, so somebody in the mob shot at the house, and somebody in the house shot back at the mob, but the mob hit the house, but the bullet from inside the house hit one of the mob and killed him, and they charged Dr. Sweat with the murder.

I will give you the rest of the story later on, but I just wanted to let you know how things went in those days. Sweat was in there, too. He was wanted to break up segregation. He was there with his brother.

Charlie, one of the first things Charlie informed us about was we were going to make Howard University Law School an approved law school, and he worked us six days a week, not only getting the law, but doing extra things like going down to the F.B.I. and learning how they did things, going out to St. Elizabeth's Insane Asylum and getting—knowing—getting something about that. Going down to the United States District Attorney's Office and seeing how they functioned, learn how things happened, because one of the things I was—it was easy to understand now, later, but Negroes had had no contact, no association with so much of this stuff that you needed to have, to know something besides just the plane law.

All right. In the first case—I mean, we worked—school started at 8:00 o'clock in the morning, we usually get out at 11:30. Thurgood and I would go down to [inaudible]. They had a restaurant downtown there, and you go in and say "Peace, 'tis truly wonderful" and you get a big meal for a quarter, and extra big meal for 35 cents. And Thurgood had a big appetite. He got the 35 cent one most of the time. I was content with the 25.

But anyway, we would have our lunch, and then we would go back to school and we would study until around 5:00 o'clock. At that time, Thurgood would go to catch the train to go up to Baltimore. He was commuting from Baltimore. I would go leave to go to the job—my job I had. I was waiting tables in the evening at one of the big apartment houses downtown.

All right, as a consequence, we worked steadily like that, and too, of course, Charlie seeing us there every day, we became his proteges. And at the first break—attempted break through was during my—our second year, a young man in Durham, North Carolina wanted to go to the School of Pharmacy, and Dr. Shepherd was President of the North Carolina Central School down there in Durham, North Carolina. And he wouldn't give—he wouldn't give us the man's transcript, and by the time it went through court and got it, all of them—made somebody persuade the man to change his mind, so nothing resulted from that effort to challenge School of Pharmacy in North Carolina.

But in the mean time, we studied and graduated in 1933. And Thurgood and some of the other students—Thurgood took the Maryland Bar, and some of the other students took the District of Columbia Bar. I was planning the whole time, that whole time to go back to Roanoke, Virginia. That's where I spent my elementary school days. And so—I hadn't applied soon enough to get the D.C.—I mean Virginia Bar until December, so when I found out that Thurgood had passed and the boys that had taken the D.C. Bar had passed, I was under a little pressure.

But anyway, in the mean time—I mean, let me back up a little bit. I was—I had finished high school in midterm, and so I didn't see any need of waiting until September to go to college. I lived three or four blocks from the college. I enrolled in the spring quarter. So—and after I learned that segregation—I mean that Plessy had—court taken our rights in Plessy, and at that time, you couldn't get a law through Congress to make it a crime to lynch a Negro. That was a big project of NAACP, to get up there, couldn't get a law passed to lynch a Negro, much less enhance any of his Civil Rights, so I determined the only thing we could do was somebody take another case to the Supreme Court and convince them that the 1896 decision was wrong. And being somebody, I went to the dean's office to see what I could do, had to do to become a lawyer, and I found that I could take one more case—one more course in foreign language, and I could go to law school at the end of my senior year, and get my degree, first degree at the end of my first year in law school, that is, upon successful transmission of it.

But anyway, at that time, I decided to take a course in Latin. They said Latin might be helpful for me in law school. And in the first year—in the Latin class, a freshman named S. W. Tucker was in the class, and I met him. So what that brings me on, when he finished college, I was finishing law school. And the next summer I was working downtown at O'Donnell's Seafood Restaurant, and I ran into him one day. I said, what are you doing? He said, studying for the bar. I said, so am I. And I had Woodbridge's notes, and I would go over to Alexandria, let him use my copy of Woodbridge's notes, and Dudley Woodbridge was a professor down at William [and] Mary that ran a bar exam course, and he was studying my notes, and I was studying—they had a 1924 Code of Virginia, I used that, and every Thursday I would go over there, and as a consequence, in December, we both took the bar and we both passed.

Hill lived a long life and later in his life achieved the notoriety and awards he deserved. "We thank Mr. Hill for the work that he has done for our freedom and for being the liberator of the Commonwealth of Virginia," said the President. On August 11, 1999, the President of the United States, William Jefferson Clinton, powerfully demonstrated the nation's gratitude to Oliver Hill when he presented him with the Presidential Medal of Freedom, the highest honor the nation can bestow on a citizen.

Speaking eloquently of Oliver Hill's contribution to the nation, President Clinton stated:

> *Throughout his long and rich life, [Oliver White Hill] has challenged the laws of our land and the conscience of our country. He has stood up for everything that is necessary to make America truly one, indivisible and equal.*

Governor Tim Kaine of Virginia speaking at Hill's funeral in August 2007 recalled the feisty Hill and his accomplishments. Kaine noted, that while Hill spent the first two thirds of his life fighting the establishment he became one of the deans of the civil rights era and was as surprised as he was delighted that so many former government agencies and elected office holders, who were his opponents, chose to honor him during the last third of his long 100 year life.

The funeral was held at the Greater Richmond Convention Center. In remarks he prepared, Virginia, Governor Timothy M. Kaine wrote of the poetic justice that a Virginia governor was delivering Hill's eulogy, since Hill often confronted the state's political establishment during his legal battles to bring equal treatment to all Virginia's citizens. Kaine said that if someone had told Hill decades ago that after his death he would "lie in state at the Governor's Mansion and be eulogized by the Virginia Governor," Hill would have laughed at the sheer outlandishness of that statement. The Richmond Times Dispatch reported on the governors eulogy:

> *"I can almost hear him now," Kaine wrote. "In fact, he probably would then have said something like 'I've known many Governors who would have been very pleased to attend my funeral—and the sooner the better."*
> *"For two-thirds of his life, Mr. Hill was basically fighting up against a civil society that wanted him to lose rather than to win," Kaine said. "But in the last third of his life, people realized that he was right. So the bar associations*

that kept him out as members gave him awards. And universities that had kept him out started naming scholarships after him."

And when Hill passed away, Kaine said, having him lie in state at the Executive Mansion was an easy decision. The last person to lie in state at the residence was Arthur Ashe; before him, it was Stonewall Jackson.

"I can't think of anybody who's had more of an impact on Virginia life the last 100 years than Mr. Hill," Kaine said. "He really believed what the Declaration of Independence said: that all people are created equal."

Inscribed on the inner liner of the casket's lid were Hill's name, his year of birth, his year of death and the following: "May the work I've done speak for me."

We will end this section about the *Brown v. Board* legal team by fast forwarding to 1995. Paul E. Wilson wrote about his experiences in defending segregation back in 1952. Wilson was the Kansas junior assistant attorney general who provided the oral arguments alongside John W. Davis to the Supreme Court in 1952. Wilson shares his very personal reason for writing about his *Brown* experiences in the dedication to his book, *A Time to Lose Representing Kansas in Brown v. Board of Education.*

For Harriet and our children, who believe I was on the wrong side. May this book mitigate their decades of embarrassment?

The book's title is from a passage in the third chapter of Ecclesiastes, and provides Wilson the podium to share his late in life redemptive views about his role in arguing for segregation. With his very personal prism on this conflicted time in America

Wilson's reflection on the words of Ecclesiastes seems to be his peace offering for being on the wrong side of history.

> *To everything there is a season, and a time to every purpose under heaven.*
> *A time to get, and a time to lose; a time to keep, and a time to cast away.*

——— THE COURT ———

If you want to see the unvarnished state of white America's 19th century's views on race just look at the Supreme Court's decisions for the 20 years following the end of the Civil War (1865). This was a court largely empanelled by Lincoln and Grant yet their racist decisions are a sobering reminder that emancipation was one thing, but an integrated society was entirely out of the question for most of the fathers and sons of the Civil War.

President Lincoln appointed five Justices to the United State Supreme Court during a critical period in American history. When he assumed the presidency in 1861 the Court had only one vacancy. However, Justice McLean soon died and Justice Campbell resigned to join the Southern Confederacy. One year later, Lincoln nominated Noah Swayne, Samuel Miller, and David Davis. In 1863 Stephen Field became the tenth Justice after Congress expanded the Court. When Chief Justice Roger Taney died in 1864, Lincoln appointed his former Treasury Secretary to succeed him—Salmon Portland Chase. During this period Justices received an annual salary of $6,000 and were expected to travel the circuit to hear federal cases as well. They met for only one term a year in the U.S. Capitol.

Nathan Clifford (August 18, 1803–July 25, 1881) who was born in New Hampshire and practiced law in Maine is one example of a judge with little sympathy for racial equality. In 1858, President James Buchanan appointed him an Associate Justice of the Supreme Court of the United States. He was confirmed by a narrow margin of 26 votes to 23 in the Senate. Senators were hesitant about placing a pro-slavery Democrat on the Supreme Court. His specialties were commercial and maritime law, Mexican land grants, and procedure and practice. Though he rarely declared any legal philosophy about the Constitution, Justice Clifford believed in a sharp dividing line between federal and state authority. He served on the Court for 23 years, beginning on January 28, 1858, and continuing until his death, in 1881, from the complications of a stroke. Clifford was viewed as a friend of the South and willing to enslave black folks all over again in the wrapper of Jim Crow.

In the years immediately following the Civil War, America appeared to possess the will and the means to end racial segregation and give the same rights enjoyed by whites to its 4 million recently freed black slaves. These noble goals, of course, were not achieved for another century. During the intervening decades, the South saw the rise of Jim Crow and Judge Lynch. In *Inherently Unequal*, constitutional scholar Lawrence Goldstone convincingly lays the blame for this tragedy at the door of the institution that could have made the difference but did not—the United States Supreme Court.

Until the early 1870s, advocates of Radical Reconstruction dominated politics in Washington. At the same time, voters approved the 13th, 14th and 15th amendments to the Constitution, granting the federal judiciary enormous power to effect change. But as the South started to roll back Reconstruction, the court became complicit by legitimizing what author Lawrence Goldstone characterized as, "the same two-tiered system of justice that had existed in the slave era." President Ulysses S. Grant in particular chose poorly, picking justices who came from corporate practices and had little interest in racial equality. In 1875, one of Grant's selections, Chief Justice Morrison R. Waite, foreshadowed what was ahead. He set aside the conviction in a lower federal court of a white man involved in an 1873 massacre in Louisiana of 100 black militiamen who, after laying down their weapons, were slaughtered by 250 armed whites. Many of those who participated were members of the Ku Klux Klan.

Such decisions did not occur in a vacuum. For most Americans, Goldstone asserts, the Civil War was fought not to liberate the slaves but to save the union. Just as important, the Republican Party was drifting away from its Lincolnesque roots and into the arms of big business, which was agnostic about the plight of defenseless blacks in the South.

In the immediate aftermath of the Civil War, Congress drafted and pushed to ratify two constitutional amendments—the 14th and 15th—intended to guarantee African Americans full equality before the law. Almost immediately, the Supreme Court began to eviscerate Congress's work. First the justices ruled that the federal government had very limited power to protect its citizens' rights; most of the time it was up to the states to ensure equal treatment. Then, bit by bit, the court gave states enormous leeway in defining equality. If Tennessee was willing to allow Klansmen to terrorize African Americans, Virginia to allow judges to block blacks from juries, and Kentucky to institute a poll tax that stripped African Americans of the vote, this court saw that as states' rights as guaranteed under the Constitution. The process peaked in the infamous 1896 case *Plessy v. Ferguson*, when the justices upheld Louisiana's claim that it was free to segregate its railroad cars because African Americans were being restricted to seats that were separate from but equal to whites. Less than 30 years after their passage, the 14th and 15th Amendments had been all but swept aside. And in their place stood the alarming figure of Jim Crow.

Constitutional scholar Goldstone, offers a clear, cogent reading of the court's machinations, no small accomplishment, since the justices generally rested their opinions on convoluted legal reasoning rather than on broad principles. And he's completely convincing when he argues that behind those carefully parsed opinions lay a deep-seated racism strengthened by the justices' embrace of social Darwinism. Before taking the bench, for instance, Chief Justice Melville Fuller helped to segregate Chicago's schools, while Associate Justice Henry Billings Brown, who wrote the *Plessy* decision, privately supported black disenfranchisement as a bulwark against the pernicious power of democracy. But Goldstone isn't satisfied with exposing the court's corruption. He also insists on slashing away at those who championed racial justice. In his telling, the Radical Republicans who wrote the amendments were zealots determined to give their particular moral code the force of law, public opinion be damned. Those activists who tried to defend black rights before the court—men such as Albion Tourgee, the lead lawyer for the *Plessy* plaintiffs—were invariably bumblers whose ham-fisted tactics undermined the cause. Even Justice John Marshall Harlan, Plessy's only dissenter, isn't spared. True, Harlan turned his dissent into a ringing defense of equal rights. But he was also a racist, Goldstone writes, who believed that African Americans were "simply equal under a benevolent set of laws created by whites." Worst of all, the author claims that the freedmen whose rights the amendments were supposed to protect "were utterly unsophisticated in either self-maintenance or self-governance," lacking "even rudimentary knowledge of social organization."

Interesting how eight of the nine Supreme Court justices were nominated by the great emancipator or his general in chief; and the ninth was an avout pro-slavery appointment by President James Buchanan. This reflects accurately the countries sentiments regarding race. It was still very much a white man's country. And while the nation just sacrificed enormously in lives and treasury to settle the slavery question, the majority of white men were certainly not willing to support miscegenation or any form of race mixing. Separate but sort of equal was good enough for most white folks.

———————

This is the way things sat until the Vinson and Warren courts took on school segregation. While Vinson sat in the Chief's chair and heard the original oral arguments in 1952, he died in September 1953 before a judgment could be rendered. President Dwight Eisenhower appointed Earl Warren as chief justice in September, 1953. His strong leadership in producing a unanimous decision to overturn *Plessey* changed the course of American history. Many historians, including Richard Kluger author of *Simple Justice*, believe that without Warren the court might not have voted to end segregation. One thing is almost certain; Vinson would never have achieved a unanimous vote.

When Earl Warren joined the court in 1953, he was moving from a distinguished career in California as a successful lawyer, Attorney General, and Governor, yet what he is most remembered for is leading the Court on the *Brown* decision. He took his judicial oath at precisely noon on October 5, 1953, and the country would never be the same.

He was also the author of the Court's written *Brown* decision. But more than just the documents author he was the one who unified a divided court to ensure that the Supreme Court issued a unanimous decision. The court Warren inherited from Vincent was one of the most bitterly dived courts in our history. Warren also had to deal with a justice who was a former member of the KKK and another who was an avowed segregationist. Justice Reed was so strongly segregationist he refused to go to the Supreme Court Christmas party if blacks were to be invited. Warren worked his magic and charm in first building a majority, and once it was clear he had the votes (6 to 3), he went about creating the unanimous decision—exactly what the country needed. In this singularly astonishing achievement—a unanimous *Brown* decision—Warren joined the ranks of the legendary Chief Justices.

All the justices saw the need for this cohesiveness to aid America, especially the South, in accepting the courts verdict—ending school segregation. They agreed with the civil rights attorneys that it was not clear whether the framers of the Fourteenth Amendment intended to permit segregated public education. The doctrine of separate but equal did not appear until 1896, they noted, and it pertained to transportation, not education.

More important, Warren wrote, that the present circumstances were the issue, not the past. Education was perhaps the most vital function of state and local governments, and racial segregation of any kind deprived African Americans of equal protection under the Fourteenth Amendment and due process under the Fifth Amendment. Jim Newton wrote a moving account of Warren's life and especially covers his deft management of the *Brown* decision [*Justice for All*, see

Bibliography item 167]. *Brown* was the Warren's courts first big verdict and it was critical to Warren, the court, and the country that he get it right.

When the decision was read to the public at 12:52 p.m. on May 17, 1954, Thurgood Marshall was of course at the plaintiff's table leading the NAACP legal team and was stunned and delighted by the news—especially a unanimous decision from such a divided court. Earl Warren addressed a packed court eager to hear the courts verdict. Here is how Jim Newton captured the moment:

> *The document before Warren then he read, "We conclude in the field of public education the doctrine of 'separate but equal' has no place. Separate educational facilities are inherently unequal." Those words were stirring enough. With them, the segregated school systems of seventeen states were struck down as unconstitutional.*
>
> *But Warren amended them as he delivered the opinion from the bench, adding a word that gave moral clarity to the legal result. "We unanimously conclude…" he read. With that, the nation took a deep and satisfying breath. Sitting before the Court, Thurgood Marshall turned his amazed look at Stanley Reed. Reed stared down from the bench and nodded almost imperceptibly. As Marshall watched, Reed wiped a tear from his cheek.*
>
> *From his seat at the center of the Court's great bench, Warren too felt the rumble of his words. "When the word 'unanimously' was spoken, a wave of emotion swept the room," he wrote in his memoirs, "no words or intentional movement, yet a distinct emotional manifestation that defies description."*

The reason Marshall turned to look at Justice Reed was his astonishment that Reed an ardent segregationist would vote in favor of integration. Marshall was hoping for a win, any kind of win, and never in his wildest dreams had he anticipated a unanimous decision—an equivalent of a Supreme Court home run. So with Warren's skill, the start of a changing tenor throughout the country, and the NAACP strategic approach the country left segregation behind at least in a legal sense on May 17, 1954. In the 335 years they resided on North America soil it can be argued; up to that point, only emancipation had a more positive impact on the life of American blacks. Of course it all started, as it always does, with a few courageous, trusting souls like Barbara Rose Johns, John A. Stokes, Oliver Brown, and Sarah Bulah, who had enough faith in the American system of justice that they willingly put at risk their comfort, lives, and futures. After all, they actually believed Jefferson had it right when he proclaimed that America was a place where "all men are created equal." In a September, 2012 New York Times article on Justice Clarence Thomas he was quoted as saying, "That the we the people did not include people who looked liked him." Justice Thomas does not leave it there, but goes on to affirm, "There was always this underling belief that we were entitled to be a full participant in 'we the people.'"

——— THE DECISION ———
AND THE AFTERMATH

The Supreme Court on May 17, 1954, issued a decree resolving the court case called *Brown v. Board.* What were not so easily resolved were the minds and hearts of whites who refused to accept integration. Every city, county, and state in the South all had their own take on reacting to *Brown.* In Prince Edward County they were calm and calculating as chronicled in Chapter Three. The good folks of Prince Edward County seemed to know that they were in this fight for the long haul; though few would have expected the struggle to last thirteen years. Even that is a misnomer since the thirteen years only cover the onset of the strike in '51 to the resumption of public schools in '64. In reality, with schools remaining de facto segregated for another decade or more and the community remaining stubbornly polarized; the struggle went on for decades.

Even today there are some combatants who still cling to their bitter memories of the Prince Edward County school strike, the creation of a white private school system, or the public school closing for five years. Jill Ogline Titus published a book in 2011, *Brown's Battleground- Students, Segregationist & the Struggle for Justice in Prince Edward County, Virginia*, that devotes considerable attention to the decades that followed the resumption of public schools in 1964. It is important to point out that by 2005 the public schools in Prince Edward County became fully integrated and doing as well as any of their contemporaries, and, to a large degree, the rancor of those past decades is kept well buried and out of sight. Not gone or forgotten, but many have decided to move on. In many ways events of the world and the maturity of the civil rights movement have overtaken the entire Prince Edward tragedy.

Richard Kluger tried to put the *Brown v. Board of Education of Topeka* decision in a historical perspective and just how long generations of blacks had waited for this moment: "...fifty-six years after segregation was approved in *Plessy,* ninety years after the Emancipation Proclamation, 163 years after the ratification of the Constitution, and 333 years after the first African slave was known to have been brought to shores of North America...." Remember, this judgment was offered by nine white men, but it was far from a gift. Blacks, fighting through the NAACP, had strategically developed a legal education system that produced the likes of Thurgood Marshall, Oliver Hill, and Spotswood Robinson. They then scraped together just enough funding to sustain a legal campaign that lasted for over 50 years. No one gave them anything—children had collected pennies to fund the legal teams, Howard University created a law school to train black attorney's to win civil rights cases, and heroes like Barbara Rose Johns took the personal risks to move the nation forward.

When the court unanimously ruled that public school segregation was unconstitutional, Chief Justice Earl Warren writing for the majority on the court explained their decision:

We come then to the question presented: Does segregation of children in public schools solely on the

*basis of race, even though the physical facilities and other
"tangible" factors may be equal, deprive the children of
the minority group of equal educational opportunities?
We believe that it does.
We conclude that in the field of public education the
doctrine of "separate but equal" has no place. Separate
educational facilities are inherently unequal. Therefore
we hold that the plaintiffs and others similarly situated for
whom the actions have been brought are, by reason of the
segregation complained of, deprived of the equal
protection of the laws guaranteed by the Fourteen
Amendment.*

*Segregation of white and colored children in public
schools has a detrimental effect upon the colored
children. The impact is greater when it has the sanction
of the law for the policy of separating the races is usually
interpreted as denoting the inferiority of the Negro group.
Any language in contrary to this finding is rejected. We
conclude that in the field of public education the doctrine
of 'separate but equal' has no place. Separate
educational facilities are inherently unequal.*

—Earl Warren, Chief Justice of the U.S. Supreme Court,
1954

The decision was something of a come from behind victory
for Marshall given the imposing legal team contesting the case,
and nearly 60 years of legal precedent he had to overcome. In
September, 2012 NY Giant's coach, Tom Coughlin, said of his
team's grit in delivering a come from behind win that Sunday, "A
lesser group of men would have had trouble," Coughlin said.
"There is plenty of stuff to correct, and we'll work to get it
corrected. But it's a lot better correcting it when you win." This
applies to Marshall and his legal team, NAACP, parents and
students; and the entire civil rights movement. They could all
feel like they had won a big victory and like coach Coughlin, it
was a lot better correcting the other wrongs from a win.

Read what others have to say about the importance of the *Brown* decision:

- *The highest court in the land, the guardian of our national conscience, has reaffirmed its faith—and the undying American faith—in the equality of all men and all children before the law.*
  —The New York Times, May 18, 1954

- *It is not too much to speak of the Court's decision as a new birth of freedom...Abroad as well as at home, this decision will engender a renewal of faith in democratic institutions and ideals.*
  —Washington Post, May 19, 1954

- *You can't imagine the rejoicing among black people, and some white people, when the Supreme Court decision came down in May 1954...Many of us saw how the same idea applied to other things, like public transportation. It was a very hopeful time. African Americans believed that at last there was a real chance to change the segregation laws.*
  —Rosa Parks

- *For all men of goodwill May 17, 1954, marked a joyous end to the long night of enforced segregation...This decision brought hope to millions of disinherited Negroes who had formerly dared only to dream of freedom.*
  —Martin Luther King Jr.

- *We concluded then that we could never win the legal battle, that you could not square a dual [school] system of that sort under our federal Constitution. ... and that the best thing for us to do would be to never admit that, of course, but to fight a delaying action in the courts. ... delay every way we could do it. ... avoid having a decision made in court, if possible, at all costs, anticipating that the decision would be against us. Now this was our approach. ... so that they'd*

> *[Blacks] have to take us on, on a broad front, in a multitude of cases.*
>
> —**John Patterson** Alabama Attorney General (and later Governor) explained his reaction to *Brown* and the South's strategy to resist
>
> - *Abolishing of the public school system as a last resort to preserve segregation of the races in the schools has been called for in a petition signed by an unprecedented 7,568 Halifax county people today.*
>
> —**Halifax Gazette**, Thursday, July 29, 1954, Lead story on front page started off with this sentence.

Cheryl Brown Henderson speaks next about her father, whose name titles the famous Supreme Court case *Brown v. Board of Education.* She discusses how the case came to be and how segregation was not only racist but defied common sense.

My father, Oliver Brown, was the lead plaintiff in the case and a welder for the Santa Fe Railroad and pastor of St. Mark AME Church.

Sadly, my father died in 1961 and he never lived to see any of this. Had he lived, I am sure he would have been amazed to see what the case ultimately accomplished and how history had made him an icon, albeit an accidental one. For contrary to some of the myths surrounding the decision, my father was not the promulgator of the Brown v. Board case. He and parents from 12 other families had been recruited by the local chapter of the NAACP to challenge the law that upheld segregation in the Topeka Elementary schools. In all probability, his name came first on the list of plaintiffs— and therefore secured for him a lasting place in history—because he was the only man among the plaintiffs, perhaps a reflection of the gender politics of the day. What all 13 plaintiffs shared, however, was a basic fact of life. Although they lived four or five blocks away from the nearest public elementary school, the school was for white children only. Therefore, some children had to be bused 30 or 40 blocks to a segregated black school. Although Kansas had a relatively progressive history in terms of race relations, the state was dragging its feet in integrating the elementary schools (all other schools were integrated at that time). To these 13 parents it made not only "civil rights sense" but common sense to end the practice.

While history may be in the eye of the beholder or more precisely for the winner to tell; a fact will always be a fact, and Cheryl Brown Henderson was mistaken about why they chose to use her dad's name for the famous case. While this theory is often repeated, in fact Darlene Brown, another plaintiff, (no relation to Oliver Brown) should have been the named plaintiff if alphabetically order was the sole criteria.

The Supreme Court was not done with *Brown* because following the May 17, 1954, decree that boldly struck down segregation they were scheduled to hear arguments to determine just how the ruling would be imposed. The country had to wait over a year for the court's next term, for the *Brown II* ruling. On May 31, 1955, the court essentially punted the heavy lifting to the district federal courts and left everyone scratching their heads over the timeline. In the end the Court set no deadline for ending segregated public education and simply ordered the states to integrate their schools with "all deliberate speed." The next chapter discusses *Brown II* and how the South did indeed respond with all deliberate speed in crafting the practices, policies and laws that came to be called "Massive Resistance."

Chapter Five

MASSIVE RESISTANCE

If there is not struggle there is no progress. Those who profess to favor freedom and yet deprecate agitation, are men who want crops without plowing up the ground, they want rain without thunder and lightning. They want the ocean without the awful roar of its many waters. This struggle may be a moral one, or it may be a physical one, and it may be a moral and physical, but it must be a struggle. Power concedes nothing without a demand. It never did and it never will....Men may not get all they pay for in this world, but they must certainly pay for all they get.

—Frederick Douglass. On August 3, 1857, Frederick Douglass delivered his, "West India Emancipation" speech at Canandaigua, New York, on the twenty-third anniversary of the event. Most of the address was a history of British efforts toward emancipation as well as a reminder of the crucial role the West Indian slaves had in their own freedom struggle. However, shortly after he began, Douglass foretold the coming Civil War when he uttered the sentence that became the most quoted of all his public orations. "If there is not struggle there is no progress."

Time Line for Chapter Five
Massive Resistance
(1954–1959)

1954, May 17. In a unanimous decree the US Supreme Court ruled in *Brown V. Board of Education* that school segregation is unconstitutional.

1955 to 1956. James J. Kilpatrick wrote editorials reviving the model of interposition as a means to fighting integration.

1955, March 2. Claudette Coleman refused to give up her seat to a white woman on a Montgomery, Alabama, bus, preceding Rosa Parks by five months.

1955, May 31. The Supreme Court handed down its decree calling on district courts to implement its school desegregation decision, often called *Brown II.*

1955, May 31. Prince Edward County Board of Supervisors met and agreed to not fund public schools for the upcoming fall school term as a means to forestall court ordered integration.

1955, July 18. A three-judge federal court ruled that Prince Edward County would not have to desegregate schools in September. The court did hold that desegregation must take place at some date in the future, but set no timeline.

1955, August 31. Emmett Till's body was discovered floating in a river in Money, Mississippi, wrapped in barbed wire and grotesquely mutilated, for presumably whistling at a white woman.

1955, December 1. Rosa Parks was arrested and thrown in jail because she refused to get up out of her seat on the bus for a white person. The ensuing boycott, coordinated by a young Reverend Martin Luther King Jr., will mark an important turning point in the African American freedom struggle.

1956. Senator Harry F. Byrd Sr., Democrat from Virginia, crafted massive resistance to resist school desegregation.

1956, February 1. The Gen. Assembly in Virginia adopted a resolution interposing the sovereignty of Virginia against the encroachment by the Federal government.

1958, September 15. In tiny Warren County Virginia, Gov. Almond closed their high school to prevent 22 blacks from attending; this was Virginia's first school closing in the state's massive resistance campaign.

1958, September 27. In Norfolk, Virginia, Gov. Almond closed six schools, but only the white schools, where blacks had petitioned for admittance.

1958, September 29. In Charlottesville, Virginia, Gov. Almond closed a high school and an elementary school.

1959, January 19. The Supreme Court of Virginia decreed the Norfolk school closing unconstitutional.

1959, January 20. Gov. Almond announced his intention to vigorously continue the fight against integration, "We have just begun to fight."

1959, January 28. Gov. Almond announced the end of massive resistance after the state and federal court rulings go against school closings.

1959, February 2. Norfolk opened the six schools it closed, essentially breaking the back of segregation in Virginia, with the notable exception of Prince Edward County.

Chapter Five
MASSIVE RESISTANCE
(1954–1959)

And the day came when the risk it took to remain tight inside the bud was more painful than the risk it took to blossom.

—Anais Nin

In the mid-1950s Americans remained deeply divided over the issue of racial equality. Segregationist viewed that the very fabric of what had been America for a hundred years was being torn to shreds by blacks and the NAACP. African Americans continued to press to have the *Brown* decision enforced, and most folks were unprepared for the intensity of resistance among white Southerners. Likewise, defenders of the "Southern way of life" underestimated the determination of their black neighbors. In the preceding Chapters we discussed how each side underestimated the other's determination, and the gap in honest communication between the races was at least a contributor to this struggle lasting for such a very long time.

By the mid 1950s the African American freedom struggle was spreading across the country. The original battle for school desegregation morphed into broader campaigns for social justice. While the *Brown* decision declared the system of legal segregation unconstitutional, the courts were slow or reluctant to push integration upon whites too far or too fast. The Supreme Court ordered only that the states end segregation with "all deliberate speed." This vagueness about how to enforce the ruling gave segregationists the opportunity to organize resistance. The segregationist employed numerous strategies to defeat integration outright, but their most often used weapon was to delay, continue to delay, and then delay more, finally giving only enough ground to appease the court without really addressing true integration.

While some whites welcomed the *Brown* decision, a large number considered it an assault on their way of life. Segregationists played on the fears and prejudices of their communities and launched a militant campaign of defiance and resistance. The movement for African American civil rights began long before the *Brown* decision and continued long after. Still, the defeat of the separate-but-equal legal doctrine undercut one of the major pillars of white supremacy in America. As discussed in Chapter 4, there may never have been a 1964 Civil Rights Bill if Thurgood Marshall had lost *Brown* in 1954.

Judge Robert L. Carter discussing the *Brown* legacy said, "…that *Brown* was done, was a thing of black intellect. Houston, Marshall, Carter. And the country, you know, is celebrating what *Brown* means and all that sort of stuff, is not really, is not really understanding that what it is celebrating, for one of few times in history, is something that has been done and achieved by black minds." While the victory was hard fought and satisfying in and of itself Thurgood Marshall put it to Kenneth Clarke this way, "you get weary from trying to save the white man's soul— especially since he was so unappreciative of the effort."

Carter was another in the long line of competent attorneys produced by the Howard University School of Law started by Charles Hamilton Houston. If there was one secret weapon in the civil rights struggle, it just might have been Houston moving the Howard Law School from a part time school to the establishment of a first-rate law school focused on social change. Most white folks paid the upstart law school no mind. Only in reflection did the opponents of integration see that the seeds of segregations destruction were planted with Houston opening a more rigors school in 1929. In 1944, upon completion of his career in the Army Air Force, Carter went to work as a legal assistant to Thurgood Marshall at the NAACP Legal Defense and Educational Fund. Robert Carter was one of the lead attorneys on noted civil rights cases, such as *Sweatt v. Painter* and *Brown*. He was the lead for presenting the arguments in the Kansas case under *Brown*. In 1956, Carter succeeded Thurgood Marshall as the NAACP Legal Defense Fund (LDF) general counsel. Over the course of his tenure at the LDF, Carter argued or co-argued and won 21 of 22 cases in the Supreme Court.

Among the most important cases Carter worked on after *Brown* was *NAACP v. Alabama* (1958), in which the Supreme Court held that the NAACP could not be required to make its membership lists public. This removed a tool of intimidation employed by some southern states as part of their massive resistance campaign to thwart implementation of the *Brown* decision.

Carter left the NAACP in 1968 and worked in a private law firm until 1972 when he was appointed to the bench as a judge of the U.S. District Court for the Southern District of New York.

——— REACTION TO BROWN ———

At the time of the May 1954 *Brown v. Board of Education* decision, 17 states and the District of Columbia had laws enforcing school segregation. By 1958, only seven states— Virginia, South Carolina, Georgia, Alabama, Florida, Mississippi, and Louisiana—maintained public school segregation. Since the settlement of the Americas by Europeans and the arrival of African slaves, the South, and essentially most of America, has had a long standing aversion to the mixing of the races. Harriet Beecher Stowe's *Uncle Tom's Cabin* had a profound effect on both the North and the South. The North was shamed into moving closer toward emancipation while the South responded with vitriol for those meddling abolitionists from the North. The South further hardened its position on slavery, denounced the book and the author, and became even more isolated, all of which contributed to their ultimate decision to succeed from the Union. Mary Eastman penned a response to Stowe's *Uncle Tom's Cabin*. Eastman's *Aunt Phillis's Cabin,* portrayed slavery as a kindness to the blacks who were incapable of taking care of themselves and the best way to deal with the Negro problem. She surely chronicled the thinking of the time, at least Southern thinking in the 1850s, on maintaining racial separation.

The author of "Uncle Tom's Cabin" speaks of good men at the North, who "receive and educate the oppressed" (negroes). I know "lots" of good men there, but none good enough to befriend colored people. They seem to me to have an unconquerable antipathy to them. But Mrs. Stowe says, she educates them in her own family with her own children. I am glad to hear she feels and acts kindly toward them, and I wish others in her region of country would imitate her in their respect; but I would rather my children and negroes were educated at different schools, being utterly opposed to amalgamation, root and branch.

—From Mary Eastman, *Aunt Phillis's Cabin.*

For many in the South, this thinking had changed little in spite of the terrible consequences they suffered from the war, the humiliation of reconstruction, and the 13th, 14th, and 15th Constitutional Amendments. Because blacks and whites did not mix in the Jim Crow South the reality for many whites was that they had no black friends, little real interactions, and no crucial conversations about race. This made it easier for whites to dehumanize and discriminate against blacks. Many forces were at work: some was from mean spirited bigots who wanted to keep someone down, as long as they were not the "bottom rail" of southern society, some was economic, some was historical, some was out of fear, some was out of peer pressure, some was because they simply did not know any blacks, and much can be attributed to long standing Southern customs. Some Southerners were not opposed to educating blacks, per se, but they feared that educating blacks, and certainly educating blacks and whites together, was a big step toward race mixing, which the vast majority of southerners strongly opposed in the 1950s. In 1903 W. E. B. Du Bois summed up the situation in the south in his iconic *The Souls of Black Folk:* "The opposition to Negro education in the South was at first bitter, and showed itself in ashes, insult, and blood; for the South believed an educated Negro to be a dangerous Negro." Remnants of this thinking were still in play throughout the South in the 1950s and undercut all attempts to integrate the schools.

But as Earl Warren was acutely aware, leaders with prestige and a will to enforce court orders, beginning with President Eisenhower, had, so far, not been willing to provide anything beyond tepid support for *Brown*. John Lewis, renowned civil rights leader, can assist us today in understanding how the initial hope of integration was smashed, for a time, on the rocks by the segregationists most used weapon—stall, stall again, and stall some more.

> *When 14-year-old John Lewis opened the paper on May 16, 1954, the headline stunned him the Supreme Court had declared segregation in schools unconstitutional. He could not believe it. Separate schools were one of the cornerstones of southern segregation. He felt his world "turned upside down." He was sure he would be attending an integrated school that coming September, a mere four months away. But Lewis' hopes will be dashed by a school desegregation process that saw only about one in 100 black students enter white schools by 1960. Lewis's broken dream captured in a microcosm the 1950s tease young African-Americans felt with the unrealized promise of racial change.*

While the court's words sounded strong, the reality was often very different. The court did not order the immediate integration of the South's segregated schools or even the immediate integration of the schools named in *Brown* case. Action was postponed for a year to give the South time to adjust. Chief Justice Earl Warren believed that time was necessary for white Southerners to accept the idea that segregation was unconstitutional and start to accept that they had lost. On May 31, 1955, the Supreme Court issued *Brown II*—this was the implementation decree long sought by the NAACP. The decree charged Federal judges with implementing *Brown*. The Federal judges were faced with considering requests on a community-by-community basis; thus putting the burden on local communities and the NAACP to fight hundreds of battles across the South. The court offered no specific guidance on how long the process should take and when segregation would end. The court did instruct officials "to make a prompt and reasonable start toward" ending school segregation and advised judges to make sure it happened "with all deliberate speed." Any delays should clearly benefit the public and be in the spirit of "good faith" compliance with the *Brown* decision.

——— JAMES J. KILPATRICK ———

One influential individual, who did not hold his tongue about the *Brown* decision, or more precisely his pen, was James J. Kilpatrick, the chief editorial writer for the *Richmond News Leader*. Kilpatrick is an important part of the massive resistance story because he became the intellectual engine of segregationist resistance. In editorials in 1955 and 1956, Kilpatrick presented what would become the foundation of massive resistance to desegregation, an invention he called interposition, a doctrine initially advanced by the 19th-century states rights advocate John C. Calhoun of South Carolina, under which a state may reject a federal mandate that it considers to be encroaching on its prerogatives.

Mr. James J. Kilpatrick, recalling that time in one of his syndicated column said, "I became the fire eating editor of the news leader. There wasn't a topic under the moon or sun on which I could not deliver a definitive opinion. I laid upon my enemies with shillelagh, tire iron and bung starter."

Kilpatrick was known, and even acknowledged by his foes as a gifted wordsmith, using words and elegant prose to make his points for segregation. This can be seen in some of his editorials from the period: "These nine men repudiated the Constitution, spit upon the 10th Amendment and rewrote the fundamental law of this land to suit their own gauzy concepts of sociology." Mr. Kilpatrick later wrote after the court ruling, "If it be said now that the South is flouting the law, let it be said to the high court: you taught us how."

Later in his life, he had had an epiphany of sorts. He wrote in the 2002 *Atlanta Journal Constitution*, "…by 1970 I had severed the last vestiges of segregation. For me, it was over. I had come to recognize the terrible evils of state sponsored racism. It'd taken a long time." Linwood Holton, Governor of Virginia from 1970 to 1974, said of Kilpatrick, "He made a bad mistake in his early years in his reaction to the Supreme Court decision on *Brown versus Board of Education*.... He redeemed himself, and he made it clear that he had gotten over any discriminatory instincts."

While his legacy is scarred, having been on the wrong side of the most important issue of his lifetime, all acknowledge his wit and brilliance with the written word. Larry Sabato, director of the Center for politics at the University of Virginia said at the time of Kilpatrick's death in 2010:

> *Kilpatrick was a superb writer and exceptionally skilled rhetorician, but unfortunately he applied those talents to help lead Massive Resistance to school desegregation in Virginia and the South in the 1950s. Massive Resistance left deep wounds which have not fully healed even 50 years later, and Kilpo's incendiary editorials in the Richmond News Leader were major reason why. Everyone deserves to have his life judged as a whole, and Kilpatrick went on to have a long, fruitful career in national journalism, representing the conservative point of view on shows such as 60 minutes and is widely syndicated column.*

Mr. James J. Kilpatrick covered the sit-ins at the fashionable lunchroom of Thalhimer's, a department store in downtown Richmond, Virginia. He recalled walking three blocks from the newspaper main office to see what was going on. He found the students were indeed in a lunch table, neatly dressed, creating no disturbance and simply asking to be served. However outside of Grace Street he found, "A dozen white punks were staging a demonstration. This was race hatred. It was ugly. I wrote an editorial supporting the students. My publisher, God rest him, made only minor changes and let it run."

Despite being adversaries and being on different sides of the integration issue, Mr. Oliver W. Hill had a cordial relationship with Kilpatrick. Mr. Oliver Hill's son, Mr. Oliver W. Hill Junior, related a conversation he had about Kilpatrick with his now deceased dad, "one of the things my father said was that Mr. Kilpatrick had such a sharp intellect, it was a shame he couldn't see what my father saw as such an eminently reasonable argument for equal rights for all people."

The final word, at least here, concerning Kilpatrick is to surmise that, while the man was undoubtedly a brilliant writer, if he had used his talents for something other than perpetuating the malevolent cause of segregation, it is widely believed he would have won one or more Pulitzer Prizes.

———— HARRY S. ASHMORE ————

As a counterpoint to James J. Kilpatrick there is Harry S. Ashmore. The *Arkansas Gazette*, Arkansas's first newspaper, was established in 1819, 17 years before Arkansas became a state. Its editorial stance for law and order during the desegregation of Central High School in 1957 earned the newspaper two Pulitzer Prizes—the first time in history one newspaper won two Pulitzers in the same year. Known for its liberal editorial pages in a conservative Southern state, the *Gazette* was led by editor Harry S. Ashmore.

In 1957, the federal courts ordered integration of the schools in the Little Rock School District, starting the Little Rock Crisis. Governor Orval Faubus defied the court order, while Ashmore editorialized for compliance with the law. This ended the friendship between the two. Ashmore became a rallying figure for moderates and liberals in Arkansas, and an object of hatred for segregationists, who labeled him a carpetbagger. The newspaper's objective news coverage was a voice of reason in an otherwise volatile media circus.

Harry S. Ashmore, writing in a front page *Arkansas Gazette* editorial, said, "the issue is no longer segregation versus integration. The question has now become the supremacy of the government of the United States in all matters of law. And clearly the federal government cannot let this issue remained unresolved no matter what the cost of this community."

After the 1954 *Brown v. Board of Education of Topeka, Kansas* ruling that mandated desegregation of American schools, the Little Rock School District put together a plan for gradual desegregation beginning in the fall of 1957. The *Gazette* editorialized that Little Rock could be a model for the rest of the country, but on the eve of the opening of the schools, Ashmore got word that Governor Orval Faubus planned to stop the school integration.

Faubus called out an armed detachment of the Arkansas National Guard to surround Central High School, ostensibly to quell mob violence. The guardsmen turned away the Little Rock Nine as they tried to enter the school. Ashmore and the *Gazette* answered vehemently with the front-page editorial, "The Crisis Mr. Faubus Made" on September 4, 1957, taking the argument beyond segregation versus integration to the supremacy of the federal government in all matters of law. As the days and weeks wore on, the *Gazette* covered all the developments of the ongoing crisis. The *Gazette's* stance for law and order and an end to segregation cost the newspaper millions of dollars in advertising and circulation losses. Circulation dropped from 100,000 to 83,000 in a matter of weeks, and Ashmore and other *Gazette* employees were threatened with violence.

In the aftermath of the Central High crisis, the *Gazette* reigned as one of the great newspapers of the country, and many of its reporters and editors moved on to other major publications such as the *New York Times*, the *Atlantic Monthly*, the *New Yorker*, the *New York Herald Tribune*, the *Philadelphia Inquirer,* and the *Chicago Tribune*. Following the integration crisis the *Gazette* was able to recruit new talent from a national pool and eventually regained its circulation lead over its cross-town rivals.

In 1958, the *Arkansas Gazette* won the Pulitzer Prize for Public Service for demonstrating the highest qualities of civic leadership, journalistic responsibility, and moral courage in the face of great public tension during the school integration crisis of 1957. The newspaper's fearless and completely objective news coverage, and its reasoned and moderate policy, did much to restore calmness and order to an overwrought community; reflecting great credit on its editors and its management. In October of that year, the *Gazette* also won the Freedom Award, presented yearly to individuals or groups who had significantly aided the cause of freedom. In that same year Harry S. Ashmore won the Pulitzer Prize for Editorial Writing, for the forcefulness, dispassionate analysis, and clarity of his editorials on the school integration conflict in Little Rock. Imagine what good a talented James J. Kilpatrick could have done for his state of Virginia during its struggle with integration?

———— THE RULE OF LAW ————

As a starting point, we should note that no blacks served in the Virginia, General Assembly for the 82 years spanning the period from Jim Crow to the run up of the modern Civil Rights movement—from 1879 to 1967. This disenfranchisement allowed the all-white General Assembly the freedom to control their "Negroes." This became especially important during the massive resistance era when the General Assembly was expected to thwart integration— legally. This was nothing new to Virginia's lawmakers who for two hundred years had always found a way to keep whites on the top rail.

To circumvent the 15th Amendment to the U.S. Constitution, which guaranteed voting rights to black men, the 1901–1902 Virginia Constitutional Convention required voters to prove their understanding of the state constitution and imposed a poll tax of $1.50 to be paid annually by registered voters. New voters had to pay $4.50, a large sum of money in those days. The Democratic majority in the General Assembly appointed all election registrars. As intended, these measures dramatically reduced voting by blacks, poor whites, and Republicans—the party of Lincoln. Within 90 days, more than 125,000 of the 147,000 black voters in the state had been stricken from the rolls of eligible voters.

Literacy tests—such as Virginia's requiring a "reasonable explanation" of any part of the state constitution— disappeared when the Civil Rights Act of 1964 stipulated that anyone with a sixth-grade education was presumed literate. The 24th

Amendment ratified in 1964, outlawed poll taxes in federal elections. In 1966 the U.S. Supreme Court reaffirmed the ban on poll taxes.

Nonetheless, the 1964 and 1965 civil rights laws enacted by Congress were never a sure thing. It took events such as "Bloody Sunday" in Selma, Alabama, to push President Lyndon Johnson to propose a Voting Rights Act, which he signed into law on August 6, 1965. Now supervision of voter registration would have oversight by federal authorities. This meant that for virtually the entire South, where fewer than half of eligible voters were registered, registration would now become open to all eligible voters. These efforts, supplemented by black freedom schools, registration drives, and voter rallies, tripled the number of black voters by 1968. The results were almost immediate. In 1967, after an 82 years absence, Dr. William F. Reid became the first African American delegate in the General Assembly. Virginia's first black Mayor, Hermanze E. Fauntleroy, Jr., became mayor of Petersburg in 1973. Lawrence Davies and Noel Taylor were elected mayors in Fredericksburg and Roanoke, respectively, in 1976. By 1977, the majority of Richmond's city council members were black. By 1985 there were seven black members of the General Assembly. And in 1989, L. Douglas Wilder became the first black governor elected in any state, with black voters providing his margin of victory. In 1992 Robert Cortez "Bobby" Scott became the first black U. S. Congressman elected from Virginia since 1888.

All of the preceding change did not come about without a struggle. Virginia was led by two Governors during the period of massive resistance, Governor Thomas Bahnson Stanley (1954 to 1958) and Governor James Lindsay Almond, Jr. (1958 to 1962).

Stanley was the Speaker of the Virginia House of Delegates and a U.S. Representative in Congress, before becoming the Governor. Almond was Assistant Commonwealth Attorney of Roanoke, Virginia, a state court judge to the Court of Roanoke and was then elected to the U.S. House of Representatives, serving in the 79th and 80th Congresses. Almond resigned his

Congressional seat in 1948, when he was elected Attorney General of Virginia. He argued and lost the state's case for segregation of public schools before the Supreme Court in the case of *Davis v. County School Board of Prince Edward County.* In 1957, he was elected Governor of Virginia, and took office in January 1958, for a single term that ended in 1962. All governors of Virginia are single-term offices because the states constitution prohibits consecutive terms for governors.

When the *Brown* decision was announced, Governor Stanley's immediate reaction to the decree was to call for, "cool heads, calm, steady and sound judgment." The Attorney General Lindsay Almond's reaction was also restrained, "Virginia will approach the question realistically to endeavor to work out some rational adjustments." These were the two men who were to lead Virginia as governor during the entire period we now call massive resistance. They were charged with the nuts and bolts of implementing massive resistance, with Sen. Byrd preferring to stay in the background while still very much the man in charge when it came to Virginia. The Byrd Organization was as vague as it was effective. Byrd described his political base not as a machine, but as "a loose organization of friends, who believe in the same principals of government." He goes on to wryly discuss his limited role: "Some people say I run a political machine in Virginia. All I do is offer a little political advice now and then." In 2003 as part of the Virginia Civil Rights Movement Video Initiative, Dr. W. Ferguson Reid, a surgeon and the first African American elected to the Virginia General Assembly since Reconstruction, describes his memory of Virginia's dominant political authority in the 1950s. Ronald E. Carrington, then President of Media Consultants Global, Inc. of Richmond, was the director-producer of the videotaping and conducted the interviews.

CARRINGTON: Now, the Byrd Machine, what did that represent in Virginia? What were the things that they wanted to make sure evolved?

REID: Okay. They were the old Carter Glass, Carter Glass was the one who wanted to perpetuate segregation, keep the status quo, to have a controlling class and a subservient class. They wanted the haves to keep having it, and the have-not's to keep not having it. So the Byrd Machine was a progression of the Carter Glass machine, and they wanted— they were the dominant political party. They wanted to maintain a segregated society. They are not interested in education. They feel that if you educate people you create problems to their existence. They wanted to have the money class. They wanted to make sure that the people who controlled government were the same class, not only state government but city government as well. They wanted to make sure that Main Street right, you know, the Main Street group and suburbia group, they wanted to keep the private clubs private. They wanted to keep the power structure as it is. They didn't want blacks or poor whites involved in any decision making.

When you look across the landscape of Virginia, the reaction to *Brown* varied widely. In the more metropolitan northern Virginia there were pockets of acceptance or at least acquiescence to the wishes of the Supreme Court. While in the Black Belt there was open resentment and hostility to the court's decree. As you will recall, the Black Belt was characterized by the 31 contiguous agricultural counties in southern and eastern Virginia where the black population often exceeded the white and strong racial prejudices prevailed. As we shall see later, these vast territories represented a real hotbed of anti-integration sentiments. In some cases, folks were willing to jeopardize their own children's educations to keep their white children from sitting next to blacks in school. Prince Edward County sits prominently within this geographic and cultural Black Belt.

Quickly following the court's decision, Governor Stanley set about developing a strategy to resist the high court's ruling on *Brown*. On May 24, 1954, he summoned to the state capital in a contingent of black leaders, including Oliver W. Hill, Dr. R. P.

Daniel, President of Virginia State College, including P. E. Young Sr., publisher of the *Norfolk Journal and Guide* (a significant black paper). During this meeting Gov. Stanley urged the black leaders to accept segregation as the rule in Virginia. They refused him.

Behind the scenes, Senator Harry Byrd pressed Governor Stanley to move forward with strong anti-integration strategies and legislation. During this early period Senator Byrd was not satisfied with the governor of Virginia's more thoughtful approach. A decade later, Atty. Gen. Stanley reported that the governor's response was viewed as too mild and in a reference to Senator Byrd's reaction, "I heard…that the top blew off the US Capitol."

On August 30, the governor appointed a 32-member legislative committee to determine the best way to resist *Brown* and to make recommendations to either kill or delay implementing *Brown*. The committee was bipartisan and all white but heavily skewed with representatives and senators from the more militant Southside. Garland Gray was appointed chairman of the committee and, thereafter, the group was known as the "Gray Commission." On January 19, 1955, the Gray Commission issued their preliminary findings. They announced that their conclusion was that the overwhelming majority of Virginians were opposed to racial integration of the public schools. These Virginians were convinced that it would quite literally destroy the public school system and their way of life. These preliminary findings were supported largely based on a single public hearing held a few months earlier. By late spring the Supreme Court finally issued its decree concerning the implementation of *Brown*. The decree mandated that integration of public schools should proceed with "all deliberate speed." The court hoped that by pushing the implementation of their integration order down to the lower courts that they could best enforce compliance with *Brown* because of their keener understanding of local conditions.

Following the late spring Supreme Court decree on implementing *Brown*, the Gray Commission issued their report to the Governor on November 11, 1955. The commission was proposing legislation under which authority for public school assignment would reside with the local boards not with the state and they favored legislation to ensure that the existing compulsory attendance laws would not force white children to attend integrated schools. They proposed that for those parents who objected to their children's enrollment in an integrated school a voucher type program would be available to receive tuition grants to support private school enrollment.

While the Gray Commission's recommendations were far from compliant to the high court's decree, they were not militant enough for the Defenders and Senator Byrd. Because of the influence of Senator Byrd most Southern politicians were expecting Virginia to play a leadership role in thwarting the implementation of *Brown*, and the commission's recommendations seem to imply a strategy of compromise rather than confrontation. Meanwhile some of the Gray Commission's recommendations were going forward at a fast clip. On November 30, 1955, the General Assembly met in special session to consider the Gray Commission's recommendation that section 141 of the Constitution of Virginia be amended to allow for tuition grants. The amendment was supported overwhelmingly by the General Assembly and a statewide referendum was scheduled for January 9, 1956.

The referendum passed and was well supported by Virginia's voters, thereby demonstrating conclusively that Virginia strongly supported the provisions of tuition assistance for private education. Regional breakdowns of white support for the amendment vary predictably along geographic lines: ranging from 84 percent in the Black Belt to 56 percent in the White Belt.

Any doubt about where Virginia's white voters stood was crystal clear after the January 9, 1956, referendum. Byrd and his machine body politic and selected white supremacist groups made sure all of Virginia was reminded about the voters' wishes to strongly oppose integration and continue to support segregation. Also joining the chorus were other vocal groups like the Defenders and editorial boards from the major newspapers of the state. The seasoned politicians clearly understood that they were expected by their voters to resist at all costs the *Brown* decision and integration.

In Virginia, the Defenders requested the General Assembly to make interposition the law of the land. In response to this, the General Assembly set a January date for voters to vote on a constitutional amendment that would make possible the use of public funds for private schools. Should anyone have doubts about how deep-seated Prince Edward County felt about the segregated school system the January vote in Prince Edward sends a clear message. The Prince Edward voters unanimously approved by 2,835 for and 350 against passage of an interposition constitutional Amendment.

James Kilpatrick of the *Richmond News Leader* dug up the old confederate states rights doctrine of "interposition"— state sovereignty trumps federal rule because of the state's belief in rights afforded them by the Constitution. Interposition was originally developed by Thomas Jefferson and James Madison, but was famously employed by John C. Calhoun to prolong slavery for the South prior to the Civil War. James Kilpatrick, who was a trusted advisor to Senator Byrd, launched an editorial campaign which touted the virtues of interposition. While the General Assembly responded by adopting an interposition resolution on February 1, 1956, many including Atty. Gen. Almond felt it was a publicity stunt that would not hold up in court.

While Virginia was dealing with integration and civil rights peacefully, one did not need to look hard for a reminder that all was not sweetness and honey in Dixie. Blacks got a chilling reminder just how little their lives were worth in the Deep South. A series of horrific revelations concerning the murder of a black boy named Emmett Till in August 1955 rocked the country. Emmett Till was a 14-year-old black boy from Chicago who allegedly whistled at a white, female store clerk while visiting his relatives in Money, Mississippi. You can see the threads of the Great Migration here. After going missing, six days later his body was found floating in a river severely mutilated and wrapped in barbed wire. The two white men who were arrested and clearly guilty were acquitted by an all-white jury. The meaning was clear—blacks could be killed by whites with impunity. Step out of line, push the status quo, or get too "uppity" and you might find yourself beaten or killed. Emmett Till became a national sensation partly because of the timing and partly because the press widely published disturbing pictures of his mutilated body.

A week after the funeral, *Jet* magazine, a widely read publication for blacks, published photos of Till's mutilated corpse. In the days that followed the black newspapers around the country followed suit. While most Northerners had heard about violence to blacks in the South; now they had graphic evidence of just how ugly things could get for blacks in the South. The Till case had a huge impact on the country—blacks in particular were frightened and angry. Blacks, especially young blacks, including blacks in the North, suddenly felt very vulnerable. Parents and their children all talked about the concern they had harbored regarding the safety of their children. Of course those in the South knew about this all along, and they were rightfully horrified but maybe not so surprised. Northerners were shocked that such horrific crime could be committed and stunned when the two murderers were acquitted in a Mississippi court even though they confessed to kidnapping and clearly had committed the crime of which they were acquitted. There for all to see and judge was old Jim Crow and just how it worked in the Deep South. The Till murder was an important backdrop to events in Virginia; becoming a rallying cry for the early years of the modern civil rights movement and a public relations disaster for segregationists.

———————

When talking about the story of Prince Edward County the question often comes up, why there was such little violence throughout the 13-year struggle? Many Northerners associate the South with: civil rights marches, angry mobs, Bull Connor beating and jailing peaceful protesters, and that awful bombing in Montgomery. So why was Prince Edward County in Virginia in general relatively devoid of violence? Well, there are two answers and they both equate to the same result. The whites in Virginia who were in power believed that violence would be counterproductive to their preferred path of a legal approach to addressing massive resistance. Further any violence could spin out of control resulting in even more federal interference and oversight. As for the blacks, somehow, they were able to retain their focus on the larger prize seeing violence as counterproductive to their larger goals. To say that black folks have had patience is one of the most understated sentences ever written. As a group, leading up to the Prince Edward County struggle, they suffered through 250 years of some of the most terrible indignities humans could impose on one another. While slavery will top most lists, many believe one of the cruelest jokes played on blacks was to give them a glimmer of the American dream with emancipation and reconstruction and then yank it away with Jim Crow and a strict segregated society, all of which lasted for many generations.

Bob Crawford strongly led the Defenders away from violence, with his views captured by a reporter in October 1955: "If this community should suffer just one instance of Klanism, our white case is lost. No matter who starts it, the whites will be blamed. We must not have it."

——— MASSIVE RESISTANCE ———

In February, 1956 just as things were about to heat up in Virginia Senator Byrd through down the gauntlet by calling for "massive resistance" to the *Brown* mandate. He went on to predict that the Southern states would organize to resist *Brown* and that the rest of the country would soon realize that racial integration would not be accepted in the South. The Senator is credited (if that is an appropriate use of the word credited) as the first congressional representative to use the term "massive resistance." To help shore up Virginia in particular and the South in general Senator Byrd and Senator Strom Thurmond of South Carolina created a declaration of principles called the "Southern Manifesto." The document was issued on March 12, 1956, and was signed by 101 Southern congressmen, the vast majority of the region's federal legislators, including both of Virginia Senators and all 10 of its representatives. The Southern Manifesto called the *Brown* decision "a clear abuse of judicial power," they pledged "to use all lawful means to bring about a reversal of this decision which is contrary to the Constitution and to prevent the use of force in its implementation."

Senator Byrd summed up the situation pretty well as he spoke from his Berryhill apple orchard that August: "Virginia stands as one of the foremost states. Let Virginia surrender to this illegal demand (the desegregation order)... and you'll find the ranks of other southern states broken... it's no secret that the NAACP intends first to press Virginia.... If Virginia surrenders, if Virginia's line is broken, the rest of the South will go down, too." Clearly all sides had decided that once again Virginia was where a line in the sand was to be drawn and battle to be made.

In response, Governor Stanley convened a special session of the General Assembly on August 27, 1956, to address additional state measures to resist the *Brown* decision. His plan, which came to be called the Stanley Plan, consisted of three principal elements: First, all local school boards would be divested of pupil placement responsibilities. Secondly, for those schools that were integrated the governor was to be given absolute authority to close the schools. The state would provide funding for private education of those students including for the salaries of teachers and principals of the closed schools. Finally, the state would deny funding to any local school board should they choose to integrate their schools.

All of these measures were in anticipation of the expected NAACP suit in an attempt to integrate five Virginia communities:

1. Arlington;
2. Warren County;
3. Norfolk;
4. Charlottesville; and
5. Prince Edward County.

Of these five communities only Arlington chose to voluntarily accept integration. The other four all allowed the closure of their public schools rather than accept integration. While Warren County, Norfolk and Charlottesville closed for six months, it was Southside Prince Edward County where the public schools remain closed for five years. The enforcement of the school closing laws in Warren County, Charlottesville, and

Norfolk in 1958 by Governor Almond was no small meanness in that it forced more than 13,000 children out of school. Each one of these five communities underwent their own particular trauma because each one of these cases was slightly different. As an example, Norfolk was hard-pressed to provide private education for 10,000 white students, whereas Prince Edward County was able to provide affordable private education for nearly all of its 1,500 white students. Another difference was that Norfolk closed only their white schools and they allowed their Negro schools to remain open. Prince Edward County closed both the white and black public schools. These differences greatly contributed to white parents demanding the resumption of public schools in Norfolk—segregated or not.

Throughout this period, most of the established papers in Virginia directly supported or at least refused to take on the Byrd machine over integration. The *Norfolk Virginian-Pilot* was one of the few who from the beginning preached moderation and acceptance. A lead editorial described the lack of merit in the Stanley Plan: "how many schools are expendable?" The editorial went on to express astonishment that the Gen. Assembly would consider adopting any legislation that would result in school closings. For five years, throughout the period of massive resistance, Lenoir Chambers editor of the *Norfolk Virginian-Pilot* conducted a campaign in support of the peaceful implementation of the court's decree. The *Norfolk Virginian-Pilot* represented one of the few established media outlets that provided this alternate view. Chambers was awarded the Pulitzer Prize in 1960 for his editorial campaign opposing massive resistance and the acceptance of school integration. In urging the rejection of Gov. Stanley's programs, the paper through its editorials, proclaimed "the threat Gov. Stanley's program poses to the public schools is an appalling reality."

In a blatant disregard for civil liberties, the Virginia Gen. Assembly undertook measures to outlaw the NAACP as an organization and attempted to obtain the names of donors and members. While the vote was surprisingly close: 59 to 39 in the House of Delegates and 21 to 17 in the Senate, the measure passed.

In most Southern states it was decided to follow Virginia's lead and attempt to force the NAACP to make available its membership lists. Charges that the NAACP was communistic or subversive were routinely cited as a justification for such actions. The intent was clear. The NAACP's opponents wanted to destroy the organization by harassing its members with economic reprisal, and other forms of repression.

By 1957, the NAACP was tied up in some form of litigation in the states of Louisiana, Texas, Virginia, Tennessee, Arkansas, Georgia, South Carolina, and Florida, and, of course, Alabama where the NAACP was completely outlawed.

Arkansas made it unlawful for any state agency to employ members of the NAACP. This act along with other racially motivated laws, resulted in the firing of seven principals and 37 teachers by the Little Rock school board. Yes, the same Little Rock that would later emerge so prominently in the national spotlight.

In 1958, the Supreme Court ruled that it was unconstitutional for the state of Alabama to require the surrender of NAACP membership lists. Although Alabama refused to allow the NAACP to operate in the state for nine more years this ruling nonetheless signaled to other Southern states that similar action would be in direct conflict with the Supreme Court. While some Southern Attorney Generals would admit privately that the law and practice were unconstitutional they did serve to divert NAACP efforts from fighting segregation.

In 2002, as part of the Virginia Civil Rights Movement Video Initiative, Oliver W. Hill Sr. describes his involvement and memory of Virginia's massive resistance period and the attacks on the NAACP. Ronald E. Carrington, then President of Media Consultants Global, Inc. of Richmond, was the director-producer of the videotaping and conducted the interviews.

CARRINGTON: What were some of the legal — some of the litigation — what was some of the litigation you did against Massive Resistance?

HILL: Well, Massive Resistance, they passed a whole lot of crazy laws, one was [inaudible] and they started holding — appointed two committees, state legislative committees. Thompson Committee in the Senate and the Boatwright Committee in the House of Representatives. They would hold hearings, and they were trying their best — biggest thing they tried to do was find — get a list of the names of the NAACP members so they could harass them. And Henry — I mean not Henry — Tucker and I successfully warded off all of those. We carried them to court.

Senator Henry L. Marsh, III describes his recollection of how the Virginia General Assembly attempted to destroy the NAACP as part of their overall resistance to *Brown.* Marsh was a civil rights attorney in 1960s before he was elected by the city council as the first African American mayor of Richmond in 1977. He was then elected to the Senate of Virginia in 1991, where he continues to serve today, representing the 16th district, consisting of the city of Petersburg, Dinwiddie County, and parts of the city of Richmond, and, Chesterfield and Prince George counties. Again, Mr. Carrington is the moderator.

CARRINGTON: Was that the Boatwright Committee?

MARSH: Well, there were several committees, but the main one was a Committee on the Offenses Against the Administration of Justice, the best — the worst misnomer you could think of because they named the committee on the Offenses Against the Administration of Justice and they were prosecuting persons who were trying to promote justice.

CARRINGTON: And what would they do — if they got the list from the NAACP, if this committee got it, what were they going to do with it?

MARSH: Oh, people would lose their jobs. People would be ostracized in the community. It wasn't popular for white people to support desegregation or to support the NAACP. In fact, some white people suffered more than black people during the civil rights revolution because they were ostracized by their community and rejected by their own community. We, meaning black people, were actually freer than whites during that time because we weren't ostracized if we took a position on civil rights. We still had our respect in the community, and we had association with blacks and whites, whereas on the other hand they would be accepted by blacks but they wouldn't be accepted by their own race.

CARRINGTON: And what were some of the activist things you did in college?

MARSH: Well, as president of the student government I read in the newspaper that the General Assembly was having a joint session to change its law so that public funds could be, for the first time, diverted to private schools, sectarian, non-sectarian private schools, and I knew that was part of the plan to use public funds to support segregation, so I went down to the General Assembly and testified against the plan. I was the only student to go down of about 36 speakers. And so the next day the picture was in the newspaper and had me, was the first time I had any public notoriety for anything.

CARRINGTON: And what was the consequence to you being in the paper being this outspoken student leader?

MARSH: Well, the first, most memorable thing was being in the room where the joint session of the General Assembly was gathered. I'd never knew much about how it functioned. There were 140 people, men, white men, mostly elderly white men, in one room. In fact, I go to a lot of joint sessions now and I think about that. And I saw basically all the political might of the State of Virginia in one room, and there were 30 some people speaking urging them not to change the laws. And of course Oliver Hill was the star. He was representing the NAACP legal staff, and he was the anchor speaker, and he blasted the General Assembly for even considering these laws, and challenged them not to pass these laws, and it was a powerful voice. He was in his prime at that time. And it made a great impression on me.

The next day I read the paper and saw my picture and said — I was surprised. And when I went to school, Dr. Henderson, who was the President of Virginia Union, Dr. Thomas Henderson, called me into his office and said, I see you went down to speak at the General Assembly. He was a close friend — I didn't know it at the time, he was a close friend of Oliver Hill's. Apparently, Oliver had said something to him because he said, I see you went down to speak yesterday at the General Assembly.

I said, yes, sir.

He said, you should have talked to me. You can't — if you are going to represent the University.

And I was surprised. I said, oh, no, sir, I wasn't representing the university. I was representing the student body. You know, I'm president of the student government.

He smiled. He said, well, I got a lot of calls from trustees. He said, you know, we raise a lot of money from our supporters from the trustees.

I said, yes, sir.

He said, I got a lot of calls today, fortunately they were all favorable. They were impressed that one of our students would go down, he said, but you know, you should have checked with me before you went down.

So I looked at him, I said, well, Dr. Henderson, if I had asked you for permission to go down yesterday, what would you have told me?

And he looked at me and he smiled. He said, well, just ask me next time before you do it. He never answered but, you know, something in our stare that told me that he knew that if I went down again I wasn't going to ask him, and he didn't, didn't really want me to, but he was doing his job in case somebody had said something to him, and I had no intention of asking him for permission to go down to speak, you know, something that meant a lot to me.

Of all the massive resistance laws Virginia put into place, the least remembered today involves the Virginia Pupil Placement Act and its governing body, the Virginia Pupil Placement Board. The three-person board was appointed by the governor and oversaw all applications for student transfers in the state. Governor Thomas B. Stanley appointed Hugh V. White, superintendent of Nansemond County schools; Beverly H. Randolph, Jr., a lawyer from Charles City County; and Andrew A. Farley, a Danville newspaper owner and Chair of the Democratic Committee for the 5th Congressional District. All three men resided in Southside Virginia, the predominately rural, heavily black region of the state. The board's actions were immediately tested in the courts. Federal Judge Walter Hoffman in Norfolk held the Pupil Placement Act, "unconstitutional on its face" and considered the board's actions a veiled attempt to segregate all students in the state on the basis of race. Other federal courts agreed and refused to even recognize the legitimacy of the state Pupil Placement Board. They consistently held local school boards responsible for following federal court orders regarding integration. However, after the federal and state courts struck down many of the massive resistance laws in January 1959, the state board continued to operate and claim authority for assigning pupils statewide. This generated considerable confusion as local boards made decisions that the state board claimed needed state approval. By 1960 the boards legacy was to become the only remaining standing pillar in Virginia's massive resistance program. In 1959, the legislature passed measures to create a "freedom of choice" approach for pupil assignment, allowing localities to manage the application process; however, the state board's members refused to acknowledge the change. In February 1960 the board's members resigned in protest over the new law. A few months later the Federal Fourth circuit Court of Appeals ruled the State Pupil Placement Board illegal and unconstitutional. The state board had refused to follow local school board recommendations for integrated pupil assignments in Norfolk, and its members admitted under testimony that they could think of no situation in which a black child would be assigned to a white school. Over the first three years of its existence, the state board members had decided on 450,000 pupil placement applications and never allowed a single black child to be assigned to a white school.

The board continued to operate even though localities made the pupil assignment decisions. The board approved a transfer of black students to a white school for the first time in July 1960. After 1960, as Virginia assigned pupils under "freedom of choice," the state board approved the localities assignment plans routinely. While it may be the least known aspect of Virginia's resistance effort, the Pupil Placement Board lasted the longest. In spite of being declared unconstitutional by federal district courts almost from its inception, the board remained active until 1966; many years after other massive resistance laws cease to exist. Its effectiveness and survival lay in the way the law was written. This particular statute never referred to race in any way. It was no coincidence that with the Byrd organization in decline in 1954, they saw the *Brown V. Board of Education* ruling as an opportunity for rallying the troops and regaining control of Virginia politics for the next two decades.

As events transpired in 1958 and 1959, with the notable exception of those in Prince Edward County, most white parents in Virginia decided they would rather have token integration than have no public schools at all, with many writing letters to the governor demanding a return of their public schools. Sarah Eskridge in her well-documented article in the Virginia Historical

Society's quarterly magazine said, "Though maligned, sometimes ignored, and even found to be unconstitutional almost from its inception, the Pupil Placement Board still managed to stay afloat and to play a role in keeping Virginia's public schools segregated for nearly a decade. The board, despite its ultimate failure and descent into obscurity, remains of vital importance because it represents a crucial link between Virginia's past racial policies and the unspoken ones of the present." The Virginia General Assembly ended the tenure of the Pupil Placement Board officially on June 30, 1966.

As a side note, Eskridge's research and article, without saying directly, pointed out the cost of segregation to whites. She documents massive forgery and lying by the Pupil Placement Board not only to the black applicants but to themselves. She finds that they routinely and deliberately misidentified the distance of black applicants' homes to the nearest school. They repeatedly judged extremely bright, talented, and proven child scholars as, "not able to perform" to the academic white schools standards. Another ploy was to arbitrarily block black students from attending white schools because of supposedly poor social skills. Eskridge cites overwhelming evidence of the thousands of lies that the white men in charge of the Pupil Placement Board were perpetuating to maintain the walls of Virginia's carefully constructed massive resistance fortifications. One wonders what they though and felt in their hearts about their work and their habitual falsifications?

After 1960, Virginia went from massive resistance to school choice and had adopted a new tactic of minimal compliance employing gradual tokenism instead of total resistance. Nonetheless, with the NAACP's continue winning of legal battles the pace of school desegregation increased rapidly after 1964 with almost 1/4 of the black students attending integrated schools by 1966.

——— **THE PRESIDENT** ———

In the earliest days following the *Brown* decision, most political leaders from the Jim Crow South either held their tongue or gave relatively non-defining responses. Also of note was the benign neglect afforded the decision by the then President Eisenhower. Of course, as the rhetoric heated up more and more resistance to *Brown* began to build in the South. Some politicians saw the opportunity for political gain, some responded to their voting base, and others just walked away, with very few mustering the political courage to do the right thing.

> *...If he had gone to the nation on television and radio telling the people to obey the law and fall in line, the cause of desegregation would have been accelerated. Ike was a hero and he was worshiped. Some of his political capital spent on the racial clause would have brought the nation closer to the constitutional standards. Ike's ominous silence on the 1954 decision gave courage to the racist who decided to resist the decision ward by ward, precinct by precinct, town by town, and county by county.*

—Associate Justice William O. Douglas, from *The Court Years, 1939-1975: the autobiography of William O. Douglas.*

While Ike said little about *Brown,* he did act decisively in the Little Rock High School crisis. Since the Supreme Court has the power neither of the sword nor the purse, it relies upon its moral authority for enforcement of its decrees, or on the aid of the president and Congress. In the years following the two *Brown* decisions, however, neither the executive nor the legislative branches moved to assist the Court; President Dwight Eisenhower believed that the federal government should not interfere in state matters; additionally the southerners in Congress prevented any action by that body.

But, finally, President Eisenhower was forced to act. In the fall of 1957, the school board of Little Rock, Arkansas, agreed to a court order to admit black students to Central High School. The governor of the state, Orville Faubus, called out the National Guard to prevent the students from entering, and when the court again ordered the students admitted, Faubus withdrew the troops.

But when the students tried to enroll, a mob attacked the students and drove them off. Eisenhower could no longer sit by passively and watch federal authority flouted. He ordered a thousand paratroopers into Little Rock, put ten thousand Arkansas national guardsmen under federal control, and used the troops to protect the black students and to maintain order in and around the school.

Jean Edward Smith, distinguished biographer, released, what is sure to be the classic and defining work on Ike in February, 2012— *Eisenhower in War and Peace*. He characterizes the great man as more cunning and calculating than previously portrayed. He also fills in some of the gaps on Ike's feelings toward civil rights. He was elected the 34th President of the United States on November 4, 1952, by a sizable majority. His views on race are today mostly characterized as a reluctant supporter. Nonetheless, Smith shares that, in February 1953, soon after assuming the Presidency and 15 months before the *Brown* decision, Ike vowed to use every power of his office to end segregation in the District of Colombia and the armed forces. Even though Truman had made the pronouncement that the military would be integrated, Ike took office with two-thirds of the Army units still segregated. Under his leadership, by October 1954, there were no more segregated units.

——— DEFENDERS VS NAACP ———

High Street sits just off Main Street in downtown Farmville. It is a picturesque spot with tree-lined sidewalks and the columns of Longwood College on the south side of the street and the Methodist Church on the other. At this spot, Confederate Veterans and the Daughters Of The Confederacy erected a Confederate monument in October, 1900. On the south side of the monument are inscribed the names of the local *Confederate Heroes 1861 — Virginia — 1865* with the words *Defenders Of State Sovereignty* included as their legacy. The monument and the inscription are emphatic of those who fought for the Confederacy. The inscription pays homage to the independent streak that runs deep within the descendents of the English and Scotch-Irish who settled Prince Edward County. Publisher Wall recalls how the monument led to the naming of the Defenders:

"...someone noticed one day that the name *Defenders Of State Sovereignty* is on the Confederate monument up on High Street up yonder. I guess we just unconsciously lifted it from that."

The Defenders were a state-wide organization primarily focused on stopping integration in Virginia and the South. The Defenders of State Sovereignty and Individual Liberties, a grassroots political organization created in Petersburg in October 1954, was dedicated to preserving strict racial segregation in Virginia's public schools. A group of prominent Southside leaders formed the group following the *Brown* decision handed down on May 17, 1954. Opening chapters across the state and employing a variety of tactics, the Defenders rigorously confronted the *Brown* mandate, influencing the state commission that bestowed its blessing on the policy of massive resistance. When massive resistance was declared unconstitutional, the Defenders organized a Bill of Rights Crusade and protested in Richmond, but the group's support and influence was on the wane. It dissolved in 1967.

Author Bob Smith discusses this topic at length in his chapter on *The Defenders of State Sovereignty*: "What the Defenders could not stand for was as important as what they could stand for. ...defender speakers bore down on the theme that violence would mean ruin for the movement. Benjamin Muse, in his *Virginia's Massive Resistance*, makes the point that the Ku Klux Klan was completely discredited by the Defenders and that the White Citizens Councils that were beginning to spring up in other parts of the South were treated with great suspicion. ...With the instincts of some of the states ablest politicians working for them, these men realize that the slightest taint could doom the organization in the eyes of the proper Virginians they must count on for support."

Robert V. Crawford held the title of President of the Defenders Of State Sovereignty And Individual Liberties, Prince Edward County Chapter. The other officers joining Crawford in the Prince Edward County Chapter were: tobacco manufacturer J. W. Dunnington, Mayor W. C. Fitzpatrick of Farmville, Dr. S. C. Patteson, J. G. Bruce of the Board of Supervisors, former school board chairman Large, and of course, publisher Wall. This local chapter of the Defenders was led by leaders of the county and city government, as well as the editor of their leading newspaper. This alignment of government, local white organizations and the press is a significant reason why Prince Edward County's version of massive resistance went to the extreme of keeping their schools closed for five years and being able to hold the white community together for the entire 13-year struggle.

Crawford was in demand as a speaker around Virginia, especially at other Defender chapter meetings. Speaking before the Charlottesville Defenders one evening in the spring of 1955 he repeated his recurring and favorite themes. He chastised the leadership of the Southern ministry: "The worst obstacle we face in the fight to preserve segregated schools in the South is the white preacher." Eschewing violence he called for restraint, "Nothing could hurt our cause more than bloodshed," and went on to identify the real villains of the peace as, "International Socialist and Communist."

May 31, 1955, turned out to be a day that the various factions surrounding Virginia's massive resistance put their cards on the table. The Supreme Court handed down its decree calling on district courts to implement it school desegregation decision. Prince Edward County was ready with a follow-on move by 8 p.m. that evening. The Board of Supervisors voted to fund only the legal minimum for public schools ($150,000) which essentially was a vote for no public schools in the county. With this move they hoped to forestall and strengthen the Board of Education's plan to continue resisting any attempt for integrated education. "In theory, they were protecting the school board from the courts by denying its funds to do the Court's bidding." Actually, they were also tying the hands of a school board whose loyalty to segregation at all costs was not necessarily absolute. "They did not believe that the courts could force them to appropriate money for schools: this was to be the bedrock of the supervisor's legal position for years to come."

Maintaining their ever hovering presence, the Defenders, were out in full force and spoke forcefully at the Board of Supervisors meeting. The mood of the heavily Defender-dominated crowd at the meeting clearly was favorable to the action of cutting school appropriations. Supervisor John G. Bruce, himself an ardent Defender, offered his assessment of the situation, "there was nothing else we could have done even if we wanted to." As the *Richmond News-Leader* put it, "It could be said that the courts ruled that noon that Negroes must be admitted to Prince Edward public schools, to which the county responded at eight o'clock that there will be no public schools."

The very next day, June 1, 1955, Chairman Edward A. Carter representing the county supervisors released a statement that was intended to rally their white base of support.

> *I believe in equal but separate schools for the children of the South as interpreted by the Supreme Court in 1896. I believe in states' rights. I believe that if we are left to work this question of schools out we will evolve a system acceptable to both races and in the best interest of all children. I believe we, both races, should work for the mutual good of all. The citizens of Prince Edward have provided for Negro children a high school second to none in the country.*
> *I don't believe integration will serve to elevate or make better citizens of either race.*
> *In view of the above facts, we shall use every legal and honorable means to continue the high type of education we propose to give the children of both races in Prince Edward County.*
>
> —As reported by the *Richmond Times-Dispatch*, June 3, 1955

Chairman Carter's above statement does a good job of crystallizing the white position in the county, or at least the official, sanitized position. While at various times over the 13-year struggle some whites would raise objections to the closing of the public schools on both financial and moral grounds, they were generally few in number and not well organized. At this point in the summer of 1955 it's fair to say that the vast majority of whites in Prince Edward County were against an integrated school, and, while hardly anyone wanted to see the schools closed, they seemed ready to drive off that cliff as well. Carter's statement was also meant to remind both whites and blacks that the new Moton High School, at a cost of $800,000, had been serving black students since the fall of 1953. He went on to say, it had an auditorium, gymnasium, cafeteria, and every modern convenience a high school should have. To whites he was saying what more should Negro children be entitled to and for the blacks he was reminding them look we gave you what you asked for.

———— CAPITULATION ————

On January 19, 1959, (Robert E. Lee's birthday, coincidentally) the massive resistance laws were struck down by the courts in two separate decisions. Governor Almond's immediate response was a ranting speech the next day, which began with the words, "To those whose purpose and design is to blend and amalgamate the white and Negro race and destroy the integrity of both races . . . ." He continued for three minutes with similar fulminations, ending with, "as Governor of this state, I will not yield to that which I know to be wrong and will destroy every rational semblance of public education for thousands of the children of Virginia. I call upon the people of Virginia to stand firmly with me in this struggle . . ."

Later, Almond would look back and refer to this moment as, "that damn speech." At that time however, Senator Byrd lauded the words, saying, "The notable speech of Governor Almond last night will further stiffen the resistance." However, Almond's resistance was not stiffened for long, perhaps because it was he who would go to jail and not Senator Byrd, if the orders of the court were defied. It only took nine days for Governor Almond to once again address the General Assembly regarding integration. With Byrd in attendance, the governor went on to explain that due to the courts recent decision he would be forced to end massive resistance. Though sounding defiant, Almond capitulated and asked the legislature to repeal the massive resistance legislation.

Almond organized a commission headed by Senator Mosby Perrow to recommend plans to integrate the schools. On February 2, 1959, 21 black students were formally integrated in

Norfolk and Arlington schools. On March 31, 1959, the Perrow Commission issued its report, which began with an outline of the history of the massive resistance laws. It then stated: "The truth is that neither the General Assembly nor the Governor has the power to overrule or nullify the final decrees of the federal courts in the school cases." The report went on to propose, "measures to bring about the greatest possible freedom of choice for each locality and each individual." This new report was, for all intents and purposes, a return to the original Gray report.

With the Governor's submission so ended one of the most divisive periods in Virginia's history. State wide massive resistance was dead, but delay and obstruction on a smaller, more local level would continue for decades. While many in the state were relieved, the Defenders of Prince Edward County would not be swayed.

The Supreme Court chose to leave the task of desegregation in the hands of the local school authorities and district courts. They ordered the courts to proceed with desegregation of public schools "with all deliberate speed." These famous words issued in 1955 meant little since the white resistance of integration resulted in nine more years of struggle before Prince Edward County would see integrated public schools. And even then it was only a few whites who joined a mostly black public school as the majority of the whites fled to the private Prince Edward Academy. Today the Prince Edward County school system is about 50% white and 50% black; and the Prince Edward Academy (renamed the Fuqua School) now admits blacks and has a policy of non-discrimination. It is not correct to say that all is forgiven and now peace reigns in Prince Edward County, because that clearly is not true. One need only spend a little time with the county residences that lived through the school closing to see, hear and feel their hurt. Most keep it buried, some have forgiven, some are learning to forgive, and others are still stuck on hate. However, no one who did not live through the strike, school closings and the County's half hearted initial attempt to resume public education should judge them. Yes Virginia had a more "genteel" way of holding their black population in check and there were numerically far less lynching's in Virginia than Mississippi, yet one might debate how genteel is denying a young person their education for five years?

Chapter Six

THEY CLOSED THEIR SCHOOLS

Cowardice asks the question: is it safe? Expediency asks the question: is it political? Vanity asks the question: is it popular? But conscience asks the question: is it right? And there comes a time when one must take a position that is neither safe, nor political, nor popular — but one must take it simply because it is right.

—Dr. Martin L. King, "Remaining Awake Through a Great Revolution," this speech was delivered at the National Cathedral, Washington, D.C., on March 31, 1968

Time Line for Chapter Six
They Closed Their Schools
(1959–1963)

1959, January 19. The Supreme Court of Virginia decreed the Norfolk school closing unconstitutional.

1959, January 28. Gov. Almond announced the end of massive resistance after the state and federal court rulings go against school closings.

1959, May 1. Prince Edward County was ordered to integrate its schools, the county instead closed its entire public school system.

1959, June 2. The board of supervisors of Prince Edward County announced its decision not to appropriate money to operate public schools for the coming year.

1960. *To Kill a Mockingbird* by Harper Lee published in 1960. The film *To Kill a Mockingbird* was released two years later.

1960. James J. Kilpatrick debates the Rev. Dr. Martin Luther King Jr. in one of the first televised debates on civil rights.

1961, August. Prince Edward Foundation learned that their funding scheme was illegal. Judge R. Lewis ruled that the state and local tuition grants as applied in Prince Edward County were invalid.

1962, September. The black children of Prince Edward County started their third year with no public school.

1963. A summer teaching program was carried out by 36 Queens College students. The New York teachers were sponsored by funds raised nationally through the United Federation of Teachers. More than 400 Negro children participated in the program of remedial instruction in fundamental academic skills.

Chapter Six
THEY CLOSED THEIR SCHOOLS
(1959–1963)

The "unthinkable", has happened, here in Virginia…

—J. Kenneth Morland, *The Tragedy of Public Schools: Prince Edward County, Virginia*, A Report for the Virginia Advisory Committee to the United States Commission on Civil Rights, Lynchburg, Virginia, January 16, 1964

At the Robert Russa Moton Museum when you walk through Gallery V, *They Closed Their Schools*, you will learn the reaction by Prince Edward County elected officials to the *Brown* decision was to abolish all public schools. Of course across the County individual reactions ran the gamut, from hard, cold political decision making to raw emotional outbursts. At the most personal level, feelings were hurt, anger was palatable on both sides and lives were irreparably harmed; with some scars lingering for generations. Through the pictures, videos and testimonials in Gallery V you can begin to understand how it must have felt to be part of a community that said no to public schools for five years.

The lead story in the September 22, 1958, issue of *Time* magazine was devoted to segregation and the public school closings—*The Gravest Crisis*. At this point, implementation of the *Brown* decision was looking grim and nowhere was it grimmer than in Prince Edward County. The cover of this particular issue had a picture of Virginia, Governor Almond adjacent to the Virginia State Seal "SIC SEMPER TYRANNIS," superimposed over a large confederate flag in the background. Once again the confederate flag resurfaces as a symbol of Southern defiance of federal authority. The article discusses how segregationist fought back hard against *Brown*. Compliance to the 1954 *Brown* decision looked no closer to actual implementation in 1958 than it had for the last 100 years. Here are some excerpts from the *Time* magazine article that portray the confusion and divisiveness that became the hallmark of this period.

Closing down the schools, Editor Jonathan Daniels of the Raleigh, N.C. News & Observer once told fellow Southerners, is "something beyond secession from the Union; [it] is secession from civilization." Last week Virginia's Governor J. Lindsay Almond Jr. and Arkansas' Governor Orval Faubus ordered certain public schools closed in answer to a Supreme Court ruling that Little Rock's Central High School must proceed immediately with its program of integration.

The essence of the Supreme Court ruling (see The Supreme Court) was that the law does not retreat from violence. Yet it was through fully arrayed state laws that Virginia's Almond closed the Warren County High School at Front Royal and Arkansas' Faubus closed all four high schools in Little Rock. The irony is that the court's ruling was brought about by and is the answer to the violence built up a year ago in Faubus' wild bid for political power. This year the South's defense is one of legal stratagems. And though both federal and state governments are pledged to avoid violence, few could doubt that the cause of integration is far worse off than it was last year.

This fact, more than any other, pointed up the need for a change in the Administration's position. Dwight Eisenhower, honorably intending to stay above the battle and base his case on the enforcement of law and order, had overlooked the fact that the U.S. needed moral leadership in fighting segregation. Without it, Southern moderates had no place to go. Without it, some of the most patient, effective integration programs were weakened as Southern die-hards mobilized their own

> *legal resources to fight the battle for segregation in the name of states' rights.*
> *It was time for the President to perceive that law enforcement must be accompanied by active effort in behalf of the principle behind the law. It was likewise time for sober Southerners to realize the enormity of the school-closing acts.*

You can sense in the article that a tipping point had been reached. One way or the other, the integration issue was coming to a head. Meanwhile, Eisenhower remained stoic, as the country, and in particular the South, was about ready to boil over. Violence was always there hanging over blacks like a ghost haunting their memory, and sometimes it was offered as an implied or a direct threat by whites. In many ways, 1958 was the year that the back of segregation was broken. While Little Rock captured the headlines, sleepy little Prince Edward County just dug in and continued to suffer on with no public schools. As other parts of the South and Virginia were starting to move forward, Prince Edward County was stuck in this time warp of their own making. They might not have been forgotten, but they were certainly left to struggle on their own as a backwater, and an anomaly of the civil rights struggle.

——— NAACP IN THE FIGHT OF ITS LIFE ———

Time and time again the NAACP found itself headed back into court to force the South to comply with the court decree's and integrate their schools. On June 2, 1959, as if it were routine business, the board of supervisors of Prince Edward County announced its decision not to appropriate money to operate public schools for the coming year.

> *The action taken today ... Has been determined upon only after the most careful and deliberate study over the long period of years since the schools in this county were first brought under the force of federal court decree. It is with*

the most profound regret that we have been compelled to take this action ... it is the fervor and hope of this board ... That we may in due time be able to resume the operation of public schools in this county upon a basis acceptable to all the people of the county.

—Minutes of the board of supervisors of Prince Edward County, Virginia, on June 2, 1959

Clearly the county was making good on its threat to close public schools rather than see them integrated. In some ways, Prince Edward County was coming to the party late. In September, 1958, under state law some 12,000 children were locked out of schools in Norfolk, Charlottesville, and Front Royal. In January 1959, the Court struck down the massive resistance laws passed by the Virginia legislature in 1956, and Gov. Almond threw in the towel admitting that massive resistance was now a dead issue. By February, 1959, in three Virginia communities, some 30 Negro children were now attending formally white schools. One might think that the crisis in Prince Edward County would be a moot point, since it appeared that massive resistance had started to crumble. The Prince Edward County case now turned on whether the courts could force them to fund public schools at all. This issue emerged as the central point in the next battleground between the NAACP and the county. In a pivotal decision made by Judge Sterling Hutchinson in 1957, no timetable was set for desegregating Prince Edward schools. His decision was overturned by an appellate court, and then, in a second look, Judge Hutchinson set the date of desegregation for Prince Edward as 1965. Fully 10 years from the time the Supreme Court implementation decision had been handed down. However, this decision, too, was overturned by an appellate court that was at great pains to point out that the county had not taken a single positive step toward eventual desegregation. The court then ordered desegregation to proceed the following September. The Board of Supervisors reacted with their mutual destruction plan at their June 1959 meeting. Many county residents could not bring themselves to believe that the public schools would ever close. The county school board argued that the supervisor's action was premature. No Negro application for attendance at any countywide school had been received by this time. Based on this, the school board's attorney thought that they had secured at least another year's delay. He further said, "with appropriations on a month-to-month basis anyway, what would the county lose by continuing its public schools until the last moment?"

———— C. D. G. MOSS ————

A few folks were doing their best to rescue the public schools in Prince Edward County. Longwood College professor C. D. G. Moss was a strong advocate of maintaining public schools in Prince Edward County. He came up with the idea of collaborating with Negro leaders to effect some sort of agreement that would permit the schools to continue in operation. Dr. Moss enlisted the help of Rev. Griffin and Willie Reed to represent the black community. The basic outline of the plan was to see if the Negro community would accept a three-year moratorium on pressing for desegregation of the public schools in return for the county's acceptance, in principle, of the Supreme Court decision and the establishment of a biracial committee charged with preparing for the eventual integration. The proposal received enough interest from the governor's office that Dr. Moss had a closed-door meeting with Gov. Almond in his office during the first week of September. While Dr. Moss intended to bring some black representatives from the county to the meeting, however representatives of the governor's office indicated, "that it would not be wise at this point for Negroes to be included in the Richmond conference." The immediate result of Dr. Moss's meeting with the governor was at least a tentative acceptance to continue with the understanding that the good doctor would now approach the white powers to be in Prince Edward County. Dr. Moss's next step was to meet with Barry Wall, who also happened to be a fellow member of the Episcopal Church. Characteristically, Wall was to the point: "Barry said that he wouldn't sit down with Griffin and Madison to discuss anything. We asked him if he would discuss with other Negroes the idea of public schools. When we pressed them on what Negroes, he wouldn't name one specifically." Wall went on to tell Dr. Moss that further talks seem pointless. Again, in his direct style, he pointed out, "they said Griffin would use his influence to keep schools clear of integration for three years. I told him I wasn't interested because if we were going to integrate the schools we'd do it now rather than three years from now. I also asked how he knew they Griffin would be able to control the situation." In the end the attempt by Dr. Moss led to nothing.

Meanwhile the private school foundation was busily preparing to open an all-white private school for the white children of Prince Edward County in September 1959. Throughout this period, Wall maintained constant pressure on the county through the *Farmville Herald* stories and his editorials. He felt that the county had the opportunity to do a great service to the greater South by rendering the Supreme Court's *Brown* decision historically ineffective. Wall also felt strongly that he need not have to test the temper of the community because he was clearly in tune with the white residents of Prince Edward County. He was especially confident that he could speak without hesitation for that part of the community that wrote the rules and articulated its public policy. When the Board of Supervisors refused to fund the public schools, editor Wall had exhorted the people of the county to "stand steady" in the August 7, 1959 *Farmville Herald*. This left some observers to wonder whether Wall was more the creator of that opinion or its principal cheer leader. Wall was often elevating the controversy beyond race, in both private and public discussions: "I see that thing as the usurpation of the rights and powers of the states. If you take this principle out of it, I have no interest in the matter at all."

In one area, Wall provided a real value to all the citizens of Prince Edward County. He repeatedly called for calm and courtesy in dealings between the black and white residents of the county, and above all counseled against violence. He also firmly articulated the point that this issue needed to be resolved in the courts, not on the streets, and yet felt assured that no court would force county residents to appropriate money to run schools. Over and over again, Wall repeated his advice to the county to "stand steady" meaning to both resist any temptation towards a rashness or violence and maintain their conviction for segregated schools. The Defenders were expecting school closings to be adopted throughout the South and were both mystified and disappointed when no school system followed the Prince Edward lead. And in fact no wide spread school closings would take place throughout the South during the entire *Brown* crisis. That left Prince Edward County alone and isolated to endure five years of no public education.

——— WHITES CREATE THE ACADEMY ———

Of course it is one thing to say that you would create a private school system and another thing to actually educate 1,500 white children. In May 1959, the Prince Edward Foundation had $11,000 in cash, $200,000 in three-year-old pledges, no teachers under contract, no school buildings, no school buses, nor any of the other necessities of a school system. The person the county chose to pull a private school system together in short order was Roy Pearson, an executive retired from Standard Oil Company. Pearson had settled in Farmville as his retirement community, but was appointed to the school board in 1957. By all accounts Pearson was an energetic, persuasive leader who could make things happen.

A visiting journalist described the "outpouring of community zeal" that whites exhibited toward the creation of the academy. Whites across the socioeconomic strata were galvanized to help in any way available to them. Local churches were solicited for building space for the school. The school needed chairs, desks, wastebaskets, blackboards, fire extinguishers, and on and on, but bit by bit almost entirely on a voluntary basis all of these needs were met. In one example Robert Redd, an assistant of Roy Pearson, remembers having about a week to make desktop attachments for some 600 folding chairs. "He set up an assembly line production and telephone volunteers, lawyers, salesmen, carpenters, for work in day and night shifts. All 600 chairs now had desktop attachments for the start of school." The creation of the Academy attracted attention across the state and country. Donations came from not only Virginia, but throughout the South. A Silver Springs, Florida, man sent along 250 pounds of used books. Used school buses were donated. One Chesterfield, VA, resident loaded his truck with books and drove it to Farmville as a gift to the new private school. By mid-August, the library of Prince Edward Academy had received 3,000 books and an unspecified amount of cash, much of it from outside the county. Sen. Byrd made public statements supporting the fundraising effort and declared that all contributions would be tax-deductible. On September 10, the foundation had a formal opening of their new school system at Farmville's white-only movie theater—the State Theatre. The Academy had enrolled nearly every white child in the county. They would be spread out over 16 buildings scattered throughout the county, mostly in churches and a few former homes, stores and even a blacksmith shop. The teachers were basically those same teachers that had been in the public school system. While the white children would now have their segregated education, the black children were left with no public education at all.

Back in June, in response to the action of the Board of Supervisors, the Negro community held a meeting on June 17, 1959. 200 Negroes packed in the New Baptist Church in downtown Farmville and heard speaker after speaker whose main purpose, according to W. Lester Banks, was to reassure them "that things were not as bad as they seemed." Oliver Hill was there and talked at length about the vote and the chance that Negroes had to unseat the offending supervisors. He also held out hope that additional court action might prevent the schools from closing. When Rev. Griffin delivered his remarks, he chose to speak on the injustices suffered by the Negroes and the necessity of standing up to them. While the main point of the meeting was a Negro equivalent of a "stand steady" message the reality was, there were no plans in place, nor were there any signs of a plan to educate black children in the coming fall. In Bob Smith's book he points out, "the truth was that the Negroes by and large could not bring themselves to believe that the whites would go this far or that the courts would permit them to go this far." Further he wrote, "The Negro plaintiffs had, after all, won the case...." Dr. N. P. Miller, summed up the feelings of the Negro community during this period, "I think that they were in full good hope that the schools would open."

Many in the community were initially concerned about their rising seniors. Most of them never imagined the schools would stay closed for more than a year, and so they worried that this group would most directly be affected by the closing of the schools. Kittrell College near Henderson, North Carolina and other institutions sponsored by the African Methodist Episcopal Church offered to educate any and all Negroes that the county could send their way. The school asked for half the normal tuition for the Prince Edward students, but made it clear that any who came would be educated even if the money could not be raised. In September, a 20-car motorcade, with 68 students, headed toward Kittrell College in North Carolina and became a visible sign of hope for the black community.

However, this positive sign was seriously negated as the county's Negro teachers began to disperse looking for jobs to support their families. The NAACP seemed to focus more on increasing voter registration than in dealing with the education crisis. There were some in the Negro community that felt the only way their children would be educated in the coming school year would be in a private school and they would need to collaborate with the whites to make that happen. Back in June, the foundation had announced that it would help the black community establish private schools of their own if they were interested. Rev. Griffin for one responded coolly that Negroes had no immediate plans other than waiting for the due process of law. In fact the foundation had gone so far, on paper at least, to create something called Southside Schools in an attempt to educate the county's black population. However, this attempt was doomed for a number of reasons:

- The effort had no enthusiastic backing among the real leaders of the Negro community; Rev. Griffin went straight to the point: "How can segregated private schools meet the need when segregated public schools were not satisfactory?"
- Blacks were leery of being manipulated. They were concerned that any support by them for private schools would either be used to continue segregation outright, or

enable the white private schools to use the available state public school building funds at their expense.
- The NAACP was strongly against blacks joining private schools, it was felt that private schools would undermine their position with the courts.

In December, the idea of private school for blacks was headed for a showdown. The NAACP, among others, had organized a Christmas party for the school age Negro children of the county. The party also became a rallying point around the NAACP's legal action and their opposition to Southside Schools. Oliver Hill spoke to the children and parents. In the long term, he said, blacks attending Southside School was a bad idea. "Some benighted individuals are trying to entice you away from your rights by promising you a private school.... Christ made the supreme sacrifice. All you will lose will be one or two years of Jim Crow education. But at the same time, in your leisure, you can gather more in basic education that you would get in five years of Jim Crow schools... A private school is being organized for one of two reasons... Either white schools are failing, need bolstering, need money, or because the white people are afraid of the pitiless spotlight of public opinion on Prince Edward."

It is of note, that Hill's remarks offered the first hint from a black leader that schools might be closed for multiple years. The idea that Negroes at that time would be able to educate themselves in their leisure time was a rather self-serving remark. Clearly the real intention was to keep the faithful, united around the NAACP's chosen legal course. Unfortunately, the cruel irony for many black children was that they would have way too much leisure time over the next four years. In the December 29 issue of the *Herald*, editor Wall spoke about the Christmas party: "The NAACP offers speeches to the adults, candy and nuts for the children they have rendered school-less, and the Southside Schools, Inc., directed by sincere white citizens, offers leadership and established education for the children. The NAACP is controlled in New York; the Southside Schools, Inc., is operated by Prince Edward people. A decision has to be made by the Negro people of Prince Edward."

Some white leaders had the idea of sending letters to every black home in the county inviting participation of the Negro community in a private Southside School. In the end, the Southside School got a total of one application, which forced the Southside group to postpone its efforts on behalf of the Negro children. The idea of a private school for the black children of Prince Edward County would come again, but the next time, its author would have the trust and favor of the black community. However, this would only transpire after four long years of no public education.

A conflict arose between the foundation and the county school board. The foundation wanted the school board to sell them the white high school building as surplus. At the heart of this request was the Board of Supervisors' belief that public schools in Prince Edward County would likely never restart unless the Supreme Court reversed its desegregation decision, an event that they thought was unlikely. When all was said and done, five of the six members of the school board walked out of the meeting and resigned from the school board rather than sell public schools. The school board, on the other hand, believed that closing the public schools was only a temporary measure. The fallout included the release of a report by the five resigning members outlining their decision to resign and their conviction and commitment to public schools for all. Here is their press release:

In its decision the school board has been guided by the fundamental belief that education must be provided for all the school age children of the entire county. Anything short of this we regard as contrary to the best interest of all of us in the long run. As we know that educated citizens are absolutely essential to the very existence of democracy in local affairs as well as in state and national ones. If the community leaves uneducated any large portion of its citizens, because they cannot afford its cost, or for any other reason, it inevitably creates for itself enormous problems in welfare, delinquency, crime, and unemployment. It means numbers of illiterate laborers which are difficult to absorb labor force. Today business and industries are demanding a higher level of training from employees than ever before.

Unless some new system of education for all can take over the whole job of the public schools and have its cost guaranteed in a reasonable manner, we fear the economic consequences to the county. This year, for example, when the people of the county have paid all of the cost of education in the county, we have seen at least half a million dollars not coming to the economic life of the county which did come in earlier years. We refer specifically here to two items. In the past we have received approximately $400,000 from the state for operation of public schools. Also in the past the large taxpaying corporations in the county have paid approximately $100,000 in local taxes. This year, this money did not come to the county in any form.

All of this occurred in April of 1960 and it had a profound and lasting effect on the citizens of Prince Edward County—black and white. After all, these were men of substance, highly regarded, and leaders in their community who were rejecting the direct wishes of the foundation. Nonetheless the county supervisors "stayed the course" and appointed a new school board that would sing the tune of the foundation and support their actions for the dismantlement of public schools in the county. Inexplicably, the foundation made no new efforts to buy the public school buildings. Instead, the foundation announced that it was launching a drive for an additional $300,000 to build an academy with at least 26 classrooms, to be ready by September 1960. Beyond just the idea for more classrooms or buildings, this campaign represented another escalation in the fight for segregated schools by adding this symbolic measure of permanence to the private school system.

So what was going on in the minds of the school board members who resigned? One of them was Lester Andrews. It seems fair to say while none of the original board members supported integrated schools, they all supported public schools for all, and when faced with the prospect of no school, they were much more interested in public education than they were in segregation. Lester Andrews, was a solid unpretentious man with who was highly respected in the community. He said, "when I was growing up, I had patches on my pants. I went to high school, public high school, and then I went to Hampden Sydney for a year and quick to go to work. If it hadn't been for public schools, I wouldn't be here." Lester felt enormous pressure to comply with the wishes of the academy foundation. He received numerous calls from friends who wanted to know why he was being obstinate and leaving schools boarded up when their children and others needed the buildings. Others wanted to be reassured that the board in general and Lester in particular really did believe that segregation was best for all. He began to sense bitterness in his daily relations with his peer business community members. Some folks started to avoid him. He recalls his son coming to him and saying, "Daddy if you sell the schools I can go to a party. Period."

The academy never was able to purchase a single public school building in Prince Edward County. Nonetheless, the effectiveness of the foundation's private schools was both a source of pride to the white community and chagrin to the county blacks and NAACP. In many substantive ways, their success represented one of the fundamental reasons that the Prince Edward County school closings went on for five long years. Both sides hardened their positions around their fundamental beliefs—segregation or integration. One might question exactly how successful the foundation schools were, but children attended class every day, and by most measures they were being educated to at least minimal standards.

For the first year of the foundation, school operations were financed entirely on a voluntary contribution basis. County taxes had been lowered proportionately; County residents were encouraged to pay the difference directly to the foundation. During the second year, the state tuition grant law kicked in additional money through the tuition-based private school funding provision. The foundation established tuitions of $240 for the lower schools and $265 for the upper school and an overall operating budget of $348,500. The state tuition grants plus local grants approved by the Board of Supervisors enabled parents to come to within $15 per child per year of being covered. Under this arrangement white private schools could continue indefinitely. The only link missing in the private school plan was school buildings. The refusal of the school board to sell the white high school forced the foundation to go to the public at large with a $300,000 fund drive to build the upper school of Prince Edward Academy. This is one of the reasons the foundation and the Board of Supervisors leaned so heavily on the school board to sell the high school.

An indication of just how committed the foundation and most of the white County community was to private schools can be seen in their actions to attain a proper high school for Prince Edward Academy. They went to the public at large with a $300,000 fund drive to build the upper school. The school construction drew heavily upon local free labor and the completed building, while valued at $400,000 it had only cost the foundation $240,000. The foundation proudly proclaimed that 90% of the contributions were from county people. However in Bob Smith's book he indicates: "This is not to say that 90% of the contributions came from within the county, however. A good source told me that one contribution of $50,000 to the building fund was received from New York."

The rosy financial picture for the foundation ended abruptly in August 1961 when federal Judge Oren Lewis ruled that the state and local tuition grants as applied in Prince Edward County were invalid. The judge pointed out that the public schools of Prince Edward County were closed, so the state's freedom of choice program offering pupils either public schools or tax paid grants to attend private schools was not operative in Prince Edward. Judge Lewis hinted that if the County reopened its public schools, it might well be eligible once again for the grants.

The foundation rose to the challenge with editor Wall leading the charge. He announced that $200,000 fund drive would be launched to provide scholarships so that no white Prince Edward child would be denied a foundation education. In October 1961, the foundation was beginning its third year of operation. Lower school pupils were still being housed in churches and other buildings spread around the county while the upper grades were enjoying their new Prince Edward Academy High School. As the foundation pressed its case for contributions both within the county, across the state and at national venues they consistently portrayed themselves as the beacon for segregation in the South—if they stood, the South would stand, and if they fell, the South would fall. While this marketing ploy undoubtedly contributed significant dollars to their cause it also contributed a hardening of the position within the black community.

By positioning themselves as the best hope of Southern segregationism, they also spurred blacks and NAACP to fight that much harder for a win in this pivotal case. Prince Edward County was visited by delegations from throughout the South to learn how they too could create private schools and sidestep segregation. And members of the foundation were called upon to visit and speak to all manners of groups throughout the South— with delegations from all of the deep southern states visiting the academy. They visited Atlanta and spoke to the Georgia Legislature at the height of that state's convulsion over school desegregation. At one visit to cosmopolitan Atlanta, Roy Pearson told the Atlanta audience that he, "judged that it would have no more trouble than Prince Edward in setting up private schools—except that it would need more of them."

The foundation drove home their message—over and over— during these visits by and to their Southern brethren. The foundation officials took great pains to explain their position. "They imagine themselves not so much stemming the black tide—although the image lay behind their words and thoughts— but turning back the minions of the federal oligarchy. They were not white supremacists really, but states' righters. Their interest was not so much in society as in law. The central issue of the Prince Edward dispute—in their view—was not whether Southern public schools should be segregated, but whether the courts could force the county to appropriate money to operate public schools at all. If they could, editor Wall warned solemnly again and again, Americans lived under true judicial tyranny."

It should be noted that, as the years dragged on, no other state or local community decided to follow Prince Edward's lead and close their public schools and create private white academies. In the middle of the five-year school closing, Attorney Gen. Robert Kennedy pointedly noted that the only places on Earth not providing free public education were Communist China, North Vietnam, Sarawak, British Honduras and Prince Edward County, Virginia. The Prince Edward County case has become known nationally and internationally as a stalemate by which the United States and the South would both be judged. Efforts were being made by the Kennedy administration to see that the schools reopened. In April, 1961 the administration attempted to intervene in the court case on behalf of the NAACP. Attorney Gen. Robert Kennedy, asked the court to bar state support for any public school in the state of Virginia until Prince Edward County schools were reopened on a desegregated basis. However, Judge Lewis rejected the Kennedy administration's effort to intervene in the suit. If the Kennedys were going to help, they were going to have to do it through direct action. Chapter 7, *Bound for Freedom* discusses the Free school started by the Kennedy administration.

———— THE BLACK RESPONSE ————

A number of circumstances arose to bog down the NAACP's attempt for a speedier legal remedy. There was the retirement of Judge Hutchinson and the delay waiting for his successor. And, then there was the NAACP's intense suspicion of state courts and healthy fear of being bottled up in endless legal wrangling at this level, since state courts were viewed as the least favorable to their cause. This compelled them to do everything possible stay within the federal court system. Also, the first stop in any Virginia state court would have been Judge Joel Flood, a relative of Senator Byrd. Judge Flood once threatened to place Reverend Griffin in jail for failure to produce NAACP records, which in the NAACP's mind clearly portrayed Judge Flood as a hostile judge. Around the time of the first anniversary of the school closings, in September, 1960, the NAACP filed a supplemental complaint with the new district judge. The burden of the complaint was that the schools of Prince Edward were remaining closed in defiance of the state constitution, which required the General Assembly to maintain a system of schools. Then, in January 1961, the NAACP filed a further supplemental complaint attacking the use of public funds—state and local tuition grants—for the foundation's private schools.

In March 1962, the State Supreme Court ruled that the supervisors could not be compelled to appropriate money to run the schools. The issue of the state's responsibilities lay undecided. In July, Judge Lewis handed down his decision: "The schools of Prince Edward could not remain closed while the schools elsewhere in the state were open; the county could not use tuition grants of a State or local nature until the situation was corrected. Judge Lewis gave the county until September to present a workable plan for compliance." The county responded that it would follow state procedure under the pupil placement act. Judge Lewis decided to stay execution of his order pending that county's appeal.

What did all of this mean? Delay, additional legal expenses for the NAACP and the continuation of the Prince Edward County school closing disaster. The appellate Fourth Circuit Court of Appeals held the case until August 1963 before they finally reversed Judge Lewis. The court held that the judge should have waited for the state of Virginia determination regarding the meaning of the Virginia Constitution. Until the Fourth Circuit concluded, it was impossible for federal courts to tell the state to operate schools or to forbid the county from using whatever tuition grants were available to it. Three years of legal effort in federal court resulted in the NAACP ending up right back where it started. While the NAACP refused to take action through state courts, the county decided that that was in their best interest. In December 1963, the state supreme court ruled that the state had no legal obligation to operate the Prince Edward schools. "In a blistering dissent, Chief Justice Eggleston labeled the decisions quote a clear invitation to the federal court to step in." In short it was the United States Supreme Court now, or nothing, for the Negro children of Prince Edward.

——— A STREET FIGHT ———

Meanwhile the push for civil rights on the national front was moving in a different direction. On February 1, 1960, in North Carolina a group of agricultural and technical college students touched off a wave of national sit-ins when they attempted to be served at a downtown Greensboro lunch counter. In one stroke, the focus of the civil rights effort moved from the courtroom to the street.

With Reverend Griffin's blessing, some young preachers of the Negro community staged sit-ins in Farmville during the spring of 1963. The Student Nonviolent Coordinating Committee brought in youthful organizers, and all that summer they marched in the streets of Farmville carrying placards, and some of them were arrested. There was also a boycott by blacks of the Farmville stores. Griffin felt that the boycott was not successful and was not the answer to achieving segregated schools.

In 1951, one of the original strikers, James Samuel Williams, was finishing up his studies to become a clergyman and was very involved in the downtown Farmville sit-ins. He was instrumental in organizing and participating in the sit-ins. Williams preached in Prince Edward County on Sundays when he was home from school, and Reverend Griffin was counting on Williams to take on considerable responsibility in his church upon graduation. But, Williams really found his footing in 1962 as chairman of the voters registration league of Prince Edward County. While he was skeptical at first, it turned out he had a knack for the job. In his own church in the Green Bay section of the county, he went from a handful of registered voters to 100% registered. In the spring of 1963 he convinced Griffin to support staging demonstrations over the spring and summer. An April 1 action was scheduled with Negro students from Hampton Institute in Virginia planning sit-ins at the local theater and lunch counters on Main Street. They failed to gain entrance on this occasion and again in July they were denied access. The demonstrations took the form of picketing with placards calling for open public schools and equal job opportunity in Farmville's business establishments.

The weekend of July 27 saw a total of 33 people arrested in demonstrations, some of them for parading without a permit and some for singing in front of the white Baptist church on Main Street during services on Sunday. Williams was one of the 22 Negroes arrested in front of the church and he was the only one who failed to go limp upon the signal. That was Williams. He had an aversion to this nonviolent technique. "I'd rather walk where I am going, to jail just like anyplace else." In August, James Samuel Williams, was sentenced to 12 months in prison—six-month suspended on good behavior for three years—for interrupting and disturbing an assembly for the worship of God, which is one of the oldest statues on the states penal books.

Residents of Prince Edward County generally treated each other cordially on the streets of Farmville and this included most of their other casual interactions. Reverend Griffin once described the strife associated with the schools, "as a dispute among gentlemen." Visitors, particularly those from the North, often expressed their surprise at the surface cordiality between the races. Helen Baker, a Friends field worker, noted her surprise at what she found when she came to the county. "I came expecting all sorts of strife and tension and I have found instead a great restraint and an unfailing courtesy. These people are not gun-toting bums; they are gentlemen." Of course the Negro in America has had a very long history of silence. Ms. Miller, a highly respected Negro leader, felt that the relations between the races had deteriorated during the period of the school struggle: "We don't say everything we think. I don't say everything I believe. Because we are silent doesn't mean that we like it." Helen Baker went on to say that it did not take her long to see behind the curtain of cordiality: "we daily exchange all of the pleasant courtesies as we meet in the stores, post office, or the streets. These pleasant greetings and our menial contacts in services are only points of contact, so that there is absolutely no communication between the races about any of the problems which have thoroughly upset our lives here. We laugh in passing about the weather as if we are each unaware of the loads in our hearts because of the children's absence. We buy sell and bargain together forever pushing back the truth—pushing back the bridge that might unite us—the bridge; the suffering, the yearning in the hearts of all of the people in this county to find a real solution to this crisis."

While each side understood little about the other's true wants and needs, it seems fair to say that since whites had access and control of the radio, TV and newspapers, their positions were better known to the blacks. And those blacks who worked as domestics in white homes had firsthand knowledge of the true feelings of their white bosses. It is also fair to say that, to a large degree, the white community had no clue what the blacks wanted or felt during this stressful period. Bob Smith points this out in his chapter on the *Crippled Generation* that the time honored communication process that whites were relying on broke down almost immediately after the school strike in 1951. Whites had always relied on a few trusted black community leaders to act as their sounding board or to gain a pulse on the black community. Those leaders lost a fair amount of their relevance because other, new leaders emerged in the strike and its aftermath. So, even when the white community did reach out to the few blacks they felt they wanted to talk to, they often received erroneous or incomplete information. Smith pointed out: "What happened, then, was the old system of communication between the races, however one-sided, was dismantled and no new system was constructed in its place."

The other factor is that the closing of the schools themselves further reduced even that contact between races. "White leaders were often invited to speak at Negro schools, and whites were in attendance at formal functions such as: graduations, dramatic and vocal presentations, and the like. With the closing of the schools the Negro community shrank visibly. And in keeping with the Jim Crow rules Negroes had no access to movies, gymnasiums, bowling alleys, pools, skating rinks, or YMCAs." And, the demonstrations in downtown Farmville and the boycott of Farmville businesses in 1963 did nothing but further degrade whatever communication there was or goodwill that remained. In fact, one particular flyer created quite a bit of ill will among the business community when a mimeograph sheet was handed out by the Negro demonstrators and reproduced in the *Herald* in August 1963.

MAKE YOUR $$$$$$$ WORK FOR FREEDOM

Our Negro children of Prince Edward County have been: segregated ... discriminate against ... locked out of schools ... denied the right to worship God ... and jailed. The above acts have been condoned if not supported directly by the merchants of Farmville.

NEGROES CAN STOP THIS ! !

Buy where you and your children will be treated with dignity and respect!!

MAKE FARMVILLE A GHOST TOWN ! !

Farmville must be as empty as a desert every day until we have public schools for all children in Prince Edward County.
Negroes of Amelia, Nottoway, Charlotte, Appomattox, Buckingham, Cumberland, and Lunenburg Counties support the BOYCOTT against the Prince Edward merchants.
DON'T BUY IN FARMVILLE! ! BOYCOTT FOR FREEDOM! !
Sponsored by the Prince Edward branch NAACP

— Street flyer used on the streets of Farmville in August, 1963

By the end of the summer of 1963 it was noted by visiting educators and activists that even the casual conversations between Negroes and whites in downtown Farmville had completely ceased.

——— EVERYONE DIGS IN ———

As the new school year opened in 1963, the white children in the foundation's Prince Edward Academy found they were able to enjoy a second year in their new campus for the upper grades. The elementary grades were still housed in various buildings like churches throughout the county, but the teachers were basically the same from the public schools. The curriculum was very similar, although some extracurricular activities were no longer offered. In order to preclude the necessity of lunch rooms or cafeterias the foundation had their classes scheduled from 8:30 a.m. until 1:30 p.m. thereby giving the children a long free afternoon. There's no evidence that the schedule in any way diminished the academic achievements of the students. Metrics like 57% of the academy graduates going on to college and the continued state board of education accreditations all speak to the quality of the private school. The foundation released figures in 1963 showing that, 376 students had paid full tuition, 371 had paid partial tuition, and 32 paid no tuition. The foundation insisted that no children would be denied an education because of inability to pay tuition.

In contrast, Smith talks about paying a visit to one of the Negro training centers in May 1962 located in the Loving Sisters of Charity Hall, a white frame building near Hampden-Sydney College. "He found children romping around the grounds during lunch break skipping rope, playing ring games, baseball, and romping through the yellow bolts of scotch broom." Inside, two classes were going simultaneously in the same classroom with a total of 45 students present." He describes how on one side of the room there where little ones learning their alphabet; while on the other side third, fourth, fifth, sixth and seventh graders were learning the rudiments of letter writing. "With the younger children singing out their "A's" and "B's" and the older ones calling out instructions to a teacher writing a letter at the blackboard, bedlam ruled. Neither of the two teachers had any professional experience (a better educated one had finished 11th grades of school). They were patient, tolerant of the noise, making out as best they could. The walls of the classroom were filled with pictures of well-known American Negroes— from Jackie Robinson to Ralph Bunch—scattered among cut out letters spelling 'Follow in the Footsteps of Great Americans.'" From the beginning, the centers had been poorly equipped and staffed. It was hoped that they would perform some of the functions of the schools—especially in keeping the children busy and together. Yet in no way could they be called schools. They just didn't have the resources necessary to replace the public schools. Originally in 1959-1960, there were 10 centers, and in 1960-1961, 15, but by 1961-1962 there were only five centers operating. The total enrollment had dropped to about 350 children. As an example, the Loving Sisters of Charity Hall was often photographed and used as a contrast between the newer buildings that the foundation was providing for the white students. Ben Powers of the *Herald*, wrote in his March 1961 article: "It is... a two-by-four sized hut, which is so overcrowded it appears to be a health hazard and a fire trap. Twenty-nine youngsters of an enrollment of forty-one were jammed like sardines into the building... Miss Margaret Hill at best could only give a good course in human endurance."

The cost of the school closing was a stain on the entire county, but no one bore the cost more than the children. Helen Baker of the Friends, was interviewed by Smith where she recalled one particular little girl named Carol. "Carol is eight years old. Last year she attended no school, but this year her parents made arrangements for her to attend school in Petersburg, Virginia, which is sixty-five miles away. Carol lives with a great-aunt; leaves home each Sunday afternoon and returns to Farmville on Friday evening. Today, while unpacking Carol's laundry bag, her mother found tucked in the dress pocket a carefully drawn note: 'I want to go home now. Mother I love you so much I want to go home. I want to go home now.' Carol is one of about 400 Negro children of all ages who must leave their home in Prince Edward County for a week—a month—a semester—a year in order to attend school. There may be as many white children who do the same: I do not know."

Of course, some children adapted better than others and for some it became the experience of a lifetime, in fact changing their life seemingly for the better. Though there always was a cost it's clear that some children and some parents rose beyond the inconvenience and unfairness to go on to achieve the best sort of revenge—living well. Barbara Ann Botts was one such young lady. She was a sixth grader when the schools closed and accepted the closing as necessary, but was struck by the inconvenience and bitterness. At 13 she was sent by the Friends to Moorestown, New Jersey and while she did well in school, though it was difficult being the only Negro in her school and classes. She went on for a second year at Morristown but then switched to Newton, Massachusetts for her final year of high school. In Newton she lived with a white family and her class of 28 students included six Negroes. "Life in school and at home were freely integrated. Perhaps more important, Barbara made lasting friendships. She was a little stunned, although very grateful, at the way she was accepted: 'Mr. H. has three daughters. From the time I came there, though, he talked about his four girls. It helped me not to feel like an outsider. I went to football games and took part in social activities just like anyone else.'"

Bob Smith talks about how the experience changed Barbara Ann Botts's life and committed her to the path of integration, but "also made it impossible for her to continue to live in the segregated South." For her part she talked about how much she appreciates all that so many, outside the county did for her and her education, but remains deeply regretful of the educational carnage she saw in her home county. "I will say that I feel that nothing much has been accomplished while the schools were closed. It seems to me that the adults could have had their little debate in court while the children continue to attend schools of some kind...."

——— THE BIGGER PICTURE ———

Virginia did its share of the heavy lifting regarding civil rights. Even the famed Freedom Riders can trace their roots back to a legal case in Virginia. Freedom riders were activists that rode interstate buses into the segregated southern United States to test the United States Supreme Court decision *Boynton v. Virginia* (issued in 1960). *Boynton v. Virginia* had outlawed racial segregation in the restaurants and waiting rooms in terminals serving buses that crossed state lines. Five years prior to the *Boynton* ruling, the Interstate Commerce Commission had issued a ruling in *Sarah Keys v. Carolina Coach Company* that had explicitly denounced the *Plessy v. Ferguson* doctrine of separate but equal in interstate bus travel, but the ICC had failed to enforce its own ruling, and thus Jim Crow travel laws remained in force throughout the South.

The Freedom Riders set out to challenge this status quo by riding various forms of public transportation in the South to confront local laws or customs that enforced segregation. The Freedom Rides, and the violent reactions they provoked, bolstered the credibility of the American Civil Rights Movement and called national attention to the violent disregard for the law that was used to enforce segregation in the southern United States. Riders were arrested for trespassing, unlawful assembly, and violating state and local Jim Crow laws, along with other alleged offenses.

The first Freedom Ride left Washington, D.C., on May 4, 1961, and was scheduled to arrive in New Orleans on May 17. Most of the subsequent rides were sponsored by the Congress of Racial Equality (CORE), while others were managed by the Student Nonviolent Coordinating Committee (SNCC, pronounced "Snick"). The Freedom Rides followed on the heels of boycotts and dramatic sit-ins against segregated lunch counters conducted by students and youth throughout the South.

The United States Supreme Court's decision in *Boynton v. Virginia* granted interstate travelers the legal right to disregard local segregation ordinances regarding interstate transportation facilities. But the Freedom Riders' rights were not enforced, and their actions were considered criminal throughout most of the South. For example, upon the Riders' arrival in Mississippi, their journey ended with imprisonment for exercising their legal rights in interstate travel. Similar arrests took place in other Southern cities.

Female Freedom Riders, particularly white ones, however presented violent racists with an perplexing dilemma, what Rider Claire O'Connor (arrested June 11, 1961) says was a sort of subconscious exploitation of sexist assumptions. "If you send women into a violent situation in which they are going to be nonviolent, there's a discontinuity: Here are men who want to be violent and yet there are women being put into harm's way." This immunity did not always last long, "Of course, many Southerners got over it and started treating women the same way as men, but it was a very useful tool because it forced people to rethink what they were doing."

Women were often underestimated by men both inside and outside the movement. As Margaret Leonard, a white Freedom Rider and Georgia native said after being arrested on June 21, 1961, "I was pretty used to being treated the way [white] women are treated in the South, which is with great courtesy but not enormous respect intellectually."

While the Freedom Rides occurred on the larger stage across the Jim Crow South, the Cold War was a geopolitical struggle that encompassed the entire globe. Nonetheless, the Cold War had direct connections back to the Prince Edward fight for integration. After all, the Prince Edward crisis overlapped almost completely with one of the iciest periods of the Cold War. The U2 incident, the Bay of Pigs invasion, and the Cuban Missile Crisis all took place between 1959 and 1964. Southern Democrats had, almost from the day of the *Brown* ruling, decided to paint civil rights and communism as one in the same and an equal threat to America. Martin L. King was often accused by his detractors as being a communist.

One aspect of the Cold War could not be painted over by the Southern Democrats was the reality of a peace time draft. In response to this Cold War threat (read Soviet Union here), President Truman announced on July 20, 1948, that the United States was re-instituting the draft and issued a proclamation requiring nearly 10 million men to register for military service in the next two months.

Following World War II, the United States moved quickly to demobilize the vast military it had constructed during that global conflict. During the war, more than 16 million men and women served in the U.S. military; when the war ended in August 1945, the American people universally demanded rapid demobilization. By 1948, less than 550,000 men remained in the U.S. Army. This rapid decline in the size of America's military concerned U.S. government officials; who believed that a confrontation with the Soviet Union was imminent. In 1947, the president issued the Truman Doctrine, which provided aid to Greece and Turkey to oppose communist subversion. In that same year, Secretary of State, George C. Marshall warned that Western Europe was on the brink of political and economic chaos that would leave it defenseless against communist aggression; the following year, Congress approved billions of dollars in financial assistance to those beleaguered nations. In June 1948, the Soviets cut all land traffic into the U.S.-British-French zones of occupation in West Berlin. The United States responded with the Berlin Airlift, in which tons of food and supplies were flown in to sustain the population of the besieged city. In light of these events, many Americans believed that actual combat with the Soviet Union was not far away.

Truman's decision to institute a peace time draft was viewed by many black men with a "here we go again" attitude and many were having nothing to do with another stint in a segregated military. Some reports forecasted 30% of the eligible black male population would not register for a segregated draft—period. As a result of this pressure Truman soon announced he would integrate the military. Just like all the other racial progress made up to this point, the fact was, pressure and only pressure yielded grudging gains by whites. The black community had enough. After just experiencing the segregated military in World War II and then returning to a segregated society back home blacks were not going to take it anymore.

On July 26, 1948, President Harry S. Truman issued Executive Order 9981. It abolished racial discrimination in the armed forces and eventually led to the end of segregation in the services. The Order's operative statement is:

> *It is hereby declared to be the policy of the President that there shall be equality of treatment and opportunity for all persons in the armed services without regard to race, color, religion or national origin. This policy shall be put into effect as rapidly as possible, having due regard to the time required to effectuate any necessary changes without impairing efficiency or morale.*

— Truman Library, 1948 Time Line

The order also established a committee to investigate and make recommendations to the civilian leadership of the military to implement the policy. The last of the all-black units in the United States military was abolished in September 1954 under the Eisenhower administration.

———— THE HUMAN COST ————

On Sunday, October 25, 2010, at 2 p.m. the author was across the street from the Moton Museum conducting an interview for the museum using the tools and techniques provided by Story Corps. Story Corps was founded in 2003, and is now one of the largest oral history projects ever undertaken. They give the famous and not-so-famous the opportunity to leave a legacy through their recorded voice for future generations.

I was supporting the Moton Museum by interviewing Gloria Locket Bowler, in, of all places, the Eggleston Funeral Establishment. The funeral parlor turned out to be a convenient place to record the interviews while the museum was undergoing renovations to facilitate their April 2011 grand opening. Gloria Locket Bowler's recording is now part of the congressional Library of Congress record. She started out talking about the poor condition of the one- and two-room school that she attended leading up to the school closings in 1959. They were basically nothing more than wooden shacks with no electricity, no running water, and no indoor toilets.

Once the schools closed, she recalled how the local churches and the NAACP did their best to provide at least some level of schooling. This allowed her to continue at least a small amount of her schooling during the four years of no public education before the free schools opened. She seemed justifiably proud when she was finally tested in 1963 and learned that she was above her grade in reading. As the interview was finishing, her emotions surfaced and she cried softly as she remembered the bitter experience she was forced to endure. It seemed to me she was crying not only for the hurt she suffered, but for the triumph she ultimately enjoyed in overcoming a system that treated her with such distain.

When the schools opened, she recalled how amazed she was to leave her farm in Prospect, after attending the local wooden schools that were no more than shacks, and to finally attend a brick school with central heat and actually ride there on a school bus. These experiences, even today, bring a wonder to her face. At the very end of the interview, Gloria Locket Bowler talked about her scary start to reentry into the public schools in 1963. The first day, when they opened the public schools, she came to her bus stop and found a crowd of white people there to protest and taunt her and the other black children. She says they surrounded the bus, chanted hateful messages and proceeded to violently rock the bus back and forth trying to intimidate and scare the children. As the bus finally pulled away the whites continued to taunt the children and ran after it throwing rocks.

Her final thoughts turned to future generations. She stated that, "to this day I value education beyond all else and so wish to pass on to the current generation, especially my grandchildren, the urgency that they pursue their education and graduate from high school as well as college." She said this was the most important message she could share with future generations.

Dorothy Lockett Holcomb, had a similar story to share. She was from Prince Edward County and was looking forward to fourth grade when she learned her school would be closed. "It was devastating, it really was," she says. "I described it to somebody one time, it's almost...a feeling like somebody dying or something, you just feel really, really, that core of sadness...What am I gonna do with no education after fourth grade?"

So Holcomb's parents sent her to school in neighboring Appomattox County, where they pretended to be residents. While some students were sent out of state as exiles, far from their families and their familiar hometown, others were just sent a few miles over the county line.

Charles Taylor was devastated when he, along with some of his classmates, was sent to North Carolina. "I was in a state of shock. You were just walking around like a zombie saying, 'When are they gonna come and get us? When are we going back to our school?'"

Most of the county's white children ended up in hastily created private schools, like Prince Edward Academy. But some white families, like Eunice Ward Carwile's, couldn't afford the tuition. "My parents couldn't afford 50 cents extra in any way, and that's when we came to a realization that we might not be able to go to school at all. So my parents decided to just move," Carwile says. "There was a time when every child in this county was denied access to free public education. It's not American."

Chapter Seven

BOUND FOR
FREEDOM

*Twelve million black men and women in this country are
proud of their American citizenship, but they are
determined that it shall mean for them no less than for
any other group, the largest enjoyment of opportunity and
the fullest blessings of freedom.*

—Dr. Robert Russa Moton. From the text of his prepared
address that he was not allowed to give at the May 30,
1922, Dedication of The Lincoln Memorial, Washington,
D. C.

Time Line for Chapter Seven
Bound for Freedom
(1963–1964)

1963, January 11. In his inaugural speech as governor of Alabama, George Wallace proclaims, "segregation now, segregation tomorrow, and segregation forever."

1963, March 19. U.S. attorney general Robert F. Kennedy says during a speech: "the only places on earth not to provide free public education are Communist China, North Vietnam, Sarawak, Singapore, British Honduras—and Prince Edward County, Virginia. Something must be done about Prince Edward County."

1963, June 11. In Alabama, federal troops force Governor George Wallace to allow black students to enter the University of Alabama.

1963, August 28. At the Lincoln Memorial, Martin Luther King makes his "I have a dream" speech.

1963, September 15. Four small girls were killed in the Birmingham bombing at 16th Street Baptist Church. Their death shocked both white and black America.

1963, September 16. Free Schools open and provide the first significant formal education for African American children in Prince Edward since 1959. This stopgap measure was initiated by the Kennedy administration to address the lack of schools for black children while the two sides continued to battle it out in court.

1963, November 22. In Dallas, President Kennedy rides in an open limousine. It passes in front of the building where Lee Harvey Oswald works. Oswald takes his rifle to work with him and shoots the president. Vice President Johnson becomes president.

1964, February 7. The Beatles land in New York, making their debut in the United States. Their record *I Want to Hold Your Hand* is a best seller.

1964, May 2. Four hundred to 1,000 students march through Times Square, New York, and another 700 in San Francisco, in the first major student demonstration against the Vietnam War. Smaller marches also occur in Boston, Seattle, and in Madison, Wisconsin.

1964, May 11. Robert F. Kennedy visited Prince Edward County to inspect the Free Schools and accept donations to the John F. Kennedy Memorial Library Fund from the students.

1964, May 25. The Supreme Court rules, in *Griffin v. County School Board*, that closing schools to avoid desegregation is unconstitutional. This ruling is the last major legal obstacle and triggers the reopening of public schools in Prince Edward in September 1964.

1964, June 19. The Senate votes on and passes the Civil Rights Act.

1964, June 21. A summer of civil rights activities occurs throughout the South. Three civil rights workers, Michael Schwerner, Andrew Goodman, and James Chaney are murdered near Philadelphia, Mississippi, by local law enforcement officials.

1964, July 2. President Johnson signs the Civil Rights Act into Law.

1964, July 18. In Harlem, New York, six days of rioting begins. According to the *New York Times*, thousands of blacks: "raced through the center of Harlem shouting at policemen and white people, pulling fire alarms, breaking windows and looting stores."

1964, August 22. At the Democratic Party's convention, Fannie Lou Hammer, representing the Mississippi Freedom Democratic Party, challenges the standing of the all-white Mississippi delegation.

1964, September 8. After five years, public schools resume in Prince Edward County for nearly 1,500 blacks and a handful of white students. While the schools are technically integrated in 1964 nearly all blacks go to the public school and nearly all whites go to the private segregated Prince Edward Academy.

1964, September 8. The former Robert Russa Moton High School building is now placed in service as Mary E. Branch Elementary School #2.

Chapter Seven
BOUND FOR FREEDOM
(1963–1964)

*Each time a man stands up for an ideal or acts to improve
the lot of others, or strikes out against injustice, he sends
forth a tiny ripple of hope, and crossing each other from a
million different centers of energy and daring, those
ripples build a current that can sweep down the mightiest
walls of oppression and resistance.*

—Robert F. Kennedy, *The Ripple of Hope* from a speech
to South African students in 1966

Gallery VI at the Robert Russa Moton Museum covers the return
to school for nearly 1,500 blacks during the years of 1963 and
1964. Following four years of no structured school, this was a
fresh start for most of the black children of Prince Edward
County. This was possible because the newly minted private
Freedom School opened in September, 1963. The gallery's name
is a direct reference to Dr. Neil V. Sullivan and his book, *Bound
for Freedom.* Sullivan was the energetic outsider who, as the
superintendent, helped create the Freedom School from the
ground up. When you walk through *Bound for Freedom* you will
learn that this gallery chronicles the period when structured
education resumed in Prince Edward County initially with the
Free School in 63', and then followed by the opening of the
public schools in September 64'.

Upon entering, the visitor is immediately struck by two
disparate situations. The happy and anxious anticipation of
children looking forward to the first day of school in Prince
Edward County, on Monday, September 16, 1963, as contrasted
with images of the Birmingham bombing at 16th Street Baptist
Church. The bombing killed four small girls on September 15,

1963—the Sunday before the Free School's opening day. As visitors move through this gallery, they begin to understand how national events directly affected the course of events in Prince Edward County. Through the Kennedy's involvement, the local story is now inextricably tied to the national story and the visitor will take this understanding with them as they explore the Free School Experiment during the 1963-64 school years. As the story of the Free Schools ends with spring commencement, the visitor will be presented one last legal case, the *Griffin* case, in which the U.S. Supreme Court mandated the reopening of the Prince Edward County public schools on an integrated basis.

Starting with the end in mind, it is clear that the black children of Prince Edward County were able to start school again in September 1963 because white men decided this injustice should no longer be allowed to continue. It is worth noting that while there were a few white men in Prince Edward who wanted to see the resumption of public schools they were relatively small in numbers and quickly censored by the triumvirate of local power: the *Farmville Herald,* county government, and The Defenders of State Sovereignty. Those who seemed to care most about the Prince Edward County black children were from outside Southside and many were from outside Virginia. Leadership came from President John F. Kennedy and his brother Attorney General Robert F. Kennedy who initiated the idea of a Free School, Superintendent Sullivan leading the implementation of the Free School, the nine white Supreme Court Justices who ruled in 1964 that it was unconstitutional to deny children a public education, and the many other white citizens throughout the country who protested and contributed books, desks, money, and time.

There are lots of reasons why these powerful, whites who played on a national and international stage decided to intervene in 1963:

- Some were embarrassed that the world press was focusing on the issue.
- The school closing ran contradictory to America's cold war propaganda campaign.
- It was hurting business not only in Southside, but Virginia and the greater South.
- Some were disturbed by the injustice of denying blacks or any children an education.
- Some thought it was more than time for the South to leave its legacy of slavery and Jim Crow behind.

Solon (638 BC – 558 BC), an Athenian statesman, lawmaker, and Lyric poet, is renowned as a founding father of the Athenian polis. He acquired a place in history and in folklore through his efforts to legislate against political, economic, and moral decline in Athens. Some of his reforms failed in the short term, yet he is often credited with having laid the foundations for Athenian democracy. Solon, of Athens the leader of Ancient Greece whose name today has become synonymous with "lawgiver" was questioned regarding how the justice in this city—state of Athens would become perfect. "When those who have not suffered an injustice are as indignant as those who have." The injured blacks of Prince Edward County were beyond simple indignation yet the resolution of the segregation question still largely rested in the hands of whites. While blacks clearly took the initiative to drive Jim Crow out of their lives, the decision makers were all within the white power structure of the day. In 1963 and 1964, blacks returned to schools because there were enough indignant whites in a position of power now willing to correct decades of injustices.

——— START OF THE FREE SCHOOL ———

By the end of 1962, the Prince Edward County struggle for integrated schools was already the most litigated case in the history of the 147-year-old civil rights movement. Although many believed the struggle ended on May 17, 1954, with the

Brown v. Board of Education Supreme Court ruling, in reality that was just a beginning point.

Five years following the *Brown* decision, the federal courts found it necessary to issue yet another order to desegregate the Prince Edward County schools. This 1959 court action precipitated the five-year closing of the public schools in Prince Edward County. As massive resistance was being beaten back in one Virginia locality after another, it was in Prince Edward County that local whites were adamant; there would be segregated schools or no schools at all. Prince Edward became famous because it was the only place in the United States, in fact the entire Western world, where children did not have free basic public schools. Both President John Kennedy and Attorney General Robert Kennedy gave speeches decrying the Prince Edward situation. In 1963 Prince Edward County, Virginia, stood alone as the only county of the 43,000 school systems in the United States that refuse to provide free public education for its children.

The story of the Free School really starts with President Kennedy. In 1963 President Kennedy could no longer tolerate and permit the further injury to the children of Prince Edward County, and through his concern, a remarkable school was built from the ground up—called the Prince Edward Free School Association, often shortened to the "Free School." The goal of the Free School was to first resume the education for upwards of 1,500 black students, second, to show the world that blacks were more than the equal of the whites, and demonstrate just how far and how much progress could be made given adequate schools and excellent teachers.

In May, 1963 William J. vanden Heuvel then working for U.S. Attorney General Robert Kennedy was called in to the office of Robert Kennedy and instructed to see what can be done to restore education in Prince Edward County. Mr. vanden Heuvel was named special assistant to the Attorney General and he had the backing of President Kennedy as well. And he was going to need all the help he could get to pull off the miracle of restarting schools in Prince Edward County after four years of a "no school stalemate."

The project was led by a remarkable group of men who formed the trustees of the Free School Association. They were all Virginians, three whites and three Negroes—all of them with the highest academic credentials. The trustee and chairman of the Free School Board of Trustees was Colgate Darden a former Governor of Virginia and President Emeritus of the University of Virginia. He later spoke about his tenure as Chairman:

> *I have been a Congressman, a Governor, a University*
> *President but*
> *this—Chairman of the Free School Board of Trustees—is*
> *the most important service I will have rendered my native*
> *state of Virginia.*

On August 14, 1963, Gov. Harrison held a press conference with Colgate Darden, Rev. Griffin, and William J. vanden Heuvel to announce the formation of the Prince Edward County Free School Association with Colgate Darden as its chairman. Also appointed were Dr. Thomas Henderson, president of the Virginia Union University, as vice chairman, and Dr. F.D.G. Ripple, the retiring dean at the University of Virginia Law School, as treasurer. The other members were Dr. Fred B. Cole, president of Washington and Lee University, Dr. Robert P. Daniel, president of Virginia State College, and Dr. Earl H. McClenney, president of St. Paul's College at Lawrenceville. An important component of the ultimate success of the Free School was the racial balance of three whites and three blacks as well as the critical aspect that they were all from Virginia. All the members were dedicated to the education of children of any race and their individual educational credentials were world-class. After four years of no school and significant negative news coverage throughout the nation and the world, this news conference garnered significant front-page interest from the likes of the *New York Times* and the *Richmond Times-Dispatch*. They boldly set the date of opening the Free Schools in Prince Edward County for September 16, 1963. You may have missed it, but to make the point, again, the date of this news conference was August 14,

1963. They were starting with nothing; no curriculum, no schools, no books, no teachers, and no administrators. The Prince Edward Free School Association was a federally initiated, state-sponsored institution that was privately financed and would be open to blacks and whites equally. This gave the team a month to organize a school system for an expected 1,500 children. They immediately set about searching for a superintendent for the school system.

Dr. Neil Sullivan was in charge of an affluent school district in New York. After a quickly arranged visit on August 19 to Washington to meet with Attorney General Robert Kennedy and his special assistant in charge of the Prince Edward project, William J. vanden Heuvel, Sullivan accepted the position of Superintendent on August 27. He later recalled that he accepted the responsibility of starting up an entire school system in 20 days "with what can only be described as improvident optimism."

On August 21, 1963, prior to accepting the superintendent position, Dr Sullivan visited Farmville and attended a meeting at the First Baptist Church with Rev. Griffin and William J. vanden Heuvel. Mr. vanden Heuvel made a presentation outlining what the Free School would do for Farmville. There were many questions and many concerns, but in the end there was a strong affirmation to go forward. One of the open questions was how the Negro community would react or support the Prince Edward County Free Schools when three years ago they rejected a private Negro Academy proposed by the local white leaders. The Negro community clearly saw their goal as attaining an integrated public education for their children and would not jeopardize their cause and legal actions by joining a private school that was, in their view, nothing more than a sham gesture with no real substance. This private Negro Academy was to be called Southside Schools Inc. But it had a governing board of 17 men—all of them white. However, the Free School had Negro involvement from the beginning and at the top, with three Negroes on the board of trustees. Another difference between the Free School and the Southside School was the Free Schools would in fact be offered at no cost to the students and their families. The Southside schools required Negroes to pay the yearly tuition of $240. For many Negro families this was impossible hurdle to surmount.

During Dr. Sullivan first visit to Farmville he discovered Negro picketers set up in front of several of the main street's larger stores. The picketers were all Negroes, mostly high-school-age children, carrying handmade signs asking for: better jobs for Negroes, for integrated churches, theaters, lunch counters, and so on. Many of the signs dealt with the educational crisis created in Prince Edward County and read: "Four years on the street is four years too long.... Why take it out on innocent Negro children?... We are not dropouts. We are lockouts." The demonstrations had been going on all summer, severely straining the local business community and local government officials, who were tired of the constant picketing and demands. The picketers were all backed by the National Association for the Advancement of Colored People. The NAACP helped keep the picketers well organized, orderly, and nonviolent. They organized shifts on a regular schedule to keep the pressure on the white business owners.

On a subsequent trip to Farmville on August 27, Dr. Sullivan spoke to a teenage girl just off the picket line. It's clear her words had a powerful effect on him; he had such difficulty getting students to talk to him and he was moved by the sheer power, sincerity, and the need expressed by this particular student.

Most of those I approached were reluctant to answer my questions, obviously suspicious of my motives. Some did talk, however, beginning with a teenage girl just off the picket line. She spoke, without self-consciousness, of being a privileged child: her parents had found it possible to send her to another community where she had lived with friends and attended school.

"But I want to come back home and live with my family now," she continued. "And I want my little brothers and sisters to go to school, too, because they've been home all these for years. That's why I'm picketing for schools." I asked her if she had heard about the free schools. "I

*have heard," she said, "and they would really be my
salvation. They would just be salvation for my whole
family."*

*... Suddenly, then, my mind was made up. I would tell the
free school trustees they have hired themselves a
superintendent.*

Many years later, writing about his decision to take on the
Prince Edward challenge, Dr. Sullivan said, "it was a wonderful
spirit that touched every part of our effort. There was a feeling
that we had broken through some terrible barriers, if there was a
possibility of creating a new and different America."

—— CHALLENGES A PLENTY——

Starting with his initial visit and continuing through those critical
early weeks, Dr. Sullivan took the time to visit with all the
stakeholders in Prince Edward County. He met with the local
government officials, who had closed the schools, the county
Board of Education, Mr. Thomas J. McIlwaine, Superintendent of
Schools, and the Reverend L. Francis Griffin, Pastor of the First
Baptist Church in Farmville. He also tried to visit with the
students, who he sought out in their rural homes. Sometimes he
had difficulty getting the children to engage with him. Whether
they were shy or not used to white men asking their opinions, the
conversations were often short and succinct, with the students
answering most questions with a simple *Yes Sir* or *No Sir*.

Dr. Sullivan was well acquainted with hurtful discrimination
and how personal it quickly became.

I knew intimately the evils of prejudice and bias.
*As a Roman Catholic, I had great difficulty securing a
teaching position back in 1936 when I looked for my first
job in New Hampshire. I had often been told by
interviewing superintendents, "you have all the necessary
qualifications, Mr. Sullivan, but I am afraid I couldn't
employ a Roman Catholic." When I was granted*

interviews by school boards in small communities I would be asked quietly, if elected what church would you attend?" When I answered, "Catholic Church," they would shake their heads and say, "sorry, there is no Catholic Church in this community. We feel that you should work where you can go to your own church." Thank the Lord times are different now—at least in New Hampshire.

The Free School would consist of the following four existing schools:

1. Mary E. Branch school number one, an elementary school.
2. Mary E. Branch school number two, an elementary school (the original Robert Russa Moton high school where the 1951 student led strike took place).
3. Robert Russa Moton high school, built in 1953 at a cost of more than $800,000.
4. Worsham elementary school in the village of Kingsville, about five miles south of Farmville.

All of these public school buildings had been closed for three years and, except for the relatively new Robert Russa Moton high school, the rest were in need of substantial repairs. The Free Schools had arranged to lease the schools from the County Board of Education.

In *Bound for Freedom* William J. vanden Heuvel discusses the challenges they faced:

On September 3, the county Board of Supervisors authorized a contract to lease the schools to the free school Association after meeting with William J. vanden Heuvel and Gov. Darden before school buildings have been padlocked for more than three years there were no books, no teaching material, the school buildings had to be repaired and cleaned. The library was practically bare, the cafeteria had to be rebuilt. In fact, the buildings are in deplorable condition. Dirt, dust and rubbished were everywhere. Floorboards were riding, plaster had fallen, water had penetrated the walls. The toilet seats were cluttered with debris and the stench was sickening. In two weeks all of this had to be changed. Mr. Jay D. Dishman was the gentleman who had responsibility for building maintenance for the Board of Education. He told Dr. Sullivan he would undertake the work would take orders only from him and not from any Negro. But, in fact, he worked around the clock, cleaned the schools on schedule, made all the necessary repairs and in time came to take orders from Negroes.

Further adding to the difficulties facing the Free School was the need to hire 100 teachers at a time when there was a national teacher shortage. And, they needed to hire excellent teachers who could help make up for three years of no school. To his credit Dr. Sullivan never said that it was his goal to erase the entire four years, but to significantly close the gap. Most of the African American teachers who had been part of the Prince Edward County segregated system had left for jobs in other counties or states when the schools were closed in 1959. The board of trustees felt it was important that at least half of the teachers hired be from Virginia and that there be a racial mix of white and black instructors. More than 30% of the faculty was white and five of those white teachers were Virginians.

As those first few frantic weeks flew by before the opening of school, Dr. Sullivan continued to have difficulty finding qualified teachers who could start in such short notice. He sent out the word for help to his board of trustees and Mr. vanden Heuvel, who said, "You'll get applicants. I'll move heaven and earth to find them for you." Dr. Sullivan responded, "That may be necessary."

Dr. Sullivan had attended mass that Sunday, September 8, and later was working the phones in his hotel room when he received a call: "A group of teachers from the Norfolk area were on their way to Farmville for an interview. Would I see them, they asked, even though it was Sunday? I assured them that I would and suggested they come directly to my hotel. One hour later they called from Main Street in Farmville. They had gone to the hotel but were refused admission! Would I interview them in the car?" Dr. Sullivan met the Norfolk teachers a few minutes later on Main Street and was impressed with "their savoir-fare, as well as their qualifications. They agreed to return on Tuesday for a second interview." As far as Dr. Sullivan was concerned, nothing was going to stand in the way of a successful opening of the Free School.

Monday morning, as Dr. Sullivan approached the Mary E. Branch school number two, he couldn't believe his eyes: "Cars were everywhere, and when I entered the school auditorium seemed almost to be overflowing with the men and woman filling out applications. There were at least 50 likely looking applicants, I estimated—many of them young, with stars in their eyes. Most were Negroes, but there were a number of whites. This, I thought, is more like it"

Dr. Sullivan decided to speak to them as a group to give them a sense of what they were in for and the challenges they would face.

Almost half of our total school enrollment will be entering a classroom for the first time in their lives. A great many will be unable to read. You'll find nine -- and 10 year olds who never heard of the alphabet and can't count to 10. Most of the 12-year-olds won't be able to tell time. Fourteen- and fifteen-year-olds will be reading at third and fourth grade level and will be unable to handle simple fractions.

Our schools are in a state of disrepair. Our supplies haven't arrived. And by the way, you had better be able to teach without textbooks. Ours probably won't be here until several weeks after school begins next Monday.
...Finally, I would say that we all have feelings about civil rights, and demonstrations seem to be the order of the day

in Farmville. But our job in the free school is teaching— and teaching must be our way of demonstrating our convictions.

I paused and looked about at the silent group. Not all people will be able to work under these conditions, I added. It will be most understandable if some of you decide not to remain for the formal interviews which will follow. Not a single person left the room. They all stayed for the interviews, and enough promising candidates were selected from this group so that, at the end of the day we found we had come near doubling our teacher roster. Things were looking up.

Despite all of the best efforts of Mr. William J. vanden Heuvel, Dr. Sullivan, and the board of trustees, with only three days left to go to the start of school, they were still short of qualified teachers. He made an emergency call to Dr. Courtland Colson, director of student teaching at Virginia State College in Petersburg on Thursday night: "I told them my problem and made a request: could you send 20 student teachers to Farmville next Monday, ready to work for a period of two weeks? That will give us the breathing spell we need to find permanent teachers." While Dr. Colson agreed to try he was not hopeful that in this late at this late point he could get his students to change their plans. Many were already signed off for teaching assignments throughout Virginia.

"The call came early Friday morning. 'Eighteen of our students have volunteered to come to Farmville,' Dr. Colson reported."

"Wonderful!" I said. "And you can tell them we will pay their board, room, travel expenses and a small salary in addition."

"I may have trouble telling them now," Dr. Colson replied. "Most of them are already on their way—some are even hitchhiking."

"I could almost see the smile of pride Dr. Colson must be wearing."

Dr. Colson finished the conversation with this, "It turned out that our students were more interested in whether or not you could get the free schools opened than in whether or not they get paid for expenses."

Miss Etta Rose Bailey of Richmond, a white elementary school principal who had retired the previous June was willing to become principal of one of the elementary schools. She "was probably the state's outstanding principal," but she had never taught Negro children before. She sought out the opportunity to directly contribute to bringing education back to the children of Prince Edward County. She voiced her feelings following the Pledge of Allegiance at the first faculty meeting.

> She said: "you're giving me an opportunity that has been denied me during all my 45 years in Virginia schools. I have always wanted to work with Negro children." As Faculty members began arriving from around the country. The Pledge of Allegiance was spoken at the end of the first meeting. As the final phrase was concluded, Etta Rose Bailey spoke: "I have repeated that oath all of my life," she said, "and only now at 70 do I really understand what it means."
>
> "... One nation under God, indivisible, with Liberty and Justice for all."

———— THE FINAL PREPARATIONS ————

Housing became a major problem as prices started escalating. Reverend Griffin used his influence in the community to keep prices at bay and ensure decent housing was available for all the teachers. This became particularly important since many of the established teachers were already absorbing significant financial sacrifices. The Free School salaries were, without exception, lower than those in competing public or private schools. In some cases, affluent school districts made up the difference so that teachers became whole, or, in other cases, they paid their entire salary.

As Dr. Sullivan worked night and day, seven days a week during those first hectic months of the school startup in August and September, he also had to put up with threatening calls, hate letters and countless other minor pettiness heaped upon him by those unfriendly to the Free School. Dr. Sullivan speaks of having a particular good day because so much had been accomplished to get the Free Schools ready that, "I felt so good that when my nightly caller paid his respects at 2 a.m., the sound of the telephone ringing seemed almost cheerful. I even smiled as I returned his profane greetings. 'Go to hell!' I told him. 'I'm staying.'"

While all this was going on, the students needed to register and vaccination inoculations were required as well. While long lines were routine in the early days of registration, everyone commented on how extremely well mannered the students were. *Bound for Freedom* captured one administrator's sense of the children as they prepared to return to class: "I noticed, too, that as they waited, the children neither laughed nor played. They didn't talk. They just stood. They were unlike any other group of children I had ever seen in my years of school experience. And this scene would be repeated, day after day, as enrollment continued." For many of them they would be entering school for the first time and this presented a significant emotional as well as intellectual first experience. All the educators who had come from outside Virginia noted how little the students talked especially when whites were present.

President Kennedy kicked off the contributions necessary to fund the nearly $2 million budget for the Free Schools. He quietly, with no publicity gave $10,000 of his own money to start the fund raising. He then went on to contact the leaders of major foundations, and, with the help of the Ford Foundation and the Marshall Field Foundation, they put together a consortium that guaranteed at least $500,000. The National Education Association (NEA) was also a significant contributor, both at the national and local level. Setting an example for other schoolchildren, the children of Cleveland gave $30,000. The teachers of Washington State gave $20,000.

In this way, hundreds of thousands of dollars were raised from teachers associations, parent-teacher groups, and schoolchildren from around America.

One of the concerns of the board of trustees was that the school would have no white students. While the Free School went out of their way to ensure that all understood this was a school for all races they found few whites in Prince Edward County willing to buck the prevailing attitudes— spoken or not, there were rules. Ultimately, a few white students did attend the Free Schools. There was Mrs. William W. Tew the wife of a white farmer who owned a small tobacco farm south of Farmville Center. Their eight-year-old daughter was not enrolled in the academy because they didn't like having a private school in Prince Edward County and believed in public education. Here is what she said as she registered her daughter for the Free School:

> *While registering her daughter for the free school Mrs. Tew told Dr Sullivan, "her daddy and I didn't want her to go to the private school," Mrs. Tew said. "It's not that we can't afford the $250 tuition, though it would be hard for us, especially this year with the tobacco crop so bad.* When Sullivan indicated that her daughter might be the only white child in the school and questioned how she would handle that, Mrs. Tew. said, *"No I wouldn't be troubled by that,"* Mrs. *Tew replied firmly. "It's just that we think school ought to be free, and that's why she's not going to the Academy. Right is right."*

Then there was Dickie Moss, the son of Dean Moss who decided that in his senior year in high school he would follow his father's courage and vision and join the Free School. In the end the Free School was overwhelming black (1,570 black to 8 white), yet those few courageous whites did add at least a speckle of integration and hope for more to come. If nothing else it became a propaganda victory for President Kennedy and his administration in proclaiming that the free schools had both white and black students.

─── OPENING DAY ───

While the Free Schools did open as scheduled on Monday, September 16, 1963, there was a shadow cast over the opening. The day before the opening, Sunday, September 15, 1963, was the day of the bombing in Birmingham, Alabama that killed four little girls as they attended church. This brutal reminder of the hate and violence still possible in the Jim Crow South cast a pall over the preparations for the opening of the Free Schools. There was even talk that many of the black parents would not send their children to school because of the bombing. As Dr. Sullivan returned to his hotel later that Sunday afternoon, he was walking through the lobby and immediately knew something was wrong: "When I walked into the lobby of the hotel, I knew at once that something had happened. Deep gloom hung like the proverbial crepe everywhere I looked." One of the reporters was the first to tell him, "Some mad man threw a bomb into a negro Sunday school down in Birmingham, Alabama. Four little girls have been killed." The news was shattering. Dr Sullivan said, "I was crushed and saddened as never before. Suddenly, for the first time, I was deeply worried—not only about our tomorrow in Prince Edward County, but for the future of mankind as well." Born and raised in Birmingham, Condoleezza Rice was with her parents in a nearby church and talks about the bombing in very personal terms.

Birmingham was clearly exposed as a city of appalling hatred, prejudice, and violence. The hatred found full expression on September 15, 1963, when a bomb at 16th St., Baptist Church killed four little girls who were on their way to Sunday school.

Ms. Rice talked about being in church that Sunday at Westminster when, *all of a sudden there was a thud and a shudder. The distance between the two churches is about 2 miles as the crow flies, but it felt like the trouble was next-door. After what seemed like hours but was probably only a few minutes, someone called to say that the 16th St., Baptist had been bombed. No one knew how many other churches might have been targeted..... An hour or so later word came that the bomb had killed four little girls who were in the bathroom. I don't remember how long it was, but as soon as we knew their names: Denise McNair, age 11, and Addie Mae Collins, Cynthia Wesley, and Carole Robertson, all age fourteen.*

The outrage would settle on our community, but at first we were just sad. Birmingham isn't that big, and everyone knew at least one of those little girls. This was a deeply personal tragedy. Denise had been a student in my father's first kindergarten. Cynthia and Denise were from the neighborhood. I knew Denise best; though she was older, we would still play with dolls together. Her father was our milkman and a part-time photographer who worked at everyone's birthday.

My uncle had been Addie Mae Collin's teacher, and he cried like a baby when he saw her picture on the news and again when he saw her empty chair the next day.

Of course all the heighted emotions were made worse by the national and international media that had come to Farmville to cover the opening of the Free Schools on Monday. So as William J. vanden Heuvel pointed out, the opening of the "Prince Edward County Free Schools was the other side of the coin. The decency of America was its message. A willingness to reach out to a fractured community distorted by attitudes of racial supremacy was the definition of our effort." The contrast between Birmingham and Prince Edward County was stark and reflected the difference between the cowards and the courageous and those who would tear down and those who would build up.

The entire world was looking to see if the Free Schools would open and what, if any, reaction would be forthcoming from those devoted to segregation. On September 16, 1963, the Free Schools opened on time in Prince Edward County. With over half of the students attending school for the first time, the excitement was palpable. Mr. William J. vanden Heuvel talks about how important the school opening was, not only to Prince

Edward County, but for the nation: "In less than a month we had enlisted more than 100 faculty members from all over America, black and white, qualified beyond any previous measure to offer the remedial education that was critical to our success."

The atmosphere that morning in Prince Edward County was charged. There were all kinds of rumors about subtle and not-so-subtle threats that had been made. The Darlington Heights bus route that was carrying one of the white children required the free schools to take some extraordinary measures. That bus not only had one of the few white children, but also news men Eric Sevareid riding along. There was enough concern by the Free School that they had arranged to send two empty buses by the critical areas were trouble was expected. When nothing happened they then completed the actual picking up of children on the Darlington Heights bus route. Just like the two empty buses the bus full of excited children had no problems making it to school on time. Darlington Heights was the home of Barbara Rose Johns and it is where she is now buried in the Triumph Baptist Church graveyard. Of course, by 1963 Barbara was a 28 year old women working in education far away from Prince Edward County.

So they came—the children neatly dressed, clean, excited, hopeful, and some touched by fear and rumors of what was going to happen. There were small opening ceremonies at all of the schools, with the official opening ceremony scheduled on the stage of the new Robert Russa Moton high school auditorium. At Branch school number two, the children gathered around the flagpole to raise the flag and say the Pledge of Allegiance. It was a little disheartening to the teachers to see some of the children confused by the distraction of the news men surrounding them: "Some of the boys and girls, trying to follow our examples, held their left hand over their right breast; others hung their heads, as if in shame."

The opening ceremonies for Branch school number two ended with a ringing of the school bell. In the principal's office, "Rudolph Doswell stood poised like a physicist at a rocket-launching countdown, with his finger on the school bell button." He wanted to make sure the first day of school started promptly on time. "These bells haven't sounded for four years," he told a newspaper man. "I'm going to make sure everyone hears them today."

The main opening ceremonies for the Free School were conducted at the Robert R. Morton high school. Those in attendance included a number of the school board trustees, observers, and friends from the United States office of education and the special representative from the U.S. Attorney General's office, Mr. William J. vanden Heuvel. There were no representatives of Prince Edward County's official government present. There were, however, numerous print media reporters, as well as television cameras recording the event for broadcast throughout the nation. Most of the boys wore sports jacket some with ties and the girls were dressed in simple but clean cotton dresses. The program started with the singing of *America the Beautiful*, which many of the children seem to know and those who didn't went through the motions and joined in with the singing. June Callaway, who was reporting for McCall's said, "the children sang *America the Beautiful* sweetly and without irony." Dr. Sullivan began by telling them, "you are coming home after four years away. It is your year. It's your school. And it's a sky is the limit kind of school where you can go as far and as fast as you like. But you're going to have to work hard. You'll find out just how hard when you get your classrooms." While a promise for hard work might bring some noticeable reaction from the students in another high school, "these young people just sat." When the ceremonies were completed the students were led to their classrooms by their teachers to begin the hard work promised by Dr. Sullivan.

—— TRAGEDY AND HOPE ——

It was when Dr. Sullivan and his wife (who taught art in the Free School) needed to find a home in Southside Virginia that he began to realize just how much the white community had closed ranks around this divisive issue and just what it meant to live in the Jim Crow South. The Sullivan's were having trouble finding someone willing to rent to them.

It was more easily said than done. There were plenty of homes available, but I found, on revealing my identity, that not all landlords would rent property to me. They wanted to know if I plan to conduct business in my home and if I would entertain Negros. Most of them wanted to know my religion. I finally made an offer for home on the outskirts of town but was told that the family needed time to think it over. Ten days later I would still be waiting for an answer.

Eventually Dr. Sullivan found someone willing to rent their home to him. Unfortunately, for much of his stay in Prince Edward County Dr. Sullivan suffered through petty and sometimes serious instances of harassment. He received hate letters, late night phone calls, garbage was dumped on his front lawn, gun shots rained through his house, and his car was damaged.

Of course, normal start up problems emerged as with any school system. There were buses that wouldn't run, there was a drought in Virginia that threatened to close the schools due to lack of water, and when the cold weather hit, some students had no warm clothing for protection. When the faculty saw increased absence because children did not have proper clothes, they sent out an emergency appeal through the media, and tons of warm clothing and heavy shoes and raincoats were delivered to Prince Edward County. While the spirit was willing and everyone in the black community was committed to educating the youngsters, the school had problems with some children falling asleep at their desks because they had not had breakfast. At least for some children, malnutrition was a recurring problem. So the schools solved that problem by having snacks and a free lunch program.

While the entire 13-year ordeal of Prince Edward County had included remarkably little violence, there was always that threat hanging over blacks at every turn. There were also, all too often, petty harassments that could be distracting, demeaning, and intimidating. Mr. William J. vanden Heuvel describes both the burdens and triumphs associated with the starting up of the Free School.

In the background was harassment, the midnight phone calls, the driving through Neil Sullivan's property dumping garbage, trees decorated with floral arrangements from the local cemeteries, bomb threats and murder threats to the Trustees. Nevertheless, the Free School faculty not only worked together but formed close bonds of friendship and association. Morale was very high. The faculty formed a successful basketball team. A choir of mixed voices gave concerts. Art classes and literary groups met. Bridge and chess tournaments were plentiful and on Tuesday nights there were free movies for students, parents and teachers.

As the Free School's teachers began to work with the students of Prince Edward County they were startled by the extent of psychological and intellectual damage done by the lack of school for four years. A grant from the United States Department of Health Education and Welfare had sponsored a study on the consequences of no school for four years and they tested over 800 of the county's children.

Michigan State University, under Dr. Robert Green, organized a team to study the implications of the failure to provide schooling to the children of Prince Edward County. The University psychologist who had done the testing found that the mean IQ of the test group of Prince Edward County students interviewed was only 69—in a representative group of normal children that number would have approximated 100. It was clear that the longer children are out of school, the more significant was the drop in their IQ. Many children did not know how old they were. The extent of the psychological intellectual damage was startling. The majority of the children under 12 had essentially lost their ability to communicate as well as their reading skills. They came

*from illiterate or semi-illiterate homes. Very few homes
had a daily newspaper or access to magazines or books.
The only library in the community was for "whites only."*

While there is no doubt that the children's unfamiliarity with
test taking and those other procedures normally taken for granted
hurt their overall IQ scores there is also no doubt that missing
school for four years had placed these youngsters at a severe
disadvantage. As an example, in one of the tests, a child was
shown a picture of a toothbrush and a hatchet, and told to circle
the one he used when he got up in the morning. Because many of
the rural children chopped wood first thing in the morning that
was their correct answer, but of course on the test it would be
marked wrong. It should be pointed out that some in the black
community disputed Dr. Sullivan's portrait in *Bound for
Freedom*, of the Prince Edward County youngsters as backward
and uncommunicative as untrue or vastly overstated.
Nonetheless, the administrators and teachers of the Free School
had legitimate concerns about the significant gap they had to
close.

While an IQ score can be viewed as just a number, the
teachers who started to work with the students in the Free School
saw firsthand the significant and awful burden placed upon these
children by being denied school for four years. These
deficiencies surfaced in a myriad of ways. Many of the
youngsters were unable to follow simple instructions like "please
turn the page" and some as old as 10 or 11 were unable to hold a
pencil properly. On the first day of school the plan was to sort
through the children by age to slot them into their initial classes.
The teachers and administrators, "overlooked one vital fact most
of the elementary school children had not the least idea how old
they were." Another issue surfaced when the teachers tried to
ascertain the reading levels of their students through a simple
reading test. Many of the students who were asked to write their
names on the cover were brought to tears because not only could
they not write their own names, but some did not even know their
own names (especially their last names). Dr. Sullivan wrote,
"Before we could notify all teachers to stop testing, a few of the

youngsters had become so upset that they ran from the building. Patient teachers followed and encourage them to return."
Dr. Sullivan writes in *Bound for Freedom*:

> *Before the day was over, it had been forcibly brought home to us that a majority of our students under 12 didn't know left from right, back from front, or top from bottom. And getting them to say even a word or two was next to impossible. They use signs. In short, they seem to have lost all ability to communicate.*

> *I visited a few elementary school classrooms during that first day and was appalled by the quiet that greeted me. And one teacher told me he was alarmed at the lack of noise he considered healthy in his teen-age classroom. What we had to realize was that back when the public schools have closed, in 1959, these children had been 11 years old and had completed only the fifth grade.*

Dr. Sullivan ends his chapter on the first day of school by sharing an ominous premonition: "…I wondered, frankly, if either teachers or students would have the courage to return a second day."

Tuesday, September 17, 1963, was a bright, sunny day in Farmville, Virginia, with temperatures in the low 80s. The superintendent need not have worried about either the students or faculty returning to the Free Schools. Not only did everyone return for the second day, but even more students joined the Free Schools as word continued to get out about the about the school. By the end of September enrolment had leveled off to about 1,570.

> *In nearly every class the teacher had a student, usually only a few, who had attended school outside of Prince Edward County during all or at least part of the preceding last four years. In all about 500 students were*

able to continue their education outside the confines of Prince Edward County. The students stood out like beacons in the classroom during the first week or two of school. They helped their teachers, pass out supplies, ran errands; they follow instructions immediately, thus setting an example for others: or, if the situation called for it, they patiently explained some mysterious direction (like "Please start at the top of the page") to their neighbors. Mostly, however, these normal healthy youngsters served as a constant reminder to their teachers of the potential that was waiting to be released in the other quiet, subdued, distant children who might otherwise have seen almost out of reach of help.

There were also those exceptional students, in about the same proportion as you find with any other school, who had IQs exceeding 150. The teachers of the Free School were especially heartened by those students, who gave them hope and encouraged them to try even harder to help the others.

Even more inspiring to the teachers were the children who had managed to progress without schooling the "resident miracles," as one teacher called them. There were, for example, the two brothers who, coached by a conscientious older sister using her own carefully save textbooks, had each advanced a full grade during the years since 1959. There was the thirteen-year-old girl who was in the third grade when the schools closed, but who had studied at home under the watchful eye of a grandmother and entered our free schools ready for eighth grade work, exactly where she would have been with schooling. Time and again, our initial grouping by ages revealed that the knowledgeable home environment was the factor that diminished learning loss. Out of some three hundred and fifty twelve-year-olds, for instance, over two hundred had serious reading problems. The others came from the homes where the parents were educated, where there were books and reading matter, or were older brothers and sisters, aware of the importance of study, had helped them.

The other good news was that the Free Schools in one year were able to help so many students recover some of the ground lost. In just a year the IQs were restored to the normal range and in fact three of the 1,570 students had IQs of over 150. One of the essential ingredients of the Free School success was that, unlike in the public schools, where 35 or more students per class was the norm, in the Free Schools, the ratio was 14 students to one teacher in high school and 21 to 1 at the elementary level.

Even after only a few weeks the teachers started to report that the students were awakening slowly, as though coming out of a long sleep. They had started to find the words to express the dreams and nightmares of the past four years.

"I wish I was six years old instead of being 10 and just starting school," one little boy said

"I didn't like to see the white children go by my house every day with books under their arms", said another.

"It seemed as if no one loved me", was the way one little girl put it. "I wished and wished I could just pass a school and see the doors open."

One of the older children asked her teacher wonderingly, "Why do you think the white people don't want us to learn?"

As Dr. Sullivan settled into life in Prince Edward County he and his wife moved from their temporary lodgings, in a local hotel, to a rented home located on Jefferson Davis Highway, five miles south of Farmville. The rural tranquility of this country location however, was frequently disturbed by the violence and harassment of racial hatred.

The House had a long semicircular driveway which, almost as soon as we moved in, became the local Indianapolis Speedway. Races began every morning about 2 A.M. and for the next two or three hours we listen to the sound of blowing horns, screeching tires, racing motors and catcalls as night riders of the local lunatic fringe roared ceaselessly in, around and out of our driveway. Our night visitors soon became more brazen. They began to leave calling cards as they drove by. First we found garbage dumped in the driveway, then on the lawn, and finally on our front steps. Trees in our yard were often decorated with floral arrangements which had obviously been taken from the local cemeteries. We got the message. Martha and I were worried enough by this time to take some precautions. We decided to sleep in separate bedrooms, figuring that if a bomb were dropped on us one night, our sons might still have at least one parent left.

Dr. Sullivan, "realized from the beginning that only a tiny minority of Prince Edward citizens were actively harassing us." Nonetheless, the constant harassment took its toll with many sleepless nights and untold worry.

As word of the Prince Edward County Free Schools got out across the country, citizens responded with notes of encouragement, boxes of books, and financial contributions. One man in New York wrote, "two weeks ago my father died after a lifetime of fighting for underprivileged, and in his memory I enclose check to help your fine work. Of course, progress is slow, but we *will* make 'the better world.' Good luck!"

When Leonard Bernstein learned that the students had no musical instruments, he helped the schools find the instruments for an entire band that was able, at graduation, to give a full dress concert playing not less than a dozen numbers.

While disciplinary problems were almost nonexistent there were problems with absenteeism. As part of Virginia's massive resistance, the General Assembly had repealed its compulsory school laws. This was felt necessary to protect the Prince

Edward Board of Supervisors from legal liability. Given that most of the students came from farms and if their help were needed on the farm it was very difficult for them to attend school under those circumstances. Here again, Rev. Griffin, his church, and NAACP contacts helped reinforce to all the families the need to send their children to school full time.

The death of President Kennedy on November 22, 1963, was especially significant to the students and parents and teachers of the Free School. President Kennedy was the one who said, "We must do something about Prince Edward County" and then he went about doing it. A special book was sent to Mrs. Kennedy signed by all of the students. The inscription read, "your sorrow is very much our own." An unexpected correlation surfaced following the president's death—much of the harassment of Dr Sullivan and his staff stopped. Why did the harassment all but stop? Dr. Sullivan felt there might have been a growing acceptance of the Free School in the general community. Or maybe folks just saw what looked like "staring into the abyss" and wanted to pull back.

Life in the Free Schools continued to march forward toward the Christmas break , yet, significant challenges remained and, fortunately, many successes were achieved as well. The schools became an exciting educational and cultural center for the children starving for this kind of attention. Some of the examples cited in *Bound for Freedom* are:

- The Robert Russa Moton high school library reported that the 700 high school students borrowed a total of 6,000 library books every month.
- Some students had started home libraries with their share of gifts from the thousands of books that poured into the Free School.
- A drama club produced an original one-act play.
- In the high school art classes, boys and girls who had never held a crayon before were now able to speaking knowingly of Italian painters and turn out sophisticated three-color soaked prints.

- In the elementary school, the Free School band was formed with the instruments provided by Leonard Bernstein of the New York Philharmonic.

- Special education teacher Madge Ship reported an 11-year-old boy had been so overjoyed after weeks of trying to read that: "He stopped. He looked up from the book. And then he shouted, 'I can read! Listen! I can read!'"

- The students were visited by notables like Bobby Mitchell, a star halfback with the Washington Redskins and Dr. Milton Coleman, head of Washington and Lee University. Also, 20 foreign exchange students from countries like Afghanistan, Pakistan, Japan, and Brazil came to visit the Free School.

- Students traveled outside of Prince Edward County, many for the first time, with trips to Richmond, Charlottesville, Washington, and New York to visit the United Nations.

In the spring of 1964, the Free Schools got a boost with a visit from Robert Kennedy, U.S. Attorney General. He toured the schools, had lunch with the children in the cafeteria, met with the families and parents of the children, and met with the county officials. Then an event occurred that was to take 46 years to come full circle. Kennedy received a portrait of his deceased brother from an aspiring artist named Louis Briel. Mr. Briel from the Hampden-Sydney College class of 1966 painted a portrait of President John F. Kennedy following the assassination heartbreak. Attorney General Robert Kennedy received the portrait while visiting the campus of Hampden-Sydney College where Briel was a student.

Briel has built upon that moment to become a distinguished portrait artist. Since 1993, his portrait of tennis great Arthur Ashe hangs in the Smithsonian Institution. In 1995 the U. S. House of Representatives added his portrait of Rep. Thomas J. Bliley, Chairman of the Commerce Committee, to its collection.

His work that should most interest the reader of this book is the portrait Briel painted, in 2010, of Barbara Rose Johns as she was preparing for the student strike.

At the unveiling on September 17, 2010, Virginia Governor, Bob McDonnell said, "It is my pleasure to unveil this portrait of a young woman who simply and gracefully formulated a dream of equality from her personal experience with inequality. It will inspire a new generation of students." He went on to reminded everyone of what he said of her in his inaugural address, "Barbara Johns was willing to risk everything for the simple opportunity of a good education. Surely, 60 years later we can work together to provide that opportunity to all Virginia children."

—— LEGAL FIGHT DRAWS DOWN ——

On Monday, March 30, 1964, a group of the Free School students traveled to Washington to observe the United States Supreme Court hearings that were to finally decide the Prince Edward County school desegregation case. Among the students who attended the Supreme Court proceedings that day was Leslie "Skippy" Griffin, the 16-year-old son of the Rev. Francis Griffin. Young Griffin possessed the highest scholastic average at the Robert Russa Moton high school. The court case was brought by Rev. Griffin to challenge the closing of the schools in Prince Edward County and the closing of all the public schools in Virginia and the Nation. The final curtain call was about to go down on the legal process that started with the original 1951 filing by Oliver Hill and Spotswood Robinson of the NAACP. For 13 years, the case had moved back and forth from Virginia courts to the Supreme Court. Today was the day it would finally be decided. However, as Chief Justice Warren closed the hearing that day, all knew they would have to wait a few more months for the written ruling to be issued. As it turned out, the ruling came on May 25, 1964, almost exactly 10 years to the day after the more famous and first ruling in this case:

On May 25, 1964, writing for a Unanimous Court, Justice Hugo Black held that the Prince Edward County Board of

Supervisors had acted unconstitutionally in closing the public schools and that the African American school children have been denied equal protection of the laws. Public education in the governmental responsibility for it had been affirmed and the insidious system of tuition grants to support segregated private education was stricken down.

The ruling meant the resumption of public schools for Prince Edward County and ensured the rest of the Nation would never go down that same rabbit hole. This left the Free Schools with one more task to complete. Nearly a month later, on June 15, 1964, it was a steamy day inside the Robert Russa Moton High School when the Free School ended its existence with their first and only graduation ceremony—the first graduation of a class of blacks from a school in Prince Edward County in five years. One measure of the Free School success was that more than half of the 23 students graduating that day were planning to attend college or continue their education in some way.

Recalling the event, Dr. Sullivan wrote, "How many good memories this year had brought to these young people—not just these 23 graduates, but all 1,578 of the students enrolled in the Free Schools. And how great had been the accomplishments of these once almost-forgotten children of Prince Edward County; and only 10 months time, they had (by tests proof) advanced an average of two years scholastically. Some boys and girls had advanced three and even four years in that time."

With the public schools returning in September, the Free Schools staff took extra efforts to help make it a smooth opening. There would no longer be any need for a Free School, with this one year experiment having done so much good, they were now slated to go out of business, yet they achieved their ultimate end which was to resume education for all the children in Prince Edward County. The Free Schools worked to help reopen all the schools, transferred thousands of books, turned over superior audiovisual gear, clean and modern facilities, and helped with those teachers who wanted to remain working in the Prince Edward County school system.

William J. vanden Heuvel recalls the years following the Free School closing. "In the few remaining years of his life, Atty. Gen. and later Sen. Robert Kennedy and I talked often about Prince Edward County. One of its legacies is an idea that was born of our witness to the extraordinary idealism of America's teachers who responded to the call almost overnight to build the Free Schools of Prince Edward County. I wrote a memorandum suggesting a National Teacher's Corps so that those wonderful teachers around the country who truly wanted to be involved in the struggle for civil rights and against poverty could enlist for a year or two, maintaining their base in their home communities, while traveling to those portions of the country where the brilliance of their commitment could bring hope to American children who might otherwise never have a chance. It became law and survives to this day, not as we had originally proposed it but nevertheless effective."

——— AN UNSETTLING QUIET ———

Visitors to Prince Edward County often commented on the quiet, dignity so often exhibited by the blacks throughout this 13-year ordeal. They never wavered in their quest for educational equality, as they continually suffered indignities from those who would keep their children forever undereducated, poor, and on the land.

Carlton Terry was 12 when he was locked out of school: "I eventually got to the point where I hated whites," he recalls. "All I knew was that I wasn't in school and I knew the reason why. I realized that the legal system was not working, at least not working for me. I remember sitting at home, watching *Amos 'n' Andy* on TV, shell shocked. I read the newspaper every day to see what would happen."

After a year, the Quakers sent him to school in Massachusetts. He went on to earn degrees from Antioch College and Princeton University, and became a Foreign Service officer for the Agency for International Development in Kenya.

"I don't know why I'm not bitter," he says. "My cousin Thelma hates Virginia with a passion. I only lost one year, and I feel like I was hurt. But imagine what it must be like for those who lost four or five years or never went back."

"I'm surprised that no one said, 'Listen, this is madness.' Why did it take so long? Why would Virginia allow that to happen? I can't understand how America let that go on."

In 1963, as a freshman in Keith Junior High School, New Bedford, Massachusetts, Terry wrote an essay for the school newspaper that chronicled the crisis up to that point—with the schools already closed for four years. The name of the essay was *The Crippled Generation*. It seems Terry was picking up where Dean Moss left off. It was Moss who first coined the expression, "The Crippled Generation," in his appearance on NBC television's *Chet Huntley Reports* in August 1962. He was of course referring to the Negro children of Prince Edward County that had been out of school for four years and were the obvious casualties. His assumption was that the white children were faring just about as well as they would have in their private schools as they would have fared in the old public schools. Carlton went on to explain that, "The name that I give this essay, *The Crippled Generation*, is an excellent title in my opinion because it is a good description of the situation as it happened. A generation left lame, and to be cured must take a great deal of money, effort, time, sweat, and a few tears to do the job accurately." Terry Carlton's essay went on to say:

> While the federal court of the United States ordered the University of Mississippi to open its doors to James Meredith, and it has not done so in the case of Prince Edward County, Virginia, where schools have been closed completely for four years[since 1959]. There have been an estimated number of one-thousand seven hundred Negro children out of school. Reason: integration against segregation.
>
> Prince Edward County is located in the southeastern part of Virginia. Its county seat is Farmville, population 4000. The county has two colleges, Hampden-Sydney for boys and the Longwood College for girls. As you can read, it

is quite educational as far as the two institutions for higher learning are concerned, but yet ignorant in the denial of public education.

We are cognizant of the fact that this problem is a disaster to the Negro children of Prince Edward and not to the white. Many of the children that have been without formal education for four years are very unlikely to return back to school when and if ever they open again. They will feel as if they are too old to be in.
I am Carlton Terry, now a freshman at Keith Junior High School. I've come to the school because I had been denied a public school education within my own county.

We, the Negro, think that the cause of this is because in 1953[sic] when my two sisters were in high school, we boycotted for a new school rather than the old 'tar top' high school that we did have.

—Carlton Terry, "The Crippled Generation", *The Keith Junior High School Chronicle*, New Bedford, Massachusetts, May 28, 1963

PUBLIC SCHOOLS RESUME

With all of this as the backdrop, the Free School staff did their best to manage expectations regarding just how much ground could be made up in one year. While Dr. Sullivan considered the situation educationally grim, he did feel hopeful of progress: "Four years loss will never be made up entirely. All I've said is that will narrow the gap." Many in the black community recognized that the older teenage Negro youths represented a special problem. In general the efforts to bring them back to school largely failed. Many had only one more year to go to attain their high school degrees, but some had been working for four years and were now wage earners well beyond the typical high school age demographic and they were unwilling or unable to make the adjustment back to being students.

Notwithstanding this group, most all of the remaining African American youngsters in the county did go back to school in 1963. While it was debated hotly whether the five years of no public education stunned the economic growth of the county, it is intriguing that Prince Edward lost population during this period, after a century of relative stability. Most observers felt that Prince Edward was seen or was part of a national trend away from rural areas but, most honest assessments contributed some of the lost population to the school closings. The African American population declined significantly more than the white.

During the same period that the schools were closed, Farmville and most of the rest of rural Virginia were increasingly courting businesses and industries to move to their community. A core group of progressive businessmen in Farmville had begun to actively try to attract industry to the town. They purchased a 20-acre site west of town and developed adequate sewage and water for development. However, they found little interest from the business community, who had no desire in coming into a community that had abandoned its public schools. The newly formed Farmville Area Development Corporation struggled to attract any prospects to even listen to their pitch. S. Waverly Putney, Junior, who was president of the corporation during this time and a member of the Board of Directors from its inception in 1950, relates that the closed schools definitely discouraged one industry and probably affected the decision of others. And he was convinced that the bad effects of the closed schools would not end even when they were reopened: "Sure it will last. You heard plenty about the aftereffects in Little Rock, didn't you?"

On June 16, 1964 taking his cue from the May 25, 1964 Supreme Court decision Judge Lewis, of the 4th District Court ordered the Prince Edward County supervisors to reopen the public schools. He also went so far as to include instructions for the supervisors regarding "appropriation of sufficient funds with ninety days to reopen schools in September." Judge Lewis was enforcing the highest court's decision that no further delay in opening integrated public schools would be tolerated. By a four-to-two vote the supervisors appropriated the $189,000 to operate the public schools. This was $41,000 less than the school board had requested and reflected grudging compliance with the court order. This appropriation reflected a 31 percent local contribution when the county average contribution across Virginia was 48 percent. Reverend Griffin's take on the appropriation was, "hopelessly inadequate" and he went on to conjecture, "an integrated school system is not intended by the supervisors." T. J. McIlwaine was still the superintendent of schools and had stunning news for the county residence in February 1965. "The main trouble is that they (the Negro pupils) are not prepared to take the courses we are offering. Reading is probably the most important problem; it is the key to everything else." Four years of no school had had their effect on the students and apparently on the memory of the superintendent. The end result was that public schools opened in September 1964 with blacks now continuing their schooling in the same schools operated by the Free Schools with only a handful of whites in attendance. This has been referred to as integration in reverse.

The Prince Edward County story does not end with the opening of public schools in 1964. Blacks and concerned whites fought the school board for many years following the opening to attain adequate funding and a quality education for their children. With the improvements in the public schools more and more whites migrated back from the Academy to the public schools. In 1971 a new superintendent took over the troubled Prince Edward County school system. James M. Anderson is credited with rebuilding the shattered school system and he stayed at it for twenty-five years. By 1974, the school had seen the white students grow to 16 percent. In 1978, fourteen years after the public schools resumed operation, under Anderson's leadership there were close to six hundred whites and seventeen hundred blacks now enrolled in the public schools. Whites attending public schools with blacks was important for a number of reasons, but not the least was the more whites in attendance the easier appropriately funding the schools became. Today Prince Edward County is often cited as an example of an effective and genuinely integrated school system with whites and blacks about evenly divided and the beneficiary of strong community support for the schools.

Time may or may not heal all wounds, but, we today can certainly gain a perspective on a moment in history once we've gotten some distance from it. Here are two separate accountings, of what was gained and lost, that were written in 1991 and 2008 respectively. As you read Egerton and Smith's account recognize they were written 17 years apart. While there are those who have never changed their minds the authors accurately reflect the softening of attitudes and the increased worth today placed on the shoulders of those fighting for integration—Barbara Rose Johns, John Stokes, Oliver W. Hill, SR. and Reverend Griffin. Many more can now see, in the light of the post 911 America, just how ridicules such an aberration as segregation would look to the world.

In 1991, twenty-seven years after the schools opened John Egerton wrote in *Shades of Gray: Dispatches from the Modern South*, "It was a reactionary step taken with deliberation by mild-mannered whites against mild-mannered blacks, and it was ultimately fruitless and destructive." He further conjectured that when it was all over, "the people of Farmville and Prince Edward County could look about them and wonder what their 'gentleman's disagreement' had wrought. Desegregation had begun, but in a way and to an extent unsatisfactory to virtually everyone; segregation still reigned, but at a cost burdensome to all."

Bob Smith, discusses his changing view in the updated preface from his re-released book in 2008, *They Closed Their Schools*. Smith's conclusion from the original publication, in 1965, was that there may not have been any winners or losers, and, at that time, he felt not enough attention had been placed on the young people who had given up so much. But, in 2008, upon further reflection, he recognized that the struggle in Prince Edward County was worth it and was one of those shaky steps the country took towards racial fairness: "For all the pain it inflicted, the battle in Prince Edward County those long years ago was hard fought and won. And the victory was not an empty one as the author feared back then; to the contrary, it now seems rich with significance."

Possibly the more profound questions are those of a moral nature. Was it right and just in 20th-century America for a community to close its public schools? And was it right for the Commonwealth of Virginia to use the powers of the General

Assembly and the governor and the attorney general's office to direct and support such closings? Frankly, these are not questions for the court, but questions of honor and humanity.

EPILOGUE

We know all too well the cruelties, hurts, and hatreds that poison life on our planet. But my daughter and I have come together to write this book because we know that a catalogue of injuries that we can and do inflict on one another is not the whole story of humanity, not by a long measure — as I hope you will see and as you no doubt know in your heart. We are indeed made for something more. We are made for goodness.

—Desmond M. Tutu, Mpho A. Tutu.
Made for Goodness: And Why This Makes All the Difference

The above quote is a fitting way to begin to end this book. This particular father and daughter team who directly felt the wrongs from others are still able to inspire us by proclaiming, "We are made for goodness." This is just how I think about the Prince Edward County integration struggle. I acknowledge the wrongs of segregation, the sacrifices made, the hurt and pain, the insanity of closing schools for five years, and yet I see the bright promise of a better world created by these civil rights pioneers.

The struggle was a test for all involved: whites, blacks, county government officials, NAACP lawyers and leaders, parents, and those who are central to this story the students. All suffered small or great anguish, trauma, and loss. So who won? In the end, the people of America won. We moved a step closer toward our ideals of a just society where all men are created equal. However, as with any struggle, there were casualties. While all the groups involved paid a price, none paid a higher price than the hundreds of African American children who had their education and future stolen from them, even before they had a chance to get started. All that we, the beneficiaries of their sacrifice, can do now is to continue to make our world a more just and caring place, be mindful of the debt we owe these pioneers, and not squander the legacy we have inherited.

The story of Barbara Rose Johns and her fellow strikers is compelling and you can feel that in their hearts they knew they deserved better and they were not being treated fairly. No one can tell where history will be forged, but certainly the strikers forged a legacy of courage and determination and, maybe most important, a belief in the American system to right wrongs that we can all admire. A child in a packed auditorium, another child, almost an adult, on a freedom ride, a man with a dream, and another man, a white president from Texas, changing the law of the land—all made history and changed our world for the better.

I hope you are able to visit the Moton Museum and learn more about our nation's rise above segregation. I am sure you will find the exhibits inspiring, educational and interesting. The words of this book will come alive through the audio, video, and images that vividly tell the story of the Prince Edward County integration struggle. Though, the biggest draw to visiting the museum is to get the feeling of "place"—that magical force that propels us into deep thought, stirs our emotions, and fills us with a desire to join in or go do something. The classrooms are still there. You can see where Principal Boyd's office was. A bell to ring the change of class periods still hangs on the wall. And, you can sit in the famous auditorium and see the stage where Barbara Rose Johns stood and raised her voice for an equal education in 1951.

Another place to visit is the Virginia Civil Rights Memorial on Capital Square in Richmond. As you walk from the Ninth Street entrance, you pass on your left, a statue of Senator Harry F. Byrd, the architect of massive resistance, and a statue of Confederate general Thomas J. "Stonewall" Jackson — aptly ironic preludes to the magnificent civil rights memorial. The four-sided memorial features: Barbara Rose Johns leading her fellow students on their fateful strike in 1951, the NAACP attorneys Robinson and Hill are on the second panel, Reverend L. Francis Griffin stands steady on a third panel, and on the final panel a diverse group of children leading the way forward to a better future. The front cover of *Reaching for the Moon* features the panel with Barbara Rose Johns striding forward to lead her community toward equality.

Further, you can just make out on the other side of the executive mansion the Oliver W. Hill, Sr. building, and, just across the street, on Ninth Street, is the Virginia Supreme Court, where so much of Virginia's civil-rights litigation was played out in the '50s and '60s. The place is suffused with irony, historical significance, and sobriety.

Every time I stand in front of the panel with the statue of Barbara Rose Johns I sense her strength, determination, and quiet dignity—serene fire indeed. And yet she seems to always be asking me questions. "Are you doing enough?" "Are you reaching for the Moon?" These are questions we all have to answer for ourselves.

If this book inspires you the reader to make a difference then the price of the words you now hold in your hands are paid in full and they have accomplished their intended purpose; and more importantly Barbara Rose Johns' legacy will have been honored. Making a difference can mean standing up to injustice like the Moton strikers, or helping someone who is having a difficult time, or a simple kind word to a stranger, or helping yourself by staying in school and reaching out to grab hold of your potential. After all the real power behind President Kennedy's words about one person making a difference is the final thought, "…every person should try."

One person can make a difference and every person should try.

—John F. Kennedy

Whatever of labor and pains may have gone into this story, I shall feel amply repaid if it encourages any member of my race to greater faith in himself, as well as in other selves, both white and black; and shall help him to make his life count for the very most in meeting and solving the great human problem which we in this country call the "race problem."

—Robert Russa Moton, Finding a Way Out: An Autobiography

Appendix I
Original Address of Dr. Robert Russa Moton (never delivered)

Below is the speech Dr. Robert Russa Moton prepared to give at the Dedication of the Lincoln Memorial, Washington, D. C., to be held on May 30th, 1922. This particular address was never given as the Harding administration censored this speech as too anti-southern and too pro civil rights.

Address of Dr. Robert Russa Moton
at the Dedication of the Lincoln Memorial
Washington, D. C.
May 30th, 1922
(Original Draft dated May 17, 1922)

When the Pilgrim Fathers set foot upon the shores of America in 1620, they laid the foundations of our national existence upon the bed-rock of liberty. From that day to this, liberty has been the watchword, liberty has been the rallying call, liberty has been the battle cry of our united people. In 1776, the altars of a new nation were set up in the name of liberty and the flag of freedom unfurled before the nations of the earth. In 1812, in the name of liberty, we bared our youthful might, and struck for the freedom of the seas. Again, in '61, when the charter of the nation's birth was assailed, the sons of liberty declared anew the principles of their fathers and liberty became co-extensive with the union. In '98, the call once more was heard and freedom became co-extensive with the hemisphere. And as we stand in solemn silence here today before this newly consecrated shrine of liberty, there still come rumbling out of the East the slowly dying echoes of the last great struggle to make freedom coextensive with seven seas. Freedom is the life-blood of the nation. Freedom is the heritage bequeathed to all her sons. For sage and scholar, for poet and prophet, for soldier and statesman, freedom is the underlying philosophy of our national existence.

But at the same time, another influence was working within the nation. While the Mayflower was riding at anchor preparing for her epoch-making voyage, another ship had already arrived at Jamestown, Virginia. The first was to bear the pioneers of freedom, freedom of thought and freedom of conscience; the latter had already borne the pioneers of bondage, a bondage degrading alike to body, mind and spirit. Here then, upon American soil, within a year, met the two great forces that were to shape the destiny of the nation. They developed side by side. Freedom was the great compelling force that dominated all and, like a great and shining light, beckoned the oppressed of every nation to the hospitality of these shores. But slavery like a brittle thread in a beautiful garment was woven year by year into the fabric of the nation's life. They who for themselves sought liberty and paid the price thereof in precious blood and priceless treasure, somehow still found it possible while defending its eternal principles for themselves, to deny that same precious boon to others.

And how shall we account for it, except it be that in the Providence of God, the black race in America was thrust across the path of the onward-marching white race to demonstrate not only for America, but for the world whether the principles of freedom were of universal application. From the ends of the earth were brought together the extremes of humanity to prove whether the right to life, liberty and the pursuit of happiness should apply with equal force to all mankind.

In the process of time, these two great forces met, as was inevitable, in open conflict upon the field of battle. And how strange it is that by the same over-ruling Providence, the children of those who bought and sold their fellows into bondage should be the very ones to cast aside ties of language, of race, of religion and even of kinship, in order that a people not of their own race, nor primarily of their own creed or color, but brethren withal, should have the same measure of liberty and freedom which they enjoyed.

What a costly sacrifice upon the altar of freedom! How costly the world can never know nor estimate! The flower of the nation's manhood and the accumulated treasure of two hundred and fifty years of unremitting toil: and at length, when the bitter strife was over, when the marshaled hosts had turned again to broken, desolated firesides, a cruel fate, unsatisfied with the awful toll of four long years of carnage, struck at the nation's head and brought to the dust the already wearied frame of him, whose patient fortitude, whose unembittered charity, whose never failing trust in the guiding hand of God had brought the nation, weltering through a sea of blood, yet one and indivisible, to the placid plains of peace. On that day, Abraham Lincoln laid down his life for America, the last and costliest sacrifice upon the altar of freedom.

We do well to raise here this symbol of our gratitude. Here today assemble all those who are blessed by that sacrifice. The united nation stands about this memorial mingling its reverent praise with tokens of eternal gratitude: and not America only, but every nation where liberty is loved and freedom flourishes, joins the chorus of universal praises for him, who with his death, sealed forever the pledge of liberty for all mankind.

But in all this vast assemblage, there are none more grateful, none more reverent, than those who, representing twelve millions of black Americans, gather with their fellow-citizens of every race and creed to pay devout homage to him who was for them, more truly than for any other group, the author of their freedom. There is no question that this man died to save the union. It is equally true that to the last extremity he defended the rights of states. But, when the last veteran has stacked his arms on fame's eternal camping ground; when only the memory of high courage and deep devotion remains to inspire the noble sons of valiant fathers; at such a time, the united voice of grateful posterity will say: the claim of greatness for Abraham Lincoln lies in this, that amid doubt and distrust, against the counsel of his chosen advisors, in the hour of the nation's utter peril, he put his trust in God and spoke the word that gave freedom to a race, and vindicated the honor of a nation conceived in liberty and dedicated to the proposition that all men are created equal.

But someone will ask: Has such a sacrifice been justified? Has such a martyrdom produced worthy fruits? I speak for the Negro race. Upon us, more perhaps than upon any other group of the nation, rests the immediate obligation to justify so dear a price for our emancipation. In answer let me review the Negroes past upon American soil. No group has been more loyal.

Whether bond or free, he has served alike his country's need. Let it never be omitted from the nation's annals that the blood of a black man—Crispus Attucks—was the first to be shed for the nation's freedom; and first his name appears in the long list of the nation's martyred dead. So again, when a world was threatened with disaster and the deciding hand of America was lifted to stay the peril, her black soldiers were among the first to cross the treacherous sea; and when the cause was won, and the record made of those who shared the cruel hardship, these same black soldiers had been longest in the trenches, nearest to the enemy and first to cross their border. All too well does the black man know his wrongs. No one is more sensible than he of his incongruous position in the great American republic. But be it recorded to his everlasting credit, that no failure on the part of the nation to deal fairly with him as a citizen has, in the least degree, ever qualified his loyalty. In like manner has he served his country in the pursuits of peace. From the first blows that won the virgin soil from the woods and wilderness to the sudden, marvelous expansion of our industry that went so far to win the war, the Negro has been the nation's greatest single asset in the development of its vast resources. Especially is this true in the South where his unrequited toil sustained the splendors of that life which gave to the nation a Washington and a Jefferson, a Jackson and a Lee. And afterwards, when devastating war had leveled this fair structure with the ground, the labor of the freedom restored it to its present proportions, more substantial than before.

While all this was going on, in spite of limitations within and restrictions without, he still found the way to buy land, to build homes, to erect churches, to establish schools and to lay the foundations of future development in industry, integrity and thrift. It is no mere accident that Negroes in America after less than sixty years of freedom own 22,000,000 acres of land, 600,000 homes and 45,000 churches. It is no mere accident that after so short a time Negroes should operate 78 banks, 100 insurance companies, and 50,000 business enterprises representing a combined capital value of more than $150,000,000. Neither is it *an accident that there are within the race 60,000 professional men, 44,000 school teachers and 400 newspapers and magazines, that general illiteracy has been reduced to twenty percent. Still the Negro race is only in the infancy of its development, so that, if anything in its history could justify the sacrifice that has been made, it is this: that a race that has exhibited such wonderful capacities for advancement should have the restrictions of bondage removed and be given the opportunity in freedom to develop its powers to the utmost, not only for itself, but for the nation and for humanity. Any race that could produce a Frederick Douglass in the midst of slavery and a Booker Washington in the aftermath of reconstruction has a just claim to the fullest opportunity for development.*

But Lincoln died, not for the Negro alone, but to vindicate the honor of a nation pledged to the sacred cause of human freedom. Upon the field of Gettysburg he dedicated the nation to the great unfinished work of making sure that "government of the people, for the people and by the people should not perish from the earth". And this means all the people. So long as any group within our nation is denied the full protection of the law; that task is still unfinished. So long as any there is abundant cause for rejoicing that sectional rancor and racial antagonisms are softening more and more into mutual understanding and increasing sectional and inter-racial cooperation. But unless here at home we are willing to grant to the least and humblest citizen the full enjoyment of every constitutional privilege, our boast is but a mockery and our professions as sounding brass and a tinkling cymbal before the nations of the earth. This is the only way to peace and security at home, to honor and respect abroad.

Sometimes I think the national government itself has not always set the best example for the states in this regard. A government which can venture abroad to put an end to injustice and mob-violence in another country can surely find a way to put an end to these same evils within our own borders. The Negro race is not insensible of the difficulties that such a task presents; but unless we can together, North and South, East and West, black and white, find the way out of these difficulties and square ourselves with the enlightened conscience and public opinion of all mankind, we must stand convicted not only of inconsistency and hypocrisy, but of the deepest ingratitude that could stain the nation's honor. Twelve million black men and women in this country are proud of their American citizenship, but they are determined that it shall mean for them no less than for any other group, the largest enjoyment of opportunity and the fullest blessings of freedom. We ask no special privileges; we claim no superior title; but we do expect in loyal cooperation with all true lovers of our common country to do our full share in lifting our country above reproach and saving her flag from stain or humiliation. Let us, therefore, with malice toward none, with charity for all, with firmness in the right as God gives us to see the right — let us strive on to finish the work which he so nobly began, to make America the symbol for equal justice and equal opportunity for all.

(THE END)

—Original speech draft from Library of Congress

Appendix II
The Speech Dr. Robert Russa Moton Delivered

Below is the speech Dr. Robert Russa Moton delivered at the
Dedication of the Lincoln Memorial, Washington, D. C., on May
30th, 1922. Moton toned down his original address to not upset
southern sensibilities as the mood of the White House, and
indeed white America was most decidedly in favor of
reconciliation between the North and South, and little attention
was to be paid to racial justice.

Address of Dr. Robert Russa Moton
at the Dedication of the Lincoln Memorial
Washington, D. C.
May 30th, 1922
(Final Draft)

When the Pilgrim Fathers set foot upon the shores of America
in 1620, they laid the foundations of our national existence upon
the bed-rock of liberty. From that day to this, liberty has been the
watchword, liberty has been the rallying call, liberty has been the
battle cry of our united people. In 1776, the altars of a new
nation were set up in the name of liberty and the flag of freedom
unfurled before the nations of the earth. In 1812, in the name of
liberty, we bared our youthful might, and struck for the freedom
of the seas. Again, in '61, when the charter of the nation's birth
was assailed, the sons of liberty declared anew the principles of
their fathers and liberty became co-extensive with the union. In
'98, the call once more was heard and freedom became co-
extensive with the hemisphere. And as we stand in solemn silence
here today before this newly consecrated shrine of liberty, there
still come rumbling out of the East the slowly dying echoes of the
last great struggle to make freedom coextensive with seven seas.
Freedom is the life-blood of the nation. Freedom is the lifeblood
of the nation. Freedom is that heritage bequeathed to all her

sons. For all who reflect upon the glory of our republic, freedom is the underlying philosophy of our national existence.

But at the same time, another influence was working within the nation. While the Mayflower was riding at anchor preparing for her epoch-making voyage, another ship had already arrived at Jamestown, Virginia. The first was to bear the pioneers of freedom, freedom of thought and freedom of conscience; the latter had already borne the pioneers of bondage, a bondage degrading alike to body, mind and spirit. Here then, upon American soil, within a year, met the two great forces that were to shape the destiny of the nation. They developed side by side. Freedom was the great compelling force that dominated all and, like a great and shining light, beckoned the oppressed of every nation to the hospitality of these shores. But slavery like a brittle thread in a beautiful garment was woven year by year into the fabric of the nation's life. They who for themselves sought liberty and paid the price thereof in precious blood and priceless treasure, somehow still found it possible while defending its eternal principles for themselves, to deny that same precious boon to others.

And how shall we account for it, except it be that in the Providence of God, the black race in America was thrust across the path of the onward-marching white race to demonstrate not only for America, but for the world whether the principles of freedom were of universal application, and ultimately to extend its blessings to all mankind.

In the process of time, as was inevitable, these great forces, the forces of liberty and the forces of bondage, from the ships at Plymouth and Jamestown, met in open conflict upon the field of battle. And how strange it is that by the same over-ruling Providence, the children of those who bought and sold their fellows into bondage should be the very ones to cast aside ties of language, of race, of religion and even of kinship, in order that a people not of their own race, nor primarily of their own creed or color, but sharing a common humanity, should have the same measure of liberty and freedom which they enjoyed.

What a costly sacrifice upon the altar of freedom! How costly the world can never know nor estimate! The flower of the nation's manhood and the accumulated treasure of two hundred *and fifty years of unremitting toil were offered up: and at length, when the bitter strife was over, when the marshaled hosts on both sides had turned again to broken, desolated firesides, a cruel fate, unsatisfied with the awful toll of four long years of carnage, struck at the nation's head and brought to the dust the already wearied frame of him, whose patient fortitude, whose unembittered charity, whose never failing trust in the guiding hand of God had brought the nation, weltering through a sea of blood, yet one and indivisible, to quietudes and peace. On that day, Abraham Lincoln laid down his life for America, the last and costliest sacrifice upon the altar of freedom.*

Today, in this inspiring presence, we racist symbol of gratitude for all who are blest by that sacrifice. But in all this vast assemblage, there are none more grateful, none more reverent, than those who, representing twelve millions of black Americans, with their fellow-citizens of every race, pay devout homage to him who was for them, more truly than for any other group, the author of their freedom. There is no question that Abraham Lincoln died to save the union. It is equally true that to the last extremity he defended the rights of states. But, when the last veteran has stacked his arms in ever-lasting peace; when only the memory of high courage and deep devotion remains to inspire the noble sons of valiant fathers; at such a time, the united voice of grateful posterity will say: the claim of greatness for Abraham Lincoln lies in this, that amid doubt and distrust, against the counsel of chosen advisors, in the hour of the nation's utter peril, he put his trust in God and spoke the word that gave freedom to a race, and vindicated the honor of a nation conceived in liberty and dedicated to the proposition that all men are created equal.

But someone will ask: Has such a sacrifice been justified? Has such a martyrdom produced worthy fruits? I speak for the Negro race. Upon us, more perhaps than upon any other group of the nation, rests the immediate obligation to justify so dear a price for our emancipation. In answer let me review the Negroes past upon American soil. No group has been more loyal. Whether bond or free, he has served alike his country's need. Let it never be omitted from the nation's annals that the blood of a black man - - Crispus Attucks - - was the first to be shed for the nation's

*freedom. So again, when a world was threatened with disaster
and the deciding hand of America was lifted to stay the peril, her
black soldiers were among the first to cross the treacherous sea;
and the last to leave the trenches. No one is more sensible than
the Negro himself of his incongruous position in the great
American republic. But be recorded to his everlasting credit, that
no failure on his part to reap the full reward of his sacrifices has
ever in the last degree qualified his loyalty or cooled his patriotic
fervor.*

*In like manner has he served his country in the pursuits of
peace. From the first blows that won the virgin soil from the
woods and wilderness to the sudden, marvelous expansion of our
industry that went so far to win the war, the Negro has been the
nation's greatest single asset in the development of its vast
resources. Especially is this true in the South where his
unrequited toil sustained the splendors of that life which gave to
the nation a Washington and a Jefferson, a Jackson and a Lee.
And afterwards, when devastating war had leveled this fair
structure with the ground, the labor of the freedman restored it to
its present proportions, more substantial and more beautiful than
before.*

*While all this was going on, in spite of limitations within and
restrictions without, he still found the way through industry,
integrity and threat to acquire 22,000,000 acres of land, 600,000
homes and 45,000 churches. After less than 60 years of freedom,
Negroes operate 78 banks, 100 insurance companies, and 50,000
business enterprises with a combined capital of more than
$150,000,000. Besides all this, there are within the race 60,000
professional men, 44,000 school teachers and 400 newspapers
and magazines; while its generally illiteracy has been reduced to
twenty percent. Still the Negro race, in these things, is but at the
beginning of its development; so that, if anything in its history
could justify the sacrifice that has been made, it is this: that a
race that has exhibited such wonderful capacities for
advancement has taken full advantage of its freedom to develop
its latent powers for itself and for the nation. A race that has
produced a Frederick Douglass in the midst of slavery, and a
Booker Washington in the aftermath of reconstruction has gone*

far to justify its emancipation. And the nation where such achievement is possible is full worthy of such heroic sacrifice.

But Lincoln did not die for the Negro alone. He freed the nation as well as a race. Those conflicting forces planted two hundred and fifty years before had slowly divided the nation in the spirit, in ideals and in policy. Passing suddenly beyond the bitterness of controversy, his taking-off served more than [unreadable word] itself to emphasize the enormity of the breach that had developed between the two sections. Not until then was there a full realization of the deep significance of his prophetic words: - - "This nation cannot endure half slave and half free."

That tragic event the Civil War shocked the conscience of the nation and stirred a great resolve to establish forever the priceless heritage so dearly bought. From that day, the noblest minds and hearts, both North and South, were bent to the healing of the breach and the restoration of the union. With a devotion that counted neither personal loss or gain, Abraham Lincoln held steadfastly to an ideal for the republic, that measured at full value, the worth of each race and section, cherishing at the same time the hope under God that all should share alike in the blessings of freedom. Now we rejoice in the far-seeing vision and unswerving faith that held firmly to its single purpose even in the midst of reproach, and preserved for all posterity the integrity of the nation.

Lincoln had not died in vain. Slowly through the years that noble spirit had been permeating every section of our land country. Sixty years ago he stood in lonely grandeur above a torn and bleeding nation, a towering figure of patient righteousness. Today his spirit animates the breasts of millions of his countrymen who unite with us to pay tribute to his lofty character and his immortal deed.

And now the whole world turns with anxious heart and eager eyes toward America. In the providence of God there has been started on these shores the great experiment of the ages - - an experiment in human relationships where men and women of every nation, of every race and creed are thrown together in daily contact Here we are engaged, consciously or unconsciously, in the great problem of determining how different races cannot only live together in peace but cooperate in working *out a higher and better civilization than has yet been achieved. At the extremes the white and black races face each other. Here in America these two races are charged under God with the responsibility of showing to the world how individuals, as well as races, may differ most widely in color and inheritance, and at the same time make themselves helpful even indispensable to each other's progress and prosperity. This is especially true in the South where the black man is found in greatest numbers and the two races are thrown in closest contact. And there today are found black men and white men who are working together in the spirit of Abraham Lincoln to establish in fact, what his death established in principle that a nation conceived in liberty and dedicated to the proposition that all men are created equal, <u>can</u> endure.*

As we gather on this consecrated spot, his spirit must rejoice that sectional rancor and racial antagonisms are softening more and more into mutual understanding and effective cooperation. And I like to think that here today, while we dedicate this symbol of our gratitude that the nation is dedicated anew by its own determined will to fulfill to the last letter the task imposed upon it by the martyred dead: that here it highly resolves, that the humblest citizen of whatever color or creed, shall enjoy that equal opportunity and unfettered freedom, for which the immortal Lincoln gave the last full measure of devotion.

And the progress of events confirms this view. Step by step has the nation been making its way forward in the spirit of the great Emancipator. And nowhere is this more true than in that section which sixty years ago seemed least in accord with his spirit and purpose, yet at this hour, in many things, is leading the rest of the nation toward the fulfillment of his hopes.

Twelve million black Americans share in the rejoicing of this hour. As yet, no other name so warms the heart or stirs the depths of their gratitude as that of Abraham Lincoln. To him above all others we owe the privilege of sharing as fellow-citizens in the consecration of this spot and the dedication of this shrine. In the name of Lincoln, twelve million black Americans pledge to the nation their continued loyalty and their unreserved cooperation in every effort to realize in deeds, the lofty principles established by his martyrdom. With malice toward none, with charity for all we dedicate ourselves and our posterity, with you and yours, to finish the work which he so nobly began, to make America an example for all the world of equal justice and equal opportunity for all.

(THE END)

—Delivered speech from Library of Congress

The legal system can force open doors and sometimes even knock down walls, but it cannot build bridges. That job belongs to you and me.

—Thurgood Marshall

Appendix III

DAVIS v. COUNTY SCHOOL BOARD OF PRINCE EDWARD COUNTY, 149 F.Supp. 431 (1957) Supreme Court Order

DAVIS v. COUNTY SCHOOL BOARD OF PRINCE EDWARD COUNTY
149 F.Supp. 431 (1957)

Dorothy E. DAVIS et al.

v.

COUNTY SCHOOL BOARD OF PRINCE EDWARD COUNTY et al.

Civ. A. No. 1333.

United States District Court E. D. Virginia, Richmond Division.

January 23, 1957.

Order Filed March 26, 1957.

Oliver W. Hill, Martin A. Martin, Spottswood W. Robinson, III, Richmond, Va., Thurgood Marshall, Robert L. Carter, New York City, for plaintiffs.

Hunton, Williams, Gay, Moore & Powell, T. Justin Moore, Archibald G. Robertson, John W. Riely, T. Justin Moore, Jr., Richmond, Va., for County School Board of Prince Edward County, Virginia, and Thomas J. McIlwaine.

J. Lindsay Almond, Jr., Atty. Gen. of Virginia, Henry T. Wickham, Sp. Asst. to Atty. Gen., for Commonwealth of Virginia.

HUTCHESON, Chief Judge.

This case originated in the Richmond Division upon the filing of a complaint on May 21, 1951. The declared object of the complaint was, in substance, to obtain a declaratory judgment holding that segregation of pupils in the public schools in the county by races constituted discrimination in violation of the Fourteenth Amendment to the Constitution of the United States. There were also allegations concerning the inequality of school facilities, which last constituted a somewhat unimportant part of the controversy.

The case was heard February 25-29, 1952, by a three-judge court which had been convened in accordance with the provisions of the statute. The opinion of that Court was filed on March 7, 1952, and is reported in D.C., 103 F.Supp. 337. An appeal was allowed on May 5, 1952, and on May 17, 1954, the Supreme Court handed down its opinion, reversing the findings and conclusions of this Court, the case having been consolidated with four other cases then pending before it. See Brown v. Board of Education, 347 U.S. 483, 74 S.Ct. 686, 98 L.Ed. 873. At the suggestion of the Court the case was further argued as to specific questions hereafter more fully discussed, and the Court filed its second opinion on May 31, 1955. 349 U.S. 294, 75 S.Ct. 753, 99 L. Ed. 1083. The mandate having been received by this Court on June 28, 1955, the case was called for further proceedings and on July 18, 1955, the three-judge court entered an order directing compliance with the terms of the mandate, but finding that it was not practicable to effect a change in the operation of the public schools of the county during the session beginning September 1955.

On April 23, 1956, plaintiffs filed a motion seeking an order fixing a time limit within which compliance with the order should be had, to which answer of the defendants was filed on June 29, 1956. On July 9, 1956, the three-judge court was reconvened and, pursuant to order previously entered, heard argument on the sole question of whether it should continue to function or if the case should be returned to the resident District Judge in whose division suit was instituted. On July 19, 1956, 142 F.Supp. 616, the Court announced its unanimous decision that since the constitutional question involved had been determined, the three-judge court should no longer function and the matter should be heard by the resident District Judge. On October 17, 1956, defendants filed a motion seeking the dismissal of the case upon the ground that the General Assembly of Virginia in extra session 1956 had provided the plaintiffs an adequate remedy at law in the courts of the Commonwealth.

The respective motions were argued on November 14, 1956, and the case is now before me as the resident District Judge for disposition of the motions upon the pleadings and certain exhibits which have been filed pertaining to the motions.

I am mindful that other District Courts have dealt with similar cases but in each case the Court was dealing with the record before it and with the problems of the particular locality affected by its order.

Consequently, those decisions afford little, if any, aid in dealing with this case.

The questions raised by the supplemental answer and motion to dismiss the motion for further relief filed by the defendants on October 17, 1956, and the arguments thereon, may be stated as follows:

(a) Should the three-judge District Court be reconvened?

| 149 F.Supp. 433 |

(b) Are certain statutes passed by the General Assembly of Virginia in extra session 1956 constitutional?; and

(c) Should plaintiffs be required to exhaust administrative remedies provided by the state statutes?

I shall first consider the questions presented in the last mentioned motion in the order stated.

From an examination of the applicable statute, Title 28, Section 2281, United States Code, and upon consideration of its purpose I reach the conclusion that in the present state of the record in this case it is not appropriate to request the convening of a three-judge court. There is no application before me for an order to restrain or enjoin the action of any officer of the state in the enforcement or execution of any state statute or order such as contemplated by the Act of Congress.

In the present state of the record of this particular case I do not consider the constitutionality of the state statutes referred to or the relief there provided proper subject of inquiry. They were the subject of argument at the hearing on November 14, 1956, and I shall dispose of the questions so raised without extended discussion.

The situation before me was aptly summed up by Judge Parker in Carson v. Warlick, 4 Cir., 238 F.2d 724, 728, in which he used the following language:

"It is argued that the Pupil Enrollment Act is unconstitutional; but we cannot hold that that statute is unconstitutional upon its face and the question as to whether it has been unconstitutionally applied is not before us, as the administrative remedy which it provides has not been invoked."

And further:

"It is to be presumed that these [the officials of the schools and the school boards] will obey the law, observe the standards prescribed by the legislature, and avoid the discrimination on account of race which the Constitution forbids. Not until they have been applied to and have failed to give relief should the courts be asked to interfere in school administration. As said by the Supreme Court in Brown v. Board of Education, 349 U.S. 294, 299, 75 S.Ct. 753, 756, 99 L.Ed. 1083:

"'School authorities have the primary responsibility for elucidating, assessing, and solving these problems; courts will have to consider whether the action of school authorities constitutes good faith implementation of the governing constitutional principles.'"

The opinion in School Board of the City of Charlottesville, Va. v. Allen (County School Board of Arlington County, Va. v. Thompson), 4 Cir., 240 F.2d 59, 64, contains language pertinent here. The Court again speaking through Chief Judge Parker, in referring to administrative remedies provided under Section 22-57 of the Code of Virginia, and after pointing out that the pupil placement law recently enacted by the General Assembly of Virginia had not become effective when the cases were heard (although it was effective at the time that opinion was rendered, as is the situation here) said:

"* * * Reliance is placed upon on our decision in Carson v. Warlick, 4 Cir., 238 F.2d 724. In that case, however, an adequate administrative remedy had been prescribed by statute, the plaintiffs there had failed to pursue the remedy as outlined in the decision of the Supreme Court of the State and *there was nothing upon which a court could say that if they had followed such remedy their rights under the Constitution would have been denied them.*" (Emphasis supplied.)

See also Hood v. Board of Trustees, etc., 4 Cir., 232 F.2d 626, and Robinson v. Board of Education, etc., D.C.Md., 143 F.Supp. 481.

The quoted language appears in point in so far as the constitutional question is concerned. While the statutes involved

| 149 F.Supp. 434 |

are not identical, the principle announced is applicable.

Turning to the proposal that the plaintiffs be required to exhaust the administrative remedies provided by the state statutes, I am again confronted by the record before me. Being of opinion I am not in a position to pass upon the constitutionality of the statutes setting up the administrative remedy, it is my thought that I should not undertake to require the plaintiffs to seek any particular remedy. They are free to do so and thereby test the constitutionality of the statutes should they desire. However, that is a right, not an obligation. In the meantime, this is a matter of school administration in which I should not interfere.

It follows that the motion of the defendants to dismiss the motion for further relief should not be granted at this time. However, I incline to the view that instead of being dismissed it should be retained on the docket of the Court for final disposition at a later time should further proceedings develop an issue properly determinable in this case.

In undertaking to approach a solution to the troublesome problems involved in this case which are presented by the record and properly before me for determination, including the motion for further relief filed by the plaintiffs, it is to be borne in mind that the Supreme Court has decided only one legal principle which is concisely stated in the syllabus appearing in 347 U.S. 483, 74 S.Ct. 686, as follows:

"Segregation of white and Negro children in the public schools of a State solely on the basis of race, pursuant to state laws permitting or requiring such segregation, denies to

Negro children the equal protection of the laws guaranteed by the Fourteenth Amendment * * *."

A study of the opinions of May 17, 1954, and May 31, 1955, reveals no other principle of law to serve as precedent or landmark in undertaking to apply the law to the facts, although certain well-recognized equitable principles are mentioned. For a clearer understanding of the question here presented, some discussion of those opinions at this point may be helpful.

In the 1954 opinion, which will be referred to as the First Brown case, 347 U.S. at page 495, 74 S.Ct. at page 692, the Court, after stating that "because of the wide applicability of this decision, and because of the great variety of local conditions, the formulation of decrees in these cases presents problems of considerable complexity", requested counsel to present further argument on questions which may be briefly summarized as follows: Whether a decree would necessarily follow providing that Negro children should forthwith be admitted to schools of their choice, or whether the Court should permit an effective gradual adjustment to be brought about to a system not based on color distinctions; whether the Supreme Court should formulate detailed decrees in the cases; if so, what specific issues should be reached thereby; if the appointment of a special master to hear evidence with a view of recommending specific terms for the decrees would be desirable; and finally, whether that Court should remand the cases to the courts of first instance with directions to frame decrees, and if that policy were followed, what general directions should the decree of the Supreme Court include and what procedures should the courts of first instance follow in arriving at the specific terms of more detailed decrees. For full text of the questions propounded and argued see 345 U.S. 972, 73 S.Ct. 1114, 97 L.Ed. 1388.

Following elaborate argument upon these questions, in which the Attorneys General of the affected states and the Solicitor General of the United States presented their views, the Court filed its opinion on May 31, 1955, which will be referred to as the Second Brown case. With knowledge of what was considered by the Court, as revealed by the questions, the language of the opinion in the Second Brown case takes on added significance,

| 149 F.Supp. 435 |

both with respect to what was not said as well as to what was said. Certain portions of that opinion follow:

"Full implementation of these constitutional principles may require solution of varied local school problems. School authorities have the primary responsibility for elucidating, assessing, and solving these problems; courts will have to consider whether the action of school authorities constitutes good faith implementation of the governing constitutional principles. Because of their proximity to local conditions and the possible need for further hearings, the courts which originally heard these cases can best perform this judicial appraisal. Accordingly, we believe it appropriate to remand the cases to those courts." [349 U.S. 294, 75 S.Ct. 756.]

The Court then proceeded to announce the following principles which should receive attention of the District Courts:

"In fashioning and effectuating the decrees, the courts will be guided by equitable principles. Traditionally, equity has been characterized by a practical flexibility in shaping its remedies and by a facility for adjusting and reconciling public and private needs. These cases call for the exercise of these traditional attributes of equity power. At stake is the personal interest of the plaintiffs in admission to public schools as soon as practicable on a nondiscriminatory basis. To effectuate this interest may call for elimination of a variety of obstacles in making the transition to school systems operated in accordance with the constitutional principles set forth in our May 17, 1954, decision. Courts of equity may properly take into account the public interest in the elimination of such obstacles in a systematic and effective manner. But it should go without saying that the vitality of these constitutional principles cannot be allowed to yield simply because of disagreement with them."

From the foregoing it is clear that the law must be enforced but the Court is acutely conscious of the variety of problems of a local nature constituting factors to be considered in the enforcement. Further emphasis upon this point is found on 349 U.S. at page 298, 75 S.Ct. at page 755, where the Court said:

"Because these cases arose under different local conditions and their disposition will involve a variety of local problems, we requested further argument on the question of relief."

Bearing in mind that the only legal issue in this case pertains to a right guaranteed by the Constitution, this language coupled with the action of the Court, takes on significance which can hardly be over emphasized. It is elementary law that one deprived of a right guaranteed by the Constitution ordinarily is afforded immediate relief. Notwithstanding this fundamental principle, the Supreme Court in this case has seen fit to specifically declare that while the plaintiffs are entitled to the exercise of a constitutional right, in view of the grave and perplexing problems involved, the exercise of that right must be deferred. With that declaration the Court used equally forceful language indicating that it realizes that conditions vary in different localities. Consequently, instead of simply declaring the right and entering a mandate accordingly, it has seen fit in the exercise of its equity powers to not only defer until a later date the time when the right may be exercised, but to clearly indicate that the time of exercising such right may vary with conditions. A realization of the effect of this action on the part of the Court is of supreme importance to an understanding of the course to be pursued by the Courts of first instance. At the risk of being repetitious, I again recall that: Before laying down these principles, the Court considered and rejected the suggestion that Negro children should be forthwith admitted to schools of their choice; rejected

[149 F.Supp. 436]

the suggestion that it formulate detailed decrees; rejected the suggestion that a special master be appointed by it to hear evidence with a view to recommending specific terms for such decrees and adopted the proposal that the Court in the exercise of equity powers direct an effective gradual adjustment under the order of the Courts of first instance. Further, the Court considered and rejected the suggestion that a specified rule of procedure be established for the District Courts but placed upon those Courts the responsibility of considering, weighing and being guided by conditions found to prevail in each of the several communities to be affected by their decrees.

In the absence of precedent, in undertaking to follow the mandate of the Supreme Court, the District Courts are confronted with the necessity of following an uncharted course in applying the sole legal principle announced in the First Brown case. One idea which emerges clearly is that procedural rules adopted in one locality may be altogether inapplicable to conditions in another.

Boiled down to its essence, in the Second Brown case the Court after pointing out that the local school authorities have the primary responsibility of finding a solution to the varied local problems, proceeded to observe that the District Courts are to consider whether the actions of the local authorities are in good faith; and that by reason of their proximity to local conditions those Courts can best appraise the conduct of the local authorities. It is then pointed out that in so appraising, the Courts should be guided by the traditionally flexible principles of equity for adjusting and reconciling public and private needs. To be considered is the personal interest of the plaintiffs, as well as the public interest in the elimination of obstacles in a systematic and effective manner. During this period the Courts should retain jurisdiction of the cases. The Court has here clearly and in unmistakable terms placed upon the District Judges the responsibility of weighing the various factors which prevail in the respective localities affected. There is here a recognition of the obvious fact that in one locality in which conditions permit, a change may be effected almost immediately. In other localities a specified period appropriate in each case may be feasible and a definite time limit fixed accordingly. In yet other communities a greater time for compliance may be found necessary. It is clear that the Court anticipated the application of a test of expediency in such cases so that an orderly change may be accomplished without causing a sudden disruption of the way of life of the multitude of people affected.

While the Supreme Court made no reference to yet another interest, there is one of a semi-public nature. This involves the teachers of the county, both white and colored, and their families, dependent upon them for support.

The conflicting rights and interests of racial and national groups in this country is nothing new. It is not confined to the Negro race but numerous illustrations might be used. A striking illustration is found in the situation of persons of Oriental origin who have come to this country. It is worthy of passing note to recall that the opinion appearing in the official reports immediately preceding the First Brown case involves the rights of persons of Mexican descent. Hernandez v. State of Texas, 347 U.S. 475, 74 S.Ct. 667, 98 L.Ed. 866. It must be borne in mind that these conflicts and the cases arising therefrom are the result of customs, traditions, manners and emotions which have existed for generations. In this particular case the customs to be changed have been not only generally accepted but repeatedly and expressly declared the law of the land since 1896.[1] While lawyers may have been conscious of the evolution of the law during this period and prepared to anticipate the possibility of a change, the average layman affected may not be charged with such prescience. Patience, time and a sympathetic

| 149 F.Supp. 437 |

approach are imperative to accomplish a change of conditions in an orderly and peaceful manner and with a minimum of friction.

In seeking a solution it is necessary to know and to understand the background upon which the factual situation is cast. In this connection it is necessary to examine briefly the present conditions in Prince Edward County, Virginia, historically and as revealed by the record in this case.[2]

Prince Edward County being inland from the easily navigable tidal reaches of the streams watering that region, was not settled until the first half of the 18th century, after the power of the Indians had been broken. At that time the pattern of life in the Colony had become established and the early residents carried with them the manners and customs prevailing in the more populous regions of Virginia. By 1783 the population consisted of 1,552 white and 1,468 colored residents. The 1950 census showed a population of 15,398, with the white and colored races approximately equal in number. During the intervening years the relations between the races have been harmonious, with a minimum of friction and tension as compared with some regions. During several decades prior to the War Between the States the processes of orderly and gradual adjustment which were becoming increasingly evident were interrupted by being involved in the political issues confronting the growing nation, with particular reference to regional differences and the clash of economic rivalries of various sections. Unfortunately this resulted in accentuating racial tension and hostility which became somewhat acute at times. While these conditions were common to the southeastern and southern parts of the country, it was felt less in Prince Edward and the surrounding area than in many other sections.

In the days following 1861-65 the entire section was poverty stricken. For the rank and file of both races there was a struggle for existence and education was of secondary importance. It is true that in this situation with the local government controlled by members of the white race and with severely limited means, there was inequality in the division, but members of the Negro race were not excluded from sharing, although to a lesser extent. This was due in part to an understandable, if erroneous, feeling that those upon whom the greater tax burden fell should receive the greater benefit. During the second quarter of the present century the economy of the section most seriously concerned has shown a marked improvement. Due to that improvement, corresponding advantages have resulted in housing, education and knowledge on the part of both races. Marked improvement in racial relationship resulted although many firmly fixed ancient customs and manners remain. With an improvement in the economic condition of the county and the resulting increase in available financial resources, an awareness of public sentiment, the mandatory requirements of the Virginia constitution and statutes upon the subject, coupled with suits brought in Federal Courts in other localities, the responsible authorities of Prince Edward County made plans for the erection of new school buildings exclusively for Negroes, which are now concededly equal if not superior to those occupied by the white pupils.

Before these plans could be completed, this suit was filed. Since the decision in the Brown case these plans have been completed. The defendants, who are the Superintendent and members of the School Board, and as such charged with the "primary responsibility for elucidating, assessing and solving" their problems, have proceeded with the operation of the schools in the county in accordance with the practice which has prevailed. They have prepared and submitted to the Board of Supervisors of the county annual budgets for the operation of the schools. In this connection it is to be borne in mind that the defendants have

| 149 F.Supp. 438 |

no authority under the law to levy or assess taxes nor to raise funds except in a limited manner by borrowing under certain conditions not pertinent here. Responsibility for providing local funds for the operation of schools rests upon the Board of Supervisors who are not defendants before this Court. The School Board consists of members appointed by the school trustee electoral board, the members of which in turn are appointed by the local state court. The members of the Board of Supervisors are elected by the people. Buttressed by popular demand of the people of the county since the decision in the First Brown case, evidenced in part by a petition signed by more than 4,000 residents, the Board of Supervisors has declined to allocate funds for the operation of schools on an annual basis. Instead it appropriates the necessary operating expenses on a monthly basis, with a publicly declared intention of discontinuing such appropriation if schools in the county are mixed racially at this time. In this connection attention is invited to the statutes recently enacted by the Virginia General Assembly under which the funds provided by the state may be withheld. Pending final interpretation of those statutes time valuable in the educational opportunities of the children involved might be irretrievably lost. Affidavits filed in this case and in no way controverted or mentioned by counsel for the plaintiffs, declare racial relations in the county to be more strained than at any time during the present generation.

In this state of facts I am called upon to fix a time when the defendants should be required to comply with the terms of the injunction issued by the three-judge court in obedience to the mandate of the Supreme Court. To do this I am to "adjust and reconcile public and private needs", by weighing and considering the personal interests of the plaintiffs as well as the interest of the public, in the elimination of obstacles in order that there may be a systematic, orderly and effective transition of the school system in accordance with the constitutional principles announced in the Brown case.

I believe the problems to be capable of solution but they will require patience, time and a sympathetic understanding. They cannot be solved by zealous advocates, by an emotional approach, nor by those with selfish interests to advance. The law has been announced by the Supreme Court and must be observed but the solution must be discovered by those affected under the guidance of sensible leadership. These facts should be self evident to all responsible people.

The children of both races, constituting an entire generation of this county, are the persons to be affected by whatever action may be taken and it follows that theirs is the real interest at stake, although closely connected with that of their parents and guardians.

Should the public schools of the county be closed for any reason, approximately three thousand children, including those of an age at which they are peculiarly impressionable, will be released from attendance. An interrupted education of one year or even six months at that age places a serious handicap upon the child which the average one may not overcome. Among those of the older age group there are some for whom it will mean the end of an education. Should the schools be resumed after an interruption, those among the younger group will be retarded in acquiring an education as compared with their contemporaries in other communities. With the release from discipline brought about by compulsory attendance at school, problems concerning juvenile conduct will be intensified with resulting injury to both children and the community and a resulting increase of racial tension with members of each race blaming the other for the lack of schools. In this connection it is to be remembered that the police protection of rural communities is different from that afforded in more populous areas. The salaries paid teachers in the state are not such as to enable them to accumulate a fund sufficient to support

[149 F.Supp. 439]

themselves and their families over a protracted period of unemployment. Loss of employment would be a serious consequence to many teachers of both races who are established in the community. Tentative and substantial plans have been made for continuation by private means of the education of white children of the county. There is no such provision for Negro children. These considerations all involve the public and private interests of the community as distinguished from the quandary of the members of the School Board.

The admonition of the Supreme Court that the personal interests of the plaintiffs in admission to public schools as soon as practicable on a nondiscriminatory basis is a consideration of which I am mindful. In response to a question from the bench, counsel for the plaintiffs stated that so far as he knew none of the original plaintiffs are now attending the schools. However, additional named plaintiffs have intervened and it is to be recalled that this is a class action. Should the plaintiffs be deprived of education or suffer an interruption in their education they will be handicapped. Concededly, their opportunities in so far as physical equipment and curriculum are concerned, are equal if not superior to those available to children of the white race. It has been held by the Court that segregation of white and colored children in public schools has a detrimental psychological effect upon the colored children. That is primarily the basis upon which the Brown case is founded. It is my belief that at this time a continuation of present methods could not be so harmful as an interrupted education.

Laying aside for the moment the probability of the schools being closed, in the present state of unrest and racial tension in the county it would be unwise to attempt to force a change of the system until the entire situation can be considered and adjustments gradually brought about. This must be accomplished by the reasonable, clear-thinking people of both races in that locality. This objective cannot be achieved quickly. It does not require the opinion of a psychologist to understand that disaffection, uneasiness and uncertainty of the adult world around them creates emotional problems for children concerned. A sudden disruption of reasonably amicable racial relations which have been laboriously built up over a period of more than three and a quarter centuries would be deplorable. At any reasonable cost, it must be avoided.

I conceive the immediate problems of the Court to be to determine whether the School Board is acting in good faith and whether the facts before the Court at this time are such that an order fixing a time limit for compliance with the decree is proper, taking into consideration the various factors outlined in the Brown case to which consideration has been given. I do not conceive it to be within the power of this Court to forecast conditions which may exist in the future. Stated differently, I must reach a conclusion based upon the facts existing at this time in the locality to be affected.

The passage of time with apparent inaction on the part of the defendants of itself does not necessarily show non-compliance. This is illustrated by the fact that after the appeal in this case was granted in May, 1952, more than three years elapsed before the mandate of the Supreme Court was received. I find that the defendants by submitting the usual budget requesting appropriations have done all that reasonably could be required of them in this period of transition. Action which might cause mixing the schools at this time, resulting in closing them, would be highly and permanently injurious to children of both races. Relations between the members of the two races in the county would be adversely affected and a final solution of the vexing problems delayed as a consequence.

At this time the children of both races are being afforded opportunities for an education under an adequate system that has been formulated over the years. If an order should result in racially integrated schools, the school system of itself would change greatly. Plans should

[149 F.Supp. 440]

be made to keep within bounds the automatic adjustments that would follow in order that society not be too drastically affected.

Many minds are now engaged in seeking an equitable solution of the problem, including those of the defendants. As was said by a great statesman, "The march of the human mind is slow".₂ It is inconceivable that any of the litigants or other persons affected would willingly see the public school system abolished or an interruption in the education of the children of the county. Either result would be disastrous to both public and private interests of the county.

It is imperative that additional time be allowed the defendants in this case, who find themselves in a position of helplessness unless the Court considers their situation from an equitable and reasonable viewpoint.

Considering all the factors, it is my conclusion that decision of the motion for further relief filed by the plaintiffs should be withheld at this time, with the reservation to the plaintiffs of the right to renew the motion at a later date after the defendants have been afforded a reasonable time to effect a solution.

In conclusion, attention is again called to the following language of the Supreme Court which is the law of this case and must be observed [349 U.S. 294, 75 S.Ct. 756]:

"But it should go without saying that the vitality of these constitutional principles cannot be allowed to yield simply because of disagreement with them."

ORDER

For reasons stated in the opinion filed herein on January 23, 1957; it is

ORDERED that (a) the Court does not pass on the matters raised in the defendant's motion to dismiss the motion for further relief (including any and all questions involving the constitutionality of the statutes of the Commonwealth of Virginia there mentioned); (b) the motion that a three-judge court be convened to consider and pass on questions before the Court at this time is denied; and (c) the motion for further relief filed by the plaintiffs herein is denied at this time.

It is further ORDERED that this action be retained on the docket of this Court for such further proceedings as may be appropriate.

Footnotes

1. Plessy v. Ferguson, 163 U.S. 537, 16 S.Ct. 1138, 41 L.Ed. 256; Gong Lum v. Rice, 275 U.S. 78, 48 S.Ct. 91, 72 L.Ed. 172.
2. See "History of Prince Edward County, Virginia" — Herbert Clarence Bradshaw — 1955.
3. Edmund Burke — "Speech on the Conciliation of America".

BIBLIOGRAPHY

The following sources are listed in order of their investigation by the author.

(1) Phillip Hoose. *We Were There Too!: Young People in U.S. History*. Canada: Douglas & McIntyre Ltd. 2001

(2) Jennifer Baszile. *The Black Girl Next Store*. New York, Touchstone Books. 2008

(3) Phillip Hoose. *Claudette Colvin: Twice Toward Justice*. Canada: Douglas & McIntyre Ltd. 2009

(4) Andrew B. Lewis. *The Shadows of Youth*. Hill and Wang. 2009

(5) *Brown v. Board of Education*, 349 U.S. (1955)

(6) Douglas A. Blackmon. *Slavery by Another Name: The Re-Enslavement of Black Americans from the Civil War to World War II*. Doubleday. 2008

(7) Harry S. Ashmore. *Civil Rights and Wrongs: A memoir of race and politics 1944 — 1994*. Pantheon Books. 1994

(8) Richard Glass. Article: *Inner-city school relishes this mark of perfection*. Richmond Times-Dispatch. July 17, 2010

(9) John A. Stokes with Lois Wolf, Ph.D. *Students on Strike - Jim Crow, Civil Rights, Brown, and Me*. National Geographic. 2008

(10) Carlotta Walls Lanier with Lisa Fraser Page. *A Mighty Long Way- My journey to Justice at Little Rock Central High School*. Ballantine Books. 2009

(11) Betty Kilby Fischer. *Wit, Will and Walls*. Cultural Innovations Inc. 2002

(12) Andrew I. Heidelberg. *The Norfolk 17- A personal narrative on desegregation in Norfolk, Virginia in 1958 — 1962*. Rose Dog Books. 2006

(13) Bob Smith. *They Closed Their Schools: Prince Edward County, Virginia 1951 — 1964*. Robert Russa Robert Russa Moton Museum. 2008
They Closed Their Schools is the most complete source on how the Prince Edward County struggle unfolded, and how it felt to the principles. *Reaching for the Moon* has permission from the publisher to use the exact words from *They Closed Their Schools* and appropriate citations were created in those instances. Additional, in chapter 6 some paraphrasing was also used to provide the reader the most direct connection to the actual events. The author is appreciative of the copyright holder's concurrence with this approach.

(14) Neil Vincent Sullivan. *Bound For Freedom: An Educator's Adventures in Prince Edward County, Virginia*. Boston Little Brown. 1965

(15) Richard Kluger. *Simple Justice: The History of Brown v. Board of Education and Black America's Struggle for Equality*. Vintage Books. 2004. Originally published in 1976 by Knopf

(16) James R. Sweeney. *Race, Reason, and Massive Resistance: The Dairy of David J. Mays, 1954- 1959*.The University of Georgia Press. 2008

(17) Terence Hicks and Abul Pitre. *The Educational Lockout of African Americans in Prince Edward County, Virginia (1959 — 1964)*. University Press of America. 2010

(18) Alexander S. Leidholdt. *Standing Before The Shouting Mob: Lenoir Chambers and Virginia's Massive Resistance to Public-School Integration*. The University of Alabama Press.1997

(19) Robert A. Pratt. *The Color Of Their Skin: Education and Race in Richmond, Virginia 1954- 89.* University Press of Virginia. 1992

(20) Jeff E. Shapiro. Article: *Brilliance and Bias.* Richmond Times Dispatch. August 17, 2010

(21) James J. Kilpatrick. OP/Ed article: *My Journey From Racism.* Atlanta Journal-Constitution. 2002

(22) Ronald E. Carrington. *Interview with John A Stokes.* Voices of Freedom: videotaped oral histories of leaders of the Civil Rights movement in Virginia by Virginia Civil Rights Movement Video Initiative. Date of interview March 21, 2003

(23) Ronald E. Carrington. *Interview with Dr. Joyce E. Glaise.* Voices of Freedom: videotaped oral histories of leaders of the Civil Rights movement in Virginia by Virginia Civil Rights Movement Video Initiative. Date of interview March 20, 2003

(24) Ronald E. Carrington. *Interview with Dr. W. Ferguson Reid.* Voices of Freedom: videotaped oral histories of leaders of the Civil Rights movement in Virginia by Virginia Civil Rights Movement Video Initiative. Date of interview March 21, 2003

(25) Ronald E. Carrington. *Interview with Oliver W. Hill, Sr.* Voices of Freedom: videotaped oral histories of leaders of the Civil Rights movement in Virginia by Virginia Civil Rights Movement Video Initiative. Date of interview November13, 2002

(26) Ronald E. Carrington. *Interview with Rev. Curtis W. Harris.* Voices of Freedom: videotaped oral histories of leaders of the Civil Rights movement in Virginia by Virginia Civil Rights Movement Video Initiative. Date of interview March 20, 2003

(27) Ronald E. Carrington. *Interview with Sen. Henry L. Marsh, III.* Voices of Freedom: videotaped oral histories of leaders of the

Civil Rights movement in Virginia by Virginia Civil Rights Movement Video Initiative. Date of interview March 20, 2003

(28) Richmond Afro-American Article. *NO TOMS CAN STOP US*. Richmond Afro-American Newspaper. May 12, 1951

(29) Martin Luther King III. The Washington Post Editorial: *Still striving for MLK's dream in the 21st century.* The Washington Post, Page A19. Wednesday, August 25, 2010

(30) Robert F. Kennedy. Address from the Kentucky Centennial of the Emancipation Proclamation. March 18, 1963

(31) Juan Williams. *Thurgood Marshall: The Man and His Enduring but Endangered Legacy*. The College Board Review, Issue 200, College Board Publications. Fall 2003

(32) Peter McCormick. *Today I Wonder How We Ever Pulled It Off: How a Band of High School Students Influenced Desegregation*. The College Board Review, Issue 200, College Board Publications. Fall 2003

(33) David Margolick. *Civil Rights- Through a Lens, Darkly*. Vanity Fair article. September 24, 2007

(34) Cheryl Brown Henderson. *Brown v. Board of Education at Fifty- A Personal Perspective*. The College Board Review, Issue 200, College Board Publications. Fall 2003

(35) David Oshinsky. *Freedom Trains, THE WARMTH OF OTHER SUNS: The Epic Story of America's Great Migration*, Review of a book By Isabel Wilkerson. NY Times Book Review. September 2, 2010

(36) Harper Lee. *To Kill A Mockingbird*. Grand Central Publishing. Copyright 1960 by Harper Lee, Reissued Edition April 2010

(37) Edward Harden Peeples. *A Perspective of the Prince Edward County Issue- Master Thesis.* University of Pennsylvania. 1963

(38) Melvin Patrick Ely. *Israel on the Appomattox: A Southern Experiment in Black Freedom from the 1790s Through the Civil War.* Alfred A. Knopf. 2004

(39) Governor Bob McDonnell. *Inaugural Address of Governor Robert F. McDonnell- A Commonwealth of Opportunity.* January 18, 2010. Richmond

(40) Sara K. Eskridge. *Virginia's Pupil Placement Board and the Practical Applications of Massive Resistance, 1956–1966.* Virginia Magazine. Published by the Virginia Historical Society, Vol.118,No.3. 2010

(41) Southern School News. May 17, 1964

(42) Bill Medic. Article: *The Blind Spot in Black History Month.* The Pro Youth Pages, http://www.proyouthpages.com/blackhistory.html. 2003

(43) Taylor Branch. *Parting the Waters: America in the King Years 1954–63.* Simon and Schuster. 1988

(44) Joan Johns Cobb. *Eye Witness to Jim Crow.* Congress of Racial Equality, An Oral History. http://www.core-online.org/History/barbara_johns1.htm. 1991

(45) Kim Urquhart. *Write from the heart.* Article on Isabel Wilkerson winner of the Pulitzer Prize in 1994 and author of *The Warmth of Other Suns: The Epic Story of America's Great Migration.* From the Emory Report, *Emory University.* http://www.journalism.emory.edu/program/wilkerson.cfm. September 25, 2006

(46) NPR Author Interview and Article. On Isabel Wilkerson winner of the Pulitzer Prize in 1994. *Great Migration: The African-American Exodus North.*

http://www.npr.org/templates/story/story.php?storyId=12982744
4. September 13, 2010

(47) DeNeen L. Brown. *Danielle Evans, an author straddling racial divides*. Article/Book Review from Washington Post on Danielle Evans book *Before You Suffocate Your Own Fool Self*. Washington Post. Thursday, October 7, 2010

(48) Ruby Bridges Hall. Article: *The Education of Ruby Nell*. *Guideposts Magazine*. pp. 3-4. March 2000

(49) Ruby Bridges Official web site:
http://www.rubybridges.com/home.htm

(50) W.E.B. Du Bois. *The Souls of Black Folk*. Barnes & Nobles Books. Published in 2003, first published in 1903

(51) Isabel Wilkerson. *The Warmth of Other Suns: The Epic Story of America's Great Migration*. Random House. 2001

(52) William W. Freehling. *The Road to Disunion: Volume I, Secessionists at Bay, 1776–1854 (Road to Disunion Vol. 1)*. Oxford University Press. Published December 5th 1991, (first published 1990)

(53) William W. Freehling. *The Road to Disunion: Volume II, Secessionists Triumphant 1854–1861*. Oxford University Press. 2007

(54) Washington Post Article. *A view from the 1950s Virginia*. May 13, 2004

(55) Nell Irvin Painter. *The History of White People*. W. W. Norton & Co. 2010

(56) Danielle L. McGuire. *At the Dark End of the Street: Black Women, Rape, and Resistance- A New History of the Civil Rights Movement from Rosa Parks to the Rise of Black Power*. Alfred A. Knopf. 2010

(57) Condoleezza Rice. *Condoleezza Rice- a memoir of my extraordinary, ordinary family and me.* Delacorte Press. 2010

(58) Eugene Robinson. *Disintegration: The Splintering of Black America.* Doubleday. 2010

(59) New York Times. *Justice Stevens on 'Invidious Prejudice'.* New York Times- Editorial. November 10, 2010

(60) Robert Russa Moton Museum, *News Letter. Barbara Rose Johns Portrait Now Featured at Virginia Capitol.* Robert Russa Moton Museum. November 2010

(61) Jesse Washington. *Article in Richmond Times Dispatch, page A9.* From the Associated Press. November 8, 2010

(62) Kathryn Edin and Maria Kefalas. *Promises I Can Keep: Why Poor Women Put Motherhood Before Marriage.* University of California Press. 2005

(63) Dr. Wayne W. Dyer. *The Power of Intention.* Hay House, Inc. 2004

(64) Charles M. Blow. *Let's Rescue the Race Debate.* NY Times-OP-ED. November 19, 2010

(65) Ron Christie. *Acting White: The Curious History of a Racial Slur.* Thomas Dunne Books. 2010

(66) Jean Edward Smith. *FDR.* Random House. 2007

(67) Ulysses S. Grant. *Ulysses S. Grant- Personal Memoirs.* Modern Library. 1999 edition, first published soon after President Grant's death with the help of Mark Twain in 1885

(68) Leon F. Litwack. *North of Slavery: The Negro in the Free States, 1790–1860.* University of Chicago Press. 1961.

(69) Leslie M. Harris. *In the Shadow of Slavery: African Americans in New York City, 1626–1863.* The University of Chicago Press. 2003

(70) C. Vann Woodward (Author), William S. McFeely (Contributor). *The Strange Career of Jim Crow.* Oxford University Press, Oxford Press USA. 3rd edition March 21, 1974, originally published in 1955

(71) Dr. Robert Russa Moton. *Dr. Robert Russa Moton Address, at the Dedication of The Lincoln Memorial, Washington, D. C., May 30th, 1922 (Original Draft). The Glouster Institute.*
http://gloucester.kma.net/Gloucester/files/ccLibraryFiles/Filena me/000000000278/Moton%20Speech-May301922.pdf

(72) Keith Eberly. *Teaching Strategy: "To Thee We Sing": Racial Politics and the Lincoln Memorial.* OAH Magazine of History, Volume 23, No 1, January 2009. Robert Russa Moton's Keynote Speech, Original Draft and Final, for 1922 Lincoln Memorial dedication.
http://oah.org/pubs/magazine/llegacy/Moton.pdf

(73) J. LeCount Chestnut. *Mock Ideal of Lincoln at Memorial-Have Jim Crow Services; Prominent Citizens Offered Insults.* Chicago Defender. June 10, 1922

(74) Chinua Achebe. *Things Fall Apart: A Novel.* Anchor. 1994, originally published in 1958

(75) Charles Mackay. *Life and Liberty in America: or, Sketches of a Tour in the United States and Canada in 1857–1858.* Harper & Brothers, 1859

(80) Euzhan Palcy, Film Director. *Ruby Bridges.* Disney DVD,1 hour- 33 minute film. 1998

(81) Richard T. Couture. *Powhatan: A Bicentennial History.* The Dietz Press, Inc. 1980

(82) Desmond M. Tutu, Mpho A. Tutu. *Made for Goodness: And Why This Makes All the Difference*. Harper Collins Publishers. 2010

(83) Marco Williams, Director/Producer. 2007 Documentary film: *Banished*. Center For Investigative Reporting And Two Tone Productions. 2007.
http://www.pbs.org/independentlens/banished/film.html

(84) James W. Loewen. *Sundown Towns: A Hidden Dimension of American Racism*. Simon & Schuster. 2005

(85) The Office of the Clerk, U.S. Capitol. *The Fifteenth Amendment in Flesh and Blood: The Symbolic Generation of Black Americans in Congress, 1870–1887*. Washington, DC. Black Americans in Congress: http://baic.house.gov/historical-essays/. 2010

(86) Eddie Gross. Article: *Region is home to 'cradle' of civil rights*. The Free Lance-Star Publishing Co. of Fredericksburg, Virginia, USA. January 19, 2009.
http://www.fredericksburg.com/News/FLS/2009/012009/011920 09/439401/index_html

(87) Richard A. Wright. *Native Son*. Harper Perennial. September 1, 1998 (Originally -published in 1940 by Harper & Brothers)

(88) James A. Miller. Article: *At 50 Years Old A Classic Still Packs a Punch*. The Crisis: A Quarterly Magazine founded by the NAACP in 1910, page 37. The Crisis Publishing Company, Inc..Winter 2008

(89) Daniel de Vise. *In Higher Education, Lessons In Equality: Md.'s Towson University conquers 'graduation gap'*. The Washington Post, page A01. Sunday, December 12, 2010

(90) Jamala Rogers. *What We Should Do Now?- Ten Black Thinkers Share ideas About the Future*. The Crisis: A Quarterly Magazine founded by the NAACP in 1910, page 23. The Crisis Publishing Company, Inc.. Winter 2008

(91) W. Lester Banks. *Prince Edward County- The Shame of a Nation (The tragedy of a Virginia county)*. The Crisis, A Record of the Darker Races, A Monthly Magazine founded by the NAACP in 1910, "the official organ of the NAACP", Vol 69, No. 4, Whole Number 593, Page 271. The Crisis Publishing Company, Inc.. May 1962

(92) Patrice Preston-Grimes. *Fulfilling the Promise: African American Educators Teach for Democracy in Jim Crow's South*. Teacher Education Quarterly. Winter 2010. Patrice Preston-Grimes is an assistant professor in the Department of Curriculum, Instruction and Special Education of the Curry School of Education at the University of Virginia, Charlottesville, Virginia.

(93) *Brown v. Board of Education of Topeka*. (I), 347 U.S. 483 (1954).

(94) Mary Eastman. *Aunt Phillis's Cabin*. Philadelphia: Lippincott, Grambo & Co.. 1852. Page 280
The novel, although obscure today, remains one of the most-read examples of the anti-Tom genre, with between 20,000 and 30,000 copies of Aunt Phillis's Cabin being sold upon its initial release in 1852. Aunt Phillis's Cabin was released in 1852 to counter Uncle Tom's.

(95) Harriet Beecher Stowe. *Uncle Tom's Cabin*. Publisher John Jewett. March 20.1852
Uncle Tom's Cabin first appeared as a 40-week serial in *National Era*, an abolitionist periodical, starting with the June 5, 1851 issue. Because of the story's popularity, the publisher John Jewett contacted Stowe about turning the serial into a book. While Stowe questioned if anyone would read *Uncle Tom's Cabin* in book form, she eventually consented to the request.

Published in book form on March 20, 1852, the novel soon sold out its complete print run.

In the first year of publication, 300,000 copies of *Uncle Tom's Cabin* were sold. Uncle Tom's Cabin was the best-selling novel of the 19th century, and the second best-selling book of that century, following the Bible.

(96) National Museum of American History. *Separate Is Not Equal: Brown v. Board of Education.*
http://americanhistory.si.edu/brown/history/6-legacy/fifty-years-after.html
Separate Is Not Equal: Brown v. Board of Education is a collective effort of the staff of the National Museum of American History, Behring Center.
This site has an informative and thorough timeline detailing the four critical years that the Supreme Court spent addressing the Brown case.

(97) Cleveland Gazette. Article: *Gen. Robert E. Lee's Daughter Arrested.* June 21,1902

(98) Nicholas D. Kristof. *Equality, a True Soul Food.* New York Times OP –ED. January 1, 2011.
Moving words about how one woman can make a difference and change the world.

(99) John L. Horton. OP-ED piece entitled: *African American History- Watch Night and New Year's Day hold special significance.* Richmond Times Dispatch. December 31, 2010

(100) Howard Hale Long. Article: *Some Psychogenic Hazards of Segregated Education of Negroes. The Journal of Negro Education,* Vol. 4, No. 3, The Courts and the Negro Separate School (Jul., 1935), pp. 336-350. URL:
http://www.jstor.org/stable/2291872
(Article consists of 15 pages.)

(101) Chas. H. Thompson. Article: *Court Action the Only Reasonable Alternative to Remedy Immediate Abuses of the Negro Separate School. The Journal of Negro Education,* Vol. 4, No. 3, The Courts and the Negro Separate School (Jul., 1935), pp. 419-434 (article consists of 16 pages). URL: http://www.jstor.org/stable/2291877

(102) Archibald G. Robertson. *Comments Mostly off the Record by Archibald G. Robertson, 11 February 1974. Davis v. County School Board of Prince Edward County, 347 U. S., 483 (1954).* Manuscript donated by the author to the Virginia Historical Society.

(103) Henry Louis Gates JR., Evelyn Brooks Higginbotham (Editors). *Biography of Vernon Napoleon Johns (1892–1965), African American National Biography.* Oxford University Press. 2008. Page 545

(104) Jamie C. Ruff. Article: *There was little notice as Barbara Johns stepped into history on April 23, 1951, but her footprints would be indelible.* Richmond Times Dispatch February 11, 2005, page D-1. Article discusses advice from the music teacher, Ms. Jones, to Barbara Rose Johns in preparing for the strike.

(105) Annette Gordon-Reed. *Race On Trial- Landmark Justice in American History.* Oxford University Press. 2002. The book discusses 12 historically important racial based litigations that have shaped American public law, policy, customs and opinion. The cases discussed start with the Amistad case in 1841, and includes Plessy, Brown, Loving and ends with the O.J. Simpson case in 1994.

(106) Time Magazine. Article: *THE NATION: Secession from Civilization.* Monday, September 22, 1958 issue. The cover for this issue of Time has a picture of Governor Almond adjacent to the Virginia State Seal " SIC SEMPER TYRANNIS" all superimposed over a large confederate flag in the background.

(107) Time Magazine. Article: *VIRGINIA: The Gravest Crisis.*
Monday, Sep. 1, 1958. The cover for this issue of Time has a
picture of Governor Almond adjacent to the Virginia State Seal "
SIC SEMPER TYRANNIS" all superimposed over a large
confederate flag in the background.

(108) Time Magazine. Article: *THE SOUTH: Stalemate on
Segregation.* Monday, Sep. 22, 1958.

(109) Kathryn Orth. *Marching their way into history / Museum
honors students' push for change.* Richmond Times Dispatch.
Monday, August 24, 1998. Times-Dispatch Staff Writer

(110) Erika Slife. *African-Americans choosing to home-school:
Statistics hard to come by, but experts say more black parents are
educating kids at home.* Chicago Tribune. January 2, 2011.
Tribune reporter

(111) Samuel L. Gravely, Paul Stillwell. *Trailblazer- The U.S.
Navy's First Black Admiral.* Naval Institute Press. August 2010

(112) Michael P. Johnson, James L. Roark. *Black Masters: A
Free Family of Color in the Old South.* W. Norton & Company.
April 17, 1986

(113) Joe Macenka. *Oliver W. Hill Sr.: 1907–2007, 200 Pay
Their Respects.* Richmond Times Dispatch Times. August 12,
2007. Dispatch Staff Writer

(114) Wes Moore. *The Other Wes Moore: One Name, Two Fates.*
Spiegel & Grau. 2010

(115) Bhelene Cooper, Jeff Zeleny. *Obama Calls for a New Era
of Civility in U.S..*New York Times. January 12, 2011
President Obama offered the nation's condolences to the victims
of the January 8, 2011 Tucson shooting rampage, urging
Americans to usher in a new era of civility in memory of the
fallen.

(116) Rev. Walter Fauntroy. *Oral History Project.* American History TV, C-SPAN3. Washington, D. C.. Saturday, January 15, 2011
The Rev. Walter Fauntroy served as the District of Columbia's first delegate to Congress from 1971 to 1991, and was a founding member of the Congressional Black Caucus. In this oral history from the collection of the CBC Foundation, Fauntroy talks about his civil rights work and his political career.

(117) Oliver W. Hill, Sr., Edited by Jonathan K. Stubbs. *The Big Bang- Brown v. Board of Education and Beyond.* Four-G Publishers. 2000

(118) Ken Woodley. *Living With The Legacies: Johns Family Members Reflect On History.* The Farmville Herald, March 2, 2001

(119) Barbara Rose Johns. *Barbara Johns' Diary.* Unfinished. Discovered by one of her daughters in 1999 on top of her dresser. "The strange thing about this was this writing lay at home on top of the bureau from about 1990 until 1999 when I left Philadelphia," said Rev. Powell, who has retired to the Cullen area. My daughter discovered it, had it (copied) and gave every member of the family a copy of it." Source:(118). The entire transcript of Barbara Rose Johns *Diary* that describes her decision to lead a student strike was published in The Farmville Herald in September 2000 and has been on display at the Robert Russa Moton Museum.

(120) Robert Shetterly. *Americans Who Tell The Truth- Portrait and Biography of Barbara Rose Johns.* 2002. http://americanswhotellthetruth.org/pgs/portraits/Barbara_Johns.php

(121) Sydney Trent. *Stand and Deliver.* The Washington Post Magazine. Apr.4, 2004. Article quotes Barbara Rose Johns: "We wanted so much and had so little . . .We had talents and abilities here that weren't really being realized, and I thought that was a

tragic shame, and that's basically what motivated me to want to see some change take place here . . .
There wasn't any fear . . . I just decided, 'This is your moment. Seize it.'"

(122) Sylvia Clute. *Beyond Vengeance Beyond Duality- A Call for a Compassionate Revolution.* Hampton Roads Publishing Company. 2010. Book was a gift from a friend who owns a book store in Richmond.

(123) Verna L. Williams. *Reading, Writing, and Reparations: Systemic Reform of Public Schools as a Matter of Justice.* University of Cincinnati College of Law Working Paper Series, Public Law & Legal Theory Working Paper No. 05-11, draft dated April 13, 2005

(124) James E. Ryan. *Five Miles Away, A World Apart- One City, Two Schools, and the Story of Educational Opportunity in Modern America.* Oxford University Press. 2010. Ryan explores the reasons for the gap between urban and suburban (Richmond and Henrico) school performance and what can be done to remedy the situation.

(125) Bob Lewis. *Civil rights memorial unveiled Monday.* The News & Advance. July 22, 2008. From Lynchburg's daily paper on the dedication of the Civil Rights Memorial in Capital Square, Richmond. The memorial includes a life size bronze of Barbara Rose Johns leading the 1951 student strike and above her inscribed in the granite are her own words: "It seemed like we were reaching for the moon."

(126) Peter F. Lau, Editor. *From Grassroots to the Supreme Court- Brown v. Board of Education and American Democracy.* Duke University Press. 2004. Discusses the strike and the adult support the students received from their teachers, principal, parents, church and black community. Describes the possibility that Ms. Davenport did indeed help Barbara Rose Johns plan the strike.

(127) James D. Anderson. *The Education of Blacks in the South, 1860–1935*. The University of North Carolina Press. September 9, 1988

(128) Nancy Whitelaw. *Mr. Civil Rights: The Story of Thurgood Marshall*. Morgan Reynolds Publishing. October 2002

(129) Emmett J. Scott. *Scott's Official History Of The American Negro In The World War- Special Adjutant to Secretary of War*. Copyright by Emmett J. Scott. 1919

(130) Matthew D. Lassiter, Andrew B. Lewis. *The Moderates' Dilemma: Massive Resistance To School Desegregation In Virginia*. University of Virginia Press. 1998

(131) Houston Baker Jr.. A. *Betrayal- How Black Intellectuals Have Abandoned the Ideas of the Civil Rights Era*. Colombia University Press. 2008

(132) Denise Watson Batts. *If the Civil Rights Movement had a home, it was here*. The Virginian-Pilot. February 20, 2011. Published on HamptonRoads.com | PilotOnline.com (http://hamptonroads.com)

(133) Robert Russa Moton. *What The Negro Thinks*. Doubleday Doran and Company. 1929

(134) Richard Wright. *12 Million Black Voices*. Basic Books. 2008. Originally published in 1941. Stunning prose and pictures from the depression.

(135) George William Van Cleve. *A Slaveholders' Union: Slavery, Politics, and the Constitution in the Early American Republic*. University Of Chicago Press. October 2010. Van Cleve makes his case that until the Thirteenth Amendment the Constitution, the laws of the land, the economy, and customs of America were from its beginning a slave state. A Slaveholders' Union demonstrates thru legal review and historical documentation that slavery was indeed an essential part of the foundation of the nascent republic. His argues that the Constitutional provisions protecting slavery were much more than mere "political" compromises—they were integral to the principles of the new nation.

(136) Peter Kolchin. *American Slavery, 1619–1877*. Hill and Wang. 2003. First edition 1993

(137) Eric Foner. *Give Me Liberty!- An American History*. W. W. Norton & Co. 2006

(138) Ken Woodley. *Moton Museum Gets Set For 'Big Reveal'- 60th Anniversary Of Historic Student Strike Approaches. The Farmville Herald*. March 24, 2011. The article is based upon a press release from the Moton Museum, with additional research and writing by Herald editor Ken Woodley. Article, for first time, publically names student strike committee members.

(139) Donald Bogle. *Toms, Coons, Mulattoes, Mammies, and Bucks: An Interpretive History of Blacks in American Films*. Continuum International Publishing Group; 3rd edition. December 1994.
This comprehensive guide covers the entire history of African Americans in films from the shocking images in Birth of a Nation to Spike Lee's controversial Malcolm X. Bogle discusses the genesis of the term Uncle Tom; and how it went from describing a black hero to black subservience.

(140) Lawrence Goldstone. *Inherently Unequal: The Betrayal of Equal Rights by the Supreme Court, 1865–1903*. Walker & Company. January 18, 2011.
A study of the post-Civil War Supreme Court decisions. Author shows how the courts narrow interpretation of the 14th amendment—bestowing "equal protection under the law" to all Americans, regardless of race—paved the way for future decisions that diminished the status of African Americans. Goldstone analyzes how politics and social Darwinism further impeded African American equality, concluding, "The Court did

not render its decisions to conform to the law but rather contorted
the law to conform to its decisions."

(141) Adam Goodheart. *How Slavery Really Ended in America.*
New York Times. April 1, 2011
This author contends that blacks forced the end of slavery where
it began.

*That historic place of first entry is Old Point Comfort near Fort
Monroe in Virginia*
*In 1619, a Dutch ship landed there and traded 20 Angolan
Africans to the English authorities for food. But Old Point
Comfort is also the place where slavery began to die. In 1861, the
commander of Fort Monroe granted the request of three escaped
slaves for sanctuary, and word of the event led thousands to join
them, creating the first Union-protected enclave of black freedom
in the South.*

*Moreover, this turning point occurred at a U.S. fort built partly
by the labor of slaves, almost 600 of them in the period from
1820 to 1822, according to records discovered by Hampton
historian Joan Charles. In a double irony, these workers were
denied the democratic freedoms they helped to protect, but their
grandchildren would call their handiwork "the freedom fort."*

*The history of Old Point Comfort, in other words, encapsulates
the entire history of American slavery. The strands of that story—
the growth of slavery and the repressive legal codes controlling
it, the actions of abolitionists, and the many-faceted resistance of
African-Americans—not only go back to the 1619 purchase of
human beings at Old Point Comfort; they also reach their
culmination in the same place.*

(142) Tomiko Brown-Nagin. *Courage to Dissent: Atlanta and the
Long History of the Civil Rights Movement.* Oxford University
Press, USA. February 9, 2011.
Discusses the civil rights struggle in Atlanta and includes the
diversity of opinions within the black community on how to
proceed, or not, with integration.

(**143**) Karin Kapsidelis. *Students retrace route of '61 Freedom Riders: 50 years later, students to follow path of Freedom Riders.* Richmond Times-Dispatch. Sunday, May 1, 2011

(**144**) Lacy Ward, Director of Robert Russa Moton Museum. Lacy Ward facebook page: http://www.facebook.com/profile.php?id=1321123223. Posted May 1, 2011. Mr. Ward is discussing the Richmond Times-Dispatch article (**143**) on the '61 Freedom Riders.

(**145**) PBS. *Virginia Currents.* Original Airdate: Thursday, April 21, 2011. http://www.ideastations.org/video/virginia-currents-2021-2011-04-28.
Televised interview with former students, Joy Cabarrus and Reverend Samuel Williams Jr. As the Robert Russa Moton Museum prepares to unveil a major exhibit, former students, Joy Cabarrus Speaks and Reverend Samuel Williams Jr., discuss what it was like to be there during the Moton High School Strike 60 years ago.

(**146**) Kelley Libby. *Once Segregated Va. School To Become Civil Rights Center.* Virginia Foundation for the Humanities. May 3, 2011

(**147**) Robert Russa Moton. *Finding a Way Out: An Autobiography.* DODO Press. 1920

(**148**) Daniel J. Sharfstein. *Black or White?: Disunion follows the Civil War as it unfolded.* New York Times. May 14, 2011

(**149**) Black Americans in Congress. *The Symbolic Generation of Black Americans in Congress, 1870–1887: The Fifteenth Amendment in Flesh and Blood.* Black Americans in Congress web site: http://baic.house.gov/historical-essays/print.html?intID=3. 2007

(**150**) Richard Goldstein. *Irene Morgan Kirkaldy, 90, Rights Pioneer, Dies.* New York Times. August 13, 2007

(151) Page Smith. *Trial By Fire, A People's History of the Civil War and Reconstruction.* Mcgraw-Hill. September 1982

(152) Annette Gordon-Reid. Pulitzer Prize winner and noted Jeffersonian scholar Annette Gordon-Reid spoke at the Philadelphia Free Library on February 8, 2011. Broadcast on Book TV. 2011. See book citation in reference (153).

(153) Annette Gordon-Reed (Author), Arthur M. Schlesinger (Editor), Sean Wilentz (Editor). *Andrew Johnson, The American Presidents Series: The 17th President, 1865-1869.* Times Books 1st edition. January 18, 2011

(154) Anna Holmes. *Spotlighting the work of women in the civil rights movement's Freedom Rides- "Who the hell is Diane Nash?".* Washington Post. June 2, 2011

(155) Sara J. Lowe. *Who Among Us Would Be Content?.* John F. Kennedy's June 11, 1963 Civil Rights Speech. Undergraduate Proseminar in History. Page 34. April, 2010

(156) W. J Woodhouse. *Solon the liberator: a study of the agrarian problem in Attika in the seventh century.* 1938. Oxford University Press

(157) The Gloucester Institute. Moton Conference Center, 6496 Allmondsville Road, Gloucester, Virginia 23061. Web site: www.gloucesterinstitute.org/home.html
The home of Dr. Robert Russa Moton now houses The Gloucester Institute. The web site provided background information on Dr. Moton life and accomplishments.

(158) James W. Loewen. *Sundown Towns.* The Home Page of James W. Loewen. Viewed on July 21, 2011.
http://sundown.afro.illinois.edu/

(159) W. E. B. Du Bois. *The Negroes of Farmville, Virginia: A Social Study*, Bulletin of the Department of Labor. January 14 1898.

(160) Kathryn Orth. Article: *Marching their way into history: Museum honors students' push for change*. Richmond Times-Dispatch. Monday, August 24, 1998

(161) Gary B. Nash. *The Unknown American Revolution*. Penguin Books. 2005

(162) Phillis Wheatley. *Poems on Various Subjects, Religious and Moral. FQ Books. July 6, 2010. Originally published in 1773*

(163) Stewart E. Tolnay and E.M. Beck. *A Festival of Violence: An Analysis of Southern Lynchings, 1882-1930*. Urbana and Chicago: University of Illinois Press. 1992

(164) Jessie P. Guzman & W. Hardin Hughes. *Negro Year Book: A Review of Events Affecting Negro Life, 1944-1946*. Tuskegee Institute. 1947

(165) Robin Washington. *You Don't Have to Ride Jim Crow! Public Television's Documentary of the 1947 Journey of Reconciliation, America's first Freedom Ride*. Film produced by Robin Washington for Corporation for Public Broadcasting. 1995

(166) Dale Brumfield. *Ghost in the Machine- Ed Peebles*. Magazine rallied against the Virginia Way. Style Weekly. August 17, 2011

(167) Jim Newton. *Justice For All- Earl Warren and the Nation He Made*. Riverhead Books. 2006

(168) Jill Ogline Titus. *Brown's Battleground– Student's, Segregationists, and the Struggle for Justice in Prince Edward County, Virginia*. University of North Carolina Press. 2011

(169) Lerone Bennett, JR. *Before The Mayflower- A History of Black America*. Penguin Books. 1993, first published in 1962

(170) Robert Russa Moton. *Draft of the Lincoln Memorial Dedication Keynote Speech*. Organization of American Historians, OAH Magazine of History, Volume 23, No 1, January 2009, ttp://oah.org/pubs/magazine/llegacy/Moton.pdf Original draft of Moton's speech for the dedication of the Lincoln Memorial scheduled for May 30, 1922. This speech was never given because white censors objected to Moton holding the country to task for failing the black man following reconstruction.

(171) Vincent West. *What was it like to grow up in segregated Richmond*. Interview by author and subsequent emails. July 29,2011

(172) Becky Rutberg. *Mary Lincoln's Dress Maker: Elizabeth Keckley's Remarkable Rise from Salve to White House Confidante*. Walker Publishing Co. 1995

(173) Elizabeth Keckley. *Elizabeth Keckley's Autobiography, Behind the Scenes or Thirty Years a Slave and Four Years in the White House*. First published by Carleton& Company in New York. 1868

(174) J. Samuel Williams, Jr. *Exilic Existence: Contributions of Black churches in Prince Edward County, Virginia During the Modern Civil Rights Movement*. AuthorHouse.2011

(175) Dr. Martin Luther King. *People in Action: Virginia's Black Belt*. N.Y. Amsterdam News. April 14, 1962

(176) Henry Louis Gates, Jr. *Life Upon These Shores: Looking at African American History, 1513-2008*. Knopf. 2011

(177) Paul E. Wilson. *A Time to Lose, Representing Kansas in Brown v. Board of Education*. Lawrence University Press of Kansas. 1995

(178) Kathryn Stockett. *the Help- Change begins with a whisper*. The Berkley Publishing Group. 2009

(179) Jean Edward Smith. *Eisenhower in War and Peace*. Random House. February, 2012

(180) Christopher Bonastia. *Southern Stalemate- Five Years without Public Education in Prince Edward County. Virginia.* The University of Chicago Press. 2012

(181) Diane Brady. *Fraternity: In 1968, a visionary priest recruited 20 black men to the College of the Holy Cross and changed their lives and the course of history*. Random House Publishing. 2012

(182) Charles Murray. *Coming Apart: The State of White America, 1960-2010*. Random House Publishing. 2012

(183) J. Kenneth Morland, *The Tragedy of Public Schools: Prince Edward County, Virginia*. A Report for the Virginia Advisory Committee to the United States Commission on Civil Rights. Lynchburg, Virginia. January 16, 1964

(184) Rachel L. Swarns. *American Tapestry: The Story of the Black, White, and Multiracial Ancestors of Michelle Obama*. Amistad, Harper-Collins Publishers. 2012

(185) Ira Berlin. *The Making of African America- The Four Great Migrations*. Penguin Books. 2010

(186) Roger W. Wilkins. *Jefferson's Pillow: The Founding Fathers and the Dilemma of Black Patriotism.* Beacon Press. July 12, 2002

(187) William O. Douglas. *The Court Years, 1939-1975: the autobiography of William O. Douglas*. Vintage Books. 1981

(188) Robert Russa Moton Museum. *BARBARA ROSE JOHNS PORTRAIT NOW FEATURED AT VIRGINIA CAPITOL.*

Posting from the Robert Russa Moton Museum web site.
September, 2012. www.motonmuseum.org/barbara-johns-portrait-unveiled-at-state-capitol/

(189) John Egerton. *Shades of Gray: Dispatches from the Modern South*. Louisiana State University Press. October 1991

(190) William Bryan Crawley, Jr. *Bill Tuck: A Political Life in Harry Byrd's Virginia*. University of Virginia Press, Charlottesville, VA. 1978

(191) Sam Borden. *With Frantic Forth, Mannin and Giants Slip Past Bucs*. New York Times article. September 16, 2012. Giants score 25 points in fourth quarter against Tampa Bay Buccaneers to win the game— 41 to 31. Cited quote is NY Giant coach, Tom Coughlin, talking about his team's grit in delivering a come from behind win, "A lesser group of men would have had trouble," Coughlin said. "There is plenty of stuff to correct, and we'll work to get it corrected. But it's a lot better correcting it when you win."

(192) Robert Barnes. *Thomas concedes that "we the people' didn't include blacks*. New York Times article. September 16, 2012.

SOURCE NOTES

These source notes use a modern convention that should be familiar to most readers of academic history. However, unlike properly trained academics I am providing some notes on the notes— the engineer in me. Below are some of the basic tenets:

- The page numbers associated with this text are listed first to identify the location of the quote or referenced work within this book,
- next in bold are quotes or referenced material from the text of the book,
- quotes use quotations and references do not use quotation marks,
- then the source is identified,
- and, finally any necessary notes of explanation are included.

CHAPTER ONE

6. **"That day"**. Joan Johns Cobb. *Eye Witness to Jim Crow.* Congress of Racial Equality, An Oral History. http://www.core-online.org/History/barbara_johns1.htm. 1991.

10. **"And then there were times"**. Barbara Rose Johns. *Barbara Johns' Diary*. Unfinished. Discovered by one of her daughters in 1999 on top of her dresser.

Barbara Rose Johns' husband discussed the diary, "The strange thing about this was this writing lay at home on top of the bureau from about 1990 until 1999 when I left Philadelphia," said Rev. Powell, who has retired to the Cullen area. My daughter discovered it, had it (copied) and gave every member of the family a copy of it." Source:(Ken Woodley. *Living With The Legacies: Johns Family Members Reflect On History*. The Farmville Herald, March 2, 2001). The entire transcript of Barbara Rose Johns *Diary* that describes her decision to lead a student strike was published in *The Farmville Herald* in

September 2000 and has been on display at the Robert Russa Moton Museum.

11. **"Some teachers tried"**. Bill Medic. Article: *The Blind Spot in Black History Month.* The Pro Youth Pages, http://www.proyouthpages.com/blackhistory.html. 2003.

14. **"It was time"**. Sydney Trent. *Stand and Deliver.* The Washington Post Magazine. Apr.4, 2004.
Article quotes Barbara Rose Johns: "We wanted so much and had so little . . .We had talents and abilities here that weren't really being realized, and I thought that was a tragic shame, and that's basically what motivated me to want to see some change take place here . . .
There wasn't any fear . . . I just decided, 'This is your moment. Seize it."

14. **"Why don't you"**. Joan Johns Cobb. *Eye Witness to Jim Crow.* Congress of Racial Equality, An Oral History. http://www.core-online.org/History/barbara_johns1.htm. 1991.

14. **"But I didn't"**. Bob Smith. *They Closed Their Schools: Prince Edward County, Virginia 1951 — 1964.* Robert Russa Robert Russa Moton Museum. 2008. 13.
They Closed Their Schools is the most complete source on how the Prince Edward County struggle unfolded, and how it felt to the principles. *Reaching for the Moon* has permission from the publisher to use the exact words from *They Closed Their Schools* and appropriate citations were created in those instances.

14. **"if we were"**. Bob Lewis. *Civil rights memorial unveiled Monday.* The News & Advance. July 22, 2008.
From Lynchburg's daily paper on the dedication of the Civil Rights Memorial in Capital Square, Richmond. The memorial includes a life size bronze of Barbara Rose Johns leading the 1951 student strike and above her inscribed in the granite are her own words: "It seemed like we were reaching for the moon."

15. **"So we knew"**. Ronald E. Carrington. *Interview with John A Stokes.* Voices of Freedom: videotaped oral histories of leaders of the Civil Rights movement in Virginia by Virginia Civil Rights Movement Video Initiative. Date of interview March 21, 2003.

15. **"But Barbara Johns"**. John A. Stokes with Lois Wolf, Ph.D. *Students on Strike - Jim Crow, Civil Rights, Brown, and Me.* National Geographic. 2008. 55.

15. **"her daughter had a temper"**. Ibid. 30.

16. **"So the coalition"**. Ibid. 22.

16. **"On Tuesday, The Herald"**. Ken Woodley. *Moton Museum Gets Set For 'Big Reveal'- 60th Anniversary Of Historic Student Strike Approaches*. *The Farmville Herald*. March 24, 2011. The article is based upon a press release from the Moton Museum, with additional research and writing by Herald editor Ken Woodley. Article, for first time, publically names student strike committee members.

17. **"I'll never forget...pull it off"**. Neil Vincent Sullivan. *Bound For Freedom: An Educator's Adventures in Prince Edward County, Virginia*. Boston Little Brown. 1965. 56.

17. **"My sister was"**. Joan Johns Cobb. *Eye Witness to Jim Crow*. Congress of Racial Equality, An Oral History. http://www.core-online.org/History/barbara_johns1.htm. 1991.

18. **"Inez Jones said"**. Jamie C. Ruff. Article: *There was little notice as Barbara Johns stepped into history on April 23, 1951, but her footprints would be indelible*. Richmond Times Dispatch February 11, 2005, page D-1. Article discusses advice from the music teacher, Ms. Jones, to Barbara Rose Johns in preparing for the strike.

18. **"They wanted to"**. Bob Smith. *They Closed Their Schools: Prince Edward County, Virginia 1951 — 1964*. Robert Russa Robert Russa Moton Museum. 2008. 40.

18. **"Mr. Griffin, who"**. Ibid. 40.

20. **"So to go back"**. James J. Kilpatrick. OP/Ed article: *My Journey From Racism*. Atlanta Journal-Constitution. 2002.

22. **"we were packed"**. John A. Stokes with Lois Wolf, Ph.D. *Students on Strike - Jim Crow, Civil Rights, Brown, and Me*. National Geographic. 2008. 65.

23. **"That day, when"**. Joan Johns Cobb. *Eye Witness to Jim Crow*. Congress of Racial Equality, An Oral History. http://www.core-online.org/History/barbara_johns1.htm. 1991.

24. **"I do not remember"**. Bob Smith. *They Closed Their Schools: Prince Edward County, Virginia 1951 — 1964*. Robert Russa Robert Russa Moton Museum. 2008. 37.

25. **"soon everyone was...up and holler"**. John A. Stokes with Lois Wolf, Ph.D. *Students on Strike - Jim Crow, Civil Rights, Brown, and Me*. National Geographic. 2008.65.

25. **"There stood Ms. Alice Marie Spraggs Stokes"**. Ibid. 66.

26. **"lots of reservations"**. Ibid. 69.

27. **"WE WANT A"**. Bob Smith. *They Closed Their Schools: Prince Edward County, Virginia 1951 — 1964*. Robert Russa Robert Russa Moton Museum. 2008. 40.

29. **"On the afternoon"**. Oliver W. Hill, Sr., Edited by Jonathan K. Stubbs. *The Big Bang- Brown v. Board of Education and Beyond*. Four-G Publishers. 2000. 149.

30. **"Herein lies the"**. W.E.B. Du Bois. *The Souls of Black Folk*. Barnes & Nobles Books. Published in 2003, first published in 1903. 161.

31. **The Robert Russa Moton High School Student Strike Committee Members.** Ken Woodley. *Moton Museum Gets Set For 'Big Reveal'- 60th Anniversary Of Historic Student Strike Approaches. The Farmville Herald*. March 24, 2011. The article is based upon a press release from the Moton Museum, with additional research and writing by Herald editor Ken Woodley. Article, for first time, publically names student strike committee members.

31. **He also chose.** John A. Stokes with Lois Wolf, Ph.D. *Students on Strike - Jim Crow, Civil Rights, Brown, and Me*. National Geographic. 2008. 75.

32. **Then there was.** Ibid. 77

32. **"he was a Christian… among the people"**. Ibid. 77.

33. **"were up against"** Bob Smith. *They Closed Their Schools: Prince Edward County, Virginia 1951 — 1964*. Robert Russa Robert Russa Moton Museum. 2008. 44.

33. **"in very few"**. Ibid. 14.

34. **"INTERVIEWER: Well, with that"** Ronald E. Carrington. *Interview with Oliver W. Hill, Sr*. Voices of Freedom: videotaped oral histories of leaders of the Civil Rights movement in Virginia by Virginia Civil Rights Movement Video Initiative. Date of interview November13, 2002

38. **"we found them"**. John A. Stokes with Lois Wolf, Ph.D. *Students on Strike - Jim Crow, Civil Rights, Brown, and Me*. National Geographic. 2008. 81.

38. **"INTERVIEWER: Let's get back"**. Ronald E. Carrington. *Interview with John A Stokes*. Voices of Freedom: videotaped oral histories of leaders of the Civil Rights movement in Virginia

by Virginia Civil Rights Movement Video Initiative. Date of interview March 21, 2003.

40. **Nearer, My God to Thee.** John A. Stokes with Lois Wolf, Ph.D. *Students on Strike - Jim Crow, Civil Rights, Brown, and Me*. National Geographic. 2008. 82.

41. **"She ended by"**. Ibid. 83.

41. **"We knew that"**. Ibid. 83.

41. **"for the progress"**. Ibid. 84.

41. "**we as Negroes**". Ibid. 84.

42. **"there is no"**. Ibid. 84.

42. **"you are saying"**. Ibid. 85.

43. **"be subject to"**. Ibid. 88.

44. "**We have been**". Ibid. 89.

45. **"REMEMBER. The eyes of… Just stand!"**. Ibid. 96.

46. **The *Afro-American* reported.** Richmond Afro-American Article. *NO TOMS CAN STOP US*. Richmond Afro-American Newspaper. May 12, 1951

46. **"quiet pastoral community…of Superintendent McIlwaine"**. Ibid. 97.

46. **"Barbara Rose Johns"**. Richmond Afro-American Article. *NO TOMS CAN STOP US*. Richmond Afro-American Newspaper. May 12, 1951.

47. **"As he headed"**. John A. Stokes with Lois Wolf, Ph.D. *Students on Strike - Jim Crow, Civil Rights, Brown, and Me*. National Geographic. 2008. 98.

47. **"Mr. Pervall has…"**. Richmond Afro-American Article. *NO TOMS CAN STOP US*. Richmond Afro-American Newspaper. May 12, 1951.

48. **"an amazing act"**. John A. Stokes with Lois Wolf, Ph.D. *Students on Strike - Jim Crow, Civil Rights, Brown, and Me*. National Geographic. 2008. 99.

48. **"We came back"**. Ronald E. Carrington. *Interview with Oliver W. Hill, Sr.* Voices of Freedom: videotaped oral histories of leaders of the Civil Rights movement in Virginia by Virginia Civil Rights Movement Video Initiative. Date of interview November13, 2002.

51. **"Just three days***"*. John A. Stokes with Lois Wolf, Ph.D. *Students on Strike - Jim Crow, Civil Rights, Brown, and Me*. National Geographic. 2008. 101.

52. **"to talk with…"**. Bob Smith. *They Closed Their Schools: Prince Edward County, Virginia 1951 — 1964*. Robert Russa Robert Russa Moton Museum. 2008. 68.

53. **"a vocal minority"**. Ibid. 69.

54. **"They were all… in North Carolina."**. Kathryn Orth. *Marching their way into history / Museum honors students' push for change*. Richmond Times Dispatch. Monday, August 24, 1998. Times-Dispatch Staff Writer.

54. **"The idea that"**. Taylor Branch. *Parting the Waters: America in the King Years 1954–63.*Simon and Schuster. 1988.

55. **"There was a tense"**. Ibid. 21.

56. **"One weekend [in 1954]"**. Joan Johns Cobb. *Eye Witness to Jim Crow*. Congress of Racial Equality, An Oral History. Web Site: http://www.core-online.org/History/barbara_johns1.htm. 1991. 44.

CHAPTER TWO

61. **"It was time".** Sydney Trent. *Stand and Deliver.* The Washington Post Magazine. Apr.4, 2004. Article quotes Barbara Rose Johns: "We wanted so much and had so little . . .We had talents and abilities here that weren't really being realized, and I thought that was a tragic shame, and that's basically what motivated me to want to see some change take place here . . . There wasn't any fear . . . I just decided, 'This is your moment. Seize it."

62. **"My days at**" Barbara Rose Johns. *Barbara Johns' Diary*. Unfinished. Discovered by one of her daughters in 1999 on top of her dresser.
"The strange thing about this was this writing lay at home on top of the bureau from about 1990 until 1999 when I left Philadelphia," said Rev. Powell, who has retired to the Cullen area. My daughter discovered it, had it (copied) and gave every member of the family a copy of it." Source of above quote: Christopher Bonastia. *Southern Stalemate- Five Years without Public Education in Prince Edward County. Virginia.* The University of Chicago Press. 2012.
The entire transcript of Barbara Rose Johns *Diary* that describes her decision to lead a student strike was published in The

Farmville Herald in September 2000 and has been on display at the Robert Russa Moton Museum.

63. **"When Barbara was 12"**. Bob Smith. *They Closed Their Schools: Prince Edward County, Virginia 1951 — 1964*. Robert Russa Robert Russa Moton Museum. 2008. 29.

64. **"My uncle was"**. Ibid. 28.

64. **"her daughter had"**. Ibid. 30.

64. **"I remember as"**. Ibid. 29.

65. **"depressing, demeaning places"**. Peter F. Lau, Editor. *From Grassroots to the Supreme Court- Brown v. Board of Education and American Democracy*. Duke University Press. 2004. Discusses the strike and the adult support the students received from their teachers, principal, parents, church and black community. Describes the possibility that Ms. Davenport did indeed help Barbara Rose Johns plan the strike. 89.

65. **Diary**. Barbara Rose Johns. *Barbara Johns' Diary*. Unfinished. Discovered by one of her daughters in 1999 on top of her dresser.

65. **"Serene, Fire"**. PBS. *Virginia Currents*. Original Airdate: Thursday, April 21, 2011. http://www.ideastations.org/video/virginia-currents-2021-2011-04-28. Televised interview with former students, Joy Cabarrus and Reverend Samuel Williams Jr. As the Robert Russa Moton Museum prepares to unveil a major exhibit, former students, Joy Cabarrus Speaks and Reverend Samuel Williams Jr., discuss what it was like to be there during the Moton High School Strike 60 years ago. Williams said he only needed two words to describe Barbara Rose Johns—"Serene Fire."

65. **"But I spent"**. Barbara Rose Johns. *Barbara Johns' Diary*. Unfinished. Discovered by one of her daughters in 1999 on top of her dresser.

66. **"Around September to May"**. Ibid.

67. **"Her classmates remember"**. Bob Smith. *They Closed Their Schools: Prince Edward County, Virginia 1951 — 1964*. Robert Russa Robert Russa Moton Museum. 2008. 31.

67. **The Warmth of Other Suns.** Isabel Wilkerson. *The Warmth of Other Suns: The Epic Story of America's Great Migration*. Random House. 2001.

68. **"Barbara went to"**. Bob Smith. *They Closed Their Schools: Prince Edward County, Virginia 1951 — 1964*. Robert Russa Robert Russa Moton Museum. 2008. 32.

69. **"One morning—I"**. Barbara Rose Johns. *Barbara Johns' Diary*. Unfinished. Discovered by one of her daughters in 1999 on top of her dresser.

70. **"It was in seizing"**. Governor Bob McDonnell. *Inaugural Address of Governor Robert F. McDonnell- A Commonwealth of Opportunity*. January 18, 2010. Richmond.

70. **"Barbara Johns was"**. Ibid.

71. **"The case remained"**. Taylor Branch. *Parting the Waters: America in the King Years. 1954–63.* Simon and Schuster. 1988.

71. **"following the strike"**. Joan Johns Cobb. *Eye Witness to Jim Crow*. Congress of Racial Equality, An Oral History. http://www.core-online.org/History/barbara_johns1.htm. 1991.

71. **"Barbara Johns would"**. Taylor Branch. *Parting the Waters: America in the King Years 1954–63.* Simon and Schuster. 1988. 21.

72 **"Long before it was"**. Taylor Branch. *Parting the Waters: America in the King Years. 1954–63.* Simon and Schuster. 1988.pp25

72. **Long before it was.** PBS. *Virginia Currents*. Original Airdate: Thursday, April 21, 2011. http://www.ideastations.org/video/virginia-currents-2021-2011-04-28. Televised interview with former students, Joy Cabarrus and Reverend Samuel Williams Jr. As the Robert Russa Moton Museum prepares to unveil a major exhibit, former students, Joy Cabarrus Speaks and Reverend Samuel Williams Jr., discuss what it was like to be there during the Moton High School Strike 60 years ago.

72. **"If a child"**. Chinua Achebe. *Things Fall Apart: A Novel*. Anchor. 1994, originally published in 1958. This is a classic African tale. The theme of the book is the destruction of village life brought about by the white man demanding changes in village culture that have unintended consequences. Additionally, this quote makes the point not to take a child for granted. *Reaching for the Moon* uses it here in

recognition of the significant contribution children made to the civil rights movement.

73. **Claudette Colvin: Twice Toward Justice.** Phillip Hoose. *Claudette Colvin: Twice Toward Justice*. Canada, Douglas & McIntyre Ltd. 2009. Book reference cited.

73. **book about her.** Betty Kilby Fischer. *Wit, Will and Walls*. Cultural Innovations Inc. 2002. Book reference cited.

74. **"Driving up I... very proud of her".** Ruby Bridges Hall. Article: *The Education of Ruby Nell. Guideposts Magazine*. pp. 3-4. March 2000.

75. **"as if she".** Ibid.

75. **"The blanket of fear".** Phillip Hoose. *We Were There Too!: Young People in U.S. History*. Canada, Douglas & McIntyre Ltd. 2001. 215.

75. **"Real men don't".** Ibid. 209.

76. **"Had there been".** National Museum of American History. *Separate Is Not Equal: Brown v. Board of Education*. http://americanhistory.si.edu/brown/history/6-legacy/fifty-years-after.html

Separate Is Not Equal: Brown v. Board of Education is a collective effort of the staff of the National Museum of American History, Behring Center.

This site has an informative and thorough timeline detailing the four critical years that the Supreme Court spent addressing the Brown case.

CHAPTER THREE

78. **"More than sixty".** Robert Russa Moton. *Draft of the Lincoln Memorial Dedication Keynote Speech*. Organization of American Historians, OAH Magazine of History, Volume 23, No 1, January 2009, ttp://oah.org/pubs/magazine/llegacy/Moton.pdf Original draft of Moton's speech for the dedication of the Lincoln Memorial scheduled for May 30, 1922. This speech was never given because white censors objected to Moton holding the country to task for failing the black man following reconstruction.

82. **"Dare we dream".** *The Birth of a Nation*. Donald Bogle. *Toms, Coons, Mulattoes, Mammies, and Bucks: An Interpretive*

History of Blacks in American Films. Continuum International Publishing Group; 3rd edition. December 1994.
This comprehensive guide covers the entire history of African Americans in films from the shocking images in Birth of a Nation to Spike Lee's controversial Malcolm X. Bogle discusses the genesis of the term Uncle Tom; and how it went from describing a black hero to black subservience.

84. ***Finding a Way Out.*** Robert Russa Moton. *Finding a Way Out: An Autobiography*. DODO Press. 1920.

84. **"For a great"**. Ibid. 139.

84. **"Of all the instruments"**. Martin Luther King III. The Washington Post Editorial: *Still striving for MLK's dream in the 21st century*. The Washington Post, Page A19. Wednesday, August 25, 2010.

85. **"the African presence"**. Henry Louis Gates, Jr. *Life Upon These Shores: Looking at African American History, 1513-2008*. Knopf. 2011.

85. **"As in the South"**. Leslie M. Harris. *In the Shadow of Slavery: African Americans in New York City, 1626–1863*. The University of Chicago Press. 2003. 11.

85. **"By the first"**. Ibid. 3.

86. **"The ratio of slaves"**. Ibid. 11.

87. **"the most famous"**. Gary B. Nash. *The Unknown American Revolution*. Penguin Books. 2005. 137.

87. **"Twas mercy brought"**. *Ibid.*

88. **"Most Northerners, to"**. Leon F. Litwack. *North of Slavery: The Negro in the Free States, 1790–1860*. Page 64. University of Chicago Press. 1961. 64.

89. **"Thus the Negro"**. Ibid. 64.

89. **"We shall not"**. Charles Mackay. *Life and Liberty in America: or, Sketches of a Tour in the United States and Canada in 1857–1858*. Harper & Brothers, 1859.

90. **"By 1860, some"**. Leon F. Litwack. *North of Slavery: The Negro in the Free States, 1790–1860*. University of Chicago Press. 1961. 151.

90. **"Douglass protested the"**. Ibid. 151.

91. **"The South claimed"**. Ulysses S. Grant. *Ulysses S. Grant-Personal Memoirs*. Modern Library. 1999 edition, first published

soon after President Grant's death with the help of Mark Twain in 1885. 114.

91, **"the most enlightened... of the Union.".** Daniel J. Sharfstein. *Black or White?: Disunion follows the Civil War as it unfolded*. New York Times. May 14, 2011.

92. **"It did not".** Ibid.

93. **"I rode in to Farmville".** Ulysses S. Grant. *Ulysses S. Grant-Personal Memoirs*. Modern Library. 1999 edition, first published soon after President Grant's death with the help of Mark Twain in 1885. 572.

93. **"I know that".** Ibid. 573.

96. **her tell-all book.** Elizabeth Keckley. *Elizabeth Keckley's Autobiography, Behind the Scenes or Thirty Years a Slave and Four Years in the White House*. First published by Carleton& Company in New York. 1868.

97. **"no negro or".** Leon F. Litwack. *North of Slavery: The Negro in the Free States, 1790–1860*. University of Chicago Press. 1961.

100. **"Examine the laws".** Black Americans in Congress. *The Symbolic Generation of Black Americans in Congress, 1870–1887: The Fifteenth Amendment in Flesh and Blood.* Black Americans in Congress web site: http://baic.house.gov/historical-essays/print.html?intID=3. 2007.

101. **"Spare us our... I am not a man.".** Ibid.

102. **"The slave went".** W. E. B. Du Bois. *The Negroes of Farmville, Virginia: A Social Study*, Bulletin of the Department of Labor. January 14 1898. 184.

103. **"being angry that".** Annette Gordon-Reid. Pulitzer Prize winner and noted Jeffersonian scholar Annette Gordon-Reid spoke at the Philadelphia Free Library on February 8, 2011. Broadcast on Book TV. 2011. See book citation number 153 in Bibliography.

104. **Plessy v. Ferguson.** The case law cited in this section is from Richard Kluger's book, *Simple Justice: The History of Brown v. Board of Education and Black America's Struggle for Equality by* Vintage Books, 2004. Originally published in 1976 by Knopf.

105. **"Public sentiment still".** Robert Russa Moton. *What The Negro Thinks*. Doubleday Doran and Company. 1929. 54.

Inclusion of this quote is to provide some evidence that Moton was not so satisfied with the current state of racial relations and less of an appeaser then many have recently portrayed him.

106. **"don't you know"**. Phillip Hoose. *Claudette Colvin: Twice Toward Justice*. Canada, Douglas & McIntyre Ltd. 2009. 8.

106. **The Jim Crow laws.** Ibid. 8.

106. **"I knew plenty"**. Ibid. 13.

107. **"The average black"**. Ibid. 4.

108. **"The number ten"**. Ibid. 8.

109. **"We could shop"**. Ibid. 17.

109. ***"Slavery by Another Name"***. Douglas A. Blackmon. *Slavery by Another Name: The Re-Enslavement of Black Americans from the Civil War to World War II*. Doubleday. 2008.

110. **"best sociological work"**. Ibid. 274.

111. **"cheap cotton depends"**. Ibid. 276.

111. **"this sense of always"**. W.E.B. Du Bois. *The Souls of Black Folk*. Barnes & Nobles Books. Published in 2003, first published in 1903. 9.

111. **"They created a"**. Roger W. Wilkins. *Jefferson's Pillow: The Founding Fathers and the Dilemma of Black Patriotism*. Beacon Press. July 12, 2002. 5.

112. **"The Tennessee River…"**. Jean Edward Smith. *FDR*. Random House. 2007. 324. The book *FDR* is also the source for the statistics quoted in the next paragraph that begins with **"Smith points out."**

113. **"2805 [documented] victims"**. Gary B. Nash. *The Unknown American Revolution*. Penguin Books. 2005. ix.

114. **"In addition to"**. Stewart E. Tolnay and E.M. Beck. *A Festival of Violence: An Analysis of Southern Lynchings, 1882-1930*. Urbana and Chicago: University of Illinois Press. 1992. 18-19.

114. **"Lethal mob violence"**. Ibid. 19.

116. **"Yes, yes, hang"**. Ibid.

116. ***"The Strange Career of Jim Crow"***. C. Vann Woodward (Author), William S. McFeely (Contributor). *The Strange Career of Jim Crow*. Oxford University Press, Oxford Press USA. 3rd edition March 21, 1974, originally published in 1955.

116. **""….the true rise"**. Ibid.

117. **"The Souls Of"**. W.E.B. Du Bois. *The Souls of Black Folk.* Barnes & Nobles Books. Published in 2003, first published in 1903. xix.

118. **"Florida did not"**. Richard Kluger. *Simple Justice: The History of Brown v. Board of Education and Black America's Struggle for Equality.* Vintage Books. 2004. Originally published in 1976 by Knopf. 327.

121. **The first migration.....**. Ira Berlin. *The Making of African America- The Four Great Migrations.* Penguin Books. 2010. 15. All four distinct migrations are from the cited text.

121. **"The Great Migration"**. NPR Author Interview and Article. On Isabel Wilkerson winner of the Pulitzer Prize in 1994. *Great Migration: The African-American Exodus North.* http://www.npr.org/templates/story/story.php?storyId=12982744 4. September 13, 2010.

122. **"His place of"**. J. Samuel Williams, Jr. *Exilic Existence: Contributions of Black churches in Prince Edward County, Virginia During the Modern Civil Rights Movement.* Author House. 2011. 16.

124. **"In the name"**. Dr. Robert Russa Moton. *Dr. Robert Russa Moton Address, at the Dedication of The Lincoln Memorial, Washington, D. C., May 30th, 1922 (Original Draft). The Glouster Institute. http://gloucester.kma.net/Gloucester/files/ccLibraryFiles/Filena me/000000000278/Moton%20Speech-May301922.pdf.*

124. **"You can't overstate…"**. Eddie Gross. Article: *Region is home to 'cradle' of civil rights.* The Free Lance-Star Publishing Co. Fredericksburg, Virginia, USA. January 19, 2009. http://www.fredericksburg.com/News/FLS/2009/012009/011920 09/439401/index_html.

125. **"With malice toward"**. Keith Eberly. *Teaching Strategy: "To Thee We Sing": Racial Politics and the Lincoln Memorial.* OAH Magazine of History, Volume 23, No 1, January 2009. Robert Russa Moton's Keynote Speech, Original Draft and Final, for 1922 Lincoln Memorial dedication. http://oah.org/pubs/magazine/llegacy/Moton.pdf.

125. **"Major Moton is"**. James D. Anderson. *The Education of Blacks in the South, 1860–1935.* The University of North Carolina Press. September 9, 1988.

126. **"The basic philosophy"**. Ibid. 272.

126. **"a DuBois ambition"** and **"a Booker Washington education."**. Ibid. 274.

126. ***What The Negro Thinks.*** Robert Russa Moton. *What The Negro Thinks*. Doubleday Doran and Company. 1929.

127. **"With some such"**. Ibid. 78.

127. **"In the midst"**. Ibid. 216.

128. **"My grandmother used"**. Marco Williams, Director/Producer. 2007 Documentary film: *Banished*. Center For Investigative Reporting And Two Tone Productions. 2007. http://www.pbs.org/independentlens/banished/film.html.

129. **"an embarrassing blend"**. Ira Berlin. *The Making of African America- The Four Great Migrations*. Penguin Books. 2010.

129. **"The best way"**. James W. Loewen. *Sundown Towns: A Hidden Dimension of American Racism*. Simon & Schuster. 2005.

130. **"the overwhelming majority"**. Douglas A. Blackmon. *Slavery by Another Name: The Re-Enslavement of Black Americans from the Civil War to World War II*. Doubleday. 2008.

130. **"something significant has…"**. James W. Loewen. *Sundown Towns: A Hidden Dimension of American Racism*. Simon & Schuster. 2005.

130. **"openly favor[ed] white supremacy"**. Ibid.

131. **"In some ways"**. Condoleezza Rice. *Condoleezza Rice- a memoir of my extraordinary, ordinary family and me*. Delacorte Press. 2010.

131. **"wove the fibers"**. Ibid. Authors Note.

131. **"So how can"**. Ibid. 47.

132. **"The City put"**. Ibid. 48.

132. **"All of these"**. Ibid. 49.

136. ***"This document began"***. Emmett J. Scott. *Scott's Official History Of The American Negro In The World War- Special Adjutant to Secretary of War*. Copyright by Emmett J. Scott. Initial publication 1919. 115.

137. **Between 1900 and.** Jessie P. Guzman & W. Hardin Hughes. *Negro Year Book: A Review of Events Affecting Negro Life, 1944-1946*. Tuskegee Institute. 1947. Source of quoted statistics.

137. **"as long as the".** James D. Anderson. *The Education of Blacks in the South, 1860–1935*. The University of North Carolina Press. September 9, 1988. 8.

140. **called the *Ghost*.** Dale Brumfield. *Ghost in the Machine- Ed Peebles.* Magazine rallied against the Virginia Way. Style Weekly. August 17, 2011.

140. **"we are able".** Ibid.

142. **"If something happens".** Robin Washington. *You Don't Have to Ride Jim Crow! Public Television's Documentary of the 1947 Journey of Reconciliation, America's first Freedom Ride.* Film produced by Robin Washington for Corporation for Public Broadcasting. 1995.

144. **"Now, Mr. Roodenko…".** Ibid.

145. **"*Thomas Jefferson noted*".** Library of Congress. President's of the United States.

146. **"60 percent in favor".** 4 Chas. H. Thompson. Article: *Court Action the Only Reasonable Alternative to Remedy Immediate Abuses of the Negro Separate School. The Journal of Negro Education,* Vol. 4, No. 3, The Courts and the Negro Separate School (Jul., 1935), pp. 419-434 (article consists of 16 pages). URL: www.jstor.org/stable/2291877. 19.

146. **The state put money.** Richard T. Couture. *Powhatan: A Bicentennial History*. The Díetz Press, Inc. 1980. 370.

147. **However, in practice… and secondary schools.** Ibid. 386.

148. **"The Richmond Times-Dispatch".** James D. Anderson. *The Education of Blacks in the South, 1860–1935*. The University of North Carolina Press. September 9, 1988. 96.

149. **"Your parents taught"** through **"our family doctor.".** Vincent West. *What was it like to grow up in segregated Richmond*. Interview by author and subsequent emails. July 29,2011.

150. **"Whenever and wherever".** John A. Stokes with Lois Wolf, Ph.D. *Students on Strike - Jim Crow, Civil Rights, Brown, and Me*. National Geographic. 2008. 7.

150. **"The white authorities".** Ibid. 7.

151. **That is a 73** through **it was $194.** Edward Harden Peeples. *A Perspective of the Prince Edward County Issue- Master Thesis*. University of Pennsylvania. 1963. Statistics from cited source, page 22.

151. **"why don't they "** through **"Moton High School.".** John A. Stokes with Lois Wolf, Ph.D. *Students on Strike - Jim Crow, Civil Rights, Brown, and Me*. National Geographic. 2008. 21.

154. **"they are coming".** Ibid. 49.

155. **"Where are the cows?".** Ronald E. Carrington. *Interview with John A Stokes.* Voices of Freedom: videotaped oral histories of leaders of the Civil Rights movement in Virginia by Virginia Civil Rights Movement Video Initiative. Date of interview March 21, 2003.

155. **"They leaked when".** Peter McCormick. *Today I Wonder How We Ever Pulled It Off: How a Band of High School Students Influenced Desegregation.* The College Board Review, Issue 200, College Board Publications. Fall 2003.

155. **"Each shack had".** Ibid.

155. **"Barbara knew what".** Kathryn Orth. Article: *Marching their way into history: Museum honors students' push for change.* Richmond Times-Dispatch. Monday, August 24, 1998.

155. **"In the tar paper".** Ibid.

155. **"The school we".** Joan Johns Cobb. *Eye Witness to Jim Crow.* Congress of Racial Equality, An Oral History. http://www.core-online.org/History/barbara_johns1.htm. 1991.

156. **"when you speak".** Ronald E. Carrington. *Interview with John A Stokes.* Voices of Freedom: videotaped oral histories of leaders of the Civil Rights movement in Virginia by Virginia Civil Rights Movement Video Initiative. Date of interview March 21, 2003.

156. **"By 1947 some".** Bob Smith. *They Closed Their Schools: Prince Edward County, Virginia 1951 — 1964.* Robert Russa Robert Russa Moton Museum. 2008.

157. **"Large felt the".** Ibid. 16.

157. **"It found Robert Russa".** Ibid. 16.

157. **Bob Smith who wrote his book.** Ibid.

158. **"the shacks were".** Ibid. 19.

158. **"In March 1948".** Ibid. 18.

162. **"I had very"** through **"community was either".** Ibid. 23.

163. **"Any Negro, every Negro".** Robert Russa Moton. *What The Negro Thinks.* Doubleday Doran and Company. 1929.

CHAPTER FOUR

165. **"Had there been"**. National Museum of American History. *Separate Is Not Equal: Brown v. Board of Education.* http://americanhistory.si.edu/brown/history/6-legacy/fifty-years-after.html.

Separate Is Not Equal: Brown v. Board of Education is a collective effort of the staff of the National Museum of American History, Behring Center.

This site has an informative and thorough timeline detailing the four critical years that the Supreme Court spent addressing the Brown case.

171. **significant legal precedents.** Richard Kluger. *Simple Justice: The History of Brown v. Board of Education and Black America's Struggle for Equality.* Vintage Books. 2004. Originally published in 1976 by Knopf.

Cited legal precedents are from this source.

173. **"In terms of the"**. Bob Smith. *They Closed Their Schools: Prince Edward County,*

Virginia 1951 — 1964. Robert Russa Robert Russa Moton Museum. 2008. 46.

174. **"by the Supreme Court's"**. Ibid. 46.

174. **"act of providence"**. Ibid. 47.

176. **"the Supreme Court"**. Richard Kluger. *Simple Justice: The History of Brown v. Board of Education and Black America's Struggle for Equality.* Vintage Books. 2004. Originally published in 1976 by Knopf.

Reaching for the Moon relied heavily on this source for the details of the *Brown* case and its various component cases.

178. **"Dorothy Davis, Dorothy Davis'"**. Ronald E. Carrington. *Interview with John A Stokes.* Voices of Freedom: videotaped oral histories of leaders of the Civil Rights movement in Virginia by Virginia Civil Rights Movement Video Initiative. Date of interview March 21, 2003.

182. **"I am of the opinion"**. National Museum of American History. *Separate Is Not Equal: Brown v. Board of Education.* http://americanhistory.si.edu/brown/history/6-legacy/fifty-years-after.html.

Separate Is Not Equal: Brown v. Board of Education is a collective effort of the staff of the National Museum of American History, Behring Center.

This site has an informative and thorough timeline detailing the four critical years that the Supreme Court spent addressing the Brown case.

183. **"We weren't in sympathy"**. Ibid.

185. **"I was for segregation"**. Richard Kluger. *Simple Justice: The History of Brown v. Board of Education and Black America's Struggle for Equality*. Vintage Books. 2004. Originally published in 1976 by Knopf. 436.

185. **"We are all"**. Ibid.

188. ***Civil Rights and Wrongs***. Harry S. Ashmore. *Civil Rights and Wrongs: A memoir of race and politics 1944 — 1994*. Pantheon Books. 1994.

188. ***"The NAACP launched"***. Ibid. 108.

188. ***"The Negro child"***. National Museum of American History. *Separate Is Not Equal: Brown v. Board of Education*. http://americanhistory.si.edu/brown/history/6-legacy/fifty-years-after.html

Separate Is Not Equal: Brown v. Board of Education is a collective effort of the staff of the National Museum of American History, Behring Center.

This site has an informative and thorough timeline detailing the four critical years that the Supreme Court spent addressing the Brown case.

190. **"WE WANT OUR"**. Library of Congress. Brown v. Board of Education.

191. **"be aimed at"**. Richard Kluger. *Simple Justice: The History of Brown v. Board of Education and Black America's Struggle for Equality*. Vintage Books. 2004. Originally published in 1976 by Knopf. 293.

191. **"The goal now"**. Ibid. 29.

193. **"on this day"**. Ibid. 572.

194. **"The personalities of each"**. Juan Williams. *Thurgood Marshall: The Man and His Enduring but Endangered Legacy*. The College Board Review, Issue 200, College Board Publications. Fall 2003.

194. **"differences in intellectual"**. Ibid.

196. **"to separate black"**. Ibid.

196. **"A lot of us"**. Oliver W. Hill, Sr., Edited by Jonathan K. Stubbs. *The Big Bang- Brown v. Board of Education and Beyond*. Four-G Publishers. 2000. 45.

197. **"In a stormy"**. Ibid. 46.

197. **"INTERVIEWER: Whenever you are"**. Ronald E. Carrington. *Interview with Oliver W. Hill, Sr*. Voices of Freedom: videotaped oral histories of leaders of the Civil Rights movement in Virginia by Virginia Civil Rights Movement Video Initiative. Date of interview November13, 2002.

202. **"We thank Mr. Hill"**. Ronald E. Carrington. *Interview with Oliver W. Hill, Sr*. Voices of Freedom: videotaped oral histories of leaders of the Civil Rights movement in Virginia by Virginia Civil Rights Movement Video Initiative. Date of interview November13, 2002.

203. **"Throughout his long"**. Ibid.

203. **"lie in state"**. Joe Macenka. *Oliver W. Hill Sr.: 1907–2007, 200 Pay Their Respects*. Richmond Times Dispatch Times. August 12, 2007. Dispatch Staff Writer.

203. **"I can almost"**. Ibid.

204. **"A Time to"**. Paul E. Wilson. *A Time to Lose, Representing Kansas in Brown v. Board of Education*. Lawrence University Press of Kansas. 1995.

205. **"To everything there"**. Ibid.

206. **"the same two-tiered"**. Lawrence Goldstone. *Inherently Unequal: The Betrayal of Equal Rights by the Supreme Court, 1865–1903*. Walker & Company. January 18, 2011. A study of the post-Civil War Supreme Court decisions. Author shows how the court's narrow interpretation of the 14th amendment—bestowing "equal protection under the law" to all Americans, regardless of race—paved the way for future decisions that diminished the status of African Americans. Goldstone analyzes how politics and social Darwinism further impeded African American equality, concluding, "The Court did not render its decisions to conform to the law but rather contorted the law to conform to its decisions."

208. **"simply equal under"** through **"of social organization"** Ibid.

209. **Justice Reed was.** Jim Newton. *Justice For All- Earl Warren and the Nation He Made*. Riverhead Books. 2006. This source is the basis for the statements made identifying Justice Reed as so strongly segregationist that he refused to go to the Supreme Court Christmas party if blacks were to be invited.
210. **"The document before".** Ibid. 324-325.
211. **"There was always".** Robert Barnes. *Thomas concedes that "we the people' didn't include blacks*. New York Times article. September 16, 2012.
212. **Brown's Battleground- Students.** Jill Ogline Titus. *Brown's Battleground– Student's, Segregationists, and the Struggle for Justice in Prince Edward County, Virginia*. University of North Carolina Press. 2011.
212. **"fifty-six years".** Richard Kluger. *Simple Justice: The History of Brown v. Board of Education and Black America's Struggle for Equality*. Vintage Books. 2004.
212. **"We come then".** National Museum of American History. *Separate Is Not Equal: Brown v. Board of Education*. http://americanhistory.si.edu/brown/history/6-legacy/fifty-years-after.html.
Separate Is Not Equal: Brown v. Board of Education is a collective effort of the staff of the National Museum of American History, Behring Center.
This site has an informative and thorough timeline detailing the four critical years that the Supreme Court spent addressing the Brown case.
213. **"A lesser group   when you win."** Sam Borden. *With Frantic Forth, Mannin and Giants Slip Past Bucs*. New York Times article. September 16, 2012.
Giants score 25 points in fourth quarter against Tampa Bay Buccaneers to win the game— 41 to 31. Cited quote is NY Giant coach, Tom Coughlin, talking about his team's grit in delivering a come from behind win, "A lesser group of men would have had trouble," Coughlin said. "There is plenty of stuff to correct, and we'll work to get it corrected. But it's a lot better correcting it when you win." This quote was the very last addition to this book. This penchant for adding quotes to *Reaching for the Moon* is one of the reasons the project took eight years.

214. **"The highest court".** Ibid.
215. **"My father, Oliver".** Cheryl Brown Henderson. *Brown v. Board of Education at Fifty- A Personal Perspective*. The College Board Review, Issue 200, College Board Publications. Fall 2003.

CHAPTER FIVE

217. **"If there is not struggle".** On August 3, 1857, Frederick Douglass delivered a "West India Emancipation" speech at Canandaigua, New York, on the twenty-third anniversary of the event. Most of the address was a history of British efforts toward emancipation as well as a reminder of the crucial role the West Indian slaves had in their own freedom struggle. However, shortly after he began, Douglass foretold the coming Civil War when he uttered two paragraphs that became the most quoted sentences of all of his public orations. They began with the words, "If there is no struggle, there is no progress."
222. **"that *Brown* was".** National Museum of American History. *Separate Is Not Equal: Brown v. Board of Education.* http://americanhistory.si.edu/brown/history/6-legacy/fifty-years-after.html
Separate Is Not Equal: Brown v. Board of Education is a collective effort of the staff of the National Museum of American History, Behring Center.
This site has an informative and thorough timeline detailing the four critical years that the Supreme Court spent addressing the Brown case.
222. **"you get weary".** Richard Kluger. *Simple Justice: The History of Brown v. Board of Education and Black America's Struggle for Equality*. Vintage Books. 2004. Originally published in 1976 by Knopf. 327.
224. **"The author of "Uncle Tom's Cabin".** Mary Eastman. *Aunt Phillis's Cabin*. Philadelphia: Lippincott, Grambo & Co.. 1852. Page 280.
The novel, although obscure today, remains one of the most-read examples of the anti-Uncle Tom Cabin genre, with between 20,000 and 30,000 copies of *Aunt Phillis's Cabin* being sold upon its initial release in 1852. *Aunt Phillis's Cabin* was released in 1852 to counter *Uncle Tom's.*

224. **"The opposition to"**. W.E.B. Du Bois. *The Souls of Black Folk*. Barnes & Nobles Books. Published in 2003, first published in 1903. 29

225. ***"When 14-year-old John Lewis"***. National Museum of American History. *Separate Is Not Equal: Brown v. Board of Education*. http://americanhistory.si.edu/brown/history/6-legacy/fifty-years-after.html.

226. **"to make a prompt…"**. *Brown v. Board of Education*, 349 U.S. (1955).

226. **"I became the"**. Jeff E. Shapiro. Article: *Brilliance and Bias*. Richmond Times Dispatch. August 17, 2010.

226. **"These nine men… taught us how."**. Ibid.

227. **"by 1970 I had"**. James J. Kilpatrick. OP/Ed article: *My Journey From Racism*. Atlanta Journal-Constitution. 2002.

227. **"He made a bad"**. Jeff E. Shapiro. Article: *Brilliance and Bias*. Richmond Times Dispatch. August 17, 2010.

227. ***"Kilpatrick was a superb"***. Ibid.

227. **"A dozen white"**. James J. Kilpatrick. OP/Ed article: *My Journey From Racism*. Atlanta Journal-Constitution. 2002.

228. **"one of the things"**. Jeff E. Shapiro. Article: *Brilliance and Bias*. Richmond Times Dispatch. August 17, 2010.

228. **"the issue is"**. Harry S. Ashmore. *Civil Rights and Wrongs: A memoir of race and politics 1944 — 1994*. Pantheon Books. 1994. 126.

229. **"The Crisis Mr. Faubus"**. Ibid.

232. **"cool heads, calm,"**. Alexander S. Leidholdt. *Standing Before The Shouting Mob: Lenoir Chambers and Virginia's Massive Resistance to Public-School Integration*. The University of Alabama Press.1997. 64.

232. **"Virginia will approach"**. Ibid. 64.

232. **"a loose organization... now and then."**. John Egerton. *Shades of Gray: Dispatches from the Modern South*. Louisiana State University Press. October 1991. 11.

232. **"CARRINGTON: Now, the Byrd"**. Ronald E. Carrington. *Interview with Dr. W. Ferguson Reid*. Voices of Freedom: videotaped oral histories of leaders of the Civil Rights movement in Virginia by Virginia Civil Rights Movement Video Initiative. Date of interview March 21, 2003.

234. **"I heard…that the"**. Alexander S. Leidholdt. *Standing Before The Shouting Mob: Lenoir Chambers and Virginia's Massive Resistance to Public-School Integration*. The University of Alabama Press.1997. 66.

234. **"all deliberate speed"**. Richard Kluger. *Simple Justice: The History of Brown v. Board of Education and Black America's Struggle for Equality*. Vintage Books. 2004. Originally published in 1976 by Knopf.

238. **"If this community"**. Bob Smith. *They Closed Their Schools: Prince Edward County, Virginia 1951 — 1964*. Robert Russa Robert Russa Moton Museum. 2008. 98.

238. **"a clear abuse…in its implementation."**. Alexander S. Leidholdt. *Standing Before The Shouting Mob: Lenoir Chambers and Virginia's Massive Resistance to Public-School Integration*. The University of Alabama Press.1997. 77-78.

239. **"Virginia stands as"**. Ibid. 78.

240. **"how many schools"**. Ibid. 79.

240. **"the threat Gov. Stanley's"**. Ibid. 79.

241. **"CARRINGTON: What were some"**. Ronald E. Carrington. *Interview with Oliver W. Hill, Sr.* Voices of Freedom: videotaped oral histories of leaders of the Civil Rights movement in Virginia by Virginia Civil Rights Movement Video Initiative. Date of interview November13, 2002.

242. **"CARRINGTON: Was that the"**. Ronald E. Carrington. *Interview with Sen. Henry L. Marsh, III.* Voices of Freedom: videotaped oral histories of leaders of the Civil Rights movement in Virginia by Virginia Civil Rights Movement Video Initiative. Date of interview March 20, 2003.

246. **freedom of choice.** Sara K. Eskridge. *Virginia's Pupil Placement Board and the Practical Applications of Massive Resistance, 1956–1966*. Virginia Magazine. Published by the Virginia Historical Society, Vol.118,No.3. 201.

Richard Kluger. *Simple Justice: The History of Brown v. Board of Education and Black America's Struggle for Equality*. Vintage Books. 2004. Originally published in 1976 by Knopf.

Both cited references fully discuss Virginia's freedom of choice plan.

247. **"though maligned, sometimes"**. Sara K. Eskridge. *Virginia's Pupil Placement Board and the Practical Applications of Massive Resistance, 1956–1966*. Virginia Magazine. Published by the Virginia Historical Society, Vol.118,No.3. 2010. 273.

247. **Nonetheless with the.** Southern School News. May 17, 1964.

248. **"*If he had*"**. William O. Douglas. *The Court Years, 1939-1975: the autobiography of William O. Douglas*. Vintage Books. 1981.

249. ***Eisenhower in War and Peace.*** Jean Edward Smith. *Eisenhower in War and Peace*. Random House. February, 2012.

250. **"someone noticed one"**. Bob Smith. *They Closed Their Schools: Prince Edward County, Virginia 1951 — 1964*. Robert Russa Robert Russa Moton Museum. 2008. 106.

250. **"What the Defenders"**. Ibid. 98.

250. **The other officers.** Ibid. 99.

251. **"The worst obstacle…"**. Ibid. 100.

251. **"They did not"**. Ibid. 102.

251. **"there was nothing… no public schools"**. Ibid. 102.

252. **"*I believe in*"**. *Richmond Times-Dispatch.* June 3, 1955 front page article. 1955.

253. **"To those whose…"**. Christopher Bonastia. *Southern Stalemate- Five Years without Public Education in Prince Edward County. Virginia*. The University of Chicago Press. 2012. 91.

253. **"that damn speech"**. Ibid. 92.

253. **"The notable speech"**. Bob Smith. *They Closed Their Schools: Prince Edward County, Virginia 1951 — 1964*. Robert Russa Robert Russa Moton Museum. 2008. 145.

254. **"The truth is"**. Ibid. 148.

CHAPTER SIX

258. **"*The "unthinkable", has happened*"**. J. Kenneth Morland, *The Tragedy of Public Schools: Prince Edward County, Virginia*. A Report for the Virginia Advisory Committee to the United States Commission on Civil Rights. Lynchburg, Virginia. January 16, 1964.

258. **"*The Gravest Crisis*"**. Time Magazine. Article: *VIRGINIA: The Gravest Crisis*. Monday, Sep. 1, 1958. The cover for this

issue of Time has a picture of Governor Almond adjacent to the Virginia State Seal " SIC SEMPER TYRANNIS" all superimposed over a large confederate flag in the background.

259. *"Closing down the schools".* Ibid.

260. *"The action taken today".* Bob Smith. *They Closed Their Schools: Prince Edward County, Virginia 1951 — 1964.* Robert Russa Robert Russa Moton Museum. 2008. 151.

262. **"with appropriations on".** Ibid. 152.

262. **"that it would".** Ibid. 154.

262. **"Barry said that".** Ibid. 155.

263. **"they said Griffin…".** Ibid. 155.

263. **I see that thing.** Ibid. 175.

264. **outpouring of community.** Ibid. 165.

264. **"He set up".** Ibid. 165.

265. **"that things were".** Ibid. 169.

265. **"stand steady".** The phrase used frequently by Barrye J. Wall the editor of the *Farmville Herald* to bolster the residents of Prince Edward County resolve to fight integration through the courts.

265. **"the truth was that… schools would open.".** Ibid. 169.

266. **"How can segregated".** Ibid. 172.

267. **"Some benighted individuals…".** Ibid. 173.

267. **"The NAACP offers".** *Farmville Herald.* Editorial. December 29, 1959.

268. **"In its decision".** Bob Smith. *They Closed Their Schools: Prince Edward County,*
Virginia 1951 — 1964. Robert Russa Robert Russa Moton Museum. 2008. 175.

270. **"when I was".** Ibid. 177.

270. **"Daddy if you".** Ibid. 178.

271. **"This is not to say".** Ibid. 186.

272. **"judged that it".** Ibid. 188.

272. **"They imagine themselves".** Ibid. 189.

274. **"The schools of".** Ibid. 199.

274. **"In a blistering".** Ibid. 200.

275. **push for civil rights.** Nell Irvin Painter. *The History of White People.* W. W. Norton & Co. 2010. Utilized as a reference on the background of modern American Civil Rights movement.

276. **"I'd rather walk"**. Bob Smith. *They Closed Their Schools: Prince Edward County, Virginia 1951 — 1964*. Robert Russa Robert Russa Moton Museum. 2008. 232.
276. **"as a dispute"**. Ibid. 246.
276. **"I came expecting"**. Ibid. 246.
276. **"We don't say"**. Ibid, 246.
276. **"we daily exchange"**. Ibid. 247.
277. **"What happened, then"**. Ibid. 246.
277. **"White leaders were"**. Ibid. 247.
278. **"MAKE YOUR $$$$$$$"**. Ibid. 248.
279. **"He found children"**. Ibid. 252
279. **"With the younger"**. Ibid. 252
280. **"It is... a two-by-four"**. *Farmville Herald*, Article. March 24, 1961.
280. **"Carol is eight"**. Bob Smith. *They Closed Their Schools: Prince Edward County,*
Virginia 1951 — 1964. Robert Russa Robert Russa Moton Museum. 2008. 255.
281. **"Life in school"**. Ibid. 256.
281. **"also made it"**. Ibid. 256.
281. **"I will say"**. Ibid. 256.
283. **"If you send... enormous respect intellectually"**. Ibid.
286. **"It was devastating"**. Kelley Libby. *Once Segregated Va. School To Become Civil Rights Center*. Virginia Foundation for the Humanities. May 3, 2011.
287. **"I was in"**. Ibid.
287. **"My parents couldn't"**. Ibid.

CHAPTER SEVEN
288. **"Twelve million black men"**. Dr. Robert Russa Moton. Dr. Robert Russa Moton Address, at the Dedication of The Lincoln Memorial, Washington, D. C., May 30th, 1922
(Original Draft). The Glouster Institute.
http://gloucester.kma.net/Gloucester/files/ccLibraryFiles/Filename/000000000278/Moton%20Speech-May301922.pdf.
294. **"when those who"**. Roger W. Wilkins. *Jefferson's Pillow: The Founding Fathers and the Dilemma of Black Patriotism*. Beacon Press. July 12, 2002.

296. **"*I have been*"**. Neil Vincent Sullivan. *Bound For Freedom: An Educator's Adventures in Prince Edward County, Virginia.* Boston Little Brown. 1965. xxiv.

297. **"with what can"**. Ibid. 3.

298. **"four years on"**. Bob Smith. *They Closed Their Schools: Prince Edward County, Virginia 1951 — 1964.* Robert Russa Robert Russa Moton Museum.2008. 232.

298. **"Most of those"**. Neil Vincent Sullivan. *Bound For Freedom: An Educator's Adventures in Prince Edward County, Virginia.* Boston Little Brown. 1965. 21.

299. **"it was a"**. Ibid. 14.

299. **"I knew intimately"**. Ibid. 28.

300. **"On September 3,"**. Ibid. xxxvi.

301. **"You'll get applicants."**. Ibid. 66.

301. **"A group of... is more like it"**. Ibid. 68-71.

302. **"Almost half of"**. Ibid. 71.

303. **"I told them"**. Ibid. 84.

303. **"The call came... paid for expenses."**. Ibid. 86.

304. **"She said: "you're"**. Ibid. xxxviii.

305. **"I felt so good"**. Ibid. 69.

305. **"I noticed, too"**. Ibid. 56.

306. **"While registering her"**. Ibid. 59.

307. **"When I walked... mankind as well."**. Ibid. 93.

307. **"Birmingham was clearly... all age fourteen"**. Condoleezza Rice. *Condoleezza Rice- a memoir of my extraordinary, ordinary family and me.* Delacorte Press. 2010. 98.

308. **"My uncle had"**. Ibid. 99.

308. **"Prince Edward County... of our effort."**. Neil Vincent Sullivan. *Bound For Freedom: An Educator's Adventures in Prince Edward County, Virginia.* Boston Little Brown. 1965. xli.

309. **"In less than"**. Ibid. xli.

309. **"Some of the"**. Ibid. 97.

309. **"These bells haven't..."**. Ibid. 98.

310. **"the children sang... people just sat."**. Ibid. 99.

311. **"It was more"**. Ibid. 45.

312. **"In the background"**. Ibid. xliii

312. **"Michigan State University"**. Ibid. 100.

313. **"overlooked one vital"**. Ibid. 102.

313. **"Before we could"**. Ibid. 103.

314. **"Before the day"**. Ibid. 103.

314. **"I wondered, frankly"**. Ibid. 104.

314. **By the end.** Ibid. 106. Cited reference used for enrolment figure of Free School.

314. **"In nearly every"**. Ibid. 114.

315. **"Even more inspiring"**. Ibid. 115.

316. **"I wish I was"**. Ibid. 120.

317. **"The House had"**. Ibid. 123.

317. **"realized from the"**. Ibid. 130.

318. **"two weeks ago"**. Ibid. 148.

318. **"your sorrow is…"**. Ibid. 155.

319. **"He stopped. He looked up"**. Ibid. 167.

320. **"It is my… all Virginia children"**. Robert Russa Moton Museum. *BARBARA ROSE JOHNS PORTRAIT NOW FEATURED AT VIRGINIA CAPITOL.* Posting from the Robert Russa Moton Museum web site. September, 2012. www.motonmuseum.org/barbara-johns-portrait-unveiled-at-state-capitol/.

320. ***"On May 25, 1964,".*** Neil Vincent Sullivan. *Bound For Freedom: An Educator's Adventures in Prince Edward County, Virginia.* Boston Little Brown. 1965. xlvi.

321. **"How many good… in that time."**. Ibid. 200.

322. **"In the few remaining…"**. Ibid. xlvii.

322. **"I eventually got… that go on."**. Bob Smith. *They Closed Their Schools: Prince Edward County, Virginia 1951 — 1964.* Robert Russa Robert Russa Moton Museum. 2008. 234.

323. **"The name that"**. Ibid. 324.

323. **"While the federal"**. Ibid. 324.

324. **"Four years loss"**. Bob Smith. *They Closed Their Schools: Prince Edward County, Virginia 1951 — 1964.* Robert Russa Robert Russa Moton Museum. 2008. 241.

325. **"Sure it will"**. Ibid. 245.

325. **"appropriation of sufficient"**. Christopher Bonastia. *Southern Stalemate- Five Years without Public Education in Prince Edward County. Virginia.* The University of Chicago Press. 2012. 221.

326. **"hopelessly inadequate... an integrated school"**.
Ibid. 222.

326. **"The main trouble"**. Ibid. 226.

327. **"It was a reactionary"**. John Egerton. *Shades of Gray: Dispatches from the Modern South*. Louisiana State University Press. October 1991. 116.

327. **Bob Smith, discusses.** Bob Smith. *They Closed Their Schools: Prince Edward County, Virginia 1951 — 1964*. Robert Russa Robert Russa Moton Museum. 2008. Preface xi.
Bob Smith, discusses his changing view in the updated preface from his re-released book in 2008, *They Closed Their Schools*. Smith's conclusion changed from the original publication, in 1965, when he did not see any winners or losers. In 2008 he felt differently and this paragraph reflects his updated assessment.

327. **"For all the pain"**. Ibid. xv.

EPILOGUE

329. **"We know all"**. Desmond M. Tutu, Mpho A. Tutu. *Made for Goodness: And Why This Makes All the Difference*. Harper Collins Publishers. 2010. 4.

331. **serene fire indeed**. PBS. *Virginia Currents*. Original Airdate: Thursday, April 21, 2011.
http://www.ideastations.org/video/virginia-currents-2021-2011-04-28.
A televised interview with former students, Reverend Samuel Williams Jr. and Joy Cabarru. As the Robert Russa Moton Museum prepares to unveil a major exhibit, former students, Joy Cabarrus Speaks and Reverend Samuel Williams Jr., discuss what it was like to be there during the Moton High School Strike 60 years ago. Williams said he only needed two words to describe Barbara Rose Johns—"Serene Fire."

Love. Freedom. Justice. A Mighty Champion.

**THE FIGHTING PREACHER
A MAN FOR ALL SEASONS
A MAN FOR ALL REASONS
A MAN FOR GREAT GALLANTRY
BEING FULL OF VALOR
COURAGE AND LIBERALITY
"YOU MAY HAVE TO BEAR IT,
BUT YOU DON'T HAVE TO GRIN"**

—The words from the plaque on the front lawn of the Robert Russa Moton Museum honoring the Reverend L. Francis Griffin (Sept. 15, 1917-Jan. 18, 1980)

INDEX